Gender and Short Fiction

Gender and Short Fiction: Women's Tales in Contemporary Britain, edited by Jorge Sacido-Romero and Laura Mª Lojo Rodríguez, is a collection of essays that explore the reasons why artistically ambitious women writers continue turning to the short story, a genre that has not yet attained the degree of literary prestige and social recognition in the modern period that the novel has. In this timely volume, the authors endorse the view that the genre still retains its potential as a vehicle for the expression of female experience alternative to and/or critical with dominant patriarchal ideology present at the very onset of the development of the modern British short story at the turn of the nineteenth century.

Jorge Sacido-Romero is Senior Lecturer in English at the University of Santiago de Compostela (Spain), where he teaches English literature. His most recent publications on the short story include *Modernism and Postmodernism in the English* (Rodopi 2012), "Ghostly Visitations" in *Atlantis* (2016) and "Liminality in Janice Galloway's Short Fiction", *ZAA* (2018).

Laura Mª Lojo-Rodríguez is Senior Lecturer in English at the University of Santiago de Compostela (Spain), where she teaches English literature and Gender Studies. Her most recent publications on the short story include "Magic Realism and Experimental Fiction: From Virginia Woolf to Jeanette Winterson" in *The Oxford Handbook of Virginia Woolf* (OUP; forthcoming 2018) and "Monica Ali's *Alentejo Blue*: Tourists at a Cultural Crossroads", *Miscelánea* (2018).

Routledge Studies in Contemporary Literature

For a full list of titles published in the series, please visit www.routledge.
com

Gender and Short Fiction
Women's Tales in Contemporary Britain

Edited by
Jorge Sacido-Romero and
Laura Mª Lojo-Rodríguez

Routledge
Taylor & Francis Group

NEW YORK AND LONDON

First published 2018
by Routledge
711 Third Avenue, New York, NY 10017

and by Routledge
2 Park Square, Milton Park, Abingdon, Oxon OX14 4RN

Routledge is an imprint of the Taylor & Francis Group, an informa business

© 2018 Taylor & Francis

The right of the editors to be identified as the authors of the editorial material, and of the authors for their individual chapters, has been asserted in accordance with sections 77 and 78 of the Copyright, Designs and Patents Act 1988.

Library of Congress Cataloging-in-Publication Data
CIP data has been applied for.

ISBN: 978-1-138-09364-5 (hbk)
ISBN: 978-1-315-10648-9 (ebk)

Typeset in Sabon
by codeMantra

For our children, Coque and Lala

Contents

Acknowledgements

We would like to thank all the contributors to this volume for their hard work and their readiness to comply with our editorial demands. Thanks are also due to the editors of the *Routledge Studies in Contemporary Literature* and the staff at Routledge, Taylor & Francis Group, particularly to Jennifer Abbott and Veronica Haggar. Sara González-Bernárdez (USC) deserves special thanks for her careful proofreading of the manuscript and Assunta Petrone (codeMantra) for her diligence and generosity. Thanks, Noemí Pereira-Ares, for your valuable comments and kindness.

We would like to acknowledge the financial support of the Ministry of Economy and Competitiveness (Government of Spain) to carry out the research collected in this volume within the framework of the *Women's Tales* project (Ref. FEM2013–41977-P—MINECO). We also thank this institution for revalidating its support to expand our research on contemporary British women short fiction along a different line in the project *Intersections* (Ref. FEM2017–83084-P—AEI /FEDER). This volume has also benefited from the generous support of the Competitive Reference Research Group *Discourse and Identity* (GRC2015/002 GI-1924) funded by the Galician Regional Government.

List of Contributors

Isabel M. Andrés-Cuevas is Lecturer in English Literature at the University of Granada, Spain. Her research focuses on the relationship between gender and contemporary British short fiction by women, and her most recent publication in this field is "'The Sap Began to Flow': Nature and the Quest for the Female Self in Margaret Drabble's 'The Merry Widow'", in *Feminism: Past, Present and Future Perspectives*, edited by Josefa Ros Velasco (Nova Science 2017)

Anne Besnault-Levita is Senior Lecturer at the University of Rouen, France. Her research focuses on modernist literature, the British short story, gender and women's studies and literary history. With Anne-Florence Gillard-Estrada, she is co-editor of *Beyond the Victorian and Modernist Divide: Remapping the Turn of the Century* (Routledge 2018).

Isabel Carrera-Suárez is Professor of English at the University of Oviedo, Spain. She has published extensively on the intersections of postcoloniality, gender and genre, particularly in novels and short stories by contemporary women authors. Recent publications include "Canadian Multicultural and Transnational Novels", in *The Oxford History of the Novel in English* (Vol 12, 2017), and "Negotiating Singularity and Alikeness: Esi Edugyan, Lawrence Hill and Canadian Afrodiasporic Writing" (*European Journal of English Studies* 21 (2), 2017).

Maria Casado Villanueva is an Associate Professor of English at the University of South-Eastern Norway. Her research focuses on the short story in the 20th and 21st century with publications on Katherine Mansfield, like "The Little Red Governess" (*Katherine Mansfield Studies* 4, 2012), as well as on D.H. Lawrence, like "A Reluctant Awakening" (*Journal of the Short Story in English* 68, 2017).

Ailsa Cox is Professor of Short Fiction at Edge Hill University, UK. Her books include *Alice Munro* (Northcote House, 2004), *Writing Short Stories* (Routledge, 2nd edition 2016) and *The Real Louise and Other Stories* (Headland Press 2009). She is also the editor of the journal *Short Fiction in Theory and Practice* (Intellect Press).

Barbara Korte is Professor of English Literature at the University of Freiburg. Her research focuses on British literature since the nineteenth century. She is the author of *The Short Story in Britain* (Tübingen 2003) and has contributed to *The Cambridge History of the English Short Story* (2016).

Carmen Lara-Rallo is Senior Lecturer in English at the University of Málaga, Spain. Her research focuses on contemporary British fiction, comparative literature and critical theory. Her works include two book-length studies of A.S. Byatt's production, one devoted to her Quartet, and another to her short stories, *La narrativa breve de A.S. Byatt: Enfoque intertextual* (2005).

Laura Mᵃ Lojo-Rodríguez is Senior Lecturer in English at the University of Santiago de Compostela. Her research focuses on the relationship between gender and contemporary British short fiction by women. Her most recent publications include: "Magic Realism and Experimental Fiction" in *The Oxford Handbook of Virginia Woolf* (OUP 2018); "Monica Ali's *Alentejo Blue*" (*Miscelánea*, 2017); "The Reception of Virginia Woolf in Hispanic-Speaking Countries" in *A Companion to Virginia Woolf* (Blackwell's 2016) or "'The Saving Power of Hallucination'" (*ZAA*, 2014).

Sylvia Mieszkowski is Professor of British literature at the University of Vienna. Her recent research in short fiction focuses on contemporary British writers in publications such as "Transnational Heterotopia and Death-Driven Narcissism in A.L. Kennedy's 'Made Over, Made Out'" (2016) and "Spectres of Domesticity: Carly Holmes's 'Piece by Piece' and Tessa Hadley's 'Bad Dreams'" (2018), both in *Short Fiction in Theory and Practice*.

Paul March-Russell teaches Comparative Literature at the University of Kent. As part of the *Women's Tales* project, he has also published articles on Zoe Lambert (*C21 Literature*, 2018) and Lucy Wood (*Short Fiction in Theory and Practice*, 2017). His other research interests include ecocriticism, modern poetry and science fiction.

Michelle Ryan-Sautour is *Maître de Conférences* (Associate Professor) at the Université d'Angers, France, where she is co-director of the "Short Fiction and Short Forms" section of the CIRPaLL research group. Her research focus is the speculative fiction and short stories of Angela Carter, Rikki Ducornet, Ali Smith, and Sarah Hall.

Jorge Sacido-Romero is Senior Lecturer in English at the University of Santiago de Compostela, Spain. He is the main researcher of the *Women's Tales* project and has concentrated on the short fiction of Janice Galloway with publications such as "Ghostly Visitations in Contemporary Short Fiction by Women" (*Atlantis*, 2016) and "Liminality in Janice Galloway's Short Fiction" (*ZAA*, 2018).

Laura Torres-Zúñiga is Assistant Professor of English at the Autonomous University of Madrid (Spain). She is a member of the *Women's Tales* and the *Intersections* research projects on the short fiction of contemporary British women writers. She is a participant in the European Network for Short Fiction Research. Her research focuses on the short story and cultural studies.

Emma Young lectures at University Campus Oldham, UK. She has published widely in the field of contemporary women's fiction, with a particular focus on the politics of gender and sexuality. Emma is the co-editor of *British Women Short Story Writers: The New Woman to Now* (EUP 2016) and author of *Contemporary Feminism and Women's Short Stories* (EUP 2018).

1 Introduction

*Jorge Sacido-Romero and Laura M^a
Lojo-Rodríguez*

The British Short Story: Still Marginal
after All These Years?

Gender and Short Fiction: Women's Tales in Contemporary Britain
grows out of an international seminar held at the University of Santiago
de Compostela in the spring of 2016. The phrase "women's tales" in the
subtitle echoes "old wives' tales", an expression commonly used to refer
derisively to superstitious and spurious beliefs that deserve no credit, or,
as Angela Carter put it: "Old wives' tales – that is, worthless stories,
untruths, trivial gossip, a derisive label that allots the art of storytelling to women at the exact same time as it takes all the values from it"
(1990: xi). Our choice of expression is, of course, ironical, as our guiding intention is, on the contrary, to give due credit to women's tales,
to explore what women authors say in and through the medium of the
short narrative form. This book thus joins the ongoing vindication of the
short story as a genuine, distinguishable and distinguished literary genre
in which women writers have excelled and go on excelling.

The unambiguous recognition of the short story as a type of fiction different from, yet not inferior to, the novel is still a far-off goal.
Unlike the case of Ireland and the United States, canonical status
and strong public support still elude the contemporary British short
story (Malcolm 2012: 52–56). Some timid progress seems, however,
to be detectable in recent overviews of contemporary British fiction.
Thus, for instance, David James's *The Cambridge Companion to
British Fiction Since 1945* (2015) does include, in its chronological
table of relevant publications, Ian McEwan's debut collection *First
Love, Last Rites* (1975), Salman Rushdie's *East, West* (1994) and
A.L. Kennedy's *Original Bliss* (1998) (xviii, xx), while Nick Bentley's
earlier *Contemporary British Short Fiction* (2008) listed only Angela
Carter's *The Bloody Chamber* (1979) under the category "Publication
of Novels" (x). In his discussion of Carter's work, however, Bentley
focused exclusively on her novels, obviating her short fiction altogether.[1] Apart from its relatively more inclusive chronology, David
James's *Cambridge Companion* does refer to one of Helen Simpson's

short story collections (2015: 87), yet when discussing the work of prominent short story writers like J.G. Ballard, Ali Smith or Michèle Roberts, only their novels deserve attention.[2]

The small degree of receptiveness towards the short story, visible only under the magnifying glass in some reference works like those mentioned above, may have something to do with the recent wave of critical interest in the short form, which has become particularly intense in the last decade (Young and Bailey 2015: 2–3). As Emma Young and James Bailey point out, one of the latest trends in this growing body of critical work is the attention paid to "women's short story writers" (2015: 3). Claire Drewery's *Modernist Short Fiction by Women: The Liminal in Katherine Mansfield, Dorothy Richardson, May Sinclair and Virginia Woolf* (2011), Kate Krueger's *British Women Writers and the Short Story, 1850–1930: Reclaiming Social Space* (2014) and Young and Bailey's own *British Women Short Story Writers: The New Woman to Now* (2015) are important in this connection as they focus exclusively on the British literary context, which compensates for the lack of book-length, systematic approaches to women's short fiction production in Britain. For, indeed, the great contribution of British women writers to the development of the modern short story is irrefutable; it is, for once, an objective historical fact, as evidenced in the long list of practitioners of the genre from Sarah Grand or Ella D'Arcy at the turn of the twentieth century through Virginia Woolf, Katherine Mansfield, Muriel Spark or Angela Carter, and to Michèle Roberts, A.L. Kennedy or Janice Galloway in our days. For well over a century, artistically ambitious women writers in Britain have turned to a genre that even today is a long way from reaching the degree of literary prestige, social recognition and even commercial value that the novel has enjoyed.[3] Though the great majority of women authors have also produced novels, the short story clearly retains its strong appeal as a literary form in the contemporary period, which is the specific focus of the present volume.

It is commonly assumed that short stories are written because they are easier to write, or less costly to publish, or because they function as preparatory experiments for the more demanding longer narrative forms. This alone does not fully explain women writers' attraction to the form and their great contribution to its development. The idea that connects all the pieces collected in *Gender and Short Fiction* is that contemporary British women writers also turn to the short story because the genre preserves its potential as a vehicle for the expression of female experience that is often critical with reality and with dominant patriarchal ideology. The attention to the ways in which formal aspects and gender concerns interrelate frames an otherwise varied array of approaches to a significant number of short stories by British women writers of the last thirty years that this volume contains.

Gender and Short Fiction: A Brief Theoretical and Historical Survey

In his 2009 book-length introduction to the genre, Paul March-Russell affirmed that "the short story has acted at various times as a resource for writers to contest the dominant beliefs in social progress and formal cohesion" (232). The ways in which women writers make use of the inherent capacities and formal features of the short story to carry out a critique of patriarchal structures cannot be removed from historical determinations and specificities. In tackling the thorny issue of the connection between gender and short fiction, indeed, one must not fall into the trap of essentialism. As Anne Besnault-Levita argued in 2007, "unless it is historicized and contextualized, the subtle question of the links between gender and the short story will not receive the theoretical answers it deserves" (484). The formal aspects intrinsically related to the genre's brevity (such as ellipsis, elusiveness, indirection, concentration, intensity and the higher degree of readerly engagement all these features demand) can be isolated and discussed as long as we attend to the ways in which these features are refashioned by individual writers in the specific context in which they are embedded. Despite its seemingly fragile status, the strength and continuity of short story is partly attributed to its capacity to respond critically to surrounding circumstances in a more immediate, unyielding and engaging manner than a longer narrative. Thus, as Ailsa Cox states, its "elusiveness and fragmentation [...] makes it harder to commodify than longer forms", and "written with intensity and immediacy, the short story is well suited to a fast changing world which may have moved on by the time you have finished, let alone published, a novel" (2015: 116, 119). Moreover, the short story's response to complex issues such as identity, gender and marginality, Cox goes on arguing, "is made possible by [... its] combination of virtuosity with accessibility, its ability to make demands on the reader which might be difficult to sustain at a longer length" (2015: 130). Because it requires more critically alert readers, Helen Simpson maintains, the short story is superior to the novel when it comes to dealing with uncomfortable questions, as novels may induce in readers a state of lethargy that blunts their critical faculties (2012: xxv).

The connection between gender and short fiction figured prominently already in the early stages of development of the modern British short story at the turn of the twentieth century – or even earlier, as Kate Krueger contends in *British Women Writers and the Short Story, 1850–1930* (2014).[4] The adversarial thrust characteristic of the modern British short story in the initial phases of its evolution was a combination of formal experimentation – breaking away from previous realistic modes and distinguishing itself from the parallel development of mass-market periodical fiction – and ideological critique of Victorian standards, particularly those related to gender roles and matrimonial harmony.[5] In the specific case of "the so-called New Women writers", Emma Liggins, Andrew Maunder and Ruth Robbins argue, they turned to the short story because "they were dissatisfied with the marriage plots of the Victorian three-volume novel and resisted the conventions of its narrative line by resisting its conventional plots. [... S]hort fiction offered an opportunity to explore new ways of being" (2011: 8).

From its inception in the late nineteenth century, the modern British short story has remained a suitable artistic mode of articulation and expression of women's ethico-political views and concerns. The small, yet lately growing, number of studies devoted to women's short fiction have revolved around this basic idea, beginning with Hermione Lee's "Introduction" to *The Secret Self: Short Stories by Women* (1985, re-edited in 1995 with the subtitle *A Century of Short Stories by Women*). There Lee suggested that the anthologised pieces by both British and American female authors contained particular "ways of seeing and talking and shaping which gave new power to, and made new versions of, women's experiences" (1995: xii). In "Gender and Genre" (1989), Mary Eagleton questioned those short story critics who stressed the genre's connection to marginality while neglecting women's short story practice: "we can see in the image they offer of the short story writer and character – non-hegemonic, peripheral, contradictory – a reflection of the position of women in patriarchal society" (62). Likewise, Clare Hanson (1989) echoed Frank O'Connor's *The Lonely Voice* (1962) in her view that alienation from dominant culture was represented more effectively in the short story than in the novel. Furthermore, Hanson considered that "the short story has been from its inception a particularly appropriate vehicle for the expression of the ex-centric, alienated vision of women" (1989: 3).

Over time, approaches to the interconnections between gender and genre became more theoretically sophisticated and context-bound. Thus, Mary Burgan related the short story by American and British women writers to *écriture féminine*, to a "female writing that counters the static forms of masculine inscription with an ongoingness that resists interruption by symbolic abstraction" (1995: 268). Drawing on Mary Burgan, Ellen Burton Harrington highlighted the elusive form's "resistance to closure and perception of a different reality, one devised through discourse but not bounded by it, offer[ing] a re-envisioning of the expansiveness essential to feminine writing" (2008: 8–9). Adrian Hunter, on his part, linked the short story to the concept of *minor literature*: namely, "that which a minority constructs within a major language" (Deleuze and Guattari 1986: 16). Like *écriture feminine*, *minor literature* is anti-totalising, intrinsically averse to finalising definitions, categorical closures, established values, assumed hierarchies and finished conceptualisations that power structures expect and enforce. Discussing Alice

Munro's treatment of colonial and postcolonial history, Hunter pointed out that the short story form is essential to the Canadian author's literary achievement of exploring areas hidden by *major* narrative forms because

> [t]he short story's interrogative economy, its failure literally to express, to extend itself to definition, determination, or disclosure, becomes, under the rubric of a theory of 'minor' literature a positive aversion to the entailment of 'power and law' that defines the 'major' literature [...] Munro stages the interrogative short story as a counter-narrative variously to the novel, the public historical record, and even the feminist revisionary project, in order to reveal how these culturally powerful narrational models fall short of the private life stories of women.
>
> (2004: 221)

Hunter linked form to gender without losing sight of the historical context of colonial and postcolonial Canada "in the counter-narratives of women's lives" (2004: 219). As a distinct way of interrogating dominant discourse, the modern short story seems to boldly inhabit a liminal space of formal and thematic exploration that is both the cause of its fragile status and the source of its strong appeal. So it was for British women modernists in the interwar period, as Claire Drewery argued, when "the short story enjoyed a resurgence in popularity" (2011: 6).[6] Women's interest in the short form continued in the decades after World War II. In her useful survey of writers from different Anglophone countries in a period whose end marks the beginning of the one under inspection in the present volume, Sabine Coelsh-Foisner concludes with a reflection on how these authors' stories adapted "the disruptive aesthetics of the genre to a feminist ethics of self-assertion via duality and discord" (2016: 301). Though it never died out, as Coelsh-Foisner showed, British women writers' attraction to the short form became more intense during the 1970s and 1980s in the wake of the Women's Liberation Movement and second-wave feminism (Young and Bailey 2015: 8). Political activism went hand in hand with intellectual and artistic work in questioning the ways in which culture produced and propagated gender stereotypes that still confined women to a position of otherness within society. As Christa Knellwolf argued, "women's groups began to spring", vindicate new rights and raise consciousness in order to gain "distance from externally imposed definitions so that it might be possible to discover an authentic understanding of female experience" (2001: 197). This led to the foundation of women's presses, such as Pandora or Virago in the 1970s, and to the revision and vindication of women's position in literary history, both past and present, through the publication of studies and republication of works which would otherwise have fallen into oblivion (Knellwolf 2001: 198–199). As Maunder, Liggins and Robbins argue, part of this editorial and critical interest in women's writing brought about the publication, particularly since the 1990s, "of a number of anthologies of short stories by women, helping to create a canon of female short-story writers from the nineteenth century to the present" (2011: 19). Apart from aiding in the construction of a female tradition, sometimes collections of stories became a form of open feminist activism. Such was the case of a volume whose title openly announced an intentional reversal of generational roles: *Tales I Tell My Mother: A Collection of Feminist Short Stories* (1978). As one of the editors and contributors, Valerie Miner, stated: "Writing stories is activism. [... S]tories are part of our work within the Women's Movement" (1978: 61, 63). *Tales I Tell My Mother* was an eighteen-month collective project and, as such, it was conceived "not [as] an anthology", but as "a book, a single entity, an accumulation of points of view", as another editor and contributor, Sara Maitland, made clear in the introductory essay to the last part of the volume (1978: 114–115). *Tales* had serious difficulties in finding a publisher and had an afterlife in *More Tales I Tell My Mother* (1987), a less structured collection of stories by the same authors: Zoë Fairbairns, Michelene Wandor, Valerie Miner, Sara Maitland and Michèle Roberts. As they stated in the expository pieces that framed the volume, short fiction was the medium of expression of the feminist "theory about women's position" that they had developed in common with the intention to "act on and change that position in the whole of society" (1978: 7). They made use of "the language and form of the short story" to question the patriarchal system in order to contribute to social transformation (1978: 9). Stories helped reinforce their sense of community not as an "imagined" one, but as "an imaginative collectivity of readers and writers" (1978: 63). Their "challenge" was conceived of in terms akin to those of *minor literature* with a clear feminist agenda: "Our challenge lies", Michelene Wandor wrote, "in the way we use the existing language to resurrect our submerged history, and convey our current feminist perspective on the world we live in" (1978: 9). The struggle took place also in the field of literary production and readership which, as Michèle Roberts writes in the "Epilogue" to *Tales*, was dominated by products, like romantic novels dealing with the Regency era, that helped to perpetuate gender stereotypes (1978:159). In the attempt to undermine disabling gender models inscribed in mainstream literature and in culture in general, the short story proved to be a particularly sharpened weapon for women. Yet anthologies and collective books were not the only outlets for politically committed short fiction. Periodical publications also carried short stories on gender questions as one of their regular features. Thus, one third of the stories collected in *Tales* had been previously published in *Spare Rib*, a feminist monthly that was very active in the Women's Liberation Movement. Running from July 1972 to January 1993, *Spare Rib* published short fiction that overtly and purposely tackled gender issues.[7]

In the heyday of second-wave feminism in Britain, the short story was the site of feminist contestation. In this connection, Angela Carter's short fiction production is a revealing and extremely influential case in the development of both the British short story and its role as a vehicle of women's resistance to patriarchal models. 1974 saw the publication of Carter's first short-fiction collection, *Fireworks: Nine Profane Pieces*. Though Carter's later collection *The Bloody Chamber* (1979) has received much more critical attention, the strikingly experimental pieces collected in *Fireworks* already exhibited many of the defining features of literary postmodernism – of which she is to be counted as one of the most prominent British initiators. The composition of the stories, tales or "profane pieces" that make up *Fireworks* was directly related to Carter's long stay in Japan, a country in which – in her own words – she "learnt what it is to be a woman and became radicalised" (1982: 28). As the course of her career shows, Carter's new awareness of women's predicaments and her idiosyncratic feminist affiliations found a privileged literary fictional expression in the short story. Significantly, before *Fireworks* Carter had published half a dozen novels (almost one per year) and three (just three!) short stories, whereas from 1974 onwards she produced four short story collections, edited three anthologies for Virago (the first one titled *Wayward Girls and Wicked Women: An Anthology of Subversive Stories* [1986], which included a story from *Fireworks*) and published her translations of Charles Perrault's fairy tales, while her novelistic output decreased dramatically (just three novels in almost twenty years).

Carter's conspicuous turn to short fiction from the mid-1970s onwards coincided in time (if we trust the teller) with her personal and political awakening and vindications as a woman writer. Drawing on Carter's own statements, we can establish how her handling of the internal capacities and conventions of the short form and her critical response to specific historical circumstances interact. To begin with, Carter considered that short fiction was endowed with a degree of artistic unity the novel lacked: "Sign and sense can fuse to an extent impossible to achieve among the multiplying ambiguities of an extended narrative" (1995: 459). In this way, short stories could have a sharp, intense impact on the reader which Carter conceived not just as an aesthetic but also as an ethical effect. Thus, she singled out the effect of "provoking unease" as "a singular *moral* function" of her Gothic tales (1995: 459; our emphasis). If Carter dubs the function of provoking discomfort "moral", it is because it can move readers into questioning conventional modes of representation: "unease [is] produced when expectations of how the world operates are called into question and even shattered" (Moss 2001: 190). The latter connects with Carter's liberating project of exposing and deconstructing the alienating ideas and models reproduced in the literary tradition, particularly those articulated in folk tales, fairy tales and myths, traditional short narrative forms: "I'm in the demy-thologising business. I'm interested in myths – though I'm much more interested in folklore – just because they are extraordinary lies designed to make people unfree" (1997: 38). The body of Carter's short fiction is a major contribution to the new wave of short story writing of the 1970s and 1980s, a period in which "the fairy tale underwent a startling trans-formation as women writers explored the feminist potential provided by the act of (re)writing the genre" (Young and Bailey 2015: 8). The ways in which the traditions, conventions, features and capacities of the short story genre are critically deployed, distorted and appropriated by Carter are outstanding instances of the rich and complex interaction between gender and genre on the eve of the period under scrutiny in the present volume.[8]

Structure of the Book

The essays collected in *Gender and Short Fiction: Women's Tales in Contemporary Britain* are distributed in six parts structured around specific topics, opening up with Anne Besnault-Levita's fresh theoreti-cal approach to the gender–genre connection which constitutes "Part I: Theorising Gender *and* Short Fiction". "Gender and Genre in British Modern and Contemporary Short Fiction: A Meta-Critical Approach" is inspired by Virginia Woolf's reflection on the open and flexible re-lationship between "women" and "fiction" in *A Room of One's Own* (1929). After providing a short history of the theorisations of the genre and an account of how gender issues entered the debate, Besnault-Levita delineates a theoretical framework based on a series of guidelines and safeguards along with a set of nine central ideas around which to bring the gender–genre link into sharper focus: *hierarchy*; women's *time* and *space*; female *subjectivity*; *voice* and *metaphor*; affect and *anger*; and *agency* and *playfulness*. These are topics and concerns present in the stories and authors discussed in the ensuing chapters which the contrib-utors to the present volume certainly do not fail to bring to the fore.

"Part II: In Carter's Wake" explores the great impact of Angela Carter's stories on contemporary British women writers. In Chapter 3, Michelle Ryan-Sautour chooses to speak about "legacy" instead of "influence" in the case of Carter, a writer whose creative imagination found a new impetus in the short narrative form. Part of Carter's leg-acy, Ryan-Sautour argues, was her crucial contribution to make the short story a suitable medium for the critical exploration of social and political questions and the search for new ways of literary expression. Short fiction was a privileged vehicle for Carter's articulation of what Ryan-Sautour calls "authorial performance": her active participation from within the literary field in topical debates that entailed a strong sense of the writer's ethical responsibility and a pursuit of the reader's active involvement. This chapter discovers traces of Carter's legacy in the short fiction of contemporary British women writers: from the more playful and metafictional ways to elicit the reader's participation found in the work of authors like Ali Smith to the more crudely sensual onslaught on readers in some stories by, for instance, Janice Galloway; from the more moderate modality of the authorial performance of Helen Simpson to the more openly provocative posturing of Hilary Mantel. If Ryan-Sautour examines Carter's impact in terms of *ethos* and authorial performance, Paul March-Russell instead focuses, in Chapter 4, on her influence on the postmodern fairy tale after the publication of *The Bloody Chamber* (1979), stressing Carter's explicit attempt to expose the violent and sexual content latent in traditional tales and myths. But Carter draws on and reworks folkloric and mythical material in ways that makes her stories generically heterogeneous, technically irreproducible and hermeneutically inexhaustible. In this chapter, March-Russell explores the different ways women writers have negotiated Carter's influence, beginning with Carter's contemporary Tanith Lee (more concerned with the manifest content of tales), continuing with the stories of Carter's near-contemporaries (A.S. Byatt, Marina Warner and Sara Maitland, more conscious of her influence) and concluding with her successors (Emma Donoghue and Sarah Hall, for whom Carter was less of a subversive figure than a part of their literary tradition).

"Part III: Body Politics" examines how short stories portray female sexuality as the site of subjection and resistance. Chapter 5, by Emma Young, finds in representations of women's bodies in recent short stories critical reassessments of neoliberal and post(-)feminist politics that revolve around the possibilities and limitations of female choice and agency. Drawing on the communicative peculiarities of the short form (ambiguity, open-endedness and readerly engagement, in particular), the authors analysed by Young – Kate Atkinson, Helen Simpson, Michèle Roberts, Kalbinder Kaur and Sarah Hall – address these issues in different ways; yet all share a resistance to unequivocal resolutions, so interpretations are largely dependent on the reader's own feminist positionality. In Chapter 6, Laura Mª Lojo-Rodríguez discusses two stories by Michèle Roberts from, respectively, her first and her last collection to date to bring to light the author's sustained effort to establish what Luce Irigaray has termed "genealogies of women", which entails a recovery of the maternal body as the material and symbolic ground upon which to found and secure collaborative ties among women, something central to a feminist agenda and indispensable in forging an emancipatory discourse for women. Chapter 7, by Isabel María Andrés-Cuevas, closes Part III with a discussion of Jeanette Winterson's short fiction. Winterson's overall tendency towards shortness is dictated by her desire to convey emotional intensity and ideological profoundness. In Winterson's collection *The World and Other Places* (1998), the combination of density and sharpness inherent to short writing serves to dismantle sex and gender standards by exploring imaginatively alternative modalities of sexual identity and sexual practices through the language of art, genre hybridity, intertextuality and intermediality ("The Poetics of Sex") and the inversion of the sexual ideology inscribed in classical myth ("Orion").

"Part IV: Voicing Differently" deals with short fiction by British women writers in which gender issues are interspersed with attention to the origins, inflections and modulations of the voice. In Chapter 8, Sylvia Mieszkowski draws on A.L. Kennedy's own statements on the short form in order to delineate what Mieszkowski designates as the author's "ballistic poetics" of the short story. Such poetics produce a sharp effect on the reader which, in the stories under inspection, entails the articulation of affect through an ambiguously (un)gendered narrative voice and the reader's hermeneutical and emotional involvement in dealing with gender inversions and ambiguities. If Mieszkowski connects Kennedy's poetics to Virginia Woolf as a privileged point of reference in the tradition of the modern short story, María Casado Villanueva (Chapter 9) refers to the aural and rhetorical richness of Katherine Mansfield's stories as particularly influential in Ali Smith's short fiction. Drawing on Mikhail M. Bakhtin's notions of dialogism and heteroglossia and their feminist appropriations, Casado Villanueva explores the ways in which gender and genre interrelate through the particular treatment of voice and multivocality in Smith's short stories in general, and in *The First Person and Other Stories* (2010) in particular. If resistance to reproducing sexual ideology through the debunking of gender expectations and the exposing of its artificial nature are central strategies in Smith's stories, the liberating ways to destabilisation of fixed identities and meanings through the voice is the focus of Jorge Sacido-Romero's discussion of Janice Galloway's short stories. Chapter 10 examines how Galloway's self-appointed task of legitimating a female perspective and its articulation in a different voice in the context of male-biased Scottish culture and society is consistently carried out in her short fiction, unlike in her novels, which perform a gradually farther removal from that context. The chapter reads a selection of Galloway's stories from her three collections to date which feature female characters that speak in the voice of care, an ethical stance that constitutes one of the most powerful alternatives to dominant patriarchal discourse. As Barbara Korte argues in Chapter 11, voice is also central in Jackie Kay's work. A major tenet of Korte's chapter is that Kay's work does not simply voice racial, national or sexual marginality, but, rather, renders experiences of liminality and transition for which the short story has proved a particularly apt vehicle. Korte reads stories from Kay's different collections to show how women of colour are not portrayed as objects of oppression, but as individuals posed in specific transitional moments in their lives that experience identity as a complex and fluid process.

"Part V: Narrating Life" collects pieces that approach short fiction by women as a way to give an ampler and more truthful account of the experience of war (Chapter 12), the encounter with racial and cultural otherness (Chapter 13) and domestic life (Chapter 14). In Chapter 12, Isabel Carrera-Suárez focuses on the contributions by three women authors to the volume *1914 – Goodbye to All That: Writers on the Conflict between Life and Art* (2014), a collection in which writers from the different countries that participated in World War I responded to Robert Graves's *Goodbye to All That* (1929) and approached the subject of artistic identity as shaped by conflict. Ali Smith's, Xiaolu Guo's and Jeanette Winterson's anti-war texts exhibit the characteristic liminality associated with the short form (a hybrid of fiction and essay in these cases) and provide contemporary views on the relationships among war, gender and art as alternative to the male-biased, Eurocentric triumphalism that permeates dominant discourses on World War I. These pieces are examples of a type of writing attentive to difference in terms of gender, ethnicity or class which, Carrera-Suárez argues, are not usually emphasised in otherwise innovative writing on war by modernists and by later generations of authors. Conflict is also the focus of Chapter 13, as Carmen Lara-Rallo examines here how A.S. Byatt's particular understanding of the short story offers a privileged site for the enactment of the East/West encounter and its conflicts in a globalised world. In stories from three different collections, Byatt explores the ways in which the experience of the encounter transforms, amplifies and problematises the female protagonists' sense of personal, (trans-)national and (trans-)cultural identity. Informed by theorists of the so-called transcultural turn like Ansgar Nünning and Zygmunt Bauman, Lara-Rallo shows how Byatt is attentive to the coexistence of cultural otherness and globalised uniformity as determining factors in the liminal experiences of the protagonists which the short story transmits to the reader more intensively and in a more engaging manner than longer narrative forms. The fact that brevity and intensity reach the reader more effectively is certainly one of the reasons which accounts for Helen Simpson's choice of the short story as her sole vehicle of literary expression. In Chapter 14, Laura Torres-Zúñiga probes into the reasons of Simpson's predilection for the short form to address women's lives and experiences. Simpson's lifelong commitment to the short story springs from the form's suitability to explore complex and controversial issues, as well as from her conviction that the home, domestic life and the hardships of maternity also belong to the realm of the political.

"Part VI: Latest News" closes the volume with Ailsa Cox's delineation of the context for the most recent developments in British short fiction by women. Thus, Chapter 15 explores the many constitutive elements of the culture of the short story in the UK, in connection with which Cox highlights the importance of Creative Writing courses in the formation of short story authors. Cox argues that they foster fruitful interactions among peers and favour the existence of a wider community of short story writers and readers. In the recent short story collections she discusses, Cox discovers new articulations of some concerns shared by women predecessors and addressed in previous chapters of this volume. The anxieties and ambiguities attached to domestic life are the focus of Carys Bray's *Sweet Home* (2012), Carter's influence is to be detected in Lucy Woods's *Diving Belles* (2012), the search for alternative ways of narrating historical events is to be found in Carys Davies's *The Redemption of Galen Pike* (2016) and the exploration of liminality in descriptions of the landscape and their counterpart in inner psychic states is the focus of K.J. Orr's *Light Box* (2016).

Notes

1 *A Concise Companion to Contemporary British Fiction*, a collective volume edited by James F. English in 2006, did not even mention Carter's *The Bloody Chamber*, a landmark in contemporary British literary history.
2 The fact that *The Cambridge Companion to American Fiction After 1945* (2012) devotes a full chapter to the short story is a clear indication of the contrast between the secure place the short form occupies in the American tradition and its exclusion from historical accounts of contemporary British literature (Lohafer 2012: 68–81). While in Britain "fiction" still means only "novels", in the United States short stories are unambiguously considered "fiction".
3 The contrast in terms of market value between the British and the American short story is also remarkable. If Alan Rinzler stated confidently in *Forbes* that "[s]hort story collections are a big business" in his article "Why Book Publishers Love Short Stories" (2010), David Malcolm lamented in 2012 that "British publishers [...] simply do not like short fiction, and have to be browbeaten by already established authors to consider publishing collections of short stories" (56).
4 For the belated development of the short story in Britain see Baldwin (1993).
5 See Hunter (2007: 34–39).
6 Drewery uses "liminality" as a trope that refers, in combination, to the marginal status of the short form and to how "modernist short fiction by women explores crises of identity encapsulated in moments or interludes of transition" (2011: 1). Kate Krueger examines how in the 1850–1930 period, the short story, on account of its formal features, became a privilege vehicle for women writers' interrogation of social space and the feminine models and ideals inscribed in it.
7 The British Library has recently made most of the contents of *Spare Rib* available online at: www.bl.uk/spare-rib
8 As we were writing this introduction, Edinburgh University Press announced the forthcoming publication of *Contemporary Feminisms and Women's Short Stories* by Emma Young, one of the contributors to the present volume. According to the information provided on the publisher's website, Young explores short stories by women writers through the concept of "the moment" in relation to contemporary feminist theories.

References

Baldwin, Dean (1993) "The Tardy Evolution of the British Short Story", *Studies in Short Fiction* 30(1): 1–10.

Bentley, Nick (2008) *Contemporary British Fiction*, Edinburgh: Edinburgh University Press.

Besnault-Levita, Anne (2007) "Gender", in *The Facts on File Companion to the British Short Story*, edited by Andrew Maunder, New York: Facts on File, 483–485.

Burgan, Mary (1995) "The 'Feminine' Short Story in America: Historicizing Epiphanies", in *American Women Short Story Writers: A Collection of Critical Essays*, edited by Julie Brown, New York: Routledge, 267–280.

Carter, Angela (1982) *Nothing Sacred: Selected Writings*, London: Virago.

Carter, Angela (ed.) (1990) *The Virago Book of Fairy Tales*, London: Virago, ix–xxii.

Carter, Angela (1995) "Afterword to *Fireworks*", in *Burning Your Boats: Collected Stories*. London: Vintage, 459–460.

Carter, Angela (1982/1997) "Notes from the Front Line", in *Shaking a Leg: Journalism and Writings*, edited by Jenny Uglow, London: Penguin, 36–43.

Cox, Ailsa (2015) "New Waves of Interest: Women's Short Story Writers in the Late Twentieth Century", in *British Women Short Story Writers: The New Woman to Now*, edited by Emma Young and James Bailey, Edinburgh: Edinburgh University Press, 114–132.

Deleuze, Gilles and Félix Guattari (1986) *Kafka: Toward a Minor Literature*, translated by Dana Polan. Minneapolis, MN: University of Minnesota Press.

Drewery, Claire (2011) *Modernist Short Fiction by Women: The Liminal in Katherine Mansfield, Dorothy Richardson, May Sinclair and Virginia Woolf*. Farnham: Ashgate.

Eagleton, Mary (1989) "Gender and Genre", in *Re-Reading the Short Story*, edited by Clare Hanson. London: Macmillan, 55–68.

English, James F. (2006) *A Concise Companion to Contemporary British Fiction*. Oxford: Blackwell.

Fairbairns, Zoë, Sara Maitland, Valerie Miner, Michèle Roberts and Michelene Wandor (1978) *Tales I Tell My Mother: A Collection of Feminist Short Stories*, London: Journeyman.

Fairbairns, Zoë, Sara Maitland, Valerie Miner, Michèle Roberts and Michelene Wandor (1987) *More Tales I Tell My Mother: Feminist Short Stories*, London: Journeyman.

Hanson, Clare (ed.) (1989) *Re-Reading the Short Story*, London: Macmillan.

Harrington, Ellen Burton (2008) *Scribbling Women and the Short Story Form: Approaches by American and British Women Writers*, New York: Peter Lang.

Hunter, Adrian (2004) "Story into History: Alice Munro's Minor Literature", *English* 53: 219–238.

Hunter, Adrian (2007) *The Cambridge Introduction to the Short Story in English*, Cambridge: Cambridge University Press.

James, David (ed.) (2015) *The Cambridge Companion to British Fiction since 1945*, Cambridge: Cambridge University Press.

Knellwolf, Christa (2001) "The History of Feminist Criticism", in *The Cambridge History of Literary Criticism, Vol. 9: Twentieth-Century Historical,*

Philosophical and Psychological Perspectives, edited by Christa Knellwolf and Christopher Norris, Cambridge: Cambridge University Press, 193–206.

Krueger, Kate (2014) *British Women Writers and the Short Story, 1850–1930: Reclaiming Social Space*, London: Palgrave.

Lee, Hermione (1995/1985) "Introduction", in *The Secret Self: A Century of Short Stories by Women*, edited by H. Lee. London: Phoenix Giant, ix–xiv.

Liggins, Emma, Andrew Maunder and Ruth Robbins (2011) *The British Short Story*, Basingstoke: Palgrave Macmillan.

Lohafer, Susan (2012) *The Cambridge Companion to American Fiction After 1945*, edited by John N. Duvall, Cambridge: Cambridge University Press, 68–81.

Malcolm, David (2012) *The British and Irish Short Story Handbook*, Oxford: Wiley-Blackwell.

March-Russell, Paul (2009) *The Short Story: An Introduction*, Edinburgh: Edinburgh University Press.

Moss, Betty (2001) "Desire and the Female Grotesque in Angela Carter's 'Peter and the Wolf'", in *Angela Carter and the Fairy Tale*, edited by Danielle M. Roemer and Cristina Bacchilega, Detroit, MI: Wayne State University Press, 187–203.

Rinzler, Alan (2010) "Why Book Publishers Love Short Stories", *Forbes*, www.forbes.com/sites/booked/2010/05/03/why-book-publishers-love-short-stories/#24487ad550c6 (accessed 10 January 2018).

Simpson, Helen (2012) *A Bunch of Fives: Selected Stories*, London: Vintage.

Young, Emma and James Bailey (eds.) (2015) *British Women Short Story Writers: The New Woman to Now*, Edinburgh: Edinburgh University Press.

Part I

Theorising Gender *and* Short Fiction

2 Genre and Gender in British Modern and Contemporary Short Fiction

A Meta-critical Approach

Anne Besnault-Levita

Introduction

The complex notions of genre and gender have been under scrutiny since their inception. But while the novel has long been a crucial site for the exploration, representation and construction of gender, in the case of the short story the question of how gender meets genre had received little critical attention before the 1980s. Mary Eagleton (1989) was among the first critics to explore the connections between gender and the short story in a theoretical way, moving beyond specific case studies. In the 1990s, Susan Hill (1991), Josephine Donovan (1998) and Elaine Showalter (1993) continued to address the issue cautiously, trying to avoid the traps of essentialism while focusing on the "angles of vision and ways of expression" that might differentiate between men's and women's novellas and short fictions (Lee 1985: ix). My own provisional conclusion on the subject in 2007 was that "unless it is historicised and contextualised, the question of the links between gender and the short story will not receive the theoretical answers it deserves" (Besnault-Levita 517).

In her postscript to *British Short Story Writers: The New Woman to Now*, Clare Hanson rightly comments: "There have been few critical studies of the British short story and none which has focused on the interaction between gender and genre" (2015: 193). My contribution to the ongoing debate obviously builds on the invaluable essays found in Young and Bailey's collection and on the recent scholarship on the subject.[1] It examines the possibility of a "separatist aesthetic theory of the twentieth-century woman's short story", to take up Hermione Lee's words in her introduction to *The Secret Self 1: Short Stories by Women* (Lee 1985: ix), first by retracing the history of the attempts at theorisation in the field, then by envisioning a method that might enable us to answer Mary Eagleton's still valid question: "Can we create a criticism which is non-essentialist, non-reductive but subtly alive to the links of gender and genre?" (1989: 66).

Theoretical Controversies

Although many recent publications on the short story include chapters on women's writing, the connection between genre and gender remains a contentious subject. Anthologies of women short story writers have existed for a few decades now, but they rarely offer new theoretical insights into the question of how gender might affect genre and how genre might articulate gender. Besides, in our poststructuralist, and for some thinkers, post-feminist era, when every claim to speak in the name of "women" is countered by so many differences of race, class, culture and sexual orientation, the attempts to look for an alternative female viewpoint or discourse appear to be paved with pitfalls. One example is Ann-Marie Einhaus's "Introduction" to *The Short Story and the First World War*, published in 2013, where she explains that:

> It serves no particular purpose to become embroiled in lengthy debates about the nature and aims of the genre. Consulting any one of the most recent works on the short story, one will inevitably come across the realisation that the short story, more than perhaps any other literary genre, is extremely hard to define, and that its definition has changed so often over time that it is virtually impossible to agree on any other common denominators than that a short story ought to be a piece of prose fiction, and that it ought to be relatively short.
>
> (10)

This comment goes against the assumptions of many short story writers and scholars who have tried to show that the short story is a unique genre offering its readers a special kind of experience – Edgar Allan Poe, Brander Matthews, Frank O'Connor, Nadine Gordimer, Clare Hanson, Mary Rohrberger or, more recently, James Bailey, Jorge Sacido, Emma Young, Andrew Maunder, Adrian Hunter, to name but a few. Similarly, the idea that genre might be shaped by gender is still greeted with scepticism, even in critical works that seek to recover gendered differences. In his introduction to a special issue on Female Gothic of *Women's Writings: The Elizabethan to the Victorian Period*, Robert Miles thus claims that early feminist criticism having reached "an impasse", the phrase "Female Gothic" has "hardened into a literary category". The essays he introduces are therefore "challenging [...] the concept of gender itself" (Miles 1994: 131). In Einhaus's approach or in Miles's, theory is presented as, at once, both a necessary starting point and a potential dead end. Viewpoints are bound to differ here, depending on whether critics believe in literary traditions and commonalities, or whether they want to focus on singularities and plurality. Charles E. May and Susan Lohafer, perhaps

the most renowned short story scholars of the time, already endorsed
these opposed approaches two decades earlier: May was still looking
for "a unified theory of the genre which would help us understand the
unique kind of experience the short story deals with and the unique
way it imitates and creates that experience" (May 1976: 10),[2] while
Lohafer saw the third wave of short story criticism as a way to assert a postmodern distrust of universal patterns of thought and of
linear narratives, whether fictional, historical or theoretical (Lohafer
1998: ix–xii). Because genre and gender are notions that might involve
essentialising forms of discourse, I would argue that they are dangerous, yet inevitable categories.

As a modernist scholar interested in the interconnectedness of genre
and gender, this paradox or dilemma reminds me of Woolf's first words
in *A Room of One's Own*, and how she would have begun were she
asked to deliver a lecture on women and short fiction:[3]

> The title women and *short fiction* might mean, and you may have
> meant it to mean, women and what they are like, or it might mean
> women and the *short fictions* that they write; or it might mean
> women and the *short fictions* that are written about them, or it
> might mean that somehow all three are inextricably mixed together
> and you want me to consider them in that light. But when I began to
> consider the subject in this last way, which seemed the most inter-
> esting, I soon saw that it had one fatal drawback. I should never be
> able to come to a conclusion. [...] All I could do was to offer you an
> opinion upon one minor point – a woman must have money and a
> room of her own if she is to write *short fiction*; and that, as you will
> see, leaves the great problem of the nature of woman and the true
> nature of *short fiction* unsolved.
>
> (Woolf 1929/1996: 3–4)

What Woolf wrote about "women and fiction" – I have here replaced
the word "fiction" in her original text with *short fiction(s)* for the sake
of my argument – provides us with irreplaceable critical guidelines and
safeguards. What matters is not so much to reach stable definitions or
to find definitive answers to complex questions, but to keep raising these
questions, in different ways and from different perspectives, without being afraid of paradoxes. Woolf insists that material culture is bound
to matter, and suggests that we should use categories and theoretical
notions and distrust them at the same time, all the while remaining
aware of our own historicity. She finally insists on our necessary hu-
mility as readers and scholars, since after all, as she argues in "Women
Novelists", "a woman's writing is always feminine; it cannot help being
feminine: the only difficulty lies in defining what we mean by feminine"
(Woolf 1918/1987: 316).

Genre and Gender in Short Story Theories: A Short History

It is commonly acknowledged that Poe's poetic comments in the 1830s led to the birth of the modern short story as a unique genre and laid the foundations of subsequent short story theories. Poe provided us with our first formal, if not formalist, definitions; paved the way for reception theories by insisting on the positive effects of brevity; placed the short prose tale midway between the short lyric and the novel by insisting on its kinship with poetry and initiated a mode of analysis that challenged the traditional hierarchy of genres. In this respect, it is striking that short story theories should have long been grounded in comparisons with the novel: a short story does what a novel does not, or cannot do. Conversely, what a novel achieves is never contrasted with what short fiction does. In the untitled metafictional story published in February 2015 as a foreword to *British Women Short Story Writers: The New Woman to Now*, Ali Smith imagines "a short story" walking into a bar, going up to the counter and asking the barmaid "what single malts do you have?" As the barmaid answers, "I'm sorry, we don't serve stories here", the short story nods "towards a group of inebriated-looking novels" and asks: "what about them, then?". A few lines further down, the barmaid explains: "we don't serve women here" (Smith 2015: viii–x). That such an acclaimed contemporary fiction writer as Ali Smith should stage a gendered competition between the novel and the short story is revealing. And yet, Poe gave the short story a new position in the traditional hierarchy of genres by showing the deliberate artistry it required. However, the conception of the short story as "counter-genre" rather than "genre" still influences the debates on its status as a potential vehicle for authors writing from a so-called marginal perspective.

The debates of the first few decades of the twentieth century saw the transformation of Poe's theories into "how-to" formulas (May 1995: 109) and prescriptive taxonomies, whether they agreed with Poe's definition of the genre or tried to contradict it. Meanwhile, in the first quarter of the twentieth century, many short story writers found a dominant image for their art, one that could symbolise its specific, "organic" form (O'Connor 1963: 22). Their intuitions empirically challenged the a-priori definitional approaches but were influenced, as the New Critics were, by the reputation of the modernist short story as an avant-garde art of ellipsis, indirection and fragmentation. The short story writers and critics of the period offered their own personal versions of a semantic and metaphorical approach to the genre. They creatively delineated the generic epistemological contours of what came to be seen as singular versions of the modern classic short story, whether one thinks of Elizabeth Bowen's "the free story" (Bowen 1936/1976: 156), V.S. Pritchett's "a piece of life as it flies" (Pritchett 1953: 31),

Nadine Gordimer's "flash of fireflies" (1968: 180) or of Eileen Baldeshweiler's "lyric short story" (1969: 443–453). During this first wave of short story criticism (from Poe's theory to the 1950s), "gender", understood to be a variable and unstable construct, had not yet become an analytical category; short story theories were elaborated in the wake of a male tradition of British and American writers and critics such as Poe, Brander Matthews, H.E. Bates, Sean O'Faolain and Charles E. May. Because their aim was mainly to understand the "philosophy" of the genre and to promote its literary status, their approach excluded a theoretical focus on women writing as women.

The 1960s, 1970s and 1980s, as Susan Lohafer reminds us, were decades of "consolidation in which anthologies of criticism replaced anthologies of stories" (in Lohafer and Clarey 1989: 8). Old theories were pursued, new ones emerged, and "the plot of short fiction theory heated up [...] with pioneering work in two areas that later drifted apart: the history and aesthetics of the form, and the social dynamics of genre" (Lohafer 1998: x). While the formal features and structural properties of the short story continued to be examined, its "nature" was still probed into by critics with, on the one hand, the use of aesthetic and ontological arguments – thus, Charles E. May explored the "nature of knowledge in short fiction" (1984) – and with political ones, on the other. In this respect, O'Connor's theory of the *lonely voice* (1963) had anticipated a shift in the scholarship on the short story whereby aesthetic considerations were related to "the sociology of culture", as Raymond Williams would define it in 1981. O'Connor defined the novel as a form which cannot "exist without a hero" and without a process of identification "with some aspect of his own conception of himself – as the Wild Boy, the Rebel, the Dreamer, the Misunderstood Idealist" (1963: 17). Conversely, he saw the short story as the art of "the Little Man", of the "mock-heroic character" representative of a "submerged population group" with whom the reader first cannot identify and for whom they will even feel a form of "horrified" distance (O'Connor 1963: 100). In the lonely voice rising from the text, the reader essentially heard "I Am your Brother" (O'Connor 1963: 17). Today, such edited volumes as Roxanne Harde's *Narratives of Community: Women's Short Story Sequences* (2007) explore short fictions in which lonely voices rather say "I am your sister", as in Ali Smith's prefatory piece in which the character of the female short story is excluded from the all-male-novels bar to be finally hailed by the barmaid of the "Ye Old Fighting Cocks" and offered to share with her a glass of whisky in the moonlight (Smith 2015: ix–x).

In the hands of the critics of the second wave of short story criticism, short story theory became, both in form and content, a more pluralistic discourse: literary histories, studies of national traditions (Irish, American and English, mostly) and individual authors appeared alongside anthologies and theoretical approaches to the genre. Although the "form of the modern short story" with its "compression", "implicativeness, singleness of effect, epiphanic peripety, psychological realism" was regularly considered explicitly or implicitly as the "indispensable suits" for a "properly modern writer", as American writer John Barth was later to regret (1998: 6), other forms of short-fiction writing and traditions started to be discussed. Thus, it was in 1988, for example, that three volumes of the new *Twayne Studies in the Short Fiction Series* devoted to individual authors were published, including one on Flannery O'Connor, to be followed in the 1990s by volumes on the short stories of Katherine Mansfield, Virginia Woolf, Elizabeth Bowen, Edith Warton, Gertrude Stein, Jean Rhys, Grace Paley, Eudora Welty, Kay Boyle and Joyce Carol Oates.

Of course, the 1980s were also a decade when gender theory and feminist criticism presented some fundamental challenges to critical orthodoxy by denouncing female stereotypes in fiction and other genres, by re-examining such categories as "subjectivity" and "identity", or by articulating a radically different vision of canonicity and literary theory. Women short story writers began to be analysed in feminist terms by critics such as Kate Fullbrook or Clare Hanson, who resorted to French theory, psychoanalysis and gender studies. At the time, though, the connections between gender and the short story as genre were not yet the rich terrain for scholarship it has recently become. Frank O'Connor's idea that the short story "remains by its very nature remote from the community" (O'Connor 1963: 88) was an insightful reflection on the genre that could explain women writers' interest in this non-hegemonic and marginal form, but, somewhat strikingly, this point was not made in O'Connor's analysis; nor was it an angle of analysis in Lohafer's *Coming to Terms with the Short Story* (1983), Valerie Shaw's *The Short Story: A Critical Introduction* (1983) or Clare Hanson's *Short Stories and Short Fictions: 1880–1980* (1985). However, things changed with Mary Eagleton's seminal article on "genre and gender" (1989) and the advent of the third phase of short story critical theory in the 1990s.

In their introduction to *British Women Short Story Writers*, Emma Young and James Bailey have clearly explained "the renewed sense of vibrancy" that enveloped short story criticism from the 1990s onwards, while referring to the recent studies that engage with women's short story writing (2015: 3). To their comments, I would like to add a few facts that underscore the difficulties that scholarship on the short story still experiences when it comes to exploring the way gender might affect genre. In her introduction to *The Tales We Tell: Perspectives on the Short Story*, Susan Lohafer (1998) evoked the spirit of this third wave of short story theory in the following terms:

> We are seeing the end of the romance of the short story critic and theorist as "outsider", fitting as that label may have been for devotees of the "lonely voice" genre. Students of the form are looking

askance now at the very boundaries that brought the field into existence [...] We're losing our defensiveness about genre; we're bored by taxonomies.

(xi)

Maybe forgetting that in many places of the world women are still a "submerged population" group, Lohafer's Western-centric and post-modernist view of the subject is currently contested, or at least qualified, by approaches nourished by cultural criticism, post-colonial studies and cross-disciplinarity. These approaches have enabled new voices to be recovered and have offered new insights into the connections between the genre and the sociology of culture. As a result, not only has the short story as a unique and singular genre been pluralised with the emergence of sub-categories such as short story cycles, micro fiction, mini fiction and serial narration; it has also been diversified in terms of the politics of aesthetic: new commonalities linked with cultural territories and identities have appeared, while chapters on "the new woman short stories", "women's stories", "British gay and lesbian short stories" or "Black British short stories" have become parts of edited volumes and companions devoted to the genre.

However, there are still studies that follow analytical paths which do not give any particular place to women's writing as a category: studies centred on the cognitive dimension of *"storyness"* and reception, for example, or on *"liminality"* as a primarily anthropological notion that contributes to the conceptualisation of the short story.[4] Interestingly, whenever the approach to the genre is definitional, philosophical or theoretical, it no longer focuses on how women's writing might enact a form of cultural and aesthetic revision, and even revolution, of the genre. As Elizabeth Frazer argues in her provocative essay "Is Theory Gendered?" (1996): "the main reason why feminists in particular should waste no time with theory is that it is *male* or *masculine*" (169). In this respect, a work such as Young and Bailey's *British Women Short Story Writers* is both timely and essential as it suggests that we do need to engage in discussions on theory as the site where historicist, feminist, formalist and postmodernist approaches can converge or be debated.

The continued rise of short fiction anthologies is another focus of interest of this third phase of short story criticism. The frequent grouping of stories according to literary categories, authorship and cultural traditions has led to the proliferation of sub-genres and has conditioned our way of reading stories. New cultural communities have appeared, some grounded in common "experiences", others linking authors writing in the same sub-genre, within the same period, or authors of the same sex, cultural background or sexual orientation. The contribution of these anthologies to the rising interest in women's writing has already been acknowledged.[5] They testify to the revived interest in how long "obscure" women writers – one example here is Elaine Showalter's 1993 *Daughters of Decadence* – have an impact on the revision of the literary canon, and offer a new publishing space for many supposedly "minor" writers. In their prefaces and introductions, some of these anthologies address the question of the intricate set of links between genre and gender. Susan Hill, in *The Penguin Book of Modern Women's Short Stories* (1990), and Hermione Lee (1985), in *The Secret Self*, both tackled the subject cautiously. Hill mentioned the "intimacy" of the form, the recurring themes of childhood and women's physical isolation and emotional solitude, and suggested that although the short stories in her collection might be enjoyed by both sexes, they "perhaps do speak, at a certain level, very particularly to other women" (Hill 1990: xii). As to Hermione Lee's rhetorical precautions – "perhaps", "at a certain level", "some distinctive angles" – they suggest that the critic did not want to mess assertively with theory and was aware of the dangers of categorising. However, when she wrote: "they are quiet, small-scale, intimate stories – a tone which suits the form best" (Lee 1985: x), we see the underlying risk of such arguments: to construct artificial commonalities and characteristics, to "obscure differences" and invite the reader to read "women's stories with gendered, stereotypical preconceptions", as Liggins, Maunder and Robins explain in their introduction to *The British Short Story* (2011: 19).

British writer Victoria Hislop's recent anthology – *The Story: Love, Loss and the Lives of Women: 100 Great Short Stories* (2013) – is a case in point. Although Hislop explains in her preface that "many of the writers in this volume have the ability to leave their gender behind in their writing", the association of "love" and "loss" in the title creates a horizon of expectations that undermines such a claim. Thus, an anthology of short fictions written by men would probably not sell well if titled *Love, Loss and the Lives of Men*, and the editor would probably not raise the question of the existence of a specific "male" voice in the anthologised stories. When Hislop evokes in the preface her "interesting conversations" about "whether there is a female 'voice' and whether women write differently from men", she does so, I would argue, in a hazy way, explaining without providing any theoretical justification, that she believes there are "quintessentially feminine writers – and some whose writing provides no clues as to their identity" (Hislop 2013: 7). The question raised by the editor's title and prefatory lines, therefore, is not so much whether "Angela Carter's 'The Bloody Chamber', for example, is [...] masculine [or] feminine" (Hislop 2013: 7), but whether contemporary women short fictions and their authors would not prefer "walk[ing] into a bar" to have a single malt (Smith 2015: viii) to being compelled, for commercial reasons, to enter the temple of "love" and "loss", or of other gendered symbolic experiences.

Genre and Gender in the Short Story: An Attempt at Theorisation

To examine old and new theories on the controversial subject of genre and gender in the short story along with the contributions of contemporary women writers in the form of fiction, essays and interviews – especially if we compare them to the writings of some of their foremothers – is an experience that sheds light both on recent theoretical breakthroughs and on sites of resistance to change. In her 1994 Cardiff lecture "The Place of Imagination", Michèle Roberts recounted how she was constantly asked whether her writing was autobiographical, "as though this kind of writing comes more naturally and easily to women, for some unspecified reason, and so is expected from us" (2012: 10). More than twenty years later, in her 2016 opening lecture of the Santiago de Compostela Gender and Short Fiction Conference, Janice Galloway still needed to explain how the phrase "as a woman writer" could still mark you "as unfit for greatness".

The critical method I propose here owes a lot to both Virginia Woolf's conception of literary history and criticism and to the recent scholarship on women's short fiction. It is also an attempt to reply to Margaret Ezell's criticism of the concepts of "female literary tradition" and "women's history" in *Writing Women's Literary History* (1993). Her arguments can indeed be used to challenge Woolf's well-known idea that "we think back through our mothers if we are women" (1929/1996: 70) as well as any attempt to explore the possibility of a gendered, literary counter-history:

> On the one hand, the search for female predecessors and the desire to establish a continuum can be seen as an indication of a belief in difference [...] On the other hand, however, the same anthologies and literary histories stress the repressive nature of being defined as "different", and of society's power to silence women through culturally maintained inhibitions, trapping the creative woman in a web of repressive definitions of "femininity".
>
> (Ezell 1993: 25)

Rather than exploring paths that might "trap" women writers in essentialism and marginality, I would like to propose a series of critical tools and safeguards that allow us to address together the subjects of genre and gender, and, along with them, those of authorship, identity, community, female tradition, voice and influence in a systematic, theoretical and historicised mode of criticism.

Definitions are Debatable, But Short Story Critics Need Them

In "Feminine Occupations", her introduction to her 2014 *British Women Writers and the Short Story, 1850–1930*, Kate Krueger uses Dorothy

Smith's conception of femininity as a "complex of actual relations vested in texts", as a "social form of social consciousness" that "can be examined as actual practices" (3).[6] Do we mean the same thing when we use the phrases "women's writing" and "female tradition"? To map a tradition and its literary genealogies is not the same as to explain whether we are talking of commonalities grounded in experience, of femininity as a gendered construction or of "women" as a symbolic position in language. One might argue that definitions are mainly dangerous – one of the reasons why Woolf herself, in *Three Guineas*, hoped that one day the word "feminist" could be burnt in a ceremony that would "clear the air" and symbolise the moment when "men and women are now working together" (Woolf 1938/1996: 221–222). In an interview with journalist Linda Richards on her novel *Clara*, Janice Galloway explains:

> I feel terribly awkward being asked a question: Is this a kind of feminist work? I don't actually know. [...] The word "feminism" is so loaded with booby traps. What it means to certain people. What it means to who you're speaking to. You can never be sure exactly what they mean when they use the word. [...] There are real gender problems in my country. If I'm labelled feminist, [some readers will be] automatically pushing me away. I think one has to be very careful of terms.
>
> (2003)

Assuredly, we want to move beyond the obstacle of preconceived womanhood in the light of what Althusser and Judith Butler call "the theory of interpellation".[7] But while we need to face the pitfalls of definition, we also need to avoid those lying in the absence of definition.

Material Culture and Institutional and Publishing Practices Matter

More than twenty years ago, the intricate set of links existing between the rise of the short story as genre and the material and institutional conditions that have always influenced its appearance in magazines, anthologies, collections, cycles or digital form was not the fruitful research field it has become. Today, all (or almost all) scholarly work on the subject takes material reality and discursive practices into account. In "Writing and Publishing the Short Story", Paul March-Russell (2016) evokes the importance of approaching the short story as a "contextual process", and not merely as a "textual product" (15). In her introduction to *The Cambridge Companion to the English Short Story*, Ann-Marie Einhaus insists on the "close relationship with [the short story's] principal media of publication, the magazine or periodical on the one hand, and the story collection or anthology, on the other" (2016: 7).

However, there is still a history to be written on the subject of how material culture has always influenced women writers in their practice of the art of the short story. In her contribution to Young and Bailey's volume, Ailsa Cox inserts her own story within the broader narrative of "short story publishing and women's writing in the late twentieth century" (2015: 114), thus providing a piece of the puzzle. Her description of the short story writer's market in the last two decades echoes José Francisco Fernández's analysis in "A Move against the Dinosaurs: The New Puritans and the Short Story": from the end of the 1990s onwards, "the commercial and sociological panorama of the literary short story [has been] bleak" (2012: 230). Even if a vast amount of the short stories are still written for women's magazines, Cox explains that "commercial publishers concentrate their efforts on the [...] 'Star players' of the literary world, leaving minority pursuits – such as the short story – to the small presses" mostly based outside London (Cox 2015: 116). For women short story writers in particular, as Cox explains, women-only publications and anthologies like *Storia*, feminist publishers like *Virago*, women's writing groups and literary journals grounded in a sense of community are of paramount importance. The exploration of the links between these material and literary communities is therefore an essential step in any critical approach to the question of genre and gender in the short story.

Beware of the Separation of Aesthetics from Politics and Ideology

In his introduction to *Modernism and Theory: A Critical Debate*, Stephen Ross examines the reasons why post-1980s literary theory "often rejected its capacity to reveal the truth about anything", whether it be "gender, identity, sexuality, race, [or] class difference" (Ross 2009: 10). Thus, if we explore short fiction and short story theories after 1970 in the light of the theoretical premises and injunctions of postmodernism, such as those challenged by Terry Eagleton in *The Illusions of Postmodernism*, we might lose the political edge that these contemporary texts possess. Ali Smith's short stories, to take just one example, certainly exhibit recognisable postmodernist characteristics such as self-reflexivity, playfulness, the blurring of the boundaries between high and popular culture, between "art" and "popular experience". But her art is not "depthless", "ungrounded"; her "first person" and "third person" may seem strangely "free-floating, contingent, aleatory" at first, but they are not utterly "atomized" or dehistoricised either (Eagleton 1996/2013: 89), otherwise her short fictions could not endorse current issues such as environmentalist ethics, nor articulate a powerful critique of contemporary disaffection and cynicism.[8] In this respect, the short history of the attempts at theorisation that I have just recounted prompts us to remember that, for various reasons and at any period of time, the question of gender might be challenged as useless or marginal. Our critical discourse constantly needs to be poised between the obstacle of preconceived womanhood and the radical deconstruction of "woman" as a valid category, social truth and individual embodied experience.

Lines of Filiation and Genealogies Cannot be Ignored

"Book begets books", Ali Smith explained in August 2012 at The Edinburgh World Writers' Conference. Smith's statement does not mean that women writers think back exclusively through their foremothers, but it certainly suggests that there is, in the history of women British short fiction, a continuity of preoccupations and anxieties related to such subjects as the construction of female identity, patriarchy, class, gender roles in the domestic and public spaces, sexuality, the body, British history and the representation of new versions of femininity. As Kate Krueger explains,

> due to its qualities of symbolic suggestiveness, intensity, and rejection of novelist premises and structures, the short story provides women a venue in which to represent their alienation from dominant ideologies of femininity and, at the same time, to offer alternative definitions.
>
> (Krueger 2014: 3–4)

This continuity of female concerns also has its breaking points as social contexts and feminist debates evolve. Antony does not systematically love Cleopatra, and Chloe might like Olivia in all sorts of ways.[9] "Mrs. Brown", as Virginia Woolf called the female character embodying the obscure lives she wanted to catch, now appears in her manifold guises. In Michèle Roberts's collection *Mud*, for example, we hear the voices and stories of a young widow recalling the male figures of her recent past ("Mud"), of a female narrator remembering her first sexual experience ("Colette Looks Back"), of the wife of a vegetarian man who cannot fit in France ("Vegetarian in France"), of Emma Bovary's *doppelgänger* ("Emma Bovary's Ghost"), of a Woolfian postmodernist ("Flâneuse"), of a contemporary Isolde ("Tristram and Isolde"), of Eva in her English sex house feeling as if she were an item on a shopping list ("Easy as ABC"), of Jane Eyre's alter ego fleeing Thornfield with Adèle ("Sleepers"), of Mary mother of Jesus ("Annunciation"). In this collection, the notion of "female tradition" implies the creative revision of stereotypes, and, as Roberts herself explains in an essay on T.S. Eliot and "impersonality as a masculine doctrine", it also entails the necessity to "go in search of [one's mother], of finding models, of making up new ones" (Roberts 1988/2012: 112). Roberts adds that only "once you find you've got many more foremothers than you ever dreamed, you can stop being amazed, à la Dr Johnson, that woman can do it all, and get on with the business of reading and writing" (1988/2012: 117).

Try Short Story Theory, Historicise Theory

My readings of contemporary British short stories by women and of recent short story theories have enabled me to track down recurring critical theories and arguments – some of them being the re-semiotisation of former ones – the relevance and adequacy of which I have tried to assess by pitting them against early and late twentieth-century short stories. In what follows, I provide an outline of key critical arguments, themes, ideas and literary categories that appear time and again in stories by women writers or in the critical discourses that study them: namely, hierarchy, time, space, subjectivity, voice, metaphor, anger, agency and playfulness.

I would argue that the notion of *hierarchy* and its continuing relevance for the discussion of both genre and gender is the first necessary stop in the investigation of the subject at stake. As differentiation implies hierarchies, hierarchies reinforce differences: both women and the short story have always struggled for recognition, advancement and equality of treatment; both have been at odds with dominant culture and have frequently refuted it. The idea of hierarchy has thus laid the groundwork for the exploration of forms of marginality, dissidence and for controversies over dominant discourses embedded in ideologies of genre and gender. I therefore argue that we still need to focus our attention on the way the hierarchy of genres and the category "women's short fiction" are consciously discussed and enacted in editorial processes, contemporary anthologies and critical discourses. Among the questions raised here, one pertains to the way contemporary mass-market magazines, literary periodicals and critical theory might use the label "women short story writers" with a short-term business approach. Another is how we assess the way such a label helps women writers to step within the margins of the canon or, on the contrary, is insidiously used to keep them out of it.

Brevity in its relation to represented and representing *time* in the short story is another indispensable term in the discussion. Because the "crisis of the short story is the short story and not as in the novel the mere logical inescapable result of what preceded it", the short story, said Frank O'Connor, "represents a struggle with Time: the novelist's Time" (1963: 105). And in her essay on literature entitled "Time", Ali Smith explains how "the difference between the short story form and the novel is to do not with length but with time", with the elasticity of the form and its insistence on the "momentousness of the moment" (2012: 28–29). But the short story's brevity can also be seen as the epitome of women's fragmented time: the time to write a letter, a diary entry, to read a "Valentine" card (Galloway 1997/1996); the time women have left between their domestic activities, the time they manage to find and whose value they reclaim, the experiential time leading them to the exploration of gendered bodily practices and experiences. This hypothesis is indirectly supported by the recent research around the issue of the social and gendered nature of time. In *Gender and the Politics of Time* (2007), for example, Valery Bryson discusses the existence of a "specifically female time-culture" in patriarchal capitalist societies – a "women's time" undermining the dominant contemporary model of time, "the linear, goal-oriented, commodified time of the clock" (121), a time that is not easily measurable and refuses the usual dichotomy of linear versus cyclical. Just as the "revisionary potential" of the short story appears to enable women writers and their female characters to "reclaim" social space (Krueger 2014: 3), the genre's struggle with time and exploration of new temporalities clearly offers a venue for contemporary women writers seeking to revise dominant time-ideologies.

As Kate Krueger explains, real and represented *spaces* are most of the time gendered; they are "locations wherein social interactions are governed by expectations surrounding masculine and feminine behaviours" (2014: 1). The "narrow stage" of the short story increases the symbolic value of its represented and representing space. Since its beginnings in the nineteenth century, she explains, the short story has produced genealogies of female characters and women writers who breach the borders of private, public and mental spaces, and thus "revise dominant narratives of femininity" (Krueger 2014: 2). Krueger's work of observing how space in the British short story is a referential and literary site enabling women writers to "depict normative spaces as sites of crisis" (2014: 3) stops in the 1930s and must be continued. Emily Horton's recent essay on "Contemporary Space and Affective Ethics in Ali Smith's Short Stories" is a significant example of how "space" as a reality and literary category can be reclaimed for "personal and social affective engagement" by postmodern subjects in general, and women writers in particular (2013: 22).

Female embodied experiences and women's shifting and plural *subjectivities* are among the major topics of twentieth-century British short fiction. Interviewed in 1999 by Cristie Leigh March, Janice Galloway explained how she wanted to distance herself from the "bloke's profile" of the contemporary Scottish literary scene: "My work is to ask what it's like to be an intelligent woman coping with the twentieth century, [...] to write as though having a female perspective is normal which is a damn sight harder than it sounds" (March 1999: 85). How contemporary women short story writers use the genre as a privileged medium to represent and construct female characters, subjectivities, bodies and sexualities, how they undermine stereotypes and play with gender fluidity and openness is another essential line of inquiry here. The difficulty obviously lies in the assessment of a difference between women's novels and women's short stories: when it comes to the literary representation of the female self, the question of how gender affects genre and vice versa is a slippery issue, as I have been arguing all along. In the case of women writers, the critical discourse on the representation of female subjectivity is still too often associated with biographical or autobiographical considerations. The inscription of female *voices* in the grammar of the short story text, on the other hand, is a subject that deserves more attention.

"Each story", explains Ailsa Cox,

> begins with the struggle to tune into the right voice; like many writers, I edit my writing aloud. And because the short story is a compressed, intensive form, orality and the rhythmic elements of language are especially pronounced in short fiction.
>
> (Cox 2015: 123)

When Frank O'Connor wrote *The Lonely Voice*, he kept away from the subject of gender; so did Michael Stephens in his valuable 1986 study of *The Dramaturgy of Style: Voice in the Short Fiction*. And although so many anthologies or monographs concerned with women's short fiction use the metaphor of voice to make a case for the importance and singularity of the chosen author, voice is rarely associated with gender along theoretical lines. However, from Katherine Mansfield's dramatic monologues and Virginia Woolf's dialogues in the seven short fictions of the Mrs Dalloway sequence to more contemporary voices – voices encoding the female self and its vulnerable presence, impersonated female voices encoded by the texts and asking for a re-vocalisation by their readers, women's voices performing in public or in the private sphere – the representation and literary construction of speech in women's twentieth-century short stories has often contributed both to the de-authorising of the voice of the traditional male narrator and to the inscription on the page of women's idiosyncratic affects, bodily rhythms and personal dramas: "Eggs, butter, sugar, flour; a lemon. Pre-heat the oven to 180 degrees. And because as you know it's the one I always make, darling girl, I have the lemon recipe pretty much by heart", we read in Helen Simpson's "Kythera" (2015: 41).

"Nana, let me tell you a story", says Eva, the narrator of Michèle Roberts's "Easy as ABC". And she goes on: "Once upon a time a girl was born in a small town far from the capital" (Roberts 2010: 129). How the short story, relying both on its oral tradition and its kinship with drama and poetry, manages to capture the still unrecorded voices of women is another promising terrain of scholarship. I would suggest that an innovative way of looking at the question might combine short story theory with scientific work such as Mary Belenky, Blythe Clinchy, Nancy Goldberger and Jill Tarule's *Women's Ways of Knowing: The Development of*

Self, Voice, and Mind (1986), which paves the way for a renewed vision of how "women ground their epistemological premises" in metaphors expressing the importance of speaking and listening (19).

While *metaphor* is currently explored in its relation to linguistics and systems of knowledge, I think it is high time to consider it not simply as a defining ingredient of the short story but as one of the places from where to examine how gender affects the practice of the genre. Many modernist and contemporary women's short stories revolve around organic, often gendered, metaphors: Katherine Mansfield's moon and sea, Elizabeth Bowen's windows, Angela Carter's mirrors or Janice Galloway's blood are but a few examples. In Roberts's eponymous story, "mud" strikingly deconstructs the more traditionally masculine and biblical notions of dust and clay to intimate images of feminine love, sex, creativity and body language. It also connotes forms of experience and writing that are not analytical but anchored in sensations, in the plasticity of words, in the flesh and in mother earth: mud, Roberts writes, may "rot [...] to good compost" inside you; it enables you to leave tracks – the imprint of your "footsteps", "names", "bodies" and "journeys" (Roberts 2010: 2, 5) – and to recover the tracks of others. Building on Susan Wolstenholme's idea that women writers form "a community characterized not by a position of marginality, [...] nor by a common bond of directly accessible experience, but rather by the symbolic exchange among the group itself" (1993: xiii), I contend that metaphors in short fiction may function as literary and epistemological sites whereby intertextual relationships lead to the creation of gendered filiations and communities.

Strikingly, metaphors having to do with affect run like a thread linking stories by women from different periods. Anger is one of these affects, conveyed more acutely through the brevity and intensity of form. In Janice Galloway's story "Blood" (1991/2001), blood itself is one of these organic metaphors that anticipate the text's entwined layers of meaning; it is also the promise of an angry, muffled shout, connecting anger to the short story's sharpness. It is obviously hazardous to see anger as a theme or a critical tool furthering our understanding of the interconnectedness of women and the short story. Like any other emotion, anger cannot be easily gendered. However, as Linda Grasso suggests in her compelling exploration of *The Artistry of Anger: Black and White Women's Literature in America, 1820–1860*, "gendered ideologies have historically precluded anger from women's emotional repertoire" as the public expression of discontent has long been culturally forbidden (2002: 5). Strikingly enough, the themes of rebellion and radicality, often embodied by female figures, are recurrent in the recent scholarship on women and the short story. The "huge offence" made to women (Smith 2007: xxvii), whether at the time of their political battles or as they now still face frustrations, oppression and unmet needs, has been a frequent preoccupation for women short story writers. From Evelyne

Sharp's *Rebel Women* in 1910 to Katherine Mansfield's "cry against corruption" (1977/1985: 98), from *fin-de-siècle Daughters of Decadence* to Doris Lessing's stories on the battle of the sexes or Galloway's "artistry of angry expression" (Grasso 2002: 5), the covert or overt feminism of short story writers has kept revealing and repairing this offence, using the genre as a forum to articulate their concerns. That the short story should be a privileged place for such an imperative is no surprise. Breaking free from the traditional narrative patterns of the novel, such as the emphasis on plot, causality and closure, it has occupied, and still does, a position that releases it from the demands of literary orthodoxy. It is obviously possible to kill "the angel in the house" in a novel; but as a theme, a voice and an instrument of resistance and condemnation, the blasting and controlled power of anger is bound to resonate differently in a short story.

While it has long been considered as a threatening sign of irrationality and mental disorder, we now know that anger, whether as a "mode of enquiry" (Grasso 2002: 5) or as an empowering energy that has accompanied each phase of women's political emancipation, can be a source of political insight, growth and *agency*. In view of recent feminist debates on how an insistence on "subordination" might perpetuate essentialist views of women as victims and men as agents, one might want to explore how contemporary women's stories create new possibilities for the fashioning of the female self. Nineteenth- and early twentieth-century women short fictions often depicted women entrapped in enclosed spaces and fixed gender roles; the limited representing space of the short story usually strengthened the impression of a limited sphere of action. Even then, though, as Kate Krueger shows, the short story was a literary site for the explorations of paths out of passivity, petrification and powerlessness. The female characters in today's British short fiction can easily get out of their rooms, boats and train cabins into the public sphere and the outer world. Their bodies, sexualities and politics are no longer subjects that need to be approached indirectly. But the compressed art of the short story is, I would argue, an engaging experimental place from which to observe the new paradigms of the female self – how it is still poised between the residual potency of the past and the prospects of the future. If we assume that the art of the short story relies on a poetics of tension and crisis, and on the balance between sophisticated constraints and experimental freedom, then the exploration of women's agency as a multifaceted resource outside subjugation is a critical aspect of the discussion on genre and gender.

"Thank God I'm writing short stories", says Janice Galloway as Celis Aston interviews her on her art in *Jellyfish*.

> You get to the end of them quicker, and you feel a sense of achievement much quicker. And I love putting them together, and I love

toying with ideas between stories and seeing how one story bounces off another – it's totally different to how chapters bounce. A completely different ball game. It's playing with the reader and saying 'I know you're out there'.

(Aston 2017)

The sense of *playfulness* imparted by the form is a feeling shared by generations of women short story writers, from Virginia Woolf looking forward to be "free" so as to write "two or more stories" after *Mrs Dalloway* and *The Common Reader* (Woolf 1953/1978: 97) to Ali Smith who, interviewed by Kenny Mathieson, stated:

You can do so much in such little space in short stories. There is such an elasticity of form there, by which I mean you can do pretty much anything you like with it and it will probably hold it.

(2006)

Again, the notion of playfulness cannot be easily gendered: irreverence, literary lightness and subversive creativity can be found in both men's and women's short stories. However, when related to the issues of authorship, voice, identity and agency, the sense of freedom and release experienced by the female practitioners of the genre sheds new light on the way genre and gender are connected. Playfulness indeed raises anew the question of how women short story writers have developed sophisticated strategies to challenge both masculine rationality and the labels, or expectations, induced by the constructed image of their femininity. Playfulness, I would argue, implies creativity, humour and the agonistic features of contestation; but more importantly, it paves the way for an alternative vision of seriousness and frivolity. The viewpoint of a snail in "Kew Gardens" (Woolf 1919/1991) is no longer irrelevant, being a "Vegetarian in France" (Roberts 2010) is no longer a trivial subject, and "Blood" (Galloway 1991/2011) does not refer to murder or a war wound but to the fluid bleeding in an adolescent's mouth and to her menstruation.

In Lieu of Conclusion: Don't Forget that Critics are Telling Stories and that Good Stories Provide Their Own Theories

My conclusion deliberately takes the form of a sixth critical proposition. We read backwards, and for those who work on contemporary literature, critical distance can be difficult to achieve. At any rate, how we discuss literary history and singular writers comes through a narrative that tells us as much about its own construction as it does about genre and gender in the short story. Conversely, and more essentially, each collection of stories, maybe even each story, enacts "her" own vision of storytelling; I am here gendering the genre on purpose, as a last debt to

Virginia Woolf and her legacy. In fact, we find the same serious play-fulness in Ali Smith's story about the short story – where the genre is first referred to as "it" before "it" is gendered as "her" by the novels around her (Smith 2015b: viii–ix) – as in the first sentence of Woolf's "The Art of Fiction", an essay ironically attacking a male tradition of literary critics, where she pictures fiction as "a lady who has somehow got herself into trouble", a thought "that must often have struck her ad-mirers" (Woolf 1927/1994: 457).

Gender does not matter, and yet it does. For once, it is always in the eye of the beholder; then, assuredly, "a woman's writing cannot help be-ing feminine", as Woolf would have it in "Women Novelists". I hope that my attempts at theorisation will have helped clarify, in a non-essentialist way, "what we mean by feminine" (Woolf 1918/1987: 316).

Notes

1 See, among others, the works of Roxanne Hard (2007), Kate Krueger (2014), Emma Liggins, Andrew Maunder and Ruth Robbins (2011), and Jorge Sacido (2012).
2 See also the first chapter of *The Short Story: The Reality of Artifice* (May 2002: 1–20).
3 I have here replaced the word fiction in the original quotation with *short fiction*.
4 Claire Drewery's own work on liminality is obviously an exception.
5 See for example Liggings, Maunder and Robbins's introduction to *The British Short Story* (2010: 1–24).
6 Krueger refers here to Dorothy Smith, *Texts, Facts, and Femininity: Explor-ing the Relations of Ruling*, London: Routledge, 1993, 163.
7 Louis Althusser popularised the idea of interpellation in his 1972 essay "Ideology and Ideological State Apparatuses". The process by which an in-dividual can acknowledge his subjecthood and subordination to ideology each time he is interpellated through various mediums was later discussed by Judith Butler, notably in *Bodies that Matter: On the Discursive Limits of Sex*. Routledge: New York (1993).
8 On these two subjects see Kotskowska (2013) and Sacido-Romero (2016).
9 My reference here is to Virginia Woolf's *A Room of One's Own* again: "'Chloe liked Olivia,' I read. And then it struck me how immense a change was there. Chloe liked Olivia perhaps for the first time in literature. Cleopatra did not like Octavia. And how completely *Antony and Cleopatra* would have been altered had she done so!" (Woolf 1929/1996: 76).

References

Aston, Celis (2017) "An Interview with Janice Galloway about *Jellyfish*", *Vimeo* 27, vimeo.com/154294004 (accessed 2 October 2017).
Baldeshweiler, Eileen (1969) "The Lyric Short Story: The Sketch of a History", *Studies in Short Fiction* 6: 443–453.
Barth, John (1998) "A Novel Perspective: 'It's a Short Story'", in *The Tales We Tell: Perspectives on the Short Story*, edited by Barbara Lounsberry, Susan

Lohafer, Mary Rohrberger, Stephen Pett and R.C. Feddersen, Westport, CT: Greenwood Press, 1–12.

Belenky, Mary Field, Blythe McVicker Clinchy, Nancy Rule Goldberger and Jill Mattuck Tarule (1986) *Women's Ways of Knowing: The Development of Self, Voice, and Mind*, New York: Basic Books.

Besnault-Levita, Anne (2007) "Gender", in *The Facts On File Companion to the British Short Story*, edited by Andrew Maunder, New York: Facts On File, 483–485.

Bowen, Elizabeth (1936/1976) "Preface to *The Faber Book of Modern Short Stories*", in *Short Story Theories*, edited by Charles May, Ohio, OH: Ohio University Press, 152–158.

Cox, Ailsa (2015) "New Waves of Interest: Women's Short Story Writing in the Late Twentieth Century", in *British Women Short Story Writers: The New Woman to Now*, edited by Emma Young and James Bailey, Edinburgh: Edinburgh University Press, 114–132.

Donovan, Josephine (1998) *Women and the Rise of the Novel, 1405–1726*, New York: St. Martin's Press.

Drewery, Claire (2011) *Modernist Short Fiction by Women: The Liminal in Katherine Mansfield, Dorothy Richardson, May Sinclair and Virginia Woolf*, Farnham: Ashgate.

Eagleton, Mary (1989) "Gender and Genre", in *Re-Reading the Short-Story*, edited by Clare Hanson, Basingstoke: Macmillan, 56–68.

Eagleton, Terry (1996/2013) *The Illusions of Postmodernism*, Malden, MA: Blackwell.

Einhaus, Ann-Marie (2013) *The Short Story and the First World War*, Cambridge: Cambridge University Press.

Einhaus, Ann-Marie (2016) "Introduction", in *The Cambridge Companion to the English Short Story*, edited by Ann-Marie Einhaus, New York: Cambridge University Press, 1–14.

Ezell, Margaret J.M. (1993) *Writing Women's Literary History*, Baltimore, MD: The Johns Hopkins University Press.

Fernández, José Francisco (2012) "A Move against the Dinosaurs: The New Puritans and the Short Story", in *Modernism, Postmodernism, and the Short Story in English*, edited by Jorge Sacido, Amsterdam: Rodopi, 229–251.

Frazer, Elizabeth (1996) "Is Theory Gendered?", *Journal of Political Philosophy* 4(2): 169–189.

Galloway, Janice (1991/2011) *Blood*, London: Vintage Books.

Galloway, Janice (1996/1997) *Where You Find It*, London: Vintage.

Galloway, Janice (2015) *Jellyfish*, Glasgow: Freight Books.

Gordimer, Nadine (1968/1976) "The Flash of Fireflies", in *Short Story Theories*, edited by Charles E. May, Athens, OH: Ohio University Press, 287–295.

Grasso, Linda M. (2002) *The Artistry of Anger: Black and White Women's Literature in America, 1820–1860*, Berkeley, CA: University of California Press.

Hanson, Clare (1985) *Short Stories and Short Fictions: 1880–1980*, London: Macmillan.

Hanson, Clare (1989) *Re-Reading the Short Story*, New York: St. Martin's Press.

Hanson, Clare (2015) "Postscript: British Women's Short Story Writing", in *British Women Short Story Writers: The New Woman to Now*, edited by

Emma Young and James Bailey, Edinburgh: Edinburgh University Press, 193–198.

Harde, Roxanne (ed.) (2007) *Narratives of Community: Women's Short Story Sequences*, Newcastle: Cambridge Scholars Publishing.

Hill, Susan (ed.) (1991) *The Penguin Book of Modern Women's Short Stories*, Harmondsworth: Penguin.

Hislop, Victoria (ed.) (2013) *The Story: Love, Loss and The Lives of Women: 100 Great Short Stories*, London: Head of Zeus.

Horton, Emily (2013) "Contemporary Space and Affective Ethics in Ali Smith's Short Stories", in *Ali Smith: Contemporary Critical Perspectives*, edited by Monica Germanà and Emily Horton, London: Bloomsbury Academic, 9–22.

Hunter, Adrian (2007) *The Cambridge Introduction to the Short Story in English*, Cambridge: Cambridge University Press.

Kotskowska, Justyna (2013) *Ecocriticism and Women Writers: Environmentalist Poetics of Virginia Woolf, Jeanette Winterson, and Ali Smith*, Basingstoke: Palgrave.

Krueger, Kate (2014) *British Women Writers and the Short Story, 1850–1930: Reclaiming Social Space*, Basingstoke: Palgrave Macmillan.

Lee, Hermione (ed.) (1985) *The Secret Self 1: Short Stories by Women*, London: Dent.

Liggins, Emma, Andrew Maunder, and Ruth Robbins (2011) *The British Short Story*, Basingstoke: Palgrave Macmillan.

Lohafer, Susan (1998) "Introduction", in *The Tales We Tell: Perspectives on the Short Story*, edited by Barbara Lounsberry, Susan Lohafer, Mary Rohrberger, Stephen Pett and R.C. Feddersen, Westport, CT: Greenwood, ix–xii.

Lohafer, Susan and Jo Ellyn Clarey (eds.) (1989) *Short Story Theory at a Crossroads*, Baton Rouge, LA: Louisiana State University Press.

Mansfield, Katherine (1977/1985) *The Letters and Journals of Katherine Mansfield: A Selection*, edited by C.K. Stead, London: Penguin.

March, Cristie Leigh (1999) "Interview with Janice Galloway", *Edinburgh Review* 101: 85–98.

March-Russell, Paul (2016) "Writing and Publishing the Short Story", in *The Cambridge Companion to the English Short Story*, edited by Ann-Marie Einhaus, Cambridge: Cambridge University Press, 15–27.

Mathieson, Kenny (2006) "Ali Smith: Listening for the Voices", in *Northings: Arts and Culture in the Highland Islands of Scotland*, http://northings.com/2006/05/01/ali-smith (accessed 30 March 2016).

May, Charles E. (1976) "A Survey of Short Story Criticism in America", in *Short Story Theories*, edited by Charles E. May, Athens, OH: Ohio University Press, 3–12.

May, Charles E. (1984) "The Nature of Knowledge in Short Fiction", *Studies in Short Fiction* 21(4): 327–338.

May, Charles E. (1995/2002) *The Short Story: The Reality of Artifice*, New York: Twayne.

Miles, Robert (1994) "Introduction", in *Women's Writings: The Elizabethan to the Victorian Period* 1(2): 131–142.

O'Connor, Frank (1963) *The Lonely Voice: A Study of the Short Story*, Cleveland, OH: World Publishing.

Pritchett, V.S. (1953) "Short Stories", *Harper's Bazaar* 87: 31, 113.

Richards, Linda L. (2003) "January Interview: Janice Galloway", *January Magazine*, www.januarymagazine.com/profiles/jgalloway.html (accessed 28 August 2017).

Roberts, Michèle (1988/2012) *On Food, Sex and God: On Inspiration and Writing*, London: Hachette Digital.

Roberts, Michèle (2010) *Mud: Stories of Sex and Love*, London: Hachette.

Ross, Stephen (ed.) (2009) *Modernism and Theory: A Critical Debate*, Abingdon: Routledge.

Sacido, Jorge (ed.) (2012) *Modernism, Postmodernism, and the Short Story in English*, Amsterdam: Rodopi.

Sacido-Romero, Jorge (2016) "Ghostly Visitations in Contemporary Short Fiction by Women: Fay Weldon, Janice Galloway and Ali Smith", *Atlantis: Journal of the Spanish Association of Anglo-American Studies* 38(2): 83–102.

Shaw, Valerie (1983) *The Short Story: A Critical Introduction*, London: Longman.

Showalter, Elaine (ed.) (1993) *Daughters of Decadence: Women Writers of the Fin-de-Siècle*, London: Virago Press.

Simpson, Helen (2015) *Cockfosters*, London: Random House.

Smith, Ali (2007) "Introduction", in *The Collected Stories of Katherine Mansfield*, London: Penguin, v–xxx.

Smith, Ali (2012) "How Should Authors Approach the Task of Writing a Novel Today?", *Edinburgh World Writers' Conference 2012–13*, www.youtube.com/watch?v=bHOSXziim9A (accessed 20 May 2017).

Smith, Ali (2015) "Foreword", in *British Women Short Story Writers: The New Woman to Now*, edited by Emma Young and James Bailey, Edinburgh: Edinburgh University Press, viii–x.

Stephens, Michael G. (1986) *The Dramaturgy of Style: Voice in Short Fiction*, Carbondale, IL: Southern Illinois University Press.

Young, Emma and James Bailey (2015) *British Women Short Story Writers: The New Woman to Now*, Edinburgh: Edinburgh University Press.

Williams, Raymond (1981) *The Sociology of Culture*, Chicago, IL: The University of Chicago Press.

Wolstenholme, Susan (1993) *Gothic Revisions: Writing Women as Readers*, Albany, NY: University of New York Press.

Woolf, Virginia (1953/1978) *A Writer's Diary*, London: Grafton Books.

Woolf, Virginia (1918/1987) "Women Novelists", in *The Essays of Virginia Woolf, Vol. 2: 1912–1918*, edited by Andrew Mc Neillie, Orlando, FL: Harcourt Brace Jovanovitch, 314–316.

Woolf, Virginia (1919/1991) "Kew Gardens", in *The Complete Shorter Fiction of Virginia Woolf*, edited by Susan Dick, Triad Grafton Books, 90–95.

Woolf, Virginia (1927/1994) "The Art of Fiction", in *The Essays of Virginia Woolf, Vol. 4: 1925–1928*, edited by Andrew Mc Neillie, Orlando, FL: Harcourt Brace Jovanovitch, 457–464.

Woolf, Virginia (1929/1938/1996) *A Room of One's Own* and *Three Guineas*, London: Vintage.

Part II
In Carter's Wake

3　The Legacy of Angela Carter

Ethics and Authorial Performance in Contemporary Short Fiction by Women

Michelle Ryan-Sautour

Introduction

In her afterword to *Fireworks* (1974), Angela Carter playfully suggests how the size of her room in Japan led her to write short fiction:

> I started to write short pieces when I was living in a room too small to write a novel in. So the size of my room modified what I did inside it and it was the same with the pieces themselves.
>
> (Carter 1995: 132)[1]

She had gone to Japan after having received the Somerset Maugham Award at the end of the 1960s, and although she had worked with the short story form in earlier texts such as "The Man Who Loved a Double Bass" (1962) and "A Very, Very Great Lady and Her Son at Home" (1965), the stories she wrote at this time attest to an affirmed exploration of a malleable genre. Pieces in *Fireworks* range from autobiography to cultural critique, fairy tale-like fantasies, parallel world fantasy and even vampire fiction. Traces of journalism blend with fiction and point to the manner in which Carter would continue to draw upon, while also defying, the tradition of short story writing.

Short stories also played a catalytic role in Carter's imaginative process. Her journals at the British Library reveal multiple entries, sometimes in the form of poems, entitled "short story",[2] fragments that appear to be forms of meditative experimentation with language and ideas. A perception of short fiction as a tool is thus present throughout much of her career, in both her journals and her writing, leading to the publication of *The Bloody Chamber* in 1979, *Black Venus* in 1985 and Carter's final, posthumous collection *American Ghosts and Old World Wonders* (1993). These stories are collected in *Burning Your Boats: The Collected Short Stories* (1995), introduced by Salman Rushdie, who emphasises how the form was adapted to Carter's voice:

> The best of her, I think, is in her stories. Sometimes at novel length, the distinctive Carter voice, those smoky, opium-eater's cadences

interrupted by harsh or comic discords, that moonstone-and-rhinestone mix of opulence and flim-flam, can be exhausting. In her stories, she can dazzle and swoop, and quit while she's ahead.

(1995: ix–x)

Angela Carter was indeed a prolific short fiction writer. Her work with the form was wide-ranging, and often provocative, as her critical fictions seek to "demythologise" (Carter 1983: 71) while also pushing the limits of the genre.[3] She indeed seems to be exploiting the "moral function" she associates with short fiction, that of "provoking unease" (Carter 1995: 459), for political ends. Carter associates this unease with the work of Poe and Hoffman, mentioning "Gothic tales, cruel tales, tales of wonder, tales of terror, fabulous narratives that deal directly with the imagery of the unconscious", and explains how short fiction allows her to move beyond daily life to a space where "the tale cannot betray its readers into a false knowledge of everyday experience" (1995: 459). Her emphasis is indeed on breaking down forms of "false knowledge" through the use of the short story form, thus also harnessing the subversive force she associates with the genre, particularly the genre of the "tale":

The tale has relations with subliterary forms of pornography, ballad and dream, and it has not been dealt with kindly by literati. And is it any wonder? Let us keep the unconscious in a suitcase, as Père Ubu did with his conscience, and flush it down the lavatory when it gets too troublesome.

(Carter 1995: 459)

The idea of short fiction as being "troublesome" is also underlined in Clare Hanson's "Postscript" to *British Women Short Story Writers: The New Woman to Now* (2015). Hanson observes how the "formal properties of the short story (disjunction, inconclusiveness and obliquity) encourage an engagement with forms of experience which may be at odds with dominant cultural narratives" (2015: 196). The disturbing effects of such properties are also part of the accusations that fall upon the short story form in Ali Smith's playful foreword to *British Women Short Story Writers* (2015a), which appears as a critical fable. A group of novels accuse a short story who "walks into a bar" of destabilising the reader: "Besides, everybody knows, a weighty literary-looking tome added. Hardly anybody buys you. You're far too short. You're far too disturbing. Difficult. Insubstantial. Quite unsettling. Deeply troubling" (Smith 2015a: ix). We can find traces here of the unease Carter mentions as being something short fiction *does*. There is a keen consciousness of ethics in the process of writing, a deep concern with how a short text can draw the reader into processes of questioning, and even outright subversion.

Carter has often been identified as being a "feminist" writer, particularly, as Clare Hanson observes, in relation to her rewriting of fairy tales in *The Bloody Chamber*, describing these stories as "hugely influential" from the 1970s onwards, notably in relation to questions of the "reshaping of patriarchal narratives, foregrounding of female sexual desire and recalibration of the power dynamic of heterosexual relationships" (2015: 196). A recent review of Edmund Gordan's biography of Carter in *The New Yorker* is tellingly titled "Angela Carter's Feminist Mythology" (Acocella 2017). Although many critics agree that Carter's fairy tales go far beyond simplistic reversal,[4] it is often these works that are cited as exemplifying her skilful use of the genre for feminist ends. However, as Helen Simpson suggests in her introduction to *The Bloody Chamber*, Carter's aesthetics are more complex: "*The Bloody Chamber* is often – wrongly – described as a group of traditional fairy tales given a subversive feminist twist. In fact these are new stories, not retellings" (2006: vii). This introduction attests to Simpson's engagement with Carter's writing and indicates the far-reaching repercussions of her work on subsequent generations of women writers. In her essay "Get Carter", Ali Smith pays homage to Angela Carter, explaining how she "revolutionised the literary and intellectual landscape and made unthinkable heights possible" (2004: 82). Smith emphasises how Carter's writing opened up new avenues for writers such as herself:

> But if Carter had become an actress and not the writer she was, I, for one, know that as a writer in post-imperialist, post-postmodern, post-post-post-feminist Britain, I would not even have had the possibility of a language, never mind the space in which to use it.
>
> (2004: 92)

It is the nature of this "language" and this "space" that will be studied in this essay. I will seek to observe how Carter's use of short fiction carries over into the work of later generations of women writers. This will not be a discussion of influence so much as one of legacy, an exploration of what Carter's work has contributed to the landscape of short fiction written by women. This includes fiction written contemporaneously to Carter, as well as the work of later generations of women short fiction writers, primarily in Great Britain. Her legacy is most evident in the increased use of short fiction as a tool for critical enquiry, as a space for the reader's creative exploration and/or destabilisation and as a genre that allows for specific forms of reflection upon what it means to be a woman author. Carter's use of the genre indeed places the question of responsibility at the forefront of aesthetics. The predominance of critical debate, questions of sexual identity and overt metafictional practices all converge to foster an ethos of playful defiance and a fearless politics. It is perhaps this ethos that spills over most clearly into the stories of contemporary women short story writers.

Short Fiction and Ethics

Helen Simpson sees Carter's fairy tales as a form of "science fiction" of the past that allows her to explore "ideas of how things might be different" (2006: ix). Indeed, Carter clearly described in interview with Kim Evans how she liked "creeping up on people from behind and sandbagging them with an idea that maybe they hadn't thought of for themselves" (1992), and in her preface to her radio play *Come Unto These Yellow Sands*, she explains how "a narrative is an argument stated in fictional terms" (1996/1985: 497). Her short fiction appears to foster creative thinking. Thus, Ali Smith observes "how the short story form allowed Carter to infiltrate story with essay, in other words narrative with discussion" (2004: 90). Simpson similarly explains how such fictional forms of critical enquiry appear in the dynamics of Carter's short story collections such as the *Bloody Chamber*, where she "uses the physical form of the story collection to approach its theme obliquely, variously, from ten-strikingly different angles" (2006: viii). Carter's works extend into many critical directions, exploring areas as varied as the visual arts, performance arts, science, philosophy, linguistics and literature, always adhering to the idea that fiction is *useful*:

> Fine art, that exists for itself alone, is art in a final state of impotence. If nobody, including the artist, acknowledges art as a means of *knowing* the world, then art is relegated to a kind of rumpus room of the mind and the irresponsibility of the artist and the irrelevance of art to actual living becomes part and parcel of the practice of art.
>
> (Carter 1979: 13)

This implies a keen consciousness of the potential for literature to propose forms of ethical enquiry. Christine Reynier and Jean-Michel Ganteau, in their introduction to *Ethics of Alterity, Confrontation and Responsibility in 19th- to 21st-Century British Literature*, speak of fiction as a space for encounters or confrontations with the other and explain how the idea of responsibility is tied up with questions of values: "the values fiction transmits wittingly or unwittingly and the way in which it transmits them: respectfully or not, falsifying, manipulating or appropriating data, the past or texts of the past" (2013: 11). In her stories, Carter appears to be examining values of the past through the lens of rewriting and re-appropriation, thus proposing an engagement with the other in culture, an effect that is in turn shared with the reader as other. Maggie Tonkin (2012), for example, comments extensively on Carter's depiction of Jeanne Duval in "Black Venus" as a rewriting of the otherness of the muse, which in turn is held out to the reader for reflection. Derek Attridge reflects upon the relational dimension of otherness as mediated by literature:

> "The other" in this situation is therefore not, strictly speaking, a *person* as conventionally understood in ethics or psychology; it is once again a relation – or a relating – between me, as the same, and that which, in its uniqueness, is heterogeneous to me and interrupts my sameness. If I succeed in responding adequately to the otherness and singularity of the other, it is the other *in its relating to me*—always in a specific time and place—to which I am responding, in creatively changing myself and perhaps a little of the world as well.
>
> (2004: 33)

Carter's short texts appear to exploit such "creative" encounters with otherness through texts that suggest a will for change. The genre of short fiction is thus infused with an ethics that reaches for the political, much in the spirit of Jacques Rancière, whose approach is aptly summarised by Ganteau and Reynier as "stressing the continuum between the ethical, the political and the aesthetic" (2013: 11).

Paul March-Russell explains how short fiction "has acted at various times as a resource for writers to contest the dominant beliefs in social progress and formal cohesion" (2009: 222). This ability to contest might stem from what Charles May sees as the capacity for short stories to open up different forms of "experience or reality", thus serving as access to "a mode of knowing which differs from the mode of knowing we find in the novel" (1994: 133). Although May does not highlight cultural critique in his study of short fiction, his idea is helpful to understand how Carter mobilises the tropes of short fiction to reach past the everyday and the ordinary and penetrate to new perceptions. Michael Basseler remarks that it is perhaps the fluidity of the short story genre that gives rise to forms of "cognitive liminality": "the notion of cognitive liminality also refers to an understanding of the short story as a genre, which stages epistemic crises and subverts our very notions of knowledge as well as the cultural hierarchies thereof" (2015: 79). Carter's short stories indeed seek to foster new ways of knowing that are tinged with a sociopolitical dimension. Whether it be the re-imagined sketch of Lizzie Borden in "The Fall River Axe Murders" or literary figures in "The Cabinet of Edgar Allan Poe", the playful romp with ideas in "In Pantoland" or the brief flashes of autobiographical reflection framed as performance in "Flesh and the Mirror", the reader of Carter's stories is invited to re-read, to rethink aspects of our history and culture through a variety of stylistic lenses. She thus challenges the reader in a way that is specific to short fiction: "Like the literary fragment, the short story is prone to snap and confound reader's expectations, to delight in its own incompleteness, and to resist definition" (March-Russell 2009: viii). It is as if Carter sensed an underlying power in the very form of short fiction and sought to deploy it in a variety of manners, often opening up areas for reflection that resist clear appropriation.

The realms for such open reflection that pass under her short fiction "pen" are wide and varied. Carter's use of the genre appears to speak to later writers on a combined level of form and ethics. Ali Smith's stories, for example, exude a playfulness that echoes Carter's formal and thematic openness, while also proposing unique twists upon the genre. The titles of her story collections speak of play with the very nature of stories as well as the structure of collections: *Free Love and Other Stories* (1995), *Other Stories and Other Stories* (1999), *The Whole Story and Other Stories* (2003), *The First Person and Other Stories* (2008), *Shire* (2013), *Public Library and Other Stories* (2015b). Smith's politics, like Carter's, are indirect, but equally probing. "true short story", for example, deals with questions of breast cancer and access to treatment through the health system (Smith 2008). The collection *Public Library and Other Stories* openly investigates the future of libraries in Great Britain and equal access to culture, proposing testimonies from critics and friends, interspersed with stories that echo these voices. Similarly, two stories in *Shire*, "the poet"[5] and "the commission", explore the question of legacy through an intricate intertwining of the histories of Virginia Woolf, Olive Fraser (a Scottish critic and writer), Helena Shire (Scottish critic) and Ali Smith herself. Smith uses both story and the dynamics of the collection in manners that reach for the "you" of the reader. Ben Davies, in reference to Jacques Derrida's "envoi", comments on Smith's strategic use of "you" in her stories and the consequent confusion of "I" and "You". Her stories highlight an awareness of the addresser and addressee, the teller and the listener, while also subverting this relationship. This dynamic is present on the level of narration as well as in dialogue, echoes, voices and the literary representation of other media. Smith's fiction openly displays a consciousness of the other, echoing in her own distinctive manner the invocation of the reader one finds in Carter's stories, such as in "The Cabinet of Edgar Allan Poe" where the "you" of the reader is brought to reflect upon Poe's biography.[6] In conversation with Kasia Boddy, Smith explains how the strategic use of dialogue and voices, as well as such forms of invocation, seek to carry the reader beyond the confines of the story:

> It's an imaginative thing. As soon as you've put a person into a role, the role becomes to some extent fixed, but when you're asking the mind of the reader to engage with the engaged minds which are in the story, then something else happens which is about connection with the reader, about connection with the imaginative scope and possibilities and hold of the person who's holding the book in their hands. And something goes out of the book at that point which then

does a kind of leap, a Chinese box effect of connection, which goes out of the intimate space of the connection, of the love, of the story, right out of itself.

(Boddy 2010: 73–74)

Smith's emphasis on the reader proposes an uncanny echo of Carter's statement in 1983 that reading is "as creative as writing" (Carter 1983: 69).

Carter's 1983 essay "Notes from the Front Line", published in Michelene Wandor's *On Gender and Writing*, enters into dialogue with essays by the likes of Sara Maitland, Michèle Roberts and Eva Figes, all in response to Wandor's question about how "writers themselves try to describe, analyse and come to terms with what the idea of 'gender' means to them in their own minds: their ideas, their imaginations, the actual pieces of writing they produce" (Carter 1983: 2). Writing from the context of 1980s feminism, Carter depicts her struggle with positioning herself:

Do I 'situate myself politically as a writer'? Well, yes; of course. I always hope it's obvious, although I try, when I write fiction, to think on my feet – to present a number of propositions in a variety of different ways, and to leave the reader to construct her own fiction for herself from the elements of my fictions.

(Carter 1983: 69)

Carter speaks of "six attempts" at asserting this political involvement, only to end with the following statement: "It's been amazingly difficult, trying to sort out how I feel that feminism has affected my work [...] Oh, hell. What I *really* like doing is writing fiction and trying to work things out *that* way" (1983: 77).

If Helen Simpson's writing appears at first sight to be very different from Carter's, with her focus on maternity and the domestic, she mobilises the tools of short fiction for similar ends. Her writing speaks of a responsibility to explore questions of femininity and family life, but also, more recently, aging, social responsibility and the environment. "The Festival of the Immortals" (2010) borders on fantasy as it brings back writers such as Shakespeare and Emily Brontë to participate in a literary festival. What first appears as a playful parody of literary events and reader culture, through the presence of dialogue between two retired women in "the early November of their lives" (Simpson 2010: 107), reveals an undercurrent of reflection about the process of aging. Mortality is juxtaposed with immortality in a story that reflects upon the identity of not only famous authors, but also of the ordinary woman, as one of the characters, Phyllis, is struggling with the task of "Life writing" (Simpson 2010: 113). This serious play with the reader is present in much of Simpson's fiction, often in association with female friendship, as is evident in her story about breast cancer in "Charm for a Friend with a Lump" (2010). Simpson delves deeply into the domestic to extract a subtle form of gender politics. Although very different from Carter's aesthetics, her short fiction has an equally incisive effect on the reader: "May you continue to pile on the years, but with more pleasure from now on. In time may your joints creak and your ears hiss, may your crows feet laugh back into the mirror at your quivering dewlaps" (Simpson 2010: 131). Here, a celebration of aging and life converge in a strategic use of the "you" that not only speaks to the friend, but also solicits the reader, as we are led to share that precarious place of heartfelt love of friendship when faced with mortality.

Like Carter, Simpson's stories also stretch the short story form. "Kentish Town" (2017a) proposes a reflection upon society and social responsibility under the surface of a seemingly banal discussion between women at a book club meeting. A discussion of Charles Dickens's *Chimes* becomes the nexus for a meditation about changes in British society through the lens of the lives of upper-middle-class women in the London area. Small details speak through the gaps of the story, as the reader is led to reconcile the domestic with larger social concerns such as poverty and child labour. A strong sense of duty can also be found in the ecological awareness that runs through many of Simpson's stories. "In Flight Entertainment", "The Tipping Point" and "Ahead of the Pack" – all from *In-Flight Entertainment* (2010) – are just a few examples of how Simpson reflects upon questions of global warming and the individual carbon footprint. Play with form is intertwined with story-writing that seeks to question, pulling the reader in. "Ahead of the Pack", for instance, is presented as a pitch for a joint venture project, as the narrator speaks to a silent addressee: "Yes, you're right, that is exactly what I'm proposing – to set up as a personal Carbon Coach! In fact, I think you'll find that very soon it'll be mandatory for every company to employ an in-house Emissions Expert" (Simpson 2010: 33).

Such investigative irony is also directed towards issues of masculinity in stories such as "Erewhon" (*Cockfosters* 2017), which is punctuated by the changing time on the clock as a husband ruminates in bed. It reads as a biting reversal of women's concerns. The representation of the body is particularly striking:

> 03:48: And the media is so disparaging of men over forty, he thought; the way it zooms in on our paunches and spindle shanks, our pendulous earlobes. Another real worry was, he was developing turkey wattles. Ella had noticed it too—she'd called him jowly the other day.
>
> (Simpson 2017a: 23)

Many of Simpson's later stories venture into the areas of masculine subjectivity, as if she is re-investigating and overtly subverting traces of what Carter has spoken of as being a "colonialization" of the mind (1983: 71).

Self-Reflective Rewriting Strategies

Such self-consciousness of how our perspectives have been trained by culture runs through Carter's short fiction. Stories such as "The Cabinet of Edgar Allan Poe", "Black Venus", "The Fall River Axe Murders" and "Our Lady of the Massacre" propose to rethink literary and historical figures, much in the spirit of what Linda Hutcheon has called historiographic metafiction. There is a self-consciousness to these forays into history and literature, and even the history *of* literature, and this metafictional thread of rewriting has woven its way into the work of many women authors, both before and after Carter. Her versions, however, are particularly forceful in their appeal to the reader. Carter's contemporary, Michèle Roberts, also rethinks the lives of authors and literary characters in a powerful manner, engaging with the likes of Colette and George Sand in "Colette Looks Back" and "Remembering George Sand" in *Mud: Stories of Sex and Love* (2010). The reader encounters major and minor characters from literature such as Adèle from *Jane Eyre*, Emma Bovary and Tristram and Isolde in the same collection. Ali Smith has spoken of such self-consciousness in Carter's writing as being essential to the story: "The self-reflectiveness comes to be part of the story and is one of its prime movers" (Boddy 2010: 81). Smith's writing also incorporates self-reflectiveness, but in her own signature manner. In "fidelio and bess" she blends the plot of Beethoven's opera *Fidelio* (with its underlying political themes) and the songs and storyline of Gershwin's *Porgy and Bess*. The story is punctuated by short exchanges between the narrator/author figure and an unidentified "you", in which the question of reworking culture through storytelling is questioned:

> Culture's fixed, you say. That's why it's culture. That's how it gets to be art. That's how it works. That's why it works. You can't just change it. You can't just alter it when you want or because you want. You can't just revise things for your own pleasure or whatever.
> Actually I can do anything I like, I say.
>
> (Smith 2008: 76)

Similarly, Michèle Roberts "does what she likes", re-examining Emma Bovary through the eyes of her maid Félicité. The maid is characterised as a storyteller in love, adding a metafictional layer to a narrative that reflects upon the act of reading and fantasy: "Stories are hard to get a hold on. They change like shadows on a day of sun and wind" (Roberts 2010: 37). The idea of ghosts, love and the fleetingness of identity are intertwined with a reflection on fiction:

> I invented her. That's what falling in love means. You make the person into your own special beloved. You think you know the person but you don't. You see her as though she were a stranger. The same as seeing ghosts
>
> (Roberts 2010: 39)

British writer Alison Macleod's collection *All the Beloved Ghosts* (2017) also engages with such processes of "ghosting" historical and literary figures through fictionalisation or re-fictionalisation as a path to storytelling. There is a notable focus on Chekhov in "Imagining Chekhov", a short series of stories in which he figures as both character and imagined author. Similarly, in "Dreaming Diana: Twelve Frames", the life and death of Lady Diana are intertwined with a narrator's reflections about her own life. Helen Simpson also scatters literary re-readings throughout her writing, often in the form of short references, drawing upon literary history, while also proposing subtle subversions, such as in the aforementioned "Kentish Town", where Dickens is at the same time summoned as a reference for socially conscious writing and also subverted for his masculine bias, as the character, ironically named Estella (a character in *Great Expectations*), explains: "Dickens couldn't do women. Not women between fifteen and thirty, anyway. They're nothing but passive characterless stooges" (2017a: 42). The story takes on the form of dialogical rewriting, as the life of Dickens and the story of *The Chimes* are recreated through the voices of the four women, positioned as figures of readers in the text, who are in turn transformed into rewriters through an astute use of dialogue. Simpson's rewriting strategies often emerge through such subtle sleights of hand, their metafictional awareness often hovering just below the surface of the story. One finds in her fiction a curious blend of the domesticity associated with Katherine Mansfield's fiction and the biting politics of Carter's stories.

The Politics of Affect

The above is just a small sample of how women have used the short story to rethink and rewrite culture and fiction, and of how modes of rewriting have become a common practice in women's fiction. However, Carter's rewriting practices also involve the power of affect. Paul Ardoin and Fiona McWilliam's recent special section on Affect and the Short Story and Cycle in *Journal of the Short Story in English* attests to the strength of short fiction as an affective form. In a round table organised by the editors, Miriam Wallace speaks of how affect is "something produced in the interaction between writer, reader, and text", and explains how this could "help us make of a particularly troubling form of fiction, the didactic or moral tale" (qtd. in Ardoin and McWilliam 2016: 177). Wallace shows how this is relevant for the study of "writing with designs on its reader" (qtd. in Ardoin and McWilliam 2016: 177). The concept of affect is rich and warrants a more in-depth study than what can be proposed in the limits of this essay. However, I suggest that we consider the importance of affect in the writer-reader exchange within the continued reach of Carter's ethics. The predominance of violence and reflections on sexuality are often orchestrated in her stories in a destabilising manner. In "The Bloody Chamber", for example, ekphrasis and a pornographic onslaught on the senses of the reader converge when the narrator describes a work by Belgian artist Félicien Rops:

> I had not bargained for this, the girl with tears hanging on her cheeks like stuck pearls, her cunt a split fig below the great blobs of her buttocks on which the knotted tails of the cat were about to descend, while a man in a black mask fingered with his free hand his prick, that curved upwards like a scimitar he held.
>
> (Carter 1995: 120)

The rape scene in the inverted world on the other side of the mirror in Carter's "Reflections" likewise proposes an onslaught on the reader's senses: "Her rape, her violation of me, caused me atrocious physical and mental pain. My being leaked away from me under the visitation of her aggressive flesh" (1993: 93).

A similar onslaught on the senses can be found in the work of Janice Galloway, particularly in *Blood* (1991), written contemporaneously to Carter. In the title story, menstruation, the violence of tooth extraction and a deep sense of alienation converge in the life of a young woman. Stella Duffy's "Martha Grace" (2002) also intensifies affect, as the main character poisons her young lover Tim Culver after he has neglected her. The emotional and physical violence that pervade the story are also evident in the language of social judgement, conveyed ironically: "No-one would ever think that Tim Culver's healthy, spent, virile young body could ever had had anything to do with an old witch like Martha Grace. As the whole town knows, the fat bitch is a dyke anyway" (Duffy 2014: 20). Like Carter, Stella Duffy's writing reaches for the reader: "You're not a storyteller unless there's someone who wants to be told", she says (Duffy 2013).

In "She Murdered Mortal He" (*The Beautiful Indifference*, 2011), Sarah Hall draws the affect charged situation of a young woman on an exotic trip with her discontent lover. The setting is saturated with fear, as evident in the woman's encounter with a dog who later becomes her companion: "A creature running toward her. She couldn't move, couldn't make a clear assessment" (Hall 2011: 126). The reader is left to wonder about the dog's benevolence towards the woman, and the blood on the dog's jowls, particularly when we learn the woman's lover has been bit by a creature in the dark:

> Oh my God, she said. Oh my God. I didn't think he would come after me.
> Her palms smelled musty, like old meat, like a sick animal. She took them away from her mouth and looked up at the man. He was watching her, nervously. His eyes kept flicking away and back towards her, as if she might react dangerously, as if she might faint or bolt. She shook her head.
> What was it? Was it a leopard?
> No, he said. No. No. There are no leopards.
>
> (Hall 2011: 147)

A breathtaking, almost silent, feminine violence is expressed through the use of the implicit in the story.

A similar edge can be found in Welsh writer Carys Davies' stories. When Davies won the Frank O'Connor prize in 2015 for *The Redemption of Galen Pike*, Irish novelist Éibhear Walshe commented on the "keenly observed stories replete with twists and turns that surprise" (qtd. in Flood 2015a) to which Davies seeks to keep the reader connected: "I'm always looking for the places in the story where I'm in danger of losing or confusing the reader" ("Interview with Davies" 2007). Surprise endings are intensified with affect in stories such as "Creed". The main character Ruth's point of view is present throughout most of the narrative, until she wanders, pregnant and bleeding, to Creed's home. The birth, with a paradoxical blend of gentleness and violence, is disquieting. Death and the numinous converge in the last few lines through Creed's point of view:

> And when the long night ended and morning came and Creed had done everything he could with his boiled cloths and his needle and his fine cotton thread, when he'd tried every desperate thing short of a prayer to stop the blood and there was nothing at all, not, that could be done and it was over, he went and stood for a long time looking out through one of his arrow-slit windows at the sloping fell aflame in the dawn with the child in his arms.
>
> (Davies 2014: 141)

One is reminded here of Carter's startling endings, such as in "The Fall River Axe Murders", where the imperative beckons to the reader:[7]

> Bridget's clock leaps and shudders on its chair, about to sound its own alarm. Their day, the Bordens' fatal day, trembles on the brink of beginning.

Outside, above, in the already burning air, see! The angel of death roosts on the roof-tree.

(Carter 1995: 317)

The reader is indeed invited to "see" a historical event redrawn in Carter's story tinged with irony and dark humour.

The Mask of the Feminist Author

Carter's short fiction has indeed contributed to an ethical thrust present in the landscape of short fiction. Writers such as Hilary Mantel appear to echo Carter's acerbic narratives, as is evident in the controversy surrounding Mantel's "The Assassination of Margaret Thatcher: 6 August 1983".[8] Mantel explains: "I believe in walking that line. You mustn't be too timid to risk getting it wrong" (qtd. in Barr 2014), suggesting how "walking that line" can trouble perceptions. Mary Eagleton observes how second-wave feminism helped women increase their presence in the "cultural sphere", and cites as proof "the reshaping in the last thirty years of our cultural history", "feminist publishing companies" and "feminist listings within mainstream companies", "feminism as an academic discourse" and the "visibility of women as not only writers but as artists, musicians, cultural workers" (2005: 1). Eagleton explains how this dynamic is reflected in the development of author characters in women's fiction. Cheryl Walker has indeed spoken of the importance of "*persona criticism*", particularly in the study of women's writing: that is, the study of the "mask of the author" and the "social configurations of the feminine" that have led to its creation (2002: 157). Carter's involvement with second-wave feminism appears historically alongside the militant writing and activities of authors such as Michèle Roberts and Sara Maitland, and this has contributed to her "mask" as feminist writer,[9] which has continued to evolve through the subsequent stages of feminism and the development of theories of gender.[10]

Carter's identity as an author is at work both within and without the frame of fiction. Jérôme Meizoz's concept of authorial "posture" might bring further clarity to this idea, inspired by Alain Viala's reformulation of Pierre Bourdieu's concept of fields and positioning:

A posture constitutes [...] a singular manner to occupy an objective 'position' in a field, which is marked out by sociological variables. It is a personal manner in which to engage with or inhabit a role, or even a status: an author replays or renegotiates his/her 'position' in a literary field through diverse modes of presentation of the self or 'posture'.

(Meizoz 2004; my translation)

As Edmund Gordan observes, Carter was keenly aware of the self as performance: "This belief – that our selves are neither false nor true, but merely roles we either master or are mastered by – is one of the central themes of Angela Carter's fiction" (2016: xiii). Carter's authorial role reflects this position, as it has evolved over time into that of the militant author. Her short fiction overflows with practices that seek to take a "position", a possibility suggested by Meizoz:

> What are the postures of enunciation that have been adopted? In what way can they be considered as taking positions in the space of literature? Whether it be that of the court poet, the gallant poet, the libertine, the honest man, the dandy, the cursed poet, these postures can be considered as a historical repertory of *ethos* that is incorporated, displayed, reversed or imitated. It is therefore possible to study in a relational manner the position in the field, the aesthetic options of an author, his/her public literary behaviour, and his/her discursive *ethos*.
>
> (Meizoz 2007: 23; my translation)

As explained above, Carter's discursive *ethos* is saturated with political, often feminist, militancy in her short fiction. Stories such as "Flesh and the Mirror" and "A Souvenir of Japan" even reflect autobiographically on how fiction can mediate feminine experience. When these texts are allied with her provocative authorial performance in interviews and editorial involvement, her presence is intensified in the literary field.

A similar effect appears in Hilary Mantel's authorial posture. Although primarily known for her historical fiction,[11] the controversy caused by her story "The Assassination of Margaret Thatcher" along with her truculent comments about the Duchess of Cambridge in 2013[12] and the unease fostered by her stories contribute to her posture as "maverick" woman writer. Her more recent story, "How Shall I Know You?", plays with the boundaries between fiction and life, as the narrator, a woman author, is invited to speak at a literary society. She invents literary influences in the story, "I went a bit wild and invented a Portuguese writer who I said knocked Pessoa into a cocked hat" (Mantel 2014), and playfully considers what A.S. Byatt or Anita Brookner would do. The character's play with proper names underlines authorial life as a form of fiction:

> I rattled smartly through my performance, throwing in the odd joke and working in one or two entirely spurious allusions. Afterward there were the usual questions. Where did the title of your first book come from? What happened to Joy at the end of *Teatime in Bedlam*? What, would I say, looking back, were my own formative influences? (I replied with my usual list of obscure, indeed

non-existent Russians.) A man in the front row spoke up: 'May I ask what prompted your foray into biography, Miss Er? Or should I say Ms.?' I smiled weakly, as I always do, and proffered 'Why don't you call me Rose?' Which created a little stir, as it is not my name.

(Mantel 2014)

The play between "Miss" and "Ms.", along with the false name, indicates a piercing playfulness with marital status as well as an ironic glance at the multiple version of the authorial self constructed by and around the woman author.

A strategic porosity between fiction and life, as connected to the author's proper name, is also evident in Smith's short fiction, particularly in "true short story". Such play takes on an increasing militancy in Smith's fiction as her promotion of women's writing grows in visibility. An article about Smith having won The Bailey's Prize in 2015 celebrates Smith as a feminist writer:

> Smith is a notable supporter of other women artists (this year's Brighton festival, for which she was guest director, featured Agnès Varda and Laurie Anderson; last year, as a guest selector at the Edinburgh international book festival, she tempted writer Nicola Barker into a rare public appearance). "My nature is feminist," she says. "How could you not be a feminist and be alive? The world is full of brilliant, interesting women."

(Higgins 2015)

Smith has been reluctant in the past to fully accept the "queer", or even the "feminist", label, and she speaks openly about this in a 2003 article in *The Guardian:* "It's just fashion, isn't it? Being a Scot and a lesbian are two big handy ticks next to my name right now. And I'm fashionable, but not that fashionable" (Denes 2003). However, there seems to be an evolution in the authorial persona that both frames her writing and appears within its structure. There is a keen consciousness of class, education, and the role of women in improving current social crises in stories that are increasingly sophisticated in their intermingling of voices and play with authorial presence.

Like Carter, she was involved with the Virago Press when she co-edited *Brilliant Careers: The Virago Book of 20th Century Fiction* (2000). Yet, unlike Carter, this persona does not appear to rule our reading of her short fiction. Smith disappears to leave room for a playful posture that continually eludes our definitive grasp, often holding up the work of other writers for our admiration. The epigraphs to her story collections overflow, for example, with quotations by favourite writers. Similarly, the aforementioned stories in *Shire* (2013), "the poet" and "the commission", as well as a few stories from *Public Library and Other*

Stories, contemplate the question of legacy for women academics and writers and for Smith herself. The two stories reveal questions of authorial haunting, as suggested in Smith's epigraph to *Shire*, which recalls the final sentences of Woolf's *A Room of One's Own* (122): "For great poets do not die; they are continuing presences; they need only the opportunity to walk among us in the flesh" (Smith 2013: 9).

If Smith oscillates between the postures of feminist writer, lesbian writer and proponent for women's writing, much in the spirit of Angela Carter, Helen Simpson's dominant posture is that of mother and wife. This posture is equally present in the way her stories have been marketed. A selection of Simpson's stories about motherhood has been published in a 2017 Vintage collection aptly titled *Motherhood*, which includes stories from three different collections. Similarly, the story "Cake" about baking a cake for her child, published in the *Telegraph* on Mother's Day in 2013, attests to Simpson's authorial "mask" as the short-story-writing mother figure both within and without her fiction. There is a curious blend of motherly advice accompanied by a gentle ethical nudge, as an awareness of global warming is interwoven with a message to her growing daughter:

> Don't give up on politics, sweetheart; don't say nothing you do will make any difference. Things change. Remember those sheep in your dream? Hedged about as we are with snake-tongued bullies and greed-merchants, the main thing is to be brave and speak up. But what do I know. The heat of the changing world will act on you and you'll rise to it.
>
> (Simpson 2017b)

This story was later re-published as "Kythera" in *Cockfosters*. In her review of *Cockfosters*, Justine Jordan suggests how Simpson's stories "have tracked the stations of life" from motherhood to menopause (2015). This collection, when viewed in relation to the whole of Simpson's works, suggests the gradual evolution of Simpson's posture, as she integrates questions of aging and world politics.

If Simpson and Smith interact with an often playful ethics of authorial positioning through the short story genre, there is in Sarah Hall's posture a dark eroticism and subtle militancy. She likes "short stories to be a powerful distilling", ones that "give you a huge wallop, one you don't see on the surface. I don't like squibs" (Thorpe 2017), and her stories appear to function in this mode. "The Beautiful Indifference" indeed echoes this position, as a woman writer rejects the art of author events:

> How do we get our children to read more? All they do is play violent video games
>   Why should they read? I don't. Given the choice I'd much rather do something else. Including blow things up.

> You're joking? You can't really be serious?
> Can't I? Why not?
> Silence. Murmurs in the crowd. She was not adopting the correct
> role of advocate.
>
> (2011: 46)

This position is heightened in *Madame Zero* (2017). The story "Evie" portrays a chilling spiral downwards as a woman's sexual relations with her husband intensify, only to learn at the end of the story that her hyper-sexuality is caused by a brain tumour. The effect of the story is heightened by an effect of masculine puzzlement and estrangement.

A similar effect is achieved in "Mrs Fox", as the growing estrangement between a husband and his wife culminates in the wife's transformation into a fox. The story reads as a woman's (re)claiming of her animal nature, an event that is also tied to a fragile landscape of a "leftover stretch of heath" in a housing development (Hall 2017). Hall speaks of this "interplay between the wild and the civilised worlds" as being "irresistible" (Haddock 2017), and underlines the importance of "human change", of "redefinition and adaptability, and the drama, conflict and meaning in our lives that comes from all that" (Haddock 2017). She also raises the question of equality between men and women in this process. Hall recognises, in particular, that an "internal revolution" is needed, a liberation that needs to "travel into the minds and the hearts, the confidence and egos of female writers" (Haddock 2017). In this same interview, Hall includes Angela Carter in a list of the short story writers who have been the most influential in her work. *Madame Zero* speaks to a growing fierceness of Hall's posture as a woman short story writer.

Conclusions

There are no easy answers to the questions raised by these women short story writers, and many pages could be written about whether these writers are more aligned with second-wave feminism, third-wave feminism, post-feminism or post-post-feminism. However, the essential notion here is that writers like Angela Carter, by using short fiction to engage with the complexity of feminism and identity, continue to open up new avenues for exploration, harnessing the genre's plasticity, its potential to concentrate affect, its use of indirection and the implicit, to push further, go deeper in seeking out new ways of thinking or rethinking gender and equality through fiction. The examples discussed above are only a small sample of evidence that Carter's writing has in many ways shifted the aesthetic possibilities offered by short fiction. The discussion could also be expanded to include writers such as A.L. Kennedy and Jackie Kay. It is as if Carter's aforementioned statement from "Notes from the Front Line" – "Oh, hell. What I *really* like doing is writing fiction and trying to work things out *that* way" (Carter 1983: 77) – continues to be deployed as a means of answering back, with short fiction being at the centre of this process. This is equally true for the fairy tale, as Paul March-Russell demonstrates in this volume. The conference organised at University of East Anglia in 2009, "The Fairy Tale After Angela Carter", indeed attests to a keen awareness of her legacy in the field of fairy tales as a specific form of short fiction. Kirsty Logan's *The Rental Heart and Other Fairy Tales* (2014), Lucy Wood's *Diving Bells* (2012), as well as Claire Dean's collection of new fairy tales, *The Museum of Shadows and Reflections* (2017), all point to a continued interest in and exploration of the potential of fairy tales to mediate questions of gender, power, culture, history and fiction. When Carter initially said in "Notes from the Front Line" that "I'm all for putting new wine in old bottles, especially if the pressure of the new wine makes the old bottles explode" (1983: 69), she probably was not thinking specifically of short fiction. However, the word "explode" indeed best describes how she has carved out a space to think within the genre. The repercussions of this legacy continue to be evident in the work of the women writing "after Angela Carter", women who continue to assert their responsibility as writers, and thus honour and perpetuate the force of her authorial presence in the landscape of short fiction.

Notes

1 All quotations from Angela Carter's stories will be taken from her collected stories *Burning Your Boats* (1995).
2 See for example, her notes on "A Souvenir of Japan" and on "The Spectral Bridegroom" in ADD Ms. 88899/1/93.
3 "I believe that all myths are products of the human mind and reflect only aspects of material human practice. I'm in the demythologising business" (Carter 1983: 71)
4 See, for example, the introduction to *Angela Carter and the Fairy Tale* by Cristina Bacchilega and Danielle M. Roemer (1998: 7–25).
5 This story also appears in *Public Library* (2015).
6 "So you say he overacts? Very well; he overacts. There is a past history of histrionics in his family" (Carter 1995: 262).
7 The imperative is repeated throughout many of Carter's short stories. See, for example, the beginning of "The Cabinet of Edgar Allan Poe" ("Imagine Poe in the Republic!" [1995: 262]), the beginning of "Overture and Incidental Music for *A Midsummer Night's Dream*" ("Call me the Golden Herm" [1995: 273]), or the end of "The Company of Wolves" ("See! Sweet and sound she sleeps in granny's bed, between the paws of the tender wolf" [1995: 220]).
8 The story proposes the imagined murder of the former British Prime Minister. It was even attacked by *The Daily Mail* as being "warped" (qtd. in Flood 2015b).
9 I have studied elsewhere how such activities, in combination with interviews and overtly political fiction, have fed the development of the aforementioned vision of Carter as a "feminist" author. See, for example: Ryan-Sautour 2007, 2012, 2013 and 2014.

10 See, for example, the introduction to Bristow and Broughton *The Infernal Desires of Angela Carter* (1997).
11 See, for example, her novel *Wolf Hall* which depicts the life of Henry VIII.
12 See, for example, Adam Sherwin (2013).

References

Acocella, Joan (2017) "Angela Carter's Feminist Mythology", *The New Yorker*, www.newyorker.com/magazine/2017/03/13/angela-carters-feminist-mythology (accessed 15 December 2017).

Ardoin, Paul and Fiona McWilliam (eds.) (2016) "Roundtable: Affect, the Short Story, and the Cycle", *Journal of the Short Story in English* 66: 163–213.

Ardoin, Paul and Fiona McWilliam (eds.) (2016) "Special Section: Affect and the Short Story and Cycle", *Journal of the Short Story in English* 66: 21–29.

Attridge, Derek (2004) *The Singularity of Literature*, [Kindle edition] London: Routledge.

Bacchilega, Cristina and Danielle M. Roemer (1998) "Introduction", in *Angela Carter and the Fairy Tale*, edited by Danielle M. Roemer and Cristina Bacchilega, Detroit, MI: Wayne State University Press, 7–25.

Barr, Damian (2014) "Hilary Mantel on Margaret Thatcher: 'I can still feel that boiling detestation'", *The Guardian*, www.theguardian.com/books/2014/sep/19/hilary-mantel-interview-short-story-assassination-margaret-thatcher (accessed 20 December 2017).

Basseler, Michael (2015) "Cognitive Liminality: On the Epistemology of the Short Story", in *Liminality and the Short Story*, edited by J. Achilles and I. Bergmann, New York: Routledge, 77–91.

Boddy, Kasia (2010) "Ali Smith: All there is, An Interview about the Short Story", *Critical Quarterly* 52(2): 66–82.

Bristow, Joseph and Trev Lynn Broughton (1997) "Introduction", in *The Infernal Desires of Angela Carter: Fiction, Femininity, Feminism*, edited by Joseph Bristow and Trev Lynn Broughton, New York: Longman, 1–23.

Carter, Angela (n.d) Angela Carter Archives at *The British Library*. ADD Ms. 88899/1/93.

Carter, Angela (1979) *The Sadeian Woman*, Harmondsworth: Penguin.

Carter, Angela (1983) "Notes from Front Line", in *On Gender and Writing*, edited by Michelene Wandor, London: Pandora Press, 69–77.

Carter, Angela (1995) *Burning Your Boats*, London: Penguin.

Carter, Angela (1996/1985) "Preface to *Come Unto These Yellow Sands*", in *The Curious Room: Collected Dramatic Works*, edited by Mark Bell, London: Vintage, 497–502.

Davies, Ben (2015) "Address Temporality and Misdelivery: The Postal Effects of Ali Smith's Short Stories", in *British Women Short Story Writers: The New Woman to Now*, edited by Emma Young and James Bailey, Edinburgh: Edinburgh University Press, 163–178.

Davies, Carys (2007) *Some New Ambush*, Cromer: Salt Publishing.

Davies, Carys (2014) *The Redemption of Galen Pike*, London: Biblioasis.

Dean, Claire (2017) *The Museum of Shadows and Reflections*, London: Papaveria Press.

Denes, Melissa (2003) "A Babel of Voices", *The Guardian,* www.theguardian.com/books/2003/apr/19/fiction.shopping (accessed 15 December 2017).

Duffy, Stella (2013) "Interview", *Structo* 9, http://structomagazine.co.uk/interviews/stella-duffy/ (accessed 1 January 2018).

Duffy, Stella (2014) *Everything is Moving Everything is Joined: The Selected Stories,* Cromer: Salt Publishing.

Eagleton, Mary (2005) *Figuring the Woman Author in Contemporary Fiction,* Basingstoke: Palgrave.

Evans, Kim (1992) "Interview", *Angela Carter's Curious Room,* BBC 2, London: BFI Film archives.

Flood, Alison (2015a) "Frank O'Connor award won by 'truly original' stories of Carys Davies", *The Guardian,* www.theguardian.com/books/2015/jul/08/frank-oconnor-award-short-stories-carys-davies-the-redemption-of-galen-pike (accessed 15 December 2017).

Flood, Alison (2015b) "Hilary Mantel's 'The Assassination of Margaret Thatcher' makes shortlist for BBC short story award", *The Guardian,* www.theguardian.com/books/2015/sep/16/hilary-mantels-the-assassination-of-margaret-thatcher-shortlist-bbc-national-short-story-award-mark-haddon (accessed 15 December 2017).

Galloway, Janice (1999/1991) *Blood,* London: Vintage.

Ganteau Jean-Michel and Christine Reynier (eds.) (2013) *Ethics of Alterity, Confrontation and Responsibility in 19th-to-21st-Century British Literature,* Montpellier: Presses Universitaires de la Méditerranée.

Gordan, Edmund (2016) *The Invention of Angela Carter,* London: Chatto & Windus.

Haddock, Sophie (2017) "'Some Internal Revolution Is Needed': An Interview with the Author Sarah Hall", *The Sunday Times Short Story Award,* http://shortstoryaward.co.uk/articles/view/168 (accessed 10 December 2017).

Hall, Sarah (2011) *The Beautiful Indifference,* London: Faber and Faber.

Hall, Sara (2017) *Madame Zero,* [Kindle edition] London: Harper Collins.

Hanson, Clare (2015) "Postscript", in *British Women Short Story Writers: The New Woman to Now,* edited by Emma Young and James Bailey, Edinburgh: Edinburgh University Press, 193–198.

Higgins, Charlotte (2015) "Baileys Prize Winner Ali Smith: 'The Canon Is Traditionally Male. That is What this Book is About'", *The Guardian,* www.theguardian.com/books/2015/jun/05/baileys-prize-winner-ali-smith-interview (accessed 15 December 2017).

Hutcheon, Linda (1995/1998) *A Poetics of Postmodernism,* London: Routledge.

"Interview with Carys Davies" (2007), *The Short Review,* www.theshortreview.com/authors/CarysDavies.htm (accessed 15 December 2017).

Jordan, Justine (2015) "*Cockfosters* by Helen Simpson Review – Dry and Tenderly Measured", *The Guardian,* www.theguardian.com/books/2015/nov/13/cockfosters-helen-simpson-review (accessed 15 December 2017).

Logan, Kirsty (2014) *The Rental Heart and Other Fairy Tales,* [Kindle edition] Cromer: Salt Publishing.

Macleod, Alison (2017) *All the Beloved Ghosts,* [Kindle edition] London: Bloomsbury.

Mantel, Hilary (2005) *Learning to Talk: Short Stories,* London: Harper.

Mantel, Hilary (2014) *The Assassination of Margaret Thatcher: Stories*, [Kindle edition] London: Henry Holt.

March-Russell, Paul (2009) *The Short Story: An Introduction*, Edinburgh: Edinburgh University Press.

May, Charles (1994) "The Nature of Knowledge in Short Fiction", in *The New Short Story Theories*, edited by Charles May, Ohio, OH: Ohio University Press, 131–143.

Meizoz, Jerome (2004) "'Postures' d'auteur et poetique (Ajar, Rousseau, Céline, Houellebecq)", *Vox Poetica*, September, www.vox-poetica.org/t/articles/meizoz.html (accessed 10 July 2017).

Meizoz, Jerome (2007) *Postures Littéraires*, Genève: Slatkine Érudition.

Roberts, Michèle (2010) *Mud: Stories of Sex and Love*, London: Virago.

Rushdie, Salman (1995) "Introduction", in *Burning Your Boats: The Collected Short Stories*, by Angela Carter, Harmondsworth: Penguin, ix–xiv.

Ryan-Sautour, Michelle (2007) "Autobiographical Estrangement in Angela Carter's 'A Souvenir of Japan', 'The Smile of Winter' and 'Flesh and the Mirror'", *Études britanniques contemporaines* 32: 57–76.

Ryan-Sautour, Michelle (2012) "Angela Carter as Fiction: Refiguring the Real Author as Performative Author", *Short Fiction in Theory and Practice* 2(1): 59–71.

Ryan-Sautour, Michelle (2013) "Affect and Authorial Performance in Angela Carter's 'Feminist' Fiction", in *Identity and Form in Contemporary Literature*, edited by Ana María Sánchez-Arce, London: Routledge, 106–121.

Ryan-Sautour, Michelle (2014) "'Am I that Name?': Authorial Identity in Writing by Contemporary British Women Authors", *Études britanniques contemporaines* 46, http://journals.openedition.org/ebc/1245 (accessed 15 December 2017).

Sherwin, Adam (2013) "Hilary Mantel Attacks 'Bland, Plastic, Machine-made' Duchess of Cambridge", *The Independent*, www.independent.co.uk/arts-entertainment/books/news/hilary-mantel-attacks-bland-plastic-machine-made-duchess-of-cambridge-8500035.html (accessed 15 December 2017).

Simpson, Helen (2006) "Introduction", *The Bloody Chamber*, by Angela Carter. London: Vintage, vii–xix.

Simpson, Helen (2010) *In-Flight Entertainment*, London: Jonathan Cape.

Simpson, Helen (2013) "Cake", *The Telegraph*, www.telegraph.co.uk/culture/books/9918478/Mothers-Day-exclusive-Cake-by-Helen-Simpson.html (accessed 24 April 2013).

Simpson, Helen (2017a) *Cockfosters*, London: Alfred Knopf.

Simpson, Helen (2017b) *Motherhood*, London: Vintage.

Smith, Ali (1999/2004) *Other Stories and Other Stories*, Harmondsworth: Penguin.

Smith, Ali (2003) "A babel of voices", *The Guardian*, www.theguardian.com/books/2003/apr/19/fiction.shopping (accessed 14 March 2016).

Smith, Ali (2003/2004) *The Whole Story and Other Stories*, London: Anchor Books.

Smith, Ali (2004) "Get Carter", in *Interrupted Lives*, edited by Andrew Motion, London: National Portrait Gallery, 80–95.

Smith, Ali (2008) *The First Person and Other Stories*, Harmondsworth: Penguin.

Smith, Ali (2012/1995) *Free Love and Other Stories*, London: Virago.

Smith, Ali (2013) *Shire*, London: Full Circle Editions.

Smith, Ali (2015a) "Foreword", in *British Women Short Story Writers*, edited by Emma Young and James Bailey, Edinburgh: Edinburgh University Press, viii–x.

Smith, Ali (2015b) *Public Library and Other Stories*, Harmondsworth: Penguin.

Smith, Ali, Kasia Boddy and Sarah Wood (eds.) (2000) *Brilliant Careers: The Virago Book of 20th Century Fiction*, London: Virago.

Thorpe, Vanessa (2017) "Interview with Sarah Hall", *The Guardian*, www.theguardian.com/books/2017/jul/02/sarah-hall-interview-madame-zero-short-stories (accessed 15 December 2017).

Tonkin, Maggie (2012) *Angela Carter and Decadence: Critical Fictions/Fictional Critiques*, Basingstoke: Palgrave.

Walker, Cheryl (2002/1990) "Feminist Literary Criticism and the Author", in *The Death and Resurrection of the Author?* edited by William Irwin, Westport: Greenwood Press, 141–159.

Wandor, Michelene (1983) "Introduction", in *On Gender and Writing*, edited by Michelene Wandor, London: Pandora Press, 1–9.

Wood, Lucy (2012) *Diving Bells*, London: Bloomsbury.

Woolf, Virginia (1977/1929) *A Room of One's Own*, London: Grafton.

4 In the Company of Wolves
Women's Fairy Tales after Carter

Paul March-Russell

Introduction

In 1992, the Jungian analyst and professional storyteller Clarissa Pinkola Estes published her spiritual self-help book, *Women Who Run with the Wolves*. Taking her cues from such works as Bruno Bettleheim's now canonical psychoanalytic study of fairy tales, *The Uses of Enchantment* (1976), the Iron John movement of Robert Bly and primarily North American women writers' exploration of the oral tradition, Estes sought to dig through "the ruins of the female underworld" and reclaim "woman's deepest nature" via "its personification in the Wild Woman archetype" (1992: 3–4). Despite or because of the mystical and biological essentialism of her account, Estes's book was popular on both sides of the Atlantic; complementing other voguish works such as John Gray's *Men Are from Mars, Women Are from Venus*, published in the same year.

The success of Estes's book attested to the enduring popular identification of women's sexual desires with animal imagery, given a further modern makeover by Neil Jordan's film adaptation of Angela Carter's *The Company of Wolves* in 1984. Carter, who also died in 1992, is not cited by Estes and, indeed, the sceptical revisioning of the fairy tale to be found in Carter's most popular book, *The Bloody Chamber* (1979), would have sat awkwardly with Estes's study. If Estes seeks psychological and emotional harmony, Carter delights in personal and social disharmony, stringent interrogation of cultural norms and often violent sexual transgression. The critical and popular success of Carter's book, not least for it being a short story collection rather than a novel, is the starting point for this chapter before it moves on to consider how Carter's influence on the postmodern fairy tale has been negotiated by contemporaries such as A.S. Byatt, Tanith Lee and Sara Maitland, author/critics such as Marina Warner and by younger writers such as Emma Donoghue and Sarah Hall.

Re-entering *The Bloody Chamber*

Much to her chagrin, following the success of *The Bloody Chamber*, Angela Carter came to be seen as a writer of myth:

> I become mildly irritated [...] when people, as they sometimes do, ask me about the 'mythic quality' of work I've written lately. Because I believe that all myths are products of the human mind and reflect only aspects of material human practice. I'm in the demythologising business.
>
> (1983/1997: 38)

As she later described to John Haffenden, her aim in writing *The Bloody Chamber* was "not to do 'versions'" of the fairy tales of the Brothers Grimm and Charles Perrault, "but to extract the latent content from the traditional stories and to use it as the beginnings of new stories" (Haffenden 1985: 84). Although Carter was more likely to have been inspired by the uses of folk tale in the work of postmodernists such as John Barth, Donald Barthelme and Robert Coover, rather than Anne Sexton's poetic metamorphosis of the Grimms in *Transformations* (1971), her emphasis upon novelty describes not so much an exhausted literature as an explosive revitalisation: "I am all for putting new wine in old bottles, especially if the pressure of the new wine makes the old bottles explode" (Carter 1983/1997: 37). The political, let alone artistic, anarchism of Carter's position not only distinguishes her reworking of fairy tale from that of her postmodern counterparts but it also points to her idiosyncratic association with the Women's Movement of the 1970s: in the same year as *The Bloody Chamber* appeared, Carter also published her advocacy of a moral pornography in *The Sadeian Woman*.

The Bloody Chamber then is not, as the short story writer Helen Simpson has observed, "a group of traditional fairy tales given a subversive feminist twist" (2006: vii). Such a designation not only caricatures the complexity of Carter's project, it also raises questions as to what is meant by a "traditional fairy tale", a "subversive" act and a "feminist" text. The term "fairy tale" is derived from the *contes de fée*, first published by Mme d'Aulnoy in 1697, only months after the first appearance in the same year of Perrault's *Histoires ou contes du temps passé* (*Stories or Tales of Times Past*). The work of d'Aulnoy and, even more so, Perrault represented the adaptation of folk material for the aristocratic tastes of the royal court and attendant families. Perrault's streamlining of folk narrative, in particular, his introduction of causality, semi-rational explanation and moral messages, cast the fairy tale as an instrument of civilising restraint upon its young and adult readers alike. By contrast, in mining the latent content of these stories, Carter's inventions return the fairy tale to an earlier phase; to the violence and sexual perversion of

Giambattista Basile and Giovan Francesco Straparola, whose early versions of "Puss-in-Boots" and "Sleeping Beauty" are more closely identified with their folk-tale roots.

Secondly, then, Carter's work is not an act of subversion (a point misunderstood by her most strenuous critics such as Patricia Duncker) but an act of inversion. Which is to say, Carter inverts what readers commonly understand to be the fairy tale in order to reveal the sex and violence that was always already present. Although Carter is often presented as a transgressive writer,[1] her inversion of the fairy tale points – as elsewhere in her fiction – to the limits of transgression and, instead, to the ultimately curtailing influences of power and ideology. Such apparent pessimism queries, lastly, what we mean by calling a text "feminist", if we understand feminism to be, at the very least, a radically reforming movement that would unsettle the basis, let alone the conduct, of patriarchy. As Carter indicated, however, such questions she preferred to explore through her fiction "and trying to work out things *that* way" (1983/1997: 43). It is the manner then, rather than the content, of the investigation that arguably allows readers to describe Carter's work as "feminist" or not.

Indeed, the odd thing about *The Bloody Chamber* was its reception and subsequent afterlives. Widely acclaimed on its original publication, the book single-handedly transformed the reputation of its author who, following early critical successes with the novels *The Magic Toyshop* (1967) and *Several Perceptions* (1968), first abandoned the UK for Japan and then alienated her readers with the New Wave Science-Fiction-inspired novel, *The Infernal Desire Machines of Doctor Hoffman* (1972).[2] At the same time, Carter made her first foray into short fiction, collected as *Fireworks* in 1974. In the accompanying afterword, Carter distinguished between the short story, which "log[s] everyday experience", and the tale, which "interprets" normative reality "through a system of imagery derived from subterranean areas behind everyday experience" (1974/1996: 459). Thus, Carter links the subject-matter of the folktale with the latent content, the political unconscious that resides within the manifestation of social reality, so as to interrogate that reality via motifs associated with Gothic literature: mirrors, castles, forests, taboo desires and objects, symbolic representations of people, baroque language and black comedy. Not only does the afterword justify what Carter has done in *Fireworks*, it also lays out the principles of the writing she would produce as an Arts Council Fellow in Sheffield from 1976 to 1978: the radio play, *Vampirella* (1976), the novel *The Passion of New Eve* (1977) and the stories that would become *The Bloody Chamber*.

Despite the seemingly transgressive content of the collection, it was welcomed not only because it adapted already familiar works from the fairy tale tradition but also because it drew so heavily upon oral techniques. As Simpson notes, despite the uniformity of Carter's revisionist project, the stories themselves vary "in length and tone"; "it is this very lack of homogeneity that gives this collection its impressive complexity" (2006: viii). Whereas the sharp, discordant shifts in tone, imagery, language and allusion to be found in Carter's preceding novels had alienated her readers, the variability of the stories – their mutability of language, register, symbol and point of view – contributed to the collection's critical success. The equally successful transition of the stories across media – *Vampirella* became the basis for "The Lady of the House of Love"; "Puss-in-Boots", published originally in an anthology edited by Emma Tennant, was subsequently adapted to radio; "The Company of Wolves", like "The Erl-King", appeared first in Tennant's magazine, *Bananas*, was also adapted to radio, and became the narrative frame for Neil Jordan's film – indicates not only the adaptability of the source material but also the extent to which Carter added to the protean storytelling tradition. In generating new narratives from the latent content of the European fairy tale, Carter also fed back into that tradition, revising it and consolidating her own position in relation to the past. Consolidation, as much as revision and transgression, contributed to Carter's critical success, an achievement that – as already indicated – Carter subsequently had to negotiate in her later works.

To that extent, Duncker is right to argue that Carter's stories, whatever her intention about the explosive effect of new wine and old bottles, nevertheless slot into "the house of fiction" (1986: 235). Yet, as she repeatedly does, Duncker overstates her argument by failing to see that – to extend the metaphor of habitation further – Carter's usage of collage knocks through into other rooms. Whatever else it is, *The Bloody Chamber* is *not* a collection composed exclusively of fairy tales. In addition to her uses of intertextuality, so that in a kaleidoscopic effect fairy tales are amalgamated both with one another and non-folktale material such as Gothic, symbolist and pornographic literature, surrealist art and high opera, Carter carefully arranges the overarching structure of the collection. Following the theme-setting title-story, Carter delivers three cat tales, two of which are transformations along the lines of "Beauty and the Beast" whilst the third is an uproarious mix of Latinate erudition and low Anglo-Saxon humour, followed by three stories that have less in common with the fairy tale tradition. "The Erl-King" is based on a German folk legend, "The Snow Child" is based on a Snow White variant suppressed by the Grimms and "The Lady of the House of Love" is adapted from Carter's aforementioned vampire play. The last three stories, although derived from variants of Little Red Riding Hood, are equally heterogeneous since, in literary terms, the werewolf legend is rooted as far back as Petronius's *Satyricon*, whilst the Gothic content of all three stories links with the recurrent transgressive imagery from the title-story through to the middle triptych. In other words, whilst Carter does indeed position her writing in relation to the past and to the fairy tale tradition in particular, so that it may be more easily appreciated as part of a body of literature, her peculiar assemblage of devices, effects and intertexts continuously reverberates, referencing and delighting in its own inventiveness. This continuous movement both within and between the stories also foregrounds the tales' latent content of erotic feeling, so that in its unceasing play, the structure of *The Bloody Chamber* becomes its own "desire machine".

The self-sufficiency of the text not only makes a mockery of over-determined attempts from both the political Right (John Bayley) and the political Left (Duncker) to interpret and pigeonhole its effects,[3] it also renders it obsolete as an experiment that can be repeated by other hands. Instead, *The Bloody Chamber*'s resistance to intelligibility – Carter's delight in the rococo tale as opposed to the minimalist short story – aspires, in Susan Sontag's words, to "an ideal plenitude to which the audience can add nothing": "A person who becomes silent becomes opaque for the other; somebody's silence opens up an array of possibilities for interpreting that silence, for imputing speech to it" (Sontag 1967: 16). If, in subsequent years, Carter was forced to negotiate the unmoveable presence of her most popular work, then so too have subsequent writers had to negotiate Carter's indelible mark on the revisioning of the fairy tale. In exploring the "array of possibilities" that *The Bloody Chamber* opened up by its very recalcitrance, successive female writers have "imput[ed] speech" to a form of storytelling that appeared to largely silence its central female characters. By contesting the subaltern status conferred upon women by the latent ideological content of the fairy tale, successive authors have implicitly engaged in a political act of re-imagination and dissidence.

Tanith Lee: Carter's Shadow

In 1982, Carter compared her lapse into obscurity in the early 1970s with what happens "when people [try] to get out of genre into mainstream" literature since the writer no longer fits with the pre-designed label (1983/1997: 35). Tanith Lee, whose prolific output switched from genre to genre but rarely received mainstream recognition, is an example of a writer popular with her peers but little-known elsewhere. One year after Carter reflected upon her ambiguous relationship with the worlds of genre and mainstream publishing, Lee published her own revisioning of the fairy tale, *Red as Blood*, subtitled "Tales from the Sisters Grimmer". There is little evidence that Carter and Lee knew each other's work. Lee later published in *Interzone*, the Science Fiction magazine for which Carter was an early contributor, and there is a possibility that Lee might have encountered Carter's stories as they were being published in magazines with Science Fiction credentials, such as *Bananas*, or adapted to radio. It is unlikely that Lee would not have known of *The Bloody*

Chamber, due to its popular and critical success, but it is equally un-likely that Lee would have been directly influenced by it, since the first of her re-imagined fairy tales was published as early as 1972. There is a possibility that Carter's success might have assisted in the design of *Red as Blood* or in its publication, but the evidence for this claim is speculative at best.[4] To all intents and purposes, the books were paral-lel developments, one operating on the cusp between genre and main-stream literature and the other appearing originally in genre titles such as *Fantasy and Science Fiction* and *Weird Tales*.

Despite the book's subtitle, Lee echoes Carter insofar as she draws upon other writers than the Grimms for the source of her material. These include Perrault, Gabrielle-Suzanne Barbot de Villeneuve and the Russian Alexander Afanas'ev. Lee plays havoc, though, with the history and geography of the stories by setting the first, based upon the medie-val legend of the Pied Piper of Hamelin, in Asia during the last century B.C.E. and the last, based upon the earliest known version of "Beauty and the Beast" by de Villeneuve, somewhere on Earth in the distant fu-ture following an alien invasion. The other stories move chronologically from the fourteenth to the twentieth centuries and geographically be-tween Asia, Scandinavia and Eastern and Western Europe. In suggesting both the universal and timeless qualities of the tales, and by focusing upon those tales most concerned with gender relations, Lee also appears to suggest that, as a consequence, the sexual struggles between men and women will also remain constant and eternal.

Despite this apparent pessimism, though, Lee also emphasises the mu-tability of the narratives. As the narrator of "When the Clock Strikes" acknowledges: "Shall I finish the story, or would you rather I did not? It is not the ending you are familiar with. Yes, I perceive you understand that, now" (Lee 1983: 51). Although universal, the stories are subject to change and there is an insistent play between what constitutes the offi-cial and unofficial version of the narrative. In that sense, whereas Carter is preoccupied with the latent, unconscious content of the fairy tales, Lee is more concerned with the manifest content – the plotting, setting and characterisation – so that her retellings are less psychological and more social in orientation. To that extent, Lee's reimagining of the fairy tales also complements more closely than Carter the feminist project through-out the 1970s and 1980s of retelling history from a female point of view.

Although hardly lacking in allusion and intertextuality, *Red as Blood* is nevertheless a less ambiguous text than *The Bloody Chamber*. By working more with the manifest content of the stories, Lee also tends to work more within the conventions of romance; to suggest ready par-allels between fairy tale and other romantic narrative forms such as allegory, Gothic, decadence and science fiction. These parameters lend her, though, great freedom and, even if Lee's stories lack the greater psy-chological depth of Carter's, she produces more narrative twists whilst the use of different times and locations gives her retellings more exotic, if not more erotic, appeal. Of particular note is the way in which Lee draws upon religious and pagan traditions. "Paid Piper", which introduces the collection, establishes a tension between the community that worships "the rat god, Raur", who therefore keeps "his folk in order" (Lee 1983: 1), and the Piper who wants them to "pray merely from the joy of being alive" (Lee 1983: 13). Although the Piper seems to allude to pagan figures such as the Green Man, his angry denunciation of Raur as a false god and the community's self-interest echoes Christ's expulsion of the moneylenders (Matthew 21: 12), whilst there is sufficient allusion to suggest that the Piper is to be read as a Christian figure: "Water can be turned into wine, or blood. I shall have to die for them, before they believe in me" (Lee 1983: 15). Nevertheless, as the title indicates, the Piper exacts a heavy payment from the disloyalty of the community by rendering them infertile. Although tempted by the Piper, the heroine Cleci sees through any opposition between true and false gods, or between Christianity and paganism, by realising that both are products of human greed: "the stupidity and avarice and hatred of mankind had finally begun to make him [the Piper] also stupid, avaricious, hating, and cruel beyond reason" (Lee 1983: 17). Lee's characters, then, are caught between two corrupt faith-systems, both of which are rooted in the failings of humanity.

Whereas Carter's characters seek to negotiate a path through a series of traps, which are ultimately connected through the network of patriarchy, Lee's protagonists are often able to take agency via magical means. The backstory to "When the Clock Strikes" is a traditional Gothic plot: the usurpation of dynastic rule by the Duke. The sole survivor of his treachery, Ashella, inherits her mother's satanic powers. Following the Duke's mysterious death, his son holds a banquet for "all men of influence and their families" (Lee 1983: 46), so as to herald a new liberal order. Ashella and her adopted family are invited to attend, where Ashella literally entrances the Prince. As the clock strikes twelve, Ashella curses him in the names of her mother, herself, his father's victims and her master, Satan:

> At the tenth stroke, he saw a change in the loveliness before him. She grew thinner, taller. At the eleventh stroke, he beheld a thing in a ragged black cowl and robe. It grinned at him. It was all grin below a triangle of sockets of nose and eyes. At the twelfth stroke, the prince saw Death and knew him.
>
> (Lee 1983: 51)

Ashella disappears, leaving behind a glass shoe, which in his insanity the Prince attempts to fit to every woman's foot in the city. Eventually, he is murdered by conspirators, the city falls to its enemies and is sacked;

its ruins becoming a site of spectacle for the visitors conducted by those who "earn a miserable existence ... showing them the dregs of the city's past" (Lee 1983: 53). The narrator's only comfort is that, someday, Ashella too will die since "None escapes Death" (Lee 1983: 53).

The next two stories, "The Golden Rope" and "The Princess and Her Future", offer contrastingly positive and negative representations of Satan. If the Christ-like figure in "Paid Piper" is corrupted by becoming a mirror image of human avarice, so Satan in Lee's stories is equally ambiguous, reflecting two sides to human nature: redemptive in the former, predatory in the latter. Such ambiguity is also apparent in the title-story, the second tale in the collection. A reworking of "Snow White", Lee imagines that both wives of the king are witches. The first secretly wishes Bianca, the Snow White figure, into being but, when she dies, it is said that her "dead flesh had smoked" after being splashed by "holy water" (Lee 1983: 19). Her successor is identified as "the Witch Queen" (Lee 1983: 18) but, despite being a Satanist, she is also a practising Christian. The ambiguity between sacred and profane belief is embodied by the dualism of the two witches, one openly recognised as such, the other disguised. The story develops into a perverse restitution of the mother-daughter relationship.[5] Bianca shuns her stepmother's piety and, after her first period, takes to wearing her mother's crown. At the same time, the plague that had disappeared with the queen's death returns, so that the Witch Queen sends a huntsman to kill Bianca. She, however, proves too deadly for him: "she buried her face in his neck, and the pain of her kiss was the last thing he felt in this world" (Lee 1983: 22). The Witch Queen poisons Bianca with a magic apple, only for it to contain "a fragment of the flesh of Christ, the sacred wafer, the Eucharist" (Lee 1983: 25). The Prince, a Christ-like figure identified by a mark upon his wrist, wakes Bianca by dislodging the Eucharist in her throat. Bianca metamorphoses into a white dove, flies to the palace where she transforms again into her seven-year-old self, and is welcomed by the Witch Queen, "her new mother", who hangs "a filigree crucifix around her neck" (Lee 1983: 27). As this brief outline suggests, Lee deliberately confuses Christian and Satanic figures, so that there is a constant slippage between the two, a slipperiness embodied by Bianca's metamorphoses culminating in the restoration with her (true? false?) mother.

The final story, projecting not only the "Beauty and the Beast" myth but also its classical antecedent, the tale of Cupid and Psyche from Apuleius's *The Golden Ass*, into the far future, breaks this pattern by – through a somewhat convoluted biological explanation – revelling in the hybridity between self and other. In its almost nostalgic use of planetary romance, the story gives a slightly rose-tinted ending to a sequence which, although less deconstructive than *The Bloody Chamber*, nevertheless plays consistently with binary oppositions between good and evil, the sacred and the profane. Like Carter, Lee generates new stories from her source material and, although more respectful of genre conventions, questions the assumptions upon which the classic fairy tales were based.

Carter's Near-Contemporaries: Byatt, Maitland and Warner

Whilst the stories that compose *Red as Blood* were written contemporaneously with the tales in *The Bloody Chamber*, authors such as A.S. Byatt, Sara Maitland and Marina Warner have openly acknowledged their debt to Carter's intervention. Maitland, who wrote for *Bananas* at the same time as Carter, has commented that "*The Bloody Chamber* taught me a thing or two" about "just how sexy the bog-standard fairy story could really be" (2012: 13). Byatt, reflecting on her award-winning, metafictional novel *Possession* (1990), has admitted:

> I can't say how important it was to me when Angela Carter said 'I grew up on fairy stories – they're much more important to me than realist narratives'. I hadn't had the nerve to think that until she said it.
> (Leith 2009)

For Warner, who has perhaps become Carter's strongest advocate since the death of Lorna Sage in 2001, Carter's reinvention of the fairy tale is central to her own revisionist project: "*The Bloody Chamber* [...] flung open that door in my head, on to the possibilities of women's re-imagining of the material that lies all about, readily to hand" (Warner 2001: 252). Despite their admiration for Carter, however, all three writers have had to find ways of writing out from under her influence – the extent to which "Carter has colonized the conception of the fairy tale among a large number of Western readers" (Benson 2001: 49) – so as to give individual voice to their characters.

Byatt's clearest excursion into the fairy story is her collection, *The Djinn in the Nightingale's Eye* (1994). More than half of the book, though, is devoted to the title-story, a tale written in the Oriental tradition that dates back to the dissemination of Antoine Galland's translation of *The Arabian Nights* (1704–1717). The first two stories are extracted from the pages of *Possession*, a translocation that, as Richard Todd has argued, opens up a dialogue between the stories and their original place of publication (1997: 43–47). Of the remaining two tales, "The Story of the Eldest Princess" was originally published in the anthology *Caught in a Story* (1992), co-edited by Caroline Heaton and Christine Park. Although omitting Carter, Heaton and Park brought together multiple generations of male and female writers from Britain, Europe and the Americas, amongst them Helen Dunmore, Ruth Fainlight and Doris Lessing. The title for the anthology was derived from Byatt's tale, an indication of her metafictional approach.

In the fairy tale kingdom of "The Eldest Princess", the blue sky has been replaced with "a pale flat green" (Byatt 1994: 43), a change that appears to be connected with the three princesses' transition from girlhood to womanhood. A wizard advises that someone should go on a quest "to fetch back the single silver bird and her nest of ash-branches" (Byatt 1994: 44) which, for unexplained reasons, will somehow restore the blueness of the sky. Rather than sending a knight, the king and queen decide to send their eldest daughter "since she was the first, and could best remember the blue sky" (Byatt 1994: 45), although why that qualifies her most is again left unclear. A reader of fairy tales, the princess realises she is part of a narrative pattern "in which the two elder sisters, or brothers, set out very confidently, failed in one way or another, and were turned to stone, or imprisoned in vaults, or cast into magic sleep" (Byatt 1994: 47). When she encounters an injured scorpion, who requires assistance from the wise woman who lives at the other end of the forest, the princess decides:

> I *could* just walk out of this inconvenient story and go my own way. I *could* just leave the Road and look for my own adventures in the Forest. It would make no difference to the Quest. I should have failed if I left the Road and then the next could set off.
>
> (Byatt 1994: 52–53)

Having realised a loophole in the injunction of fairy tales not to leave the beaten path, the princess heads off into the forest, acquiring further animal companions along the way, until she arrives at the wise woman's house. Here, as the old lady comments, there is "no story": "we are free, as old women are free, who don't have to worry about princes or kingdoms, but dance alone and take an interest in the creatures" (Byatt 1994: 66). Whereas in "The Company of Wolves" Carter associates the grandmother with the role of storyteller, and hence an instrument of patriarchy, Byatt reclaims the figure of the spinster as someone released from the bonds of sexual desire and the patriarchal narratives of marriage and inheritance. The relationship that the wise woman has with the princess is grandmotherly without it being filial.

In the same year as she published *The Djinn in the Nightingale's Eye*, Byatt contributed a translation to Marina Warner's collection of seventeenth- and eighteenth-century stories by women, *Wonder Tales*. This anthology, alongside Warner's short story collection *The Mermaids in the Basement* (1993), the BBC Reith Lectures of 1994 (*Managing Monsters: Six Myths of Our Time*) and her study of the fairy tale, *From the Beast to the Blonde* (also 1994), all amounted to one revisionist project. As Warner summarised:

> Fairy tale offers a case where the very contempt for women opened an opportunity for them to exercise their wit and communicate their

ideas: women's care for children, the prevailing disregard for both groups, and their presumed identity with the simple folk, the common people, handed them fairy tales as a different kind of nursery, where they might set their own seedlings and plant out their own flowers.

(1995: xix)

Whilst in her cultural history Warner reclaimed the experience of women's storytelling, in her own tales Warner followed Roland Barthes as much as Carter by describing how mythological patterns are inscribed within the fabric of everyday life.

Although the opening story to *The Mermaids in the Basement*, "Be My Baby" (1992), reworks the fairy tale motif of the abducted child, most of the stories draw their inspiration from the Bible and classical myth. "Ballerina: The Belled Girl Sends a Tape to an Impresario" (1996) also "forms part of this sequence" (2001: 252) according to Warner.[6] As Warner continues, the "immediate inspiration was a bronze sculpture called 'Ballerina' by the Spanish contemporary artist Juan Muñoz which shows a girl with staring eyes and bells for hands, but it echoes the theme of the maid-without-hands" (2001: 252), a folkloric motif that Warner ascribes to a medieval romance by Philippe de Beaumanoir, but which also recurs in stories by, amongst others, Basile, Straparola and the Grimms. Although the purpose of the sequence was "to give voice" (Warner 2001: 252) to the female protagonists of myth and legend, in "Ballerina" the voice of the central character is embedded, first as a tape recording, and then framed by the accompanying letter from her doctor to the impresario, Orlowski.

The doctor describes his patient, Phoebe, as suffering from "body dysmorphic disorder" (Warner 2001: 253), such that she believes her hands have been removed and replaced by bells. Having seen Orlowski describe his most "recent production [...] about the therapeutic power of performance and participation" (Warner 2001: 253) on a BBC2 arts programme, Phoebe desires to impress Orlowski with an account of her singing, dancing and ringing skills whilst her doctor hopes that he will at least listen to her, since Orlowski has already shown an ability to reach "out to those who are so often kept out of the light, as if society [...] were ashamed of admitting them as members" (Warner 2001: 253). What the reader knows about Orlowski, though, is only what is gleaned from the TV interview. His name, however, echoes the title-character of *The Hands of Orlac*, Maurice Renard's 1920 thriller filmed on numerous occasions about a surgeon whose hands are replaced with those of a serial killer. Like the surgeon's hands that cure rather than kill, Phoebe's hands have – as we learn – been fetishised by others as her defining characteristic, such that the rest of her has, as in the transactions that occur in the early fairy tales, been objectified and traded-in for the special quality of her hands.

In her account, Phoebe relates how she was the star pupil at her local ballet school and, although "still titchy" (Warner 2001: 256), she
gained entry to a London dance academy. Her best features, however,
are not her legs but her hands. The dance mistress describes them as
Phoebe's "capital" (Warner 2001: 256), a commodity to be invested
in for future prosperity, whilst her boyfriend – a choreographer and
would-be impresario like Orlowski – insists that they should be in-
sured. Prohibited from doing anything physical, let alone sexual, with
her hands, Phoebe is compelled by her boyfriend to take the lead in
"a puppet version of The Little Mermaid, with my hands in whiteface
dancing the parts in a black box like a Punch and Judy booth" (Warner 2001: 256–257). As she struggles with the role, Phoebe begins to
psychologically deteriorate, imagining that her hands have become
"wrinkled", "the joints thickening", "the tips flattening and the colour
changing" (Warner 2001: 257), until paralysis sets in. Finally, in her
paralysed state, she imagines a doctor coming to her and persuading
her to have a transplant, since "[p]lenty of people would be glad of
a pair of hands like mine [...] even if they didn't do me any good any
longer" (Warner 2001: 257). In her fantasy, the hands are bloodlessly
removed and displayed in a shoe box whilst she, in return, gains bells,
singing and movement. Phoebe remains addicted to fame so that, if
earlier versions of the story were primarily about sexual anxiety and
the unsexing of the female, in Warner's version, sexuality is constituted
within the desire that drives Phoebe towards self-mutilation in the hope
of celebrity, glamour and personal recognition.

While Maitland echoes Byatt by self-consciously rewriting fairy tales,
she also resembles Warner by analysing contemporary social situations
through the framework of myth and folklore. Unlike either of them,
she is the one most dedicated to the short story form; her earlier work
being collected in *Angel Maker* (1996). A later volume, *On Becoming a
Fairy Godmother* (2003), typifies her writing up to that point. On the
one hand, there are stories such as the opening tale, a variant of Hans
Christian Andersen's "The Little Mermaid" (1837), in which a betrayed
and grieving housewife discovers a tiny mermaid trapped within the toi-
let bowl whilst, on the other hand, there are more direct rewrites of fairy
tale, such as "The Wicked Stepmother's Lament", in which Cinderella's
stepmother attempts to justify her actions:

> I just wanted her to *see*, to see that life is not all sweetness and light,
> that people are not automatically to be trusted, that fairy godmoth-
> ers are unreliable and damned thin on the ground, and that even
> the most silvery of princes soon goes out hunting and fighting and
> drinking and whoring.
>
> (Maitland 2003: 31)

The title-story sums up, in many respects, Maitland's project of reclaiming those aspects of female identity that have been suppressed by the civilising constraints of church, government, family and patriarchy:

> Witches are glamorous. Glamour is what witches are and what their power is. There is an element of excitement and an element of deceit in all glamour.
> This is crucial. Witches are neither good nor bad. They are powerful.
> (Maitland 2003: 129)

The ambiguity of the witch figure underwrites Maitland's later story, "Moss Witch", which was the runner-up in the BBC National Short Story Award for 2009, and which began a new phase in Maitland's output. Originally published in Geoff Ryman's anthology, *When It Changed*, the story – like all the other collaborations – was written in consultation with a scientist. Maitland took bryophytes as her starting point and conceived a witch who is a sentient form of moss. This thought experiment lent a detailed scientific gloss to the folkloric motifs of tree nymphs and wood sprites and to the doomed encounter between humans and fairy folk who lead them astray. In Maitland's story, a bryologist meets the moss witch by chance, and although by her words and actions she gives a believable account of her true nature, he fails to understand her, lulled by her ability to turn "the language of science [...] into a love song" (2009: 33–34). Finally, his impatience gets the better of him, he breaks the spell and he begins collecting moss samples. Whereupon, and without any implied judgement from Maitland, the witch kills him: "She was sorry of course, but for witches it is always duty before pleasure" (2009: 35–36), the duty, that is, to protect her habitat even at the expense of her would-be human lover.

Since then, Maitland has produced a further collection, *Moss Witch and Other Stories* (2013), based upon a series of collaborations with scientists. At the same time, however, and reflecting Maitland's religious and spiritual beliefs, she has also explored the deep relationship between forests and fairy tales in a book, *Gossip from the Forest* (2012), which combines examples of nature writing with retellings of stories from the Grimms. Whether Maitland's inspiration is coming from the realms of evidence-based science or pantheistic faith, her goal is holistic, seeking the connections between the natural world and the folkloric imagination so that both are "protected, valued, seen for what they are" (Maitland 2012: 20). To that end, Maitland contributes an idiosyncratic strand to what has been termed "the new nature writing" (Cowley 2008: 7–12), idiosyncratic insofar as it is rooted within the feminist and countercultural politics of the 1970s.

Carter's Successors: Emma Donoghue and Sarah Hall

Since the 1980s, then, and whatever Carter's personal misgivings about fairy tales might have been, fable and folklore have become sources of inspiration for male and female writers alike. Indeed, to see this as solely a female project and not to consider modern-day fabulists such as Neil Gaiman or China Miéville would be to skew the entire act of reclamation. Equally, a consideration of postcolonial and magical realist writers, such as Carter's near-contemporaries Ben Okri and Salman Rushdie, and relative newcomers, such as Helen Oyeyemi, would open up this retrieval to the knitting-together of indigenous literary traditions. Nevertheless, for the Irish writer Emma Donoghue, who in *Kissing the Witch* (1997) eschews Gaelic folk culture for the European fairy tale, and the Cumbrian author Sarah Hall, Carter is less a subversive figure than an integral part of the literary tradition to which they belong. If Carter's near-contemporaries had to find ways of negotiating her influence, for Donoghue and Hall it is more a case of acknowledging her presence and then charting their own course.

Kissing the Witch, although currently available only as an e-book, has received more critical attention than most of the texts discussed here. This may be because, as the title indicates, gender and sexual relations are foregrounded, including the homosexuality that Carter omitted. Two broad readings have emerged within the scholarship. Firstly, critics have analysed the text's gender relations as indicative of its feminist content. Susan Sellers, for example, concentrates on the centrality of female relations in the text but, almost like Duncker on Carter, is frustrated by its lack of a coherent "feminist" message (2001: 98). By contrast, Elizabeth Wanning Harries focuses upon Donoghue's multiple use of the frame-tale, so that each story runs into its successor, and circumvents the phallogocentrism of a linear narrative (2001: 129–134). Other critics have concentrated upon Donoghue's rewriting of familiar character types, such as Cinderella and Prince Charming (Crowley and Pennington 2010: 307–309), or generational and family relationships in the stories (Martin 2010: 4–25; Palko 2015: 917–939). Secondly, critics have explored the text's queering both of its form and content. For example, Martine de la Rochère has examined the mother-daughter relationship but in the context of Adrienne Rich's writings on heterosexism, whilst Jennifer Orme, rejecting the character-based approach of other critics, has focused on the narrative construction as a queering of literary form (de la Rochère 2009: 13–30; Orme 2010: 116–130).

What has been less appreciated is the extent to which *Kissing the Witch*, Donoghue's first foray into short fiction, extended her own revisionist project. Donoghue's first published book, *Passions Between Women* (1994), was a history of lesbian culture from the end of the seventeenth to the start of the nineteenth centuries. Her first two novels were both realistic and set in contemporary locations, but with the emphasis again upon lesbian relations. At the same time, though, Donoghue also wrote three stage plays, the first a dramatisation of Anne Lister's Regency diaries, the second vaudevillian in structure and the third based upon a seventeenth-century witch trial. Donoghue's early output, although preoccupied with the reclamation of women's history and, in particular, lesbian history, ranges across different media, tonal registers and narrative forms. *Kissing the Witch*, although open-ended as a short story sequence, is nevertheless concentrated as a formal experiment and so synthesises the foci that were emerging in Donoghue's *oeuvre*: buried histories, female relationships, fantasy and folklore, realism and the authenticity of women's experience. For example, despite the erotic overtone of her stories, accentuated by the intimacy of the first-person address, Donoghue avoids both the baroque prose of Carter and the Gothicism of Lee for a spare, deliberately repetitive style:

> What about the shoe? she asked.
> It was digging into my heel, I told her.
> What about the prince? she asked.
> He'll find someone to fit, if he looks long enough.
> What about me? she asked. I'm old enough to be your mother.
> Her finger was spelling on the back of my neck.
> You're not my mother, I said. I'm old enough to know that.
>
> (1998: 8)

In concert with these stylistic techniques, Donoghue eschews the violent collage effects of Carter for a more harmonious redistribution of fairy tale motifs throughout her tales. If for Carter fairy tales were "extraordinary lies designed to make people unfree" (Carter 1983: 38), Donoghue works within the lie, redistributing and reshaping it, so as to reveal the contours of a covert history.

In comparison, Sarah Hall turns away from the history of social and sexual relations to dwell more upon the domestic space. "Mrs Fox" won the BBC National Short Story Award in 2013 and has since been republished as the lead story to Hall's most recent collection, *Madame Zero* (2017). The immediate intertext, as indicated by the characters' surname, is David Garnett's 1922 novella, *Lady into Fox*, although both Garnett's original and Hall's rewriting are locatable within a long history of literary metamorphoses from Ovid to Carter. In her version, Hall focuses more upon the reactions of the unnamed husband to his wife's transformation.

Following Sophia's metamorphosis, he first experiences an "acute discerning" as she allows him to study her "like a curious lover" (Hall 2014: 16). He then experiences overwhelming grief as he locks both himself and his wife into the house, disturbed only by the cleaning lady's brief appearance. Ushering her out, he decides to research what might have happened in a desperate attempt to "avail himself of understanding, reason, definition" (Hall 2014: 21). All he discovers from the fiction, fables and medical textbooks that he reads is a lack of coherence apart from one stubborn detail: *"an act of will"* (Hall 2014: 21). Whereas before he had believed in the romantic illusion of their existence, and in his wife's constant availability, he now realises that she was in her possession of her own agency, merely never before acted upon. Unable to adjust not only to Sophia's new state but also to the realisation of how "even before this" could she have been "his pet" (Hall 2014: 24), he lets her go.

He goes back to work and gradually mourns for his wife. Just before Christmas he returns to the edgeland where he last saw her before the change and "his mind begins to ease" (Hall 2014: 28). Hall knowingly announces the epiphany – "It is in such mindful moments, when everything is both held and released, that revelation comes" (Hall 2014: 28) – and in the early spring Sophia, still a fox, returns. He discovers that she has a den and, within, four fox-cubs that he realises "must be, his" (Hall 2014: 31). Each week he visits the den, and "although they pay him no heed" (Hall 2014: 33), he commits himself to this new duty. "What will become of them he does not know" (Hall 2014: 35–36) but "[h]e has given up looking for meaning" (Hall 2014: 36). Instead, whereas before, the loss of Sophia would have been unendurable, it is now the fox that gives his life purpose: "how could life mean anything without his unbelonging wife?" (Hall 2014: 37). Although the story is premised upon the conflict of gender relations, its trajectory is one that expands into other forms of alterity, in particular, in the relationship between the human and animal worlds. The latter, no longer treated as an anthropomorphic extension of the former as in the fairy tale tradition through to Carter, but as an object in itself that demands an ethical response from the human subject.[7]

Conclusion

What this chapter has shown is the extent to which *The Bloody Chamber*, a landmark in contemporary British women's short fiction, did not so much negate the fairy tale tradition as make it possible for Carter's contemporaries and successors to use it for their own purposes. Since the fairy tale is itself suspended between its origins in folk culture and its literary development in or around of the royal courts of the seventeenth century, so we should also regard Carter and Lee, her popular counterpart, as engaged in a fruitful dialectic. Byatt, Maitland and Warner all develop responses to Carter that both negotiate her influence and take her inspiration in different directions – metafiction, contemporary social criticism and an engagement with the worlds of science and spirituality that can also be seen in Hall's emphasis upon the otherness of the animal kingdom. Lastly, Donoghue develops an implosive, as compared to Carter's more explosive, strategy in order to unearth from the mediations of official history a covert history that celebrates women's social and sexual relations with one another.

Notes

1 Again, it suits Patricia Duncker to initially present Carter on these terms so as to then upbraid her for her failure to represent gay sexuality (Duncker 1986: 222–236; Duncker 1996: 58–68).
2 Carter acknowledged her debt to Michael Moorcock's Science Fiction magazine, *New Worlds*, in an interview with David Pringle on 10 August 1979 (Pringle 1979). Speaking at the annual Science Fiction convention, Eastercon, in 1982, Carter noted that after publication of her novel, "I stopped being able to make a living" (Carter 1983/1997: 35).
3 See Hermione Lee's response to Bayley's accusation of political correctness in Carter's work (Lee 2007: 315–327).
4 I am grateful, for this discussion of Carter and Lee, to an email conversation (dated 20 July 2017) with Nadia Van Der Westhuizen.
5 Veronica L. Schanoes (2014) also discusses mother-daughter relationships but in relation to Lee's later novel, *White as Snow* (2000).
6 The story was later republished in Warner's 2002 collection *Murderers I Have Known*.
7 See also Jochen Achilles's blurring of the boundary between humans and animals in relation to Judy Bunditz's short story, "Dog Days" (1998) (Achilles 2015: 41–45).

References

Achilles, Jochen (2015). "Modes of Liminality in American Short Fiction: Condensations of Multiple Identities", in *Liminality and the Short Story: Boundary Crossings in American, Canadian, and British Writing*, edited by Jochen Achilles and Ina Bergmann, New York: Routledge, 35–49.

Benson, Stephen (2001) "Angela Carter and the Literary Märchen: A Review Essay", in *Angela Carter and the Fairy Tale*, edited by Danielle M. Roemer and Cristina Bacchilega, Detroit, MI: Wayne State University Press, 30–58.

Byatt, A.S. (1994) *The Djinn in the Nightingale's Eye: Five Fairy Stories*, London: Chatto & Windus.

Carter, Angela (1974/1996) "Afterword to *Fireworks*", in *Burning Your Boats: Collected Stories*, London: Vintage, 459–460.

Carter, Angela (1983/1997) "Notes from the Front Line", in *Shaking a Leg: Journalism and Writings*, edited by Jenny Uglow, London: Chatto & Windus, 36–43.

Cowley, Jason (2008) "Editor's Letter: The New Nature Writing", *Granta* 102: 7–12.

Crowley, Karlyn and John Pennington (2010) "Feminist Frauds on the Fairies? Didacticism and Liberation in Recent Retellings of 'Cinderella'", *Marvels and Tales* 24(2): 307–309.

De la Rochère, Martine (2009) "Queering the Fairy Tale Canon: Emma Donoghue's *Kissing the Witch*", in *Fairy Tales Re-Imagined: Essays on New Retellings*, edited by Susan Reddington Bobby, Jefferson, NC: McFarland, 13–30.

Donoghue, Emma (1998) *Kissing the Witch*, London: Penguin.

Duncker, Patricia (1986) "Re-Imagining the Fairy Tales: Angela Carter's Bloody Chambers", in *Popular Fictions: Essays in Literature and History*, edited by Peter Humm, Paul Stigant and Peter Widdowson, London: Methuen, 222–236.

Duncker, Patricia (1996) "Queer Gothic: Angela Carter and the Lost Narratives of Sexual Subversion", *Critical Survey* 8(1): 58–68.

Haffenden, John (ed.) (1985) *Novelists in Interview*, London: Methuen.

Hall, Sarah (2014) *Mrs Fox*, London: Faber.

Harries, Elizabeth Wanning (2001) *Twice Upon a Time: Women Writers and the History of the Fairy Tale*, Princeton, NJ: Princeton University Press.

Heaton, Caroline and Christine Park (eds.) (1992) *Caught in a Story: Contemporary Fairytales and Fables*, London: Vintage.

Lee, Hermione (2007) "'A Room of One's Own, or a Bloody Chamber?': Angela Carter and Political Correctedness", in *Flesh and the Mirror: Essays on the Art of Angela Carter*, edited by Lorna Sage, London: Virago, 315–327.

Lee, Tanith (1983) *Red as Blood, or Tales from the Sisters Grimmer*, New York: DAW Books.

Leith, Sam (2009) "Writing in Terms of Pleasure: Interview with A.S. Byatt", *The Guardian*, www.theguardian.com/books/2009/apr/25/as-byatt-interview (accessed 27 July 2017).

Maitland, Sara (2003) *On Becoming a Fairy Godmother*, London: Maia.

Maitland, Sara (2009) "Moss Witch", in *When It Changed: Science into Fiction*, edited by Geoff Ryman, Manchester: Comma, 27–38.

Maitland, Sara (2012) *Gossip from the Forest: The Tangled Roots of Our Forests and Fairytales*, London: Granta.

Martin, Ann (2010) "Generational Collaborations in Emma Donoghue's Kissing the Witch: Old Tales in New Skins", *Children's Literature Association Quarterly* 35(1): 4–25.

Orme, Jennifer (2010) "Mouth to Mouth: Queer Desires in Emma Donoghue's *Kissing the Witch*", *Marvels and Tales* 24(1): 116–130.

Palko, Abigail L. (2015) "'No Mother nor Nothing to Me': Excavating the Maternal Figure in *Kissing the Witch*", in *Fairy Tales Reimagined: Essays on New Retellings*, edited by Susan Reddington Bobby, Jefferson, NC: McFarland, 13–30.

Pinkola Estes, Clarissa (1992) *Women who Run with Wolves: Contacting the Power of the Wild Woman*, London: Rider.

Pringle, David (1979) "Exclusive New Interview with Angela Carter", *Angela Carter Online*, https://angelacarteronline.com/2017/05/07/exclusive-new-interview-with-angela-carter/ (accessed 24 July 2017).

Schanoes, Veronica L. (2014) *Fairy Tales, Myth, and Psychoanalytic Theory: Feminism and Retelling the Tale*, Farnham: Ashgate.

Sellers, Susan (2001) *Myth and Fairy Tale in Contemporary Women's Fiction*, Basingstoke: Palgrave.

Simpson, Helen (2006) "Introduction", *The Bloody Chamber*, by Angela Carter. London: Vintage, vii–xix.

Sontag, Susan (1967) "The Aesthetics of Silence", in *Styles of Radical Will*, London: Vintage, 3–34.

Todd, Richard (1997) *A.S. Byatt*, Plymouth: Northcote House.

Warner, Marina (1994) *The Mermaids in the Basement*, London: Vintage.

Warner, Marina (1995) *From the Beast to the Blonde: On Fairy Tales and Their Tellers*, London: Vintage.

Warner, Marina (2001) "Ballerina: The Belled Girl Sends a Tape to an Impressario", in *Angela Carter and the Fairy Tale*, edited by Danielle M. Roemer and Cristina Bacchilega, Detroit, MI: Wayne State University Press, 250–257.

Part III
Body Politics

5 Tales of Femininity and Sexuality

Competing Discourses and the Negotiation of Feminisms Today[1]

Emma Young

Introduction

In the twenty-first century the discourses of choice and agency have animated feminist debates. Indeed, many feminist critics have highlighted the significance of these tropes in the context of post(-)feminisms and neoliberalism. In using the term "post(-)feminism", this chapter acknowledges the multiple meanings associated with the term. Thus, "post(-)feminism" refers to both the *postfeminist* approach to gender and sexuality which aligns itself with postmodern and poststructuralist thinking, as well as the *post-feminist* tendencies more commonly affiliated with backlash theories and notions of women's sexual liberation in the twenty-first century. This nuanced recognition of differences between these two terms is especially important in the context of neoliberalism, given neoliberalism's perpetuation of rational self-interest as autonomously achieved and devoid of situational context. The tropes of choice and agency, therefore, are a site of coming together for feminist politics and neoliberal discourses. While Angela McRobbie views these tropes as "inextricably connected with the category of 'young women' [meaning] feminism is decisively aged" (2004: 255), Rosalind Gill has argued that more than men, "women are required to work on and transform the self, to regulate every aspect of their conduct, and to present all their actions as freely chosen" (2008: 443). Moreover, Shelley Budgeon positions this increasing focus on autonomy and choice as key descriptors for "contemporary ideals of femininity" (2011: 131). In light of such observations, this chapter considers the ways in which British women short story writers negotiate the competing discourses of contemporary feminisms through their exploration of women's femininity and sexuality. In the process, this chapter foregrounds the politics of choice and agency and thereby engages with a key site of contemporary feminist discourse.

Most frequently, the politics of choice and agency are manifest on the female body. By focusing on the representation of femininity and sexuality in these short story narratives it is possible to reveal some of the ways in which neoliberalism and post(-)feminist politics are mapped, reflected and critiqued in contemporary women's writing. Kate Atkinson's "Transparent Fiction", Michèle Roberts's "Annunciation", Sarah Hall's "The Agency", Helen Simpson's "Diary of an Interesting Year" and Kalbinder Kaur's "When English Girls Hold Hands" all address these themes in differing ways. Crucially, I suggest, across all of these stories, it is by drawing on the potential of the short story as a literary vehicle – a form defined by ambiguity, open-endedness and a particular requirement on the part of the reader – that facilitates this feminist dynamic. Therefore, this chapter also highlights the importance of affective textual relations for perpetuating an engagement with feminist politics. Undoubtedly, the short story provides a unique literary vehicle for these fictional representations of and engagements with feminist politics and, I would suggest, in the hands of certain women writers the short story becomes a feminist vehicle for expression.

In discussing the all-women shortlist for the BBC National Short Story Award 2013, the Chair of the judging panel, Mariella Frostrup, heralded this event as evidence that "the short story is a form much suited to the innovative brilliance of women writers" (Bury 2013). Although Frostrup's statement tends towards the general, it usefully signals the timeliness of discussing contemporary British women writers and their relationship with the short story. In 2014, for the third time in seven years, the BBC National Short Story Award celebrated an all-female shortlist. In the wider international context, 2013 saw the Canadian short story writer Alice Munro receive the Nobel Prize for Literature. In considering the work of a group of contemporary British women short story writers (Atkinson, Hall, Kaur, Roberts and Simpson), this chapter draws on voices from the literary mainstream, those who have solely published short stories, authors who have worked across a variety of genres, as well as those who are less well known in the academy and are positioned as non-canonical. In itself, this breadth of women short story writers illuminates the versatility and significance of the genre.

The question of genre, what defines a genre and what do we mean by the term "short story" are enduring literary debates. In the context of women's writing and feminist politics, I would argue that there are particular formal features of the short story which are especially resonant: open endings, ambiguity, time and brevity. All of these features overlap and tend to inform one another, and, crucially, these formal tendencies all tend to impact on the experience of and demands placed on the reader. For example, short stories tend to employ two types of narrative ending that can be categorised as either conclusive, and therefore revealing, or open-ended and subsequently ambiguous. Regardless of which approach is utilised by an author, both of these endings entice the reader towards this narrative moment with high expectations, as the story's "meaning" is either uncovered or the reader is left to imagine it for him/

herself. In both situations a tension arises between the reader and the story. In interrogating the function of the short story's ending and its generic specificities, Ursula Hurley suggests that "reader autonomy is a gift of the genre" but that it requires "imaginative and intellectual engagement [by the reader]; it does not tolerate passivity" (2011: 29). The idea of "reader autonomy" is problematic because it implies that a reader is unconstrained, when in fact the reader always functions within the confines of a narrative, no matter how ambiguous a narrative. It is the reader's investment in the story which gives moments of epiphany and narrative resolution their power. In instances in which the ending is left open or is ambiguous, this structure encourages the reader to think beyond the ending. This, I suggest, is particularly resonant in the context of feminisms in which the reader is asked to actively engage with the text's politics. Arguably, then, the reader's own feminist positionality is drawn into question either overtly or covertly in the reading of short fiction.

Kate Atkinson: Conflicts of Character

In her short story "Transparent Fiction", Kate Atkinson introduces us to the character of Meredith, a young woman who has "gone through life borrowing other people's personalities rather than going to the trouble of developing her own" (2002: 48). An American currently living in the UK, Meredith is established as a woman who lives from moment to moment. Her relationship with Fletcher is viewed as a "temporary liaison" and she experiences an "odd malaise" in England which she suspects is due to "an overabundance of history" (Atkinson 2002: 53). What is especially interesting about Meredith is the tension which resides at the heart of her character. She is depicted as pursuing a carefree existence, devoid of material attachments, yet her doctoral research is into Telomeres, which as the narrative informs us, is all about the longevity of life, since "the longer our telomeres, the longer we live" (Atkinson 2002: 57). Thus, while on the surface Meredith is seen to live in the moment, her work is focused on research into DNA that impacts on human cells and ageing. In this narrative space, the reader is confronted with conflicting and quite contradictory messages about Meredith which subsequently signal the performative and temporary nature of identity and, indeed, existence. There is a level of subtle critique around femininity and desire in Atkinson's narrative embodied in the Meredith's character: "Meredith knew that most men would rather have Air Stewardess Barbie in bed with them than a girl with a doctoral thesis" (Atkinson 2002: 50–51). The conflict between authenticity and performance of self is here brought to the fore, but this time it is expressed through the imagery of the female body and what makes a woman attractive and desirable to a man.

The heteropatriarchal lens is the model by which Meredith is measuring her own existence and worth in this story, and arguably it is this framework from which she seeks to escape via her carefree lifestyle. As the story closes, "Meredith Zane ran into the future for ever" (Atkinson 2002: 67), and with a poetic twist, Atkinson's closure is both forward-facing and conflicted as the future and eternity merge in this narrative moment. Atkinson's story illuminates the way in which women writers engage with the politics of femininity and sexuality in the most diverse, and sometimes subtle, ways. It is through the gestures towards characterisation and small narrative remarks that the reader is made aware of the prevalence of heteropatriarchal norms in shaping and defining Meredith. In this respect, "Transparent Fiction" is a telling critique of the normalisation of gender discourses that assign value and meaning to women's bodies based on their perceived femininity and sexual attractiveness as defined by men. As such, the notions of choice and agency are at the heart of Meredith's story, which can be read as an individual battle between the competing demands of sociocultural expectations and individual agency and desire. The oppositional motifs, whether the old/new, short/long or even the intelligent/attractive, that resonate throughout "Transparent Fiction" all accentuate the conflicting experiences that shape Meredith's existence. In many ways, the experiences of Meredith in "Transparent Fiction" illuminate the fact that choice is "a modality of constraint" and that the "individual is compelled to be the kind of subject who can make the right choices" (McRobbie 2004: 261). Positioned in this way, Meredith's run into the future at the end of the narrative could be read as an attempt to shed the constraints that demand such choices to be made. Crucially, it is the open-ended conclusion to the story that affords such a possibility and perpetuates this line of interpretation.

Helen Simpson's Dystopian Nightmare

"Diary of an Interesting Year", set in 2040, examines how the political issue of global warming, or, more specifically, the after-effects of planetary disaster, affect the lives of "G" and his wife. If, as Shelley Budgeon argues, "[a]utonomous choices are reached through a process of careful self-reflection and, therefore, are seen to be grounded in an authentic expression of what is right or true for that particular person" (2011: 130), then the diary format of Simpson's narrative is arguably the ultimate medium through which to critique the notion of free choice for women. Following the first entry for "12th February 2040", the diary entries become increasingly more disturbing with references to "nothing to be done about the cholera" (Simpson 2012: 351) and rats in the house "gnawing away at the breadbin" (Simpson 2012: 352). While the narrator does reveal some personal detail (she married "G", her university tutor), the main focus of the diary entries is the everyday living conditions, including food rations, car-sharing, bartering for goods and washing out rags by hand. Even in this dystopian future, the domestic setting is at the forefront of Simpson's narrative, and the entries reveal the personal battles faced by the protagonist. Thus, the personal choices of the individual are contextualised in the situation and circumstances in which they are being made, a situation which – as the diary reveals – becomes increasingly distressing and dangerous.

Eventually (on 1st August 2040) the couple flee their home in a bid to survive, but "G" is killed. The narrator is then captured by her husband's murderer, "M", and her existence comes to depend entirely on "M". The narrative device of the diary reinforces the personal perspective of the story. Further, the brevity of the entries and their terse language contribute to the harrowing effect the story has upon the reader. After murdering "G" and abducting the narrator, "M" systematically rapes her: "What he does to me is horrible. I don't want to think about it, I won't think about it" (Simpson 2012: 361). Writing a fortnight later, she confides to the diary that "M can't seem to get through the day without at least two blowjobs. I'm always sick afterwards (sometimes during)" (Simpson 2012: 361). This is the entirety of the entry, thus illuminating how the violence against her becomes the dominant focus of the story at this point. The confidential space of the diary is transformed into the only site of safety for the narrator and the space in which she can acknowledge the lack of choice and agency afforded by her current situation. In this instance, the brevity of the short story is replicated in the shortness of the diary entry, with both features serving to illuminate the intensity of experience and female suffering.

With "Diary of an Interesting Year" the potential consequences of global warming, or the "Big Melt" as "G" coins it, are pushed to the extreme and Simpson fictionalises the potential aftermath. The bleak, harrowing and traumatic account foregrounds the humanitarian implications, particularly for women. After all, in the dystopian mayhem it is the narrator that is raped, abused, beaten and impregnated, highlighting the gendered threat in the context of a prevailing dystopian world. The diary contains accounts of repeated beatings, before the protagonist writes of her suspected pregnancy. Attempting to abort the child she drinks a self-made potion of "rank juice" (Simpson 2012: 362), but it fails to work. Eventually she reports in the diary, on the 10th November 2040, that "[i]t's over" (Simpson 2012: 363). When drunk on his vodka, the narrator entices "M" up to the platform in the trees where he has been keeping her before pushing him over the edge. The final diary entry of the story sees the protagonist bury the baby in the ground and the "[l]ast line: good luck, good luck, good luck, good luck" (Simpson 2012: 364), before she heads north with only the rucksack of goods for survival. Significantly, ambiguity prevails at the story's ending as the forward-facing statement leaves the reader in a state of uncertainty as to the future of the protagonist. Thus, despite the narrative being built on explicit details as shared in the diary, the ending shifts to more uncertain terrain and sees a glimmer of utopian hope arise for the protagonist. The ability to be both explicit and ambiguous in this story is significant: while agency and free choice are far from accessible modalities for the protagonist, the story's ending leaves space for alternative possibilities to be realised.

Michèle Roberts: A Woman's "Choice"?

In "Annunciation", a young Catholic girl, Marie, is subject to and overrun by the dichotomy of the virgin or the whore or, as she phrases it, "[s]lag or saint: you're allowed to choose" (Roberts 2010: 153).[2] The discourse of choice is foregrounded, yet these choices are construed as being either morally good or bad. Such comments highlight the way that "[s]exual reputation is still policed punitively and at great cost to some girls whose behaviour is reframed within more negative discourses of female sexuality" (Gill 2007: 73). Thus, female sexuality is pulled between narratives of empowerment and refrains of judgement. As the story unfolds, this aspect of "choice" is problematised further as the lines become blurred regarding when, if and even whether Marie makes free choices. After she leaves school and goes to work at the General Post Office, with her first pay packet she buys a new outfit as well as "eyebrow tweezers, curlers, hair spray" and other instruments of feminine beauty (Roberts 2010: 154). Attempting to achieve a social life, she goes to night venues on her own, including the cinema. However, "[t]he moment the lights dim a man will arrive in the neighbouring seat and start to bother her, nudging and whispering, opening his flies" and this harassment causes Marie to leave the cinema (Roberts 2010: 155). Nonetheless, "[s]he doesn't complain to the manager. It's just how men are and you put up with it. The women at work [...] say she should take it as a compliment: I should be so lucky" (Roberts 2010: 155). There is a gendered assumption that this male behaviour is "acceptable", it is natural, and women should be appreciative of such attention. Through this matter-of-fact commentary it is left to the reader to judge the acceptability of such behaviour. By drawing attention to the feminisation of Marie's body, with her purchase of beauty products, the story positions femininity at the heart of Marie's characterisation and illuminates how an act of female self-empowerment results in unsolicited male harassment.

Such sexual harassment by men is depicted as persistent: when Marie "walks around the city, men spring out at her from every crack and crevice" (Roberts 2010: 156). Over time she "lets some of these men steer her into a pub, buy her a drink, then take her back to their hotels" as she sees them as travellers in need of company, like herself (Roberts 2010: 156). Believing they only want to chat and "feeling daring", she goes up to their Bloomsbury hotel room and "lets one or two of them fuck her" (Roberts 2010: 156). There is a disconnection between the narrative voice and the action which suggests a consequential trail of events over which Marie lacks control or choice. After all, it is "what she's there for, isn't it: he buys her a gin and tonic, she drinks it, which shows she's willing. She doesn't know how to say no" (Roberts 2010: 156). According to this story, for Marie sex is less a choice and more a social expectation, as authored by men, who tell her this is the appropriate course of action. Like Eva, who remembers her manners with the double-edged "thank you", Marie has been brought up "to be accommodating and polite. Not to say boo to a goose. So you can't call it rape. Slag. She lies there and goes through the motions and feels nothing" (Roberts 2010: 156). Far from feeling desire or demonstrating sexual agency, Marie is passive, too polite to say no, but suggestively she fails to consent either. Here, Roberts provokes the reader to question whether female silence should be taken as consent.

Issues of consent and compliance are taken further with the insertion of the authoritative voice of the "psychiatrist [whom] her GP suggests she see, later on, during a bad patch in her early twenties" (Roberts 2010: 157). He reinforces this earlier thought-pattern of Marie's: that she is "asking for it" and perpetuates the victim-blaming culture. He asks her "you pretend to be so innocent but you must have wanted it. Why deny it?" before accusing her of seeking "out situations of seduction" (Roberts 2010: 157). Further, one night when Marie's "three flatmates sort themselves out a partner each, and lie down on the floor and begin having sex, Marie feels in the way" (Roberts 2010: 160). Realising "the fourth man is making his way across the room towards her" Marie "manages to get up, avoid her would-be swain's clutch, [and] stumble out" of the flat (Roberts 2010: 161). Recounting this traumatic event to the psychiatrist he merely comments that she is "sitting there, isn't she? [...] So she's joined in" (Roberts 2010: 160); verbal consent does not matter in this framework as female silence becomes consent. In discussing the limits of choice, Budgeon suggests that

> [w]omen are incited to make choices by discourses that obscure the conditions that make choice possible – or impossible, for that matter. When these conditions are concealed, the choices that are on offer appear to be 'natural' or inevitable, and therefore beyond the bounds of critique.
>
> (2011: 131)

In "Annunciation", Roberts makes visible the conditions that limit choice for Marie, and in the process offers a scathing critique of institutional and societal responses to women's sexual well-being and identity.

As a consequence of this, the story also becomes a powerful criticism of the impregnation of the Virgin Mary, who was not offered a choice. When running away from her house to escape this fourth man, Marie falls in the street and here, "enter the angel. Joe" (Roberts 2010: 161). Despite his name suggesting synergies with Joseph, Mary's husband in the Bible, Joe is clearly Marie's "archangel Gabriel", the bringer of good news, or at least this is how he appears initially. Although "Joe's her mother" with his "[s]ilky hands" of protection (Roberts 2010: 167), Marie is described as "falling in with Joe" (Roberts 2010: 165) not falling *for* him and, subsequently, sex is again not a pleasant experience for Marie: "she doesn't come. He fingers her too abruptly, impatient for her to heat up and be ready" (Roberts 2010: 166). With language that conjures up Marie as being like a vehicle, warming up in cold weather ready for its driver, she once again becomes a passive receptacle of man's desire. The psychiatrist diagnoses Marie as "faking it", as she is "pretending to be so innocent but really wanting to bite men's penises off" (Roberts 2010: 166). In actuality, the only faking Marie does is in her orgasm, "because that helps shorten the whole experience and also you don't get told off for failing to come" (Roberts 2010: 166). Sexual pleasure is a performance for Marie, a "show" that is orchestrated by social convention and phallocentric definitions of "good sex".

Moreover, Joe's sexual control soon spills over into domestic violence. Joe takes Marie to the home of one of his customers, Anne, who is buying a piece of artwork from him. When Marie does not speak to Anne, Joe "gives her [Marie] a quick slap for her bad manners" (Roberts 2010: 173). The apparent rudeness on the part of Marie is caused by fear, as she wants nothing more than "to hurl herself at Anne" and for Anne to take care of her (Roberts 2010: 172). Joe's violence towards Marie increases and he becomes "good Joe bad Joe [...] who'll hit her kiss her hit her kiss her" until, in the end, a pregnant Marie leaves Joe (Roberts 2010: 174). Pregnant, and attempting to escape the sexual and physical violence of Joe, she runs away to a hostel and tells herself that "you can get money, easy, just charge men for sex" (Roberts 2010: 180). Prostitution is considered an option, a means to an end for Marie, not a choice.

However, Marie does not resort to selling her body to survive; instead, she tracks down Anne's phone number and calls her to explain all. She is greeted with the soothing "Oh baby" of Anne, which reinforces the biblical connections of the story: Anne is the name of Mary's mother, and she becomes a symbolic mother-figure to Marie in the story (Roberts 2010: 180). Subsequently, Marie moves in with Anne's goddaughter, Lizzie, in a shared house "[f]ull of girls" (Roberts 2010: 180). She forms a strong sisterly bond with Lizzie, who helps "Marie in her cheerful, slapdash way" (Roberts 2010: 181) by looking after Marie's baby. Thus, the story's resolution establishes this shared home as a space outside male gaze and control. Waking in the middle of the night, Lizzie and Marie both care for the baby and the "three of them sit peacefully together" (Roberts 2010: 182), an ending that marks a turn towards the second-wave politics of sisterhood and community. Thus, "Annunciation" appears to offer a sceptical critique of post-feminist politics, especially notions of women's sexual agency and "free choice", while simultaneously reasserting the value of sisterhood and, subsequently, second-wave feminism.

The discourses of second-wave feminism and post(-)feminisms both have a tendency to prioritise the politics of sex. In *Straight Sex* (1994), Lynne Segal reflects on the 1960s milieu and her experiences of the sexual liberation movement. However, Segal also considers how this period caused women to equate sex with liberation and, subsequently, provoked women into seeking liberated sex (1994: 30). By comparison, reflecting on the contemporary context, McRobbie argues that, in a postfeminist (her usage) era, there is an

> uncritical relation to the dominant, commercially produced, sexual representations that actively invoke hostility to assumed feminist positions from the past in order to endorse a new regime of sexual meanings based on female consent, equality, participation, and pleasure, free of politics.
>
> (2004: 34)

This "uncritical" and therefore normalised assumption that this is an age in which women can have sex "free of politics" is problematic. Instead, Rosalind Gill argues, it is necessary to listen to women's stories about their personal choices and "to contextualise these stories, to situate them, to look at their patterns and variability, to examine their silences and exclusions, and, above all, to locate them in a wider context" (2007: 77). Roberts critiques this "new regime of sexual meaning based on female consent" (McRobbie 2004: 34) by telling stories and situating them and "their patterns and variability [...] in a wider context" (Gill 2007: 77). As a result, sex is revealed to always be a choice that must be negotiated within a given set of socio-economic and cultural parameters. In this respect, across these various waves of feminism emerges an enduring reminder that, in the context of gender discourses, choice is always a subjective concept.

With this negotiation of feminist politics, Roberts's story attests to the importance of recognising the nuances and multiplicity often merged in the term "postfeminism". Sarah Gamble notes that the "postfeminist debate tends to crystallise around issues of victimisation, autonomy and responsibility" (2001: 43). Because of this stance, Gamble asserts, postfeminism is often unwilling to condemn pornography and is sceptical of the date-rape phenomenon (2001: 44). Gamble's outline concludes that, "because it tends to be implicitly heterosexist in orientation, postfeminism commonly seeks to develop an agenda which can find a place for men" (2001: 44). Crucially, like third-wave feminism, postfeminism is an attempt to develop earlier feminist thought, while incorporating some of the tenants of postmodernism and post-structuralism in its treatment of knowledge and identity. Conversely, post-feminism is a notably media-driven notion which results in the discourse often being manipulated to produce provocative headlines. Female celebrities are heralded for their iconic status and deployed as symbols of women "having it all". In *Backlash* (1991), Susan Faludi argues that post-feminism *is the backlash* and that women are told (particularly by the media) that, "[y]ou may be free and equal now, [...] but you have never been more miserable" (1). The subtext of Faludi's claim is that feminism is blamed for the woes of women *and* men today. In the 1990s moment, feminism becomes a problematic term and an ideology troubled by fissures which are compellingly captured in Roberts's short fiction, as she reworks biblical motifs and engages in an act of revision. Significantly, in Roberts's "Annunciation", the fissures that ensue throughout the story are redressed in the story's conclusion through the image of women's coming together.

Kalbinder Kaur: "We'll get used to it"

Kalbinder Kaur's "When English Girls Hold Hands", published in *Kin: New Fiction by Black & Asian Women* (2003), is narrated by an unnamed young woman who is acting as "the tour guide" for her friend Milla (34). The women are currently in India, as suggested by the description of banyan trees and markets where mini Taj Mahals are located (Kaur 2003: 34). While the opening description paints a still-life portrait of these two women sat beneath the banyan tree with Milla writing a postcard, the cultural tensions at the heart of the narrative seep to the fore as the narrator, who assumes a sense of belonging and authority in this space, berates her friend "for wearing shorts" (Kaur 2003: 34). The narrator has clearly lived in the United Kingdom for a considerable period of time, and her diasporic identity is foregrounded in the story as in India, her "homeland", she assumes a position of knowledge with her white, English school friend Milla. In contrast to Milla, who is clearly a tourist in this country based on the manner in which she behaves and the fact that every experience is "shiny to her, exotic" (Kaur 2003: 35), the narrator appears to claim an "authentic" connection with the country which is demonstrated through her knowledge of the bus routes and geography of the city. However, the narrator's desire to assert this authority and maintain appearances for Milla is undercut, and indeed undermined from the reader's perspectives, due to the narrator's unspoken thoughts which pervade the narrative: "I should [know] but I don't, so I change the subject" (Kaur 2003: 34), "my speech is clumsy and in the end I speak English" (Kaur 2003: 35). The narrator's identity is constantly under scrutiny and in contention throughout the narrative. By taking up the position of a returned citizen, she uses Milla's position as the cultural "Other" to assert her identity. On the one hand, she appears to feel superior to Milla in this space, in which she is mistaken by other women who say they knew her mother (due to the colour of her skin and an assumed familiarity), yet, on the other hand, a critique runs through the narrative which reveals her lack of knowledge about the country and therefore her own "foreignness".

Although the narrator celebrates this "in-betweenness" – "I am floating in the air between nations" (Kaur 2003: 35) – her desire to play the role of tour guide, or superior, to Milla during this trip has significant consequences. When the young women take a bus back to the hotel, the narrator once again takes an assertive stance and insists that Milla sits between two village women while she stands in the overcrowded space "trying to slot in the best way I know how" (Kaur 2003: 36). The desire to "slot in" on the bus is symbolic of the narrator's attempts to fit in the wider culture, but, as in other situations, this does not progress as anticipated. The narrator's knowledgeable position is cruelly undermined by the fact that on this journey she learns something new: "I didn't know what a tweak was before, but now I do. It is about mechanics; a twist, not a stroke or an aim at arousal. He tweaked my right nipple" (Kaur 2003: 37). The ensuing narrative describes how the narrator is sexually assaulted on the bus by "a pair of thick black eyebrows, and heavy eyelashes, that's all I can see even though his whole face is there" (Kaur 2003: 37). The emphasis of the narrative falls on the response this provokes in the narrator and her internal thoughts: "People have seen, and they are silently watching me, judging me. I am afraid they think I want this" (Kaur 2003: 37). What scares the narrator more than the assault itself is the response of those around her and her fear at being judged, replicating her experience throughout the trip more broadly.

As the women step off the bus the narrator cannot bring herself to look at Milla, who eventually breaks her silence and admits that she saw the assault. The narrator's response is poignant:

> I don't say that I had been protecting her, that knowing she was watching all that time makes me feel sick, that my sacrifice was obviously a mistake. I try to reassert my identity as expert, and say that I hadn't slapped him or made a scene, as I didn't want her to feel uneasy. I didn't say I was so shocked that I couldn't slap him, so shocked I couldn't speak as I bumped against his body, his hands on my hips holding me in place.
>
> (Kaur 2003: 37–38)

Yet again the narrator is striving to maintain her "identity as expert", and her concern of not behaving in the manner expected by others, by society and culture, fuels her fear of speaking out. However, this response also acknowledges the trauma of the experience itself, and, even though she cannot bring herself to admit it to others, her shock at the assault is revealed to the reader. With this description, an element of sympathy for the narrator is created, and the story attempts to illuminate the plethora of reasons that she did not speak out. It therefore offers a scathing critique of sexual assault and the ways in which women who are victims are often silenced, whether because of stigma, fear or any other reason. The assault itself happens quickly, and the narrative detailing it is only a page and a half of the short story (which in total is four pages), thus there is a swiftness and immediacy to the action. In this respect the reader is suddenly confronted with the realities of the situation, which are made even more vivid given that throughout the story the narrator has worked to create an aura of authority, control and power which here is overturned.

Finally, Milla's response to her friend is telling and it reveals the way in which this incident is perceived through a white, Western lens. As the unnamed protagonist reports of Milla's words:

> She tells me I was wise to keep quiet. She tells me that this is common here. With the crowded buses, and all. It's the heat [...,] this type of weather makes the locals obscene. She says there is nothing that we can do. She has heard of men murdering women for much less than a raise voice in countries like these. She tells me we'll get used to it, and squeezes me hand.
>
> (38)

Importantly, the narrator continues to reinforce the difference between the two women (as she perceives it) with the repeated usage of the pronoun "she" throughout this paragraph. Implicitly, Milla's opinion and view is not the same as the narrator's. However, despite this, Milla's use of "we", as being reported here, still infiltrates this narrative and therefore the narrator cannot escape her conflation with Milla, who she sees as the foreign "other". The sexual assault, then, is still mediated through the lens of "them" and "us" and, in this instance, the narrator's identity is further conflicted as her victim status seems to mean she can no longer be a citizen or part of this "other" community. Furthermore, Milla's words of comfort to her friend also offer a host of stereotypes, from the behaviour of local men being put down to the weather (a "scientific" fact she read in a Western newspaper) to the phrasing of "we'll get used to it", which places the emphasis on women adjusting to the sociocultural context because this is "normal" behaviour.

Importantly, published in 2003, this story tragically fictionalises similar events which enraged a global audience in 2012, when a young woman was raped and murdered on a bus in Delhi. This was not the first time that such an atrocity had taken place but the media attention the incident received brought the issue to the fore of Western consciousness. Such permissive attitudes towards sexual abuse and sexual politics are problematic in India (as can be seen in the frequency of media articles that cover this topic). Thus, while the narrator's self-proclaimed expertise is undermined through this traumatic experience, Milla's response is perhaps more challenging for the reader, as she normalises such an event and the abuse of women, and thereby unconsciously complies with the sociocultural status quo. These synergies between fact and fiction highlight the way in which literature, the telling of stories, can act as a political vehicle. Kaur tells an important story in "When English Girls Hold Hands", one which is, sadly, a fabulation of a dark reality. It is in the brevity of the short story, with the narrative space being far more concentrated, which renders this event in a sharp and hard-hitting way for the reader. Moreover, the differing positionality of both characters, firmly established from the story's opening by the unnamed narrator and protagonist, works to bring the reader into the text as they are encouraged to navigate between these two characters to evaluate the situation for him/herself.

Sarah Hall's Sexual "Agents"

In stark contrast to Roberts's portrayal of sexual harassment and domestic violence, Sarah Hall's "The Agency" positions women's unspoken sexuality as a "private act" (2011: 96). In fact, "unspoken" is a key word here because Hall's narrative's intensity is built on ambiguity as the reader attempts to unravel events and decode the unspoken meaning behind the women's conversation and actions. The reader is immediately submerged into the action as the protagonist Hannah tells of the phone call she has just received from a "polite male voice" on a private number (Hall 2011: 89). Quite rapidly, it becomes apparent that something significant is about to unfold in the story, and that prior to the story's point of commencement, arrangements have already been made. Over the subsequent pages Hannah's narrative takes the reader back to the initial conversation in which Anthea King – another mother she had met at the school gates of her children's primary school – had recommended Hannah to join a "company" who are "private and reliable". Indeed, Anthea herself had been a "member" for "over a year" (Hall 2011: 90).

The narrative continues to move back in time and reveal how Anthea and Hannah's friendship developed – lunches with the girls, shopping trips and time spent confiding the secrets of marriages, relationships and affairs. It is only once Hannah reveals how she had almost entered into an affair with her husband's brother that Anthea hands her the card for The Agency, encouraging Hannah not to be embarrassed: "I am a great believer in private acts" (Hall 2011: 96). The language of the narrative is professional yet elusive. The instructions Hannah receives from Anthea about ringing reception and asking for an "initial consultation" are all the register of business, a professional transaction (Hall 2011: 97). This is furthered when on the day of the "first appointment" Hannah dresses in a burgundy suit and heads to the city (Hall 2011: 97) to be greeted by Alistair at The Agency, who offers her champagne and a form to complete simply to identify her "preferences" (Hall 2011: 108). While throughout the narrative the reader acts like a detective, piecing together the clues, suspecting that this is about sex, or sexual liaisons but never being sure. It is only when Hannah shares the contents of the form with the words "companion", "*Film, Restraints, Doll, Defecation*" (Hall 2011: 109) that these suspicions are validated. However, the air of professionalism permeates the narrative as sexual desire is enshrouded in the language of business. Thus, "The Agency" exploits the potential for ambiguity in the short story and, in doing so, also blurs the boundaries between genres as well. The innuendo effect that emerges at the level of reading, with the reader encouraged to fill in the blanks, plays on erotic imagination. At the same time, the story edges towards erotica, while never quite stepping across the genre's threshold.

While the reader's suspicions are seemingly verified, there is no point in the narrative in which sex is explicitly named. The scene at The Agency closes with Alistair asking Hannah to wait in a room upstairs before the story recommences with Hannah returning home. At home, her everyday life continues, with Hannah putting on the washing and checking that all signs of her afternoon's exploits are hidden: she removes her laddered stockings and puts them in the bin, her shoes are only lightly scuffed, which could have been done bedding them in on the gravel path outside, and the bruise that was already appearing under her hip? "I would tell John that the car door had swung shut against it in the wind" (Hall 2011: 112). Suddenly the words of Tamar (one of the women from the lunch group) ring incredibly true: "Women can live far more comfortably with secrets" (Hall 2011: 94). The professionalism and mystery surrounding women's sexuality in Hall's story is not because of shame; instead, it leaves the reader with a sense of women's empowerment and critically reflects on the traditional binary position of women's sexuality as either virgin or whore. Crucially, it is the ambiguity of the narrative which facilitates this depiction and which enables the short story to act as a vehicle of feminist expression in this instance.

From the very beginning of the narrative, sexuality is positioned as vital to health and well-being, as Anthea remarks: "You have to look after your health. It's amazing how truly discordant life seems if you feel wrong within yourself" (Hall 2011: 91). A women's sexual gratification becomes important to her sense of identity, her mental and emotional well-being. In "The Agency" it is also a means of women's coming together. In the closing scene Hannah returns Anthea's call and confirms that she can mind her daughter Laura the following evening. Hannah describes how: "We spoke for a moment or two. There was a pause in the conversation, and then came her gay, indecorous laughter" (Hall 2011: 114). Anthea's laughter lifts the narrative as she asks Hannah if she had a "jolly time in the city today". When Hannah responds that she was just "visiting a relative", Anthea "laughed again. Yes. Of course, darling. Of course" (Hall 2011: 114). Here the unspoken, shared knowledge between these two women unites them. It cements their friendship and the laughter suggests not just an act of pleasure but also an act of subversion. "The Agency" challenges the stereotype of women's sexual subservience, tropes of defiance and instead locate sexuality as a site of pleasure, intimacy and – through the professionalisation of "The Agency" – normal, everyday occurrence in a woman's life.

In Hall's narrative, women are agents of their sexual lives, and The Agency facilitates their ability to choose sexual encounters without fear of judgement. In this respect, The Agency as a space challenges the sociocultural discourses that often entrap women's bodies. However, in itself this is potentially problematic as it risks overlooking "how ascribed statuses and external realities continue to circumscribe agency in ways that actually limit both the freedom women have to exercise choice and the kinds of choices they have access to" (Budgeon 2011: 133). Therefore, even though The Agency is designed by and for women, the fact it is run by a man (Alistair) complicates this initial sense of escape from heteropatriarchal norms. Instead, I suggest that, the story renegotiates understandings of and approaches to female sexuality which do not refute the engagement with men, but establish a different "contractual" understanding. Such an understanding in "The Agency" creates limitations of choice, which are most prominent in the form that Hannah fills in. It provides her with a set of boxes to choose from, so that she is being offered choices about her sexuality; however, these are predetermined by the options on the form. Following the understanding that "The Agency had been conceived by a woman" (Hall 2011: 11), these are women's choices on the page, but they still establish parameters and place limitations on the individual being asked to choose. In this way, even a seemingly empowered woman who is acting with agency is still unable to make autonomous choices.

Conclusion

Critiquing a perceived mobilisation of the terms choice, agency and autonomy in recent scholarship, Gill questions "[t]o what extent do these terms offer analytical purchase on the complex lived experiences of girls and young women's lives in postfeminist, neoliberal societies?" (2008: 435). If these terms are being increasingly deployed to perpetuate a narrative of female empowerment and free choice, and to create base evidence for post-feminist arguments, then the work of Atkinson, Simpson, Roberts, Kaur and Hall provides, a timely reminder that the situation for women is far more complex than purported by such language. Throughout all of these stories, regardless of the slant of the commentary around the issues of femininity and sexuality, the realities of lived experience are all realised and provide compelling portrayals of how sociocultural discourses shape individual existence. Crucially, these narratives recognise the significance of cultural influence (which Gill sees as being increasingly side-lined in neoliberal times) and thereby reinforce the way in which the politics of gender, sexuality and ethnicity all contribute to the possession of agency and autonomy. As such, the work of these women short story writers can be seen as an attempt to complicate, rather than remain complicit with, post-feminist and neoliberal discourses in which individual are "entrepreneurial actors who are rational, calculating and self-regulating" (Gill 2008: 436).

All of the stories discussed in this chapter have provided accounts that "tell us about the production of contemporary femininity" and sexuality in some way (Budgeon 2011: 135). Arguably, if deeper understandings of agency, autonomy, choice and subsequently feminism come through analysing the social relations, processes and realities of the individual, then literature is a vital vehicle for engaging with such debates. Perhaps one of the greatest powers of fiction is the ability to capture both external and internal realities. Gill's analysis poses a crucial question about the relationship between culture and subjectivity: "how is it [...] that social constructed ideals of beauty or sexiness are internalized and made our own, that is, really, truly, deeply our own, felt not as external impositions but as authentically ours" (Gill 2008: 436). Narrative voice is a core element of storytelling, and in the short story the reader's heightened awareness of being told a story enables a coming together of culture and subjectivity. More specifically, the short story provides a textual space in which ambiguity is fostered, characters can and may remain more elusive, and the reader is often left asking further questions about the story just been told. In this regard, such formal features enable women writers to ask the reader: do these women have free choice and agency?

Notes

1 Parts of this chapter were originally published in *Contemporary Feminism and Women's Short Stories* (Edinburgh University Press, 2018). I am grateful to Edinburgh University Press for permission to reproduce this work here.
2 The title, "Annunciation", refers to the Feast of the Annunciation, when the archangel Gabriel visited the Virgin Mary to tell her she would be the mother of Jesus Christ (Luke 1: 26–28).

References

Atkinson, Kate (2002) *Not the End of the World*, London: Doubleday.

Budgeon, Shelley (2011) *Third Wave Feminism and the Politics of Gender in Late Modernity*, London: Palgrave Macmillan.

Bury, Liz (2013) "All-woman shortlist for BBC short story award 2013" *The Guardian*, www.theguardian.com/books/2013/sep/20/bbc-short-story-shortlist-2013-woman (accessed 15 March 2017).

Faludi, Susan (1991/1993) *Backlash: The Undeclared War Against Women*, London: Vintage.

Gamble, Sarah (2001) "Postfeminism", in *The Routledge Companion to Feminism and Postfeminism*, edited by Sarah Gamble, London: Routledge, 43–54.

Gill, Rosalind (2007) "Critical Respect: The Difficulties and Dilemmas of Agency and 'Choice' for Feminism: A Reply to Duits and van Zoonen", *European Journal of Women's Studies* 14(1): 69–80.

Gill, Rosalind (2008) "Culture and Subjectivity in Neoliberal and Postfeminist Times", *Subjectivity* 25: 432–455.

Hall, Sarah (2011) *The Beautiful Indifference*, London: Faber.

Hurley, Ursula (2011) "Look Back in Wonder: How the Endings of Short Stories Can Be Their Most Powerful and Effective Distinguishing Features", *Short Fiction in Theory and Practice* 1(1): 25–35.

Kaur, Kalbinder (2003) "When English Girls Hold Hands", in *Kin: New Fiction by Black & Asian Women*, edited by Karen McCarthy, London: Serpent's Tail, 34–38.

McRobbie, Angela (2004) "Post-Feminism and Popular Culture", *Feminist Media Studies* 4(3): 255–264.

Roberts, Michèle (2010) *Mud: Stories of Sex and Love*, London: Virago.

Segal, Lynne (1994) *Straight Sex: The Politics of Pleasure*, London: Virago.

Simpson, Helen (2012) *A Bunch of Fives: Selected Stories*, London: Vintage.

6 Genealogies of Women

Discourses on Mothering and Motherhood in the Short Fiction of Michèle Roberts

Laura Mª Lojo-Rodríguez

Introduction: Maternal Power

"What is woman, apart from her social and material function in re-producing children, nursing, renewing the work force?" Luce Irigaray's question in the opening pages of *Sexes and Genealogies* (1987: 10) encapsulates the feminist challenge in articulating alternatives to women's access to culture, in defining women in their full ontological dimension, in rediscovering or inventing

> the words, the sentences that speak of the most ancient and most current relationship we know – the relationship to the mother's body, to our body – sentences that translate the bond between our body, her body, the body of our daughter.
>
> (Irigaray 1987: 18–19)

Because of their natural capacity to engender and nourish life, women have been relegated to the role of "eternal mediators" for the incarnation of the body in a social order predicated upon the sexual division of labour (production *versus* reproduction), which always ends up in neglecting the singularities of women's bodies and their own world (Irigaray 1993: 103). The foundations of culture and of language operate, according to Irigaray, on the "basis of an original matricide" (1987: 11) aiming to destroy maternal power (*puissance*) to maintain women's silence in order to control and even prevent love for the mother, for the daughter, for the sister, "love of same" (1993: 105). Under the rule of patriarchy women are separated from their mothers "if the woman is to enter into desire for the man-father" (Irigaray 1993: 101), and is thus transplanted into the genealogy of fathers and husbands:

> The bond between mother and daughter, daughter and mother, has to be broken for the daughter to become a woman. Female genealogy has to be suppressed, on behalf of the son-Father relationship, and the idealization of the father and husband as patriarchs.
>
> (Irigaray 1993: 108)

According to Irigaray, our task as women is to give life back to the mother "who lives with us and among us" (1987: 18) in order not to be accomplices in their murder if we aim at achieving a full status as subjects, at carrying out an active social role, at, in sum, truly becoming women. Such a move requires what she defines as a "genealogy of women", an ethical order which would grant the fluidity of affect among women as well as the establishment of the necessary conditions for women's action: "This world of female ethics would continue to have two vertical and horizontal dimensions: daughter-to-mother, mother-to-daughter; among women, or among 'sisters'" (Irigaray 1993: 108). The aim of this essay is to explore Irigaray's "genealogies of women" in Michèle Roberts's short fiction, or the establishment of an ethical order which necessarily requires the recovery of the maternal body – or vertical dimension – in order to successfully accomplish bonds of collaboration among women – or horizontal dimension. This essay will be examining two short stories by Michèle Roberts: "Anger" and "Annunciation" – compiled in, respectively, her first and last, to this date, short fiction collections: *During Mother's Absence* (1993) and *Mud: Stories of Sex and Love* (2010). The presence of "vertical" and "horizontal" dimensions in each narrative illustrates Roberts's consistent ethical and political position as a feminist writer from her early years to this date, while also showing how such a commitment necessarily requires a thorough re-examination of bonds among mothers, daughters, sisters and friends, as well as a reassessment of the various ways traditional discourses have rendered those relationships, often uncritically assumed.

Genealogies of Women: Michèle Roberts

Roberts herself has often acknowledged the influence of French feminism in her writing. French feminist thought has aided her as an artist to first understand the "burning hate, sizzling despair [and] rage" springing from "the earliest experience that is the loss of my mother" (Roberts 1983: 64), poetically articulated in a body of fiction aiming to re-imagine fullness, completion and, above all,

> the maternal body, my mother's body, alive and warm and generous, an image of that body which says that is how she was, that is how we were, once, together. Blissful mutual giving and taking. What the French call *la jouissance* and what the French feminists like Julia Kristeva and Hélène Cixous say we find again through writing and reading.
>
> (Roberts 1998: 20)

Roberts's fiction is a literary attempt to come to terms with the loss of the mother, whether that is literal ("Charity") or metaphorical (Lojo-Rodríguez 2012: 33): "Everything I wrote went back to maternal loss, maternal absence, and now dares to re-image maternal presence, full-ness" (Roberts 1998: 21). Without a firm hold to that bond, Roberts's characters experience a void which results in a frustrated desire for completion. These narratives represent a move to mend what was broken, to recuperate the maternal bond through memory and writing. Put differently, the sense of the maternal loss becomes for Roberts a powerful, inspiring and fruitful tool which relates to woman's imagination and the power of the written word. In other words, the mother's absence paradoxically fuels a desire to overcome despair, abandonment and rage in order to construe something new:

> Out of this *chaos* of feeling, out of this overwhelming sadness at *absence*, we learn to create something beautiful: our words, later on our gifts, later still our works of art. We re-create the mother inside ourselves, over and over again.
>
> (Roberts 1998: 21)

Michèle Roberts often infuses women's genealogies with a mythical dimension, encompassing various narratives which have historically encapsulated particular visions of femininity, aiming at eventually challenging many of their received assumptions that ultimately mirror patriarchal ideology. Roberts's fiction represents an empowering counter-narrative for women, which implies both a reassessment of gender roles and a readjustment of the literary conventions which had sustained them. Such a mythical dimension of women's genealogies finds, I will argue, a privileged literary site in Roberts's short fiction. Roberts's genealogies often turn to Classical and Christian myths and to fairy tales which, as Irigaray explains, lay down traces and remains of the elements which prefigure human subjectivity in "myths and folk tales as *mysteries*, those stories of birth, initiation, love, war, death, and passion delivered in images and actions with all innocence of knowledge" (1987: 58). Of course, Roberts has explored such concerns in novel form, but she has also argued how many of her novels are often composed of short stories, and her use of different narrative voices responds to "different stories being plaited together" in such a way that the combination of the short story and the novel is her "greatest contribution" to the novel form (Bastida Rodríguez 2003: 104).

The short story form, both as a source in myths and tales and as a constituent element, plays a central role in Robert's project of recovery of the maternal bond. For Roberts, fairy tales and storytelling lie at the heart of her writing impulse which, in her case, is linked to a matrilineal inheritance: "My English grandmother, who lived with us, was a great storyteller. So, she, I think, gave me a sense of the magic of storytelling" (García-Sánchez 2011: 140). Most importantly, and as Marina Warner has suggested, the fairy tale could be regarded as an inherently feminist genre and has been popularly considered as a woman's activity, something produced by women – "old wives' tales", with all its connotations of error and lack of critical judgement – but the genre may be put to the opposite use of disrupting "the apprehensible world in order to open spaces for dreaming alternatives" (1995: xvi). Along with Warner, whose influence she has often acknowledged, Roberts is well aware of the "transforming power of fairy stories and that therefore this could be good for women" (Bastida Rodríguez 2003: 105). For Roberts, the transformative power of literature, the universality of myths and archetypes, and the specificity of history intertwine in the poetic language of the unconscious, the

> place of imagination [...] at the heart of each of us, at the heart of culture, of society [...] in which to let go of old certainties, let boundaries dissolve, experience the kind of chaos necessary for new life, new ideas.
>
> (1998: 22)

Formally speaking, the short story is, like the fairy tale itself, a radically unstable genre which questions narrative norms and defies immutability. The short story can be certainly viewed as an example of what Deleuze and Guattari have termed "minor literature", as "that which a minority constructs within a major language" (1986: 16) entailing resistance, challenge and the reassessment of new forms working upon the remains of culture (March-Russell 2009: 248).

Significantly, Robert's first collection of short fiction was entitled *During Mother's Absence* (1993), a series of permutations of the mother/daughter plot. Four of the narratives – "Charity", "Fish", "God's House" and "*Une Glossarie*/A Glossary" – are rendered by a peripheral first-person female child narrator on the threshold of the adult world. Their narratives reveal a woman's painful rite of passage from childhood to maturity where love for the mother and frustration at her loss intertwine in an acute and conflicting interaction of ambivalent feelings. In addition, such perspectives also dramatise what Roberts has dubbed as a young girl's rebellion against her own father's "omniscient narrative [...]; I felt trapped in his story of who I was in life" (Newman 2003). In so doing, Roberts puts forward an interesting feminist rewriting of the traditional male pattern of maturation – or Oedipus complex – by exclusively focusing on the mother/daughter relationship, articulated in the text through Roberts's rejection of omniscience – or of the powerful paternal pattern of familiar dominance along with the elision of the male figure. In this way, Roberts undoes the dominant logic denounced by Irigaray: "Under the rule of patriarchy the girl is separated from her mother and from her family in general. She is transplanted into the genealogy of her husband; she must live with him, carry his name, bear his children" (Irigaray 1987: 2). These narratives undermine this premise by foregrounding a female genealogy that is essential to create an ethical order that would enable the necessary conditions for women's action, a "world of female ethics" beyond the idealisation of the son-Father relationship and the other suppressed "vertical dimension" of the relationship "daughter-to-mother, mother-to-daughter" (Irigaray 1993: 108). If motherhood, as Kristeva would have it, is "a threshold where 'nature' confronts 'culture'" (1980: 238), the desire to recover the maternal body, a blissful communion between mother and daughter is, for Roberts, only realised in fiction, and this conflicting mixture of love for the mother, anger at her loss, and pain for her absence is what fuels her writing. Because of this conflicting mixture of feelings, of the inner "chaos" of woman's relationship with her mother, maternal presences, motherhood and relationships between mothers and daughters are most often described at once as a painful and complex processes of rediscovery.

Maternal Absence: Michèle Roberts's "Anger"

Roberts's *During Mother's Absence* opens up with the story entitled "Anger", which sets the keynote for the collection as a whole. The narrative pivots on Roberts's reassessment of the Melusine myth – "clearly a story about the relationship to the mother, and mother nature, and how she fits into society", according to Irigaray (1987: 59) – as well as on a writer's anger at failing to successfully articulate the maternal body, encapsulating the perspective of an "angry daughter" (Bastida Rodríguez 2003: 106). "Anger" intertwines different narrative modes which move from the opening oral voice of a community in a fairy-tale fashion, the third-person omniscient voice focalised by a male character, both attached to "authority figure[s]" (García-Sánchez 2011: 151), to a final first-person "blissful babble" (Newman 2003) of a woman's monologue which dismantles authorial control. In so doing, Roberts infuses the mother-daughter bond with a mythical dimension which intertwines both literary assessments of the Melusine legend (as recounted by Jean d'Arras in *Roman de Mélusine ou l'Histoire des Lusignan*, 1478) and the comparable stories in the Andersen and Grimm collections of fairy tales and Roberts's interpretation of them all, or her own "retelling [of] old stories with that personal link on", as she herself has explained (García-Sánchez 2011: 150).

According to the ancient Melusine legend, the fairy Melusine married Guy de Lusignan, Count of Poitou, under condition that he should never attempt to intrude upon her privacy and bore the count many children. Their harmony was interrupted when Melusine's husband broke the conditions of their union in order to behold his wife as she bathed in a tub. When Melusine discovered the indiscreet intruder, she transformed herself into a dragon, and disappeared leaving her children behind. As Kevin Brownlee argues, the Mélusine text possesses "potent female-gendered categories of the erotic and the 'natural'", and suggests that the equation between the female body and power may eventually carry disastrous consequences (1994: 18). In a sense, Melusine's monstrosity may also signal patriarchal fears of women's power.

"Anger" opens with a fairy tale formula to introduce Bertrande, Melusine's mother, a most unconventional woman questioned by villagers for her improprieties: "Once upon a time, there was a red-haired country woman called Bertrande living with her husband, Guillaume Tarentin, in their small house tucked into the side of a steep hill in Provence" (Roberts 1993: 1). Bertrande's unusual physical attributes match an improper behaviour that puzzles villagers with her unwomanly attitude and with her propensity to produce odd artefacts from ordinary objects:

> She saved everything, and found a use for it. Bits of string, knotted together, mended chair seats and baskets; she grew flowers in old saucepans, which she then stuck in the windowsill; out of old boxes she made cupboards and stools; out of old cardboard she made patches for broken windows, mats for the kitchen floor of trodden earth, trays on which to store vegetables.
>
> (Roberts 1993: 2)

Bertrande's use of low and ordinary elements to produce amazing objects mirrors a writer's craft to reassess an inherited tradition, while also upsetting the sexual division of labour in terms of production and reproduction, refusing to bear her husband a child: "But what you never saw Bertrande's hands doing was caressing a child. Married for ten years, she appeared incapable of conceiving an heir" (Roberts 1993: 4). Despite Bertrande's efforts to refuse being walled up in a single function as a wife and mother, she eventually becomes pregnant for which she would be welcomed "as one of themselves". Yet, and as villagers notice, she "snubbed every attempt at friendliness", becomes "even more sullen and quiet" (Roberts 1993: 4), and is suspected by women villagers to have an improper and dangerous behaviour during pregnancy in order to consciously provoke a miscarriage (Roberts 1993: 5).

When Bertrande gives birth to a baby daughter, she develops a strong feeling of disaffection for the child, which culminates in her failed attempt to kill the baby by dropping her in the fire:

> Guillaume said the fire was out. No, Bertrande said that the fire was out. She was cold, and so was the baby. She needed fire. She needed to be warm. She wanted to go back to bed, not to sit in a

cold kitchen with no fire. The fire was not out. The fire was near
Bertrande. Bertande was near the fire. She made more fire with the
poker. The flames licked up. She held the baby to the fire to make it
warm, like the fire inside her. She held the fire to the baby. Bertrande
dropped the baby in the fire. She said it was not an accident.

(Roberts 1993: 9)

In the passage Roberts voices prejudice and gossip, to eventually confirm
Bertrande's infanticidal intentions, which come to villagers as the eventual evidence of Bertrande's unnatural, monstrous nature:

The priest came puffing up the hill to christen the child. They named
her Melusine. No one knew where the name came from, and no one
dared ask. Guillaume simply said that it would be so. Bertrande
went to bed and stayed there and was silent. They brought the child
for her to be fed, and they watched her to make sure that she did not
try to harm it again. Downstairs in the kitchen, drinking unhappy
toasts to the bandaged newborn, they whispered to each other that
Bertrande was a monster.

(Roberts 1993: 10)

Significantly, Bertrande names her daughter Melusine, an index of the
foundational representation of the maternal as both body and symbol, yet
also a signal that Bertrande's recognition as a mother will be problematic.
Furthermore, Bertrande's failed infanticide recalls Medea, culturally constructed as the archetypal murderous mother figure, an example of how
maternal generative power most often collides with the communal representatives of paternal control. The Medea myth addresses what Adrienne
Rich has called "the heart of maternal darkness" (1976: 258), the complex
ambivalence of motherhood tinged by a tension of opposites which collide.
Medea's act of infanticide inspires horror as the expression of an unthinkable crime because it undermines the supposed naturalness of women's
position in the private sphere as wives and, especially, as mothers, suggesting the ambivalent relationship between prohibition and desire.[1]

Bertrande's refusal to comply with women's social expectations as a
wife and as a mother eventually drives her towards death, and the parish
priest decides that her grave should be placed in a liminal position "close
enough to the church to be included in the company of the righteous, and
at a sufficient distance not to cause offence" (Roberts 1993: 11). She will
not be mourned or missed, since her existence is being violently blotted
out from the villagers' memory and the family history:

It was a poor funeral, people said afterwards: like a pauper's. They
understood why Guillaume would not allow any flowers, and why
he did not invite them back to his house afterwards, and why he

marked the grave with a plain cross made of cheap wood with no
words cut on it other than his wife's name.

(Roberts 1993: 11)

The figure of the dead mother, as Ruth Cain has observed, is important
"for what it tells us about the positioning of maternal subjects within
Western thought" (2013: 409). In the narrative, Bertrande's suppression
and silencing implies that Melusine will be deprived of her matrilineal
inheritance and literally "transplanted" into the genealogy of her father,
Guillaume, and later into that of her husband, the schoolmaster Pierre
Caillou, a process which formally signals the inception of the story's second section. Likewise, Melusine's actions will be monitored from Pierre's
standpoint, aware of the extent to which Bertrande's scandalous life and
death had "shaped" Melusine, but also of the fact that "she had a secret" (Roberts 1993: 12). Despite Melusine's tendency to day-dreaming,
Pierre notices her talented nature as particularly manifested in her skilful though awkward drawings, such as

> the portrait of some mythical creature she must have seen in a pic-
> turebook somewhere: a wild being of the woods, half-man, half-
> beast, covered from head to toe in thick curly fur, and with little
> breasts peeping out that proved her to be female,

which the girl argues to have seen "in the mirror" (Roberts 1993: 14).
   Much like the monstrous semi-human figures that Melusine colours
in her picture book, Pierre eventually discovers that Melusine has also a
double nature:

> He [Pierre] knew, of course, as did everyone in the village, that she
> [Melusine] had been burnt as a baby, and that the midwife had said
> that the skin would grow back but should be shiny and puckered
> and red, that she would be grotesque in the place where the women
> of that country were smooth milky white. What he had not expected
> were the little breasts. He had thought her too young. What he had
> not expected was the thick, silky thatch of bright red hair that curled
> from her neck down around her breasts and on down to her waist.

(Roberts 1993: 15)

Puzzled by this discovery, Pierre discusses Melusine's nature with her father and stepmother, who admit that Bertrande had delivered "herself a
monster" and that "the most disturbing aspect of the whole business [...]
was that the hair regularly disappeared of its own accord after four or
five days, and reappeared with equal regularity a month later" (Roberts
1993: 17), during the course of which Melusine locked herself and
refused human intercourse.

On the condition never to disturb Melusine during those critical days of confinement, Pierre marries her, and by "studying her peculiarities he began to love her, and to hope that she loved him in return" (Roberts 1993: 19). Despite Pierre's encouragement of her artistic vocation, soon Melusine grows "silent, irritable and finally rebellious [... and] was turning out as undomestic as her mother had been" (Roberts 1993: 21) and the days of confinement increase in number. As in most versions of the Melusine myth, Pierre feels overwhelmed with doubts – "Had he married a real wild woman of the woods, half-human and half-beast" (Roberts 1993: 23) – and eventually breaks the promise made to Melusine's parents by intruding in her confinement:

> He [Pierre] knelt down and peered in through the keyhole. The pantry was ablaze with light. Standing in the centre of the tiny room [...] was the most beautiful woman Pierre had ever seen. She was naked. She was tall, and creamy skinned, and her long red hair flowed down her back like streams of fire. There was no blemish anywhere on her. She turned her head and smiled at someone he could not see, someone just standing outside his line of vision. Her lips moved, and she spoke. He could not read her words, nor could he, squinting, make out their shape by lip-reading. The she turned her head and looked straight at the door.
>
> (Roberts 1993: 24)

Pierre's is puzzled by his discovery; expecting to find a hybrid monster he learns that his wife has actually transformed into "the most beautiful woman" he had ever seen, her horrid birthmark – reminiscent of original sin – being miraculously removed from her body. Melusine's metamorphosis "runs counter to notions of unique, individual integrity in the Judaeo-Christian tradition" (Warner 2002: 2), expressing a sense of eternal flux, "a prevailing law of mutability and change" (Warner 2002: 4) which undermines traditional models of femininity by presenting an empowering monstrosity which can lead to further transformations (Castagna 2010: 61). Such transformations are signalled in the text by the abandonment of third-person omniscience – related to male, authorial control over Bertrande and Melusine's bodies and consciousness – in favour of the fluid first-person narrative which comes next and which intertwines the consciousness of mother and daughter.

The section brings together motifs and images which relate to the characters' thoughts in an attempt to reconstruct their family history, which necessarily stems from the assumption of guilt and the will to forgive. The purifying nature of fire (which has branded Melusine's body and her mother's nature as "monstrous") articulates the whole section with its illuminating, purifying force, reminiscent of Christian iconography and rituals. The coherent, ordered and logical discourse of the rest of the sections gives way to full physicality, maternal lamentation, sexual desire in a subjective yet powerful discourse which aims to reconstruct a bond between mother and daughter by restoring a female genealogy, suppressed in the preceding male-controlled sections. Forgiveness – realised through the burning tears running down Melusine's body, washing away her scar, her sins, her hatred and resentment – enacts the final reparation, signalling the restorative power of love, of sexual love, of filial love through the waters of a particular kind of baptism: "I kiss and lick all of your skin between your neck and waist. I am crying because I love you so much. My tears fall on you and are warm on your scars" (Roberts 1993: 25).

The narrative thus leaves behind male authorial control by recalling a pre-Oedipal state, a restoration of the loving mother-daughter bond in an identification which culture suppresses and silences, where mother and daughter blissfully commune making possible reparation and forgiveness:

> Look in the mirror, the mother says, and see how beautiful you are. Silly, you're holding the mirror in the wrong place. Hold it lower down. See the red fire glowing there, in the secret place between your legs. See how beautiful you are. You are like me. You are my daughter. I will love you for ever. You can leave me and you can always come back.
>
> (Roberts 1993: 26)

In the passage, the mirror becomes a tool which the mother provides for the daughter for self-contemplation, for "our own becoming" which can supplement and support "the different houses, the different bodies that have borne me" (Irigaray 1987: 65) in a movement towards self-knowledge. By emphasising affinity between mother and daughter, the mirror's reflection confirms the "sameness", or "the maternal-feminine which has been assimilated before any perception of difference" (Irigaray 1993: 98), which restores Melusine's mother to her rightful place in the constitution of a female vertical genealogy. Formally speaking, the insertion of the third section in an otherwise omniscient, male-controlled narrative implies a destabilisation of the Symbolic Order signalling a pre-Oedipal, semiotic realm existing before and below language.

Despite the complexities of maternal relationships in the narrative, Roberts evokes reparation and forgiveness as a restorative image of an imagined original unity between mother and daughter, a sense of oneness with the body of the mother (Frampton 2006: 657), a feminist myth of origins whose function is, as Roberts herself has put it, to "remember us": "My mother dropped me in the fire, but she will heal me" (Roberts 1993: 26). The linguistic fluidity of this section is reminiscent of Kristeva's formulation of the pre-Oedipal, semiotic *chora* which "is analogous only to vocal or kinetic rhythm" (1984: 25–26), an evocative and fluid use of bodily language able to

> speak of the most ancient and most current relationship we know – the relationship to the mother's body, to our body – sentences that translate the bond between our body, her body, the body of our daughter. We need to discover a language that is not a substitute for the experience of *corps-è-corps* as the paternal language seeks to be, but which accompanies that bodily experience, clothing it in words that do not erase the body but speak the body.
>
> (Irigaray 1987: 19)

The narrative closes with a final restorative moment by recalling the perspective of Melusine's father, Guillaume. Aware of his daughter's increasing alienation, Guillaume approaches Melusine's house and taps her window, but she refuses to speak to him. Guillaume observes Melusine's scars "as angry as though she had been dropped in the fire that very day", and weeps on "the scarred skin around his daughter's breasts and [...] on to his hands, warm and stinging" (Roberts 1993: 28). Guillaume's act of contrition and her daughter's forgiveness enables Melusine's final metamorphosis, which turns her skin "as creamy and smooth as it had been on the day she was born" (Roberts 1993: 28–29). Roberts closes the narrative with a footnote, which acknowledges the inspiration provided by Toni Morrison in the story's composition process, and which clarifies Bertrande's murderous intentions towards her daughter, performed out of love rather than of hatred in order to spare Melusine the pain which her object position could bring about. In so doing, Robert's enhances the narrative's power to rehabilitate the dead mother, who keeps coming back to haunt Melusine as a ghost, and whose encounters are presumably rendered in the story's penultimate section.

Roberts's reassessment of Melusine, a myth of female agency, articulates a powerful counternarrative which questions received assumptions pertaining to models of femininity and propriety, intertwining traditional oral formulae from fairy tales with suggestive literary rewritings. "Anger" is about the complexities of the mother-daughter relationship, about the traumatic trajectory of a female child to restore the lost maternal body in order to place it in a genealogy of women, which Roberts takes as the necessary point of inception to produce an ethical discourse of female empowerment. Roberts's reassessment of the Melusine myth exemplifies the painful inadequacies of motherhood, but also as an opportunity to consider the necessity of coming to terms with expected roles and models, to confront the complexities of the mother/daughter relationship and to restore the mother to her rightful place in a woman's genealogy "if we are not to be accomplices in the murder of the mother [...] Let us try to situate ourselves within that female genealogy so that we can win and hold on to our identity" (Irigaray 1987: 19).

Marian Myths and Postmodern Reassessments: Michèle Roberts's "Annunciation"

The second narrative under examination is "Annunciation", compiled in Robert's last short story collection to date entitled *Mud: Stories of Sex and Love* (2010). This compilation articulates Roberts's visitation of a full range of female experiences, which comprise the lives of anonymous women, as well as a rewriting of iconic women writers and characters, such as Emma Bovary, George Sand, Jane Eyre, Rapunzel, Colette or Little Red Riding Hood, whose ghosts have haunted women's imagination and conditioned their relationship with the literary canon. The fourteen stories of the collection explore women's sexual desire through the discovery of their own bodies and their physicality – as the word "mud" in the collection title suggests. These stories entail a variety of female perspectives which journey through pleasure, pain, sexual encounters, virginity, prostitution, sensuality, death of the loved ones and most notably, loneliness and the earthly strategies that some women develop to face solitude.

Mud: Stories of Sex and Love is also a powerful rumination on the role of the writer's imagination, its impact on the reader and on culture at large. The narrator of the opening story makes this point obvious by alluding to the collection's metafictional nature and to the material quality of literature, which the word "mud" encapsulates:

> I picked up the curls of mud and balanced them on my palms. Loops and circles of mud. Mud words. Mud commas and full stops. Bits of writing, broken apart, like the pieces of an old pot you dig up when going over your allotment. I'd piece them back together again, make something new with them.
>
> (Roberts 2010: 7)

The passage becomes a metafictional commentary on the writer's craft, on the collection's simultaneously fragmentary and unitary nature, on the materiality of writing, and on a woman's urge to reassess the inherited literary tradition in order to "make it new". As a result, Robert's deployment of such imagery becomes an inspiring reflection on the female capacity to produce life, not only in biological terms, but also in social ones by producing a powerful counter-narrative which reflects on the nature of things, truth, myth and origins, as the protagonist of the first narrative indicates:

> Yes I could have eaten a handful of earth, dry-damp-delicious in my mouth, and I could have eaten the long woven hedges and the bright grass and the black thorns glossy as silver. I wanted to lick all of it, taste it and swallow it and be one with it. And then, dissolving, I wasn't myself, I wasn't myself any more. I'd gone. I was just part of

the mud, fresh in the rain and the sun and I was fed by the world, mouth open, full, churning with joy.

(Roberts 2010: 4)

The narrator's metamorphic experience – swallowing the word and being swallowed by it – allows her to assume alternative identities by fusing and influencing others in turn, in a fluid movement which eventually becomes an inspiring reflection on female subjectivity, gender roles, cultural constructions, power and inheritance, and on the ways to relate to the literary tradition. In this collection, Roberts's point of inception entails the fragmentation of the authorial self and progresses "towards the intention to renew tradition by reaffirming an underlying order in history accessible at the level of myth" (1983: 66).

"Mud" actually becomes a powerful motif which recurs in all the narratives, taking the reader back to one of the foundational myths on artistry, life and inspiration in Genesis, whose narrative depicts God as a craftsman, creating life *ex nihilo* by modelling both man and woman, and endowing them with life with his breath, a most powerful image juxtaposing creation and inspiration, as Roberts herself has claimed: "I needed to name myself in a way that connected female-powerful-creator" (1983: 63). While drawing from this Biblical image, Roberts also departs from it by reinventing the Christian myth and placing mud on a woman's mouth, an image which virtually recurs in each of the narratives in the collection. In theological terms, the Word actualises God's creative power; God creates the world through the Word in Genesis – "Let there be light", and there was light (Genesis 1: 3), an image which finds its counterpart in the Gospel of St John announcing the Advent of God the Son – the Word – to save the World: "In the beginning was the Word, and the Word was with God, and the Word was God [...] Through him all things were made; without him nothing was made that has been made" (St John 1: 1–3).

Roberts's eleventh narrative in the collection, "Annunciation", examines the discursive and ideological repercussions of the relationship between creativity and the power of the written word by playfully bringing together two foundational myths related to birth and creation in the Christian tradition: God the craftsman creating life *ex nihilo* in Genesis and its counterpart in the New Testament, the Advent of God the Son of woman born. Roberts herself has discussed in numerous occasions how her writing was heavily influenced by "the rituals and forms of worship of the Catholic church, by their language and rhythms" which she acknowledges to have inside like "my mother's milk: a French Roman Catholic" (1983: 66). In "Annunciation" Roberts re-examines the Marian myth and its repercussions on women's sexuality: Mary's Immaculate Conception spares her death and vice, to the point that the relationship to Mary has become the prototype of the love relationship, courtly love and love of the child, as matrix within which various other relations are measured (Kristeva 1985: 136, 138). In Western thought, Mary represents a feminine ideal subsumed under the maternal and thus becomes extremely influential as a role model. However, in "Annunciation" Roberts powerfully questions the role of women in general – and of Mary in particular – as "eternal mediators for the incarnation of the body and the world of man, women [who] seem never to have produced the singularity of their own body and world" (Irigaray 1993: 109).

As Warner explains, in Christian theology "Mary's consent to the Incarnation [...] exemplifies the most sublime fusion of man's free will with the divine plan. The free cooperation of man and God for salvation bears the metaphysical name of synergy" (1976: 177). In the Gospel, both Matthew and Luke were most likely influenced by the classical tradition of virgin birth when they wrote their accounts of Christ's origins (Warner 1976: 34). By doing so, both writers were concerned with stamping an enduring seal of approval on the birth of Christ in accordance with classical accounts of miraculous births which would mirror heroic qualities. In this context of Christ's marvellous birth – a sign of his divine nature – the humanity of the Virgin Mary is not always evident, since the Mother of God is alone of her sex distinguished from the human race in her freedom from sin (Kristeva 1985: 134).

However, Roberts displaces the miraculous and magic elements from the myth, focusing instead on Mary as an ordinary woman, a helpless working-class girl whose efforts to struggle and survive in a class-conscious, indifferent society are indeed epic and miraculous in themselves. In "Annunciation" Roberts reassesses the conjunction between woman's free will and the divine plan by liberating her main character, Marie, from male constraints and designs. Thus, she is presented as a brave single mother deserted by her divorced lover, Joseph, but helped out by a community of women whose generous love culminates in advent of the Son of God, a miracle entailing female agency and bonds of cooperation among women, or Marie's discovery of a "horizontal dimension" upon which women's world is grounded. Marie's sexual and emotional relationships with men prove painful and traumatic: the different men in her life abuse and degrade her, but she finds the necessary love and security in Anne and Lizzie (Mary's mother and cousin in the Scriptures) who align with Marie in an alternative female Trinity to secure protection for her child.

In doing so, Roberts subverts conventional representations of Mary as an invisible mediator, as the submissive receptacle of God's son by placing the emphasis on Mary's emotional struggle and agency, thus foregrounding God's matrilineal – rather than paternal – inheritance. In Roberts's story, Christ's birth will be possible only when "love of same" is actually enacted through the establishment of a woman's genealogy, a horizontal dimension of "love among women" (Irigaray 1993: 102), thus "achieving, through their relations with each other, a path into infinity that is always open" (Irigaray 1993: 105, 106).

In establishing models of female behaviour and propriety, Mary's virginity – related to life and grace – is articulated in opposition to Eve, who propitiated the Fall, death and sin into the world (Kristeva 1985: 137). Roberts questions the premise that women's sexual behaviour may propitiate falling into either the virgin or the whore category by making her character move in between the two: Marie is an "open-mouthed", "vulnerable and soft" "good girl in the early 1960s, and that's how the nuns in the grey stone convent school bring her up", prepared "for the angel when he whirrs into her life" (2010: 153), but, at the same time, she is prepared to discover her own sexuality when entering adulthood. Roberts playfully intertwines here the figure of the "spiritual" mother, the iconic Madonna, and the eroticised woman, the prostitute, recalling Mary Magdalene. The biblical prostitute reconciles the spiritual and the sexual in the female, a motif which has been extensively explored by Roberts in her fiction and essays. Against the Catholic denial of the body, there emerges Mary Magdalene as "a highly-coloured version of the eternal feminine", as the very image of the "return of the repressed: the numinous body, sexiness and holiness intertwined", "a figure of glorious contradiction" (Roberts 1998: 27–29).

Marie leaves school at eighteen, "having failed her exams" and starts work as a clerk in the General Post Office on the Euston Road. Her first pay packet is spent on new clothes and make-up to match a new social life out of her "Catholic ghetto", out of her non-Catholic new friends, "iconoclast bullies", "deluded heathens who eat sausages on Fridays, who refer to the Blessed Virgin Mary just as Mary and think she is just another woman" (Roberts 2010: 155). While Marie leads an innocent life at the office during daytime, she ventures out at night on her own and finds out that men often approach her "nudging and whispering", but thinks "it's just how men are and you put up with it" (Roberts 2010: 155). Thus, we are told, "[w]hen she walks around the city, men spring out at her from every crack and crevice, edging too much close, rubbing up against her, asking how much she charges" (Roberts 2010: 156).

Marie experiences a number of sexual encounters with men she does not even like, since "she doesn't know how to say no. She's been brought up to be accommodating and polite" (Roberts 2010: 156). Marie still believes that "good men exist", and hopes one day to find a perfect partner whom she will recognise "because he'll treat her so well" (Roberts 2010: 156), yet all male figures in Marie's life eventually disappoint her. In this sense, a revealing situation occurs when Marie decides to visit a psychiatrist "during a bad patch in her early twenties" (156). The psychiatrist's diagnosis of Marie's emotional state summarises the prevailing atmosphere of male prejudice and aggressiveness towards women disguised as scientific, objective medical discourse: "'You pretend to be so innocent but you must have wanted it. Why deny that? Why can't you take some responsibility for what happened?'" (Roberts 2010: 157). The psychiatrist, sitting in his armchair like a *Pantocrator*, stands for patriarchal, normative power and control:

> The round metal window behind his office chair forms his painted white halo; frame scarred with rust, peeling. The eyes of this mind-saint bur her up. Marie slumps on her orange vinyl chair. Mouth full of mud. She can't explain. He's like the parish priest. You don't talk back to that fiery judge.
>
> (Roberts 2010: 157)

After his advice, Marie learns to "keep her eyes down in the street, and not to look around her; so fewer men try it on" (Roberts 2010: 158), but this does not prevent other undesirable situations from taking place. Marie rents a flat with three girls from work; they hold a Saturday night party which turns out to be an orgy with satanic decorations and sex as the night unfolds: Marie runs away from her flat and meets Joe, simultaneously "the angel" (Roberts 2010: 161) – archangel Gabriel, who announces Mary the good news – and Mary's husband, whom she immediately likes for being "nice" and "respectful" (Roberts 2010: 164), leaves her flat and moves to Joe's. Marie believes to have found her twin soul and rapidly falls in love with Joe, but she soon learns that she is actually entrapped in a sadistic relationship:

> He ties her up. He knots Marie's hands and feet to the bedstead with silk scarves. He touches and rubs her, gently now, taking his time, until she comes. Then he photographs her. Then he fucks her. Then he photographs her again. Then he unties her. Sometimes he doesn't fuck her at all, just ties her up and photographs her splayed legs. Gorgeous, darling: gorgeous. Sometimes he dresses her up: lipsticked nun flashing her knickers; pouting little First Communicant shedding her dress, her veil. Marie feels taken care of; as though Joe's her mother, the scarves her mother holding her. Silky hands saying come on darling this is for your own good. Rapture of surrender to those hands, to those eyes, to that camera. Rapture of giving Joe everything he asks for; her attention, her love, her crisis.
>
> (Roberts 2010: 167)

Marie enters into a spiral of violence and abuse, loses her job, drinks too much, and feels she is to blame since, according to her psychiatrist, she is actually "promiscuous and frigid; she hates men and wants to castrate them. She's faking it: pretending to be so innocent but really wanting to bite men's penises off" (Roberts 2010: 166). Marie's life experiences a turning point when she finds out she is pregnant; she feels unprepared to become a mother, and abortion is an illegal practice:

> What was the game with the flower petals you ripped off? He loves me he loves me not. I'll have a baby no I'll not. How can I possibly become a mother? It wouldn't be fair on the child. Poor little tyke. She can't ring her parents and ask for help. To them abortion is a mortal sin. Herod's Slaughter of the Innocents all over again, punished by an eternity in hell-fire. She has lost touch with her former flatmates and good riddance [...] She's got no friends. Stupid girl, she berates herself: stupid girl.
>
> (Roberts 2010: 175)

When Marie eventually finds the courage to desert Joe, she turns to Anne as her only hope, an upper-middle class woman whom Marie remembers as one of Joe's patrons and as one of the few people who had treated her with kindness and affection since her arrival in London. In her despair, Marie recalls their first meeting at Anne's flat, and how she had wished to "sit in the armchair with her and feel her arms around her" and to "lie in her lap like a baby" (Roberts 2010: 172). Anne does not disappoint Marie and helps her out, driving her over to her god-daughter's, Lizzie (briefly recalling Mary's cousin Elizabeth in the Bible), who offers her to move in to her own flat.

Aided by these two women, a female version of the Holy Family, Marie eventually "gives birth the following December, at the London Hospital" (Roberts 2010: 181). The baby's arrival to the flat humorously echoes the Adoration of the Three Magi, a ceremony involving the acknowledgment of the Child's divine nature by the three Wise Men, who venerate Jesus as both Man and God. In Roberts's story, this ceremony becomes a welcome party, where women sincerely celebrate Marie's courage as a single mother and joyfully drink beer, cider, and gin-and-tonic:

> Once the baby is brought home the household throws a party in the kitchen, to bless and welcome him. They encircle his head with a wreath of tinsel and evergreen, hang strings of lights above his basket, light candles, splash drops of gin and tonic on his brow, sing to him.
>
> (Roberts 2010: 181)

The disinterested love and generosity these women show to Marie propitiate both the material means and emotional climate for the advent of God's Son: "Lizzie helps Marie in her cheerful, slapdash way. She takes the baby out for airing, to give Marie a chance to catch up on her sleep, helps her fill in forms for the DHSS, soaks nappies in buckets" (Roberts 2010: 181).

The narrative closes with images with suggest both a "vertical dimension" of mother-and-child bonds of affection, as well as a "horizontal dimension" of love and solidarity among women, which suggestively intertwine. Mother and child communion is encapsulated in Marie's breast-feeding her baby in the story's closing pages, which simultaneously incorporates Lizzie to the picture, recalling an alternative and blissful Holy Family as well as suggesting honest bonds of affection among women:

> Sometimes, when the baby wakes at three or four a.m. and cries for a feed, Lizzie hears him. She creeps out of her own room, peeps round Marie's door. Marie, still half asleep, pulling a blanket around her shoulders, fumbling to fit the baby to her breast, looks up and nods: come in. Lizzie, wrapped in a second blanket, perches on the end of the bed in darkness. Then gradually she sprawls across the eiderdown, propped on one elbow. Sometimes they chat; exchange confidences. Sometimes they remain in silence [...] The room holds them. The baby gulps and burps. They swim in an ordinariness that feels safe, and lets their edges blur and loosen [...] The three of them sit peacefully together, part of the London night.
>
> (Roberts 2010: 181–182)

The traditional holy family is here replaced by a sisterhood of women who experience motherhood in an alternative and inspiring way. By doing so, these women construct a "world of female ethics" (Irigaray 1993: 108), envisioning a women-structured world pivoting on the miracle of motherhood, here deprived of supernatural constituents and explained in its full ambivalence, complexities and physicality. In "Annunciation" Roberts gives us a modern version of Mary void of her epic or divine attributes, and constructs her as a plain, confused and tormented working-class girl facing unwanted motherhood. In addition, Roberts reassesses the Marian myth by bringing to the fore the relevance of God's matrilineal inheritance, thus downplaying the persistent equation between femininity and the Maternal with silence and submissiveness which Christianity brings to its peak (Kristeva 1985: 134). Traditionally, the Virgin Mary has worked as the ideal representation of motherhood in its fullness and perfection, despite her exemption by special privilege "from intercourse, from labour, and from other physical processes or ordinary childbearing" (Warner 1976: 192–194). By questioning the Christian dogma of Mary's "immaculate conception" and other elements related to it, Roberts places Mary in a human context of sin, mortality and death which Marie's mouth "full of mud" suggests (Roberts 2010: 157). In the story Roberts turns Marie's initial subjection and powerlessness to potential empowerment by allowing her to find an inspiring alternative to the bourgeois, normative family. Such a possibility is, indeed, encapsulated in Irigaray's productive notion of "love of same", namely, a world of love and affection which Marie eventually finds in new models of parenting and motherhood, as entailed by her sisterhood with Anne and Lizzie, whose disinterested love and charity pave the way for the Saviour to be born.

Conclusion

The two stories under examination here, "Anger" and "Annunciation" – compiled in Roberts's first and last collection of short fiction, *During Mother's Absence* (1993) and *Mud: Stories of Sex and Love* (2010), respectively – exemplify the early and later stages of Michèle Roberts's aesthetic development as a writer. These narratives unfold Roberts's feminist agenda as integral to her artistry, an ethical position which informs her narrative and which necessarily requires thorough examination of received models of femininity and relationships among women. As Roberts herself has always acknowledged, the search for the maternal body has fuelled her narrative, which is at stake in both "Anger" and "Annunciation". Whereas "Anger" revises folk traditions, such as the Melusine myth, which ultimately address the relationship between mother and daughter from a secular perspective, "Annunciation" reassesses the impact of the Marian myth on women's femininity and sexuality. Furthermore, both stories become mutually complementary in their attempt to recover "genealogies of women", the matrilineal inheritance which Western culture has often deemed invisible by transplanting women's offspring to a genealogy of fathers and husbands. Through the short story, Roberts sharply conveys the message that recovering such a female inheritance enables women to establish fruitful bonds of collaboration among them, which marks the point of inception for the production of the emancipatory, liberating discourse of a female ethics.

Note

1 In *Totem and Taboo*, Sigmund Freud posited such a tension between prohibition and desire as crucial to the concept of taboo, "a primaeval prohibition forcibly imposed (by some authority) from outside, and directed against the most powerful longings to which human beings are subject" (1955: 34–5). Freud's particular intuition about the nature of those wishes led him to assert that Sophocles' *Oedipus the King* dramatised repressed incestuous and parricidal wishes which are virtually universal. Whereas the Oedipal narrative has been, since Freud, consistently utilised to dramatise psychic processes of growth and maturation, the figure of the murderous mother continues to incite rejection and disgust in most readers. Freud himself showed a selective enthusiasm for the Oedipus myth: the index to his collected works contains a long list of references to Oedipus and only one

to Medea – in spite of the conspicuous similarities between the two myths – which may respond to Freud's idealisation of maternal love, described as "the most perfect, the most free from ambivalence of all human relationships" (1965: 133).

References

Bastida Rodríguez, Patricia (2003) "On Women, Christianity and History: An Interview with Michèle Roberts", *Atlantis: Journal of the Spanish Association of Anglo-American Studies* 25(1): 93–107.

Brownlee, Kevin (1994) "Mélusine's Hybrid Body and the Poetics of Metamorphosis", *Yale French Studies* 86: 18–38.

Cain, Ruth (2013) "The Buried Madonna: Matricide, Maternal Power and the Novels of Michèle Roberts", *Women's Studies* 42(4): 408–438.

Castagna, Valentina (2010) *Shape-Shifting Tales: Michèle Roberts's Monstrous Women*, Bern: Peter Lang.

Deleuze, Gilles and Félix Guattari (1986) *Kafka: Toward a Minor Literature*, translated by Dana Polan, Minnesota, MN: University of Minnesota Press.

Frampton, Edith (2006) "'This milky fullness': Breastfeeding Narratives and Michèle Roberts", *Textual Practice* 20(4): 655–678

Freud, Sigmund (1965) *New Introductory Lectures on Psychoanalysis*, in *The Standard Edition of the Complete Psychological Works of Sigmund Freud*, Vol. XXII, edited by James Strachey and translated by Anna Freud, London: The Hogarth Press.

García-Sánchez, M. Soraya (2011) "Talking about Women, History and Writing with Michèle Roberts", in *Travelling in Women's History with Michèle Roberts's Novels*, Bern: Peter Lang, 139–154.

Irigaray, Luce (1987), *Sexes and Genealogies*, translated by Gillian C. Gill, New York: Columbia University Press.

Irigaray, Luce (1993) *An Ethics of Sexual Difference*, translated by Carolyn Burk and Gillian C. Gill, Ithaca, NY: Cornell University Press.

Kristeva, Julia (1980) "Motherhood According to Giovanni Bellini", in *Desire in Language*, edited by Leon Roudiez and translated by Thomas Gora et al., Oxford: Blackwell, 237–270.

Kristeva, Julia (1984) *Revolution in Poetic Language*, translated by Margaret Waller, New York: Columbia University Press.

Kristeva, Julia (1985) "Stabat Mater", *Poetics Today* 6(1/2): 133–152.

Lojo-Rodríguez, Laura Mª (2012) "Recovering the Maternal Body as Paradise: Michèle Roberts's 'Charity'", *Atlantis: Journal of the Spanish Association of Anglo-American Studies* 34(2): 33–47.

March-Russell, Paul (2009) *The Short Story: An Introduction*, Edinburgh: Edinburgh University Press.

Newman, Jenny (2003) "An Interview with Michèle Roberts", *Cercles: Revue pluridisciplinaire du monde Anglophone*, www.cercles.com/interviews/roberts.html (accessed 14 May 2016).

Rich, Adrienne (1976) *Of Woman Born: Motherhood as Experience and Institution*, London: Virago.

Roberts, Michèle (1983) "Questions and Answers", in *On Gender and Writing*, edited by Michelene Wandor, New York: Thorsons, 62–68.

Roberts, Michèle (1993) *During Mother's Absence*, London: Virago.

Roberts, Michèle (1998) *Food, Sex and God: On Inspiration and Writing*, London: Virago.

Roberts, Michèle (2010) *Mud: Stories of Sex and Love*. London: Virago.

Warner, Marina (1976) *Alone of All Her Sex: The Myth and the Cult of the Virgin Mary*, New York: Alfred Knopf.

Warner, Marina (1995) *From the Beast to the Blonde: On Fairy Tales and Their Tellers*, London: Vintage.

Warner, Marina (2002) *Fantastic Metamorphoses, Other Worlds*, Oxford: Clarendon Press.

7 "Oh Yes, Women Get Erect"

Dismantling Sexual Standards in Jeanette Winterson's Short Fiction

Isabel María Andrés-Cuevas

Introduction

In her essay "Imagination and Reality", Jeanette Winterson insists on the capacity of the imagination – and of art, as a direct product of the latter – to allow us to apprehend a reality beyond the sensorial world:

> I see no conflict between reality and imagination. They are not in fact separate. Our real lives hold within them our royal lives; the inspiration to be more than we are, to find new solutions, to live beyond the moment.
>
> (1996: 142)

As Winterson remarks, the imagination provides us with clues about our identities, desires and existential cravings. Narratives, as products of the imagination, do give us an answer to life's problems. Yet, because of the limitations intrinsic to human existence, these answers are always partial and provisional:

> Here we are, with all the pieces in place and the final moment waiting. I reach this moment, not once, many times, have been reaching it all my life, it seems, and I find there is no resolution [...] That's why I write fiction – so that I can keep telling the story.
>
> (Winterson 2005: 137)

This chapter aims to examine the role of the imagination in some of Jeanette Winterson's short stories from her volume *The World and Other Places* (1998) inasmuch as they devise critical strategies to demystify traditional standards pertaining to female roles and women's sexuality. In addition to this, I argue how Winterson's particular deployment and understanding of the short story serves a subversive, critical purpose connected to the genre's peripheral position in relation to hegemonic literary discourses. In keeping with this, Winterson even goes as far as to refrain from calling her fictions "novels" or "romances", under the conviction that "the calling of the artist, in any medium, is to make it new" (Winterson 1996: 12). Even though her fictional production is mainly novelistic, the truth is that Winterson's narratives come close to the short story in that they resemble Virginia Woolf's idea of female novels. For Woolf, these narratives needed to be shorter than conventional novels, should be essentially concerned with physicality and the human body, and had to be written in a prose capable of expressing the emotional complexity inherent to "the poetry in her" (Woolf 1929/1989: 77). Furthermore, Winterson favours a type of shorter fiction that allows her to combine both emotional intensity and ideological profoundness: "In my own fiction I try to drive together lyric intensity and breadth of ideas. It is not possible, not desirable, I think, to maintain lyrical intensity over long stretches" (Winterson 1996: 173). She conceives of fiction as the "realisation of complex emotion" (Winterson 1996: 111), considering that through fiction the writer should manage to "bring back to us starts of feeling that can volt through the thickness of the day" (Winterson 1996: 185). In this regard, the short story is certainly an apt vehicle to convey conceptual concentration and emotional intensity.

In tune with this density and sharpness, Winterson envisions art and imagination as instruments with a powerful contesting value whose function is to awaken our critical awareness about socio-economic factors and a concomitant defence of individual freedom of choice. As she observes, "[a]rt is dangerous" since "art, by its nature, objects" (Winterson 1996: 139). The stories in *The World and Other Places* attest to this challenging power of fiction, especially as they can buttress the invalidation of gender conventions associated with sexual categories. "The Green Man" is a cautionary tale against the dangers of misconceiving masculinity by neglecting its fluid, multiple and ever-changing nature (Connell 2005: 76). Its protagonist, called simply "the Green Man", leads a life of growing frustration because he is anchored to a traditional notion of masculinity, impervious to changes in the conception of gender roles and to the rapidly evolving sexual politics of the late twentieth century. A similar rigidity of mind characterises Duncan, the male protagonist of "Atlantic Crossing". When confronted with the idea of having to share his boat cabin with a woman, as Carla Arnell argues, "both the disruption of his conventional expectations as well as his belief in the proper order of things for men and women make him uncomfortable" (2005: 166). He is obsessed about keeping both genders properly detached from each other, compartmentalised: "men and women don't mix" (Winterson 1998: 21). However, despite his restlessness about gender differences, he paradoxically ends up falling in love with someone whose sexual identity was initially mistaken on account of her seemingly male name: Gabriel Angel. Sexual stereotypes are also subverted in "O'Brien's First Christmas", in which Winterson "mocks and parodies [the] overestimating of the aesthetic model of femininity" (Front 2009: 25). O'Brien is perceived as an unfulfilled woman, as she has failed to comply with social ideals: "Marriage, children, a career, travel, a home, enough money, lots of money" (Winterson 1998/1999: 81). Yet the story has a rather ironic twist when O'Brien's life changes – literally – after she receives the visit of a fairy godmother who turns her blonde using her magic powers. "Disappearance I" – set in a dystopian world where sleep is discouraged as "dirty, unhygienic, wasteful and disrespectful to others" (Winterson 1998/1999: 105) – has been interpreted as a metaphor of the way in which sex, in different sociocultural contexts, has been banished from the sphere of the morally acceptable (Oates 1998: 26). In "Holy Matrimony", the hypocrisy of a society devoid of true feelings, in which capitalism takes over the purity of genuine emotions, is debunked in favour of an unhindered, honest and convention-free type of relationship. This unconstrained type of love the story's female narrator endorses requires the demystification of established models. Thus, she does not aspire to the iconic freedom and innocence Adam and Eve enjoyed before the fall, but to the lovers' association with the more universal and less mythical notions of heaven and earth (Winterson 1998/1999: 185).

As a detailed analysis of all of these narratives would exceed the space limitations of this chapter, I will concentrate on two of the stories in the volume, "The Poetics of Sex" and "Orion", which are particularly clear representations of the challenging capacities of art and imagination to transform both the existing order and our own perception of reality. These two stories offer suggestive ways to critically question preconceptions regarding same-sex relationships and compulsory heterosexuality, while validating alternative sexual practices and sexual identities in order to suggest the possibility of new such models and paradigms, which entails a more open and democratic understanding of gender. Thus, in "The Poetics of Sex", Winterson deconstructs sex-tied preconceptions in the context of a homosexual relationship through the language of art and through genre hybridity, as the story has the form of an interview whose dialectical dynamics intensifies the narrative's sharpness, itself a defining feature of the short story. As for "Orion", Winterson rewrites the story of Orion and Artemis, yet inverting the traditional power hierarchy and the sexual ideology inscribed in the mythic tale – a genre considered one of the most ancient predecessors of the short story form (March-Russell 2009: 4). Winterson's revision of the myth, therefore, confers a new archetypal value on the original narrative which, as myths did in ancient societies, establishes models – alternative ones in this case – for the understanding of gender identity. As will be argued, in this collection Winterson deviates from realism, seen as a banal attempt to transform art into "a version of everyday reality" (Winterson 1996: 31) in order to focus on fantasy and the imagination because of their capacity to offer lavish spectacles and verbal explosions whose glossy surface nevertheless encapsulates a power to question and transform social structures and gender constructions.

The Power of Art

In *Art Objects*, Winterson holds the idea that artistic creation is a way to confront the reality hidden underneath layers of our own taboos and self-restrictions: "The rebellion of art is a daily rebellion against the state of living death routinely called real life [...], a fragmented society afraid of feeling" (Winterson 1996: 108–109). Winterson advocates here the visionary capacity of the artist – whom she significantly refers to as "she". The artist's imagination opens up for the audience new "multiple and vast" paths of reality that lead to an encounter with an unhampered, freer version of both self and existence:

> The artist is an imaginer. The artist imagines the forbidden because to her it is not forbidden. If she is freer than other people it is the freedom of her single allegiance to her work. Most of us have divided loyalties, most of us have sold ourselves. The artist is not divided and she is not for sale. Her clarity of purpose protects her although it is her clarity of purpose that is most likely to irritate most people.
> (Winterson 1996: 116)

That "clarity of purpose" enables the artist to envision other dimensions of existence underneath what she calls "notional reality", by which she refers to purely sensorial or uncritically apprehended experience (Winterson 1996: 134). Art must allow us to "see beyond the view from the window, even though the window is its frame" (Winterson 1996: 136), and so enable us to accept perceptions of the world that clash against our own. In that sense, art for Winterson "offers the challenge we desire but also the shape we need" in order to reconsider our system of values, particularly those concerned with aspects of our lives which involve strong taboos, such as sex, love, birth and death (Winterson 1996: 113–114). Winterson conceives of art and imagination as means of defying certain pre-established conventions, often regarding gender roles, which curtail individual freedom, as well as the possibility of full realisation independent of sexual identity. In Winterson's work, this subversive power of art has a double edge: on the one hand, the imagination is obviously present inasmuch as her stories are fictional works, and therefore products of the mind; on the other hand, the imagination has a more complex role in the narratives analysed here since it challenges fixed categories related to gender, particularly through intertextual practices. In "The Poetics of Sex", the undermining of gender stereotypes is realised through the choice of narrative discourse along with some pictorial images and

references to the poetry of Sappho. These elements enable the demystification of certain generalised prejudices against lesbian relationships as
well as the validation of a more heterogeneous and fluid conception of
literature that attests to the multiple nature of reality, also in terms of
gender. Winterson's re-appropriation of the classical myth of Orion and
Artemis in "Orion" allows her to challenge hegemonic masculinity and
condemn violence in all its forms, as well as to highlight the true value of
forgiveness and compassion through the character of Artemis. Indeed, as
she repeats in a refrain that recurs in "Imagination and Reality": "The
reality of art is the reality of the imagination" (Winterson 1996: 133).

In her conception of the potential encapsulated by the imagination,
allied with the suggestive capacities of language, Winterson adheres to
a Romantic notion of art. In *Art Objects*, she emphasises the role of art
as the vehicle leading us towards a timeless world that is also capable of
opening to us layers otherwise unseen: "Imagination takes in the world
of sense experience, and rather than trading it for a world of symbols, delights in it for what it is" (Winterson 1996: 150). Likewise, for Winterson,
the artist is a prophet or visionary that allows us to elevate above the
mundane and enables a connection with the sublime in the material.
This is possible because they live "more intensely than the rest of us",
and therefore permit us to "rediscover the intensity of the physical world"
(Winterson 1996: 151). She somewhat subscribes to the Blakean view of
the imagination as spiritual sensation that will result in a revolutionary
transformation of external reality, and thus perceives art as an instrument
to counter the effects of capitalism, as well as of an educational system
devised to transform individuals into a homogeneous uncritical mass of
consumers (Denby 2007: 100–101). The stories analysed below illustrate
that conception of art as a powerfully subversive tool even capable of
shaking the pillars of our mental and sociocultural scaffolding.

Un-straightening the Short Story: "The Poetics of Sex"

Probably, the story that best illustrates that convention-defying power
of art in *The World and Other Places* is "The Poetics of Sex". Here, the
discourse of artistic creation works as a strategy to deconstruct established female roles and heteronormative prejudices. Structured in a series of sections with headings that reproduce traditional misconceptions
about same-sex love, the story takes the form of an interview in which
questions such as "Were You Born a Lesbian?" or "What Do Lesbians
Do in Bed?" are answered. Despite the narrative's fragmented nature,
the development of the story is clear: two women meet, experience bliss,
break up and are reunited to live together for fifty years.

Little in the text agrees with conventional standards of form. Both the
intermedial quality of the text (a story narrated through the "evocation or
imitation" [Rajewsky 2005: 52] of the techniques of the interview, both

in an oral and written form) and the author's choice of title (more typical of an academic essay than of an interview or a story) are in line with Winterson's purpose of subverting stereotypes and traditional expectations. Brian Richardson has commented on the "six rude rhetorical questions [...] in a large font" that divide the text (2006: 84) and that seem to imitate the visual array of printed interviews. Nevertheless, these headings fail to confer on the text a desirable degree of coherence as, for instance, some of them are repeated for no apparent reason. Neither do they fulfil the function of real epigraphs, as the ensuing texts do not necessarily work as adequate replies to these interrogative headings, but rather recreate the love story between the two women in a predominantly metaphorical style. As pointed out above, the pretended interview has an uncertain, liminal quality as it is situated at an intersection between written and oral discourse. Hence, in spite of the headings characteristic of printed interviews, the narrative often includes some repetitions of the questions allegedly made by the interviewer which seem to suggest that the narrator is at times unable to understand her interlocutor. The latter, in keeping with the postmodern quality of the writing, remains absent for the reader all throughout the text.[1] In this regard, the story mocks the occasionally inquisitive nature of the interview as a genre, and in particular the prejudices inscribed in the questions. Richardson has noted the pastiche quality of "The Poetics of Sex":

> It is a parody of a dialogue, a total transformation of the question and answer scenario. Instead of eliciting information, the questions serve to generate the narrative. In this, it is typical of the way the postmodern interlocutor and respondent defy conventional norms, particularly [...] the primordial one between narrator and (dramatized) narratee.
>
> (2006: 84)

Along with the aspects discussed above, the vindication of lesbian love in a largely homophobic society is conveyed through the discourse of art interwoven throughout the story as references to poetry and painting recurrently contribute to the discrediting of sex-tied preconceptions. The story is narrated in the first person by someone called Sappho, one of the protagonists of the love affair. Like her literary namesake, the Greek lyric poet temporarily banished in her native island, Lesbos, Winterson's Sappho allegorically places herself on an island along with her lover. Cath Stowers reads this motif of seeking for shelter on "lesbian islands" as an image of displacement from the "dark continent" (Freud 1926: 212) in which the founder of psychoanalysis situated women as a whole (Stowers 1996: 74). It is only here, Sappho argues, and not on the "Mainland", where this kind of genuine, unadulterated woman can "be found growing wild" (Winterson 1998/1999: 41). In her depiction of this feminine haven, Sappho debunks the social stereotype that automatically encases lesbian women within a standardised monadic category by affirming that a Mainland Woman – the metaphoric term for heterosexual women in heteronormative society – can only be found in "a couple of obvious forms":

> On this island where we live, [...] we have found the infinite variety of Woman. On the Mainland, Woman is largely extinct in all but a couple of obvious forms. She is still cultivated as a cash crop but is never to be found growing wild.
>
> (Winterson 1998/1999: 40–41)

This uncanny uniformity that reduces women to "cash crop" is probably enforced by the capitalist system of most Western societies which promotes "streamlined homogeneity" (Winterson 1996: 134). The implicit reference to the Greek poet's island of Lesbos, which represents for Winterson's Sappho a recurring retreat "where she likes to come back" (1998/1999: 39), also allows the narrator to present her own imaginary island, where women love other women, as an ideal place in which women in their multiple varieties represent an alternative to the oppressive and impoverishing materialism of the heterosexual Mainland.

Phaon, the ferryman for whose unrequited love Sappho killed herself by jumping off the Leucadian cliffs – according to a legend seemingly resulting from a desire to assert Sappho as heterosexual (Hallett 1979: 456) – is given a role in the story. The character's correlate in the narrative is Phaeon, to whom the narrator ironically attributes the occupation of "run[ning] a little business called LESBIAN TOURS" (Winterson 1998/1999: 43). He pilots his motorboat round the island for sightseers, and at the same time he pathetically fantasises that "[t]hey are all in love with [him]" (Winterson 1998/1999: 44). Likewise, Sappho's poetry is echoed in the text as Winterson's Sappho's critical attention to language and its imposition of heteronormative standards evokes the poet's "Words":

> When I see a word held hostage to manhood I have to rescue it [...] I like to be a hero, like to come back to my island full of girls carrying a net of words forbidden them. Poor girls, they are locked outside their words just as the words are locked into meaning. Such a lot of locking up goes on on the Mainland but here the doors are always open. [...] On this island where we live [...] we have found the infinite variety of Woman.
>
> (Winterson 1998/1999: 39–41)

That male tyranny of the compulsorily heterosexual Mainland and the manipulation it effects upon language is ironically suggested through the narrator's depiction of the latter as a place where "[s]weet trembling word[s]", just like the frail princesses of popular fairy tales, are "locked in a tower, tired of [their] Prince coming and coming"[2] as they wait for their liberation and relocation on Sappho's island (Winterson 1998/1999: 39). The idea of openness and unrestraint on this island, along with the idea of a multiple, uninhibited sense of womanhood there, is reminiscent of the sense of freedom and unmitigated potentiality in Sappho's "Words":

> Although they are
> Only breath, words
> Which I command
> Are immortal.
>
> (Sappho 2004: 91)

In these lines, the poet extols words as instruments of female empowerment which can be passed down to other generations and thus create a network of liberated women who "command" their own lives. In a like manner, present-day Sappho vindicates the importance of releasing language from the patriarchal constraints that transform it into an element for the entrapment of women in a network of masculine-oriented premises. Her discontent echoes Judith Butler's denunciation of the impossibility for homosexuality to be named or recognised under a "set of culturally prevalent prohibitions" imposed by the hegemonic tyranny of heterosexual rules (1997: 139). As she wrote in *Gender Trouble*:

> the repressive law effectively produces heterosexuality, and acts not merely as a negative or exclusionary code, but as a sanction and, most pertinently, as a law of discourse, distinguishing the speakable from the unspeakable [...], the legitimate from the illegitimate.
>
> (Butler 1990: 65)

These constraints on language emerge from the dictates of a male-dominated society. For Luce Irigaray, that patriarchal construction of gender in terms of the opposition male/female, as well as the language that classifies individuals in terms of this dyad, is part of the hegemonic signifying politics that limits the definition of feminine in a male-operated system. Hence, only the possibility of another language – in which words can be rescued from their being "hostage[s] to manhood" (Winterson 1998/1999: 39) – will enable the female sex to escape the mark of gender which, for Irigaray, represents a phallogocentric annihilation of the feminine:

> If we don't invent a language, if we don't find our body's language, it will have too few gestures to accompany our story. We shall tire of the same ones, and leave our desires unexpressed, unrealized. Asleep again, unsatisfied, we shall fall back upon the words of men – who, for their part, have "known" for a long time. But *not our body*.
>
> (1985: 214)

For Monique Wittig, there is also an urgent necessity of attending to bodily reality and rescuing desire from the unnaturalness of compulsory heterosexuality and normative discourse: "If desire could liberate itself, it would have nothing to do with the preliminary marking by sexes" (1979: 114).

In the imaginary location Winterson's Sappho metaphorically flees to, those patriarchal impositions which fully operate on the heterosexual Mainland have lost their coercing effects. On "[t]his delicious unacknowledged island" (Winterson 1998/1999: 39), which escapes the understanding of Salami and the rest of males,[3] women are free to act and love each other. Against the prevalent prohibitions on the Mainland – "[s]tay inside, don't walk the streets, bar the windows, keep your mouth shut, keep your legs together, strap your purse around your neck, don't wear valuables, don't look up, don't talk to strangers, don't risk it, don't try it" (Winterson 1998/1999: 39) – on the island these women inhabit "doors are always open" (Winterson 1998/1999: 39). As Wittig proposes, here desire is unleashed, and women can freely rejoice "naked with each other" (Winterson 1998/1999: 39). Winterson's Mainland indeed resembles Irigaray's view of the patriarchal encasement of the female under a hegemonic male-centred system of discursive marking. Marilyn B. Skinner highlights the connection between Sappho's poetry and Luce Irigaray's argument about "speaking (as) woman" in "When Our Lips Speak Together", the essay that concludes *This Sex Which Is Not One*. As Skinner puts it: "troping speech as lesbian erotic play, Irigaray gives substance to her conception of a polysemous feminine language enacted through the female body. Communication between her lovers takes place on a timeless, almost wordless plane beyond patriarchal 'compartments' and 'schemas' [...], where only the body's truths are valid" (1996: 189).

At the end of the story, Winterson's Sappho invites Picasso to love her and allows herself to be loved – and "leaf[ed] through" – in a passage structured around images of harvesting and vegetation (Winterson 1998/1999: 44). Bright colours – ruby red and orange – predominate:

> Hang on me my darling like rubies round my neck [...] Give me your rose for my buttonhole. Let me leaf through you before I read you out loud [...] We are fresh and plentiful. She is my harvest and I am hers. She seeds me and reaps me, we fall into one another's laps [...] The room is orange with effort.
>
> (Winterson 1998/1999: 44–45)

The exaltation of sensual love calls to mind a poem by Sappho titled "One Girl", especially the first stanza, constructed around the image of apple harvesting and presided over by a "sweet" and "redden[ing]" piece of fruit (Sappho 2004: 53). The poet insists on the pertinence of the moment for the fruit to be caught, as it has reached its precise degree of maturation. Here, the sexual implications of the sumptuousness evoked by the image of the apple – the forbidden fruit – at its highest point of redness and sweetness cannot be ignored:

> Like the sweet apple which reddens upon the topmost bough,
> A-top on the topmost twig – which the pluckers forgot, somehow –
> Forget it not, nay, but got it not, for none could get it till now.
>
> (Sappho 2004: 53)

In the story, the couple formed by Sappho and Picasso has just gone through a major crisis that ended up in the lovers' separation. However, in the last part of the story, headed by the same question that precedes the initial section – "Why Do You Sleep with Girls?"[4] – a reconciliation is suggested. After the sensuous exhortation to love each other – "Hang on me" (Winterson 1998/1999: 44) – seemingly uttered by the narrator, she continues to describe their sexual encounter, in which agricultural images, as seen above, are combined with images of fire, all of which result in a passion materialised in the bright colour of the room, now turned orange (Winterson 1998/1999: 45).

As suggested earlier, Winterson's use of pictorial imagery works towards the debunking of homophobic prejudice and the validation of the feminine body. Particularly significant are those associated with Picasso, the artist that gives name to Sappho's partner in "The Poetics of Sex". Here, Picasso continues to be a painter, yet his identity is now that of a lesbian woman who has a love relationship with Sappho, the narrator. The female body occupies the centre of the text along with the couple's passionate sexual encounters. Even though Winterson's Picasso is also an artist, the periods that define her art are not necessarily the chronological stages in her production, but an undefined blend between her vital processes and her menstruation. Hence, a pun on the word "period" playfully fuses a reference to the different creative phases in the famous painter's work – the earliest of which are traditionally known as "blue period" (1901–1903) and "pink period" (1905–1906), respectively ("Picasso" 2010) – with the woman's menstrual cycles. By incorporating the female reality of menstruation into the text, the narrator defies the standards of a society eminently ruled by patriarchal – and obviously, heterosexual – authority. Even the "periods" in Winterson's Picasso – first red and then blue – follow a logic of their own, different from those of the real-life painter:

> My lover Picasso is going through her Blue Period. In the past her periods have always been red. Radish red, bull red, red like rose-hips bursting into seed. Lava red when she was called Pompei and in her Destructive Period.
>
> (1998/1999: 31)

Winterson's focus on bodily processes in the story is in line with some of the vindications of second-wave feminism, such as Julia Kristeva's critique of the process of demonisation and alienation to which the female body has been subjected. Thus, Kristeva highlights how menstrual blood has been systematically considered as a polluting element, and like other female bodily processes, abject (1982: 71). Following Kristeva, Kelly Oliver insists on this idea of abjection of the menstrual body as opposite to the mystified maternal body (Oliver 1993: 61). And for Elizabeth Grosz, this position of abjectness of the menstruating body is linked to the Western ontological dichotomy between, on the one hand, solid, perfected objects/bodies as controllable and, on the other, fluid elements/bodies as out of control, and, therefore untrustworthy. Within this paradigm, Grosz situates the menstruating body as a fluid entity that deviates from the desirable norm:

> For the girl, menstruation, associated as it is with blood, with injury and wound, with a mess that does not dry invisibly, that leaks uncontrollably, not in sleep, in dreams, but whenever it occurs, indicates the beginning of an out of control status that she was led to believe ends with childhood.
>
> (1994: 205)

The process of female empowerment through the affirmation of the menstruating body is reinforced by the ludicrously sarcastic description of this female Picasso's creative technique. The openness in her rhetorical question "Don't you know I paint with my clit?" (Winterson 1998/1999: 37) validates the reality of the female body, at the same time as it aims to scandalise narrow-minded representatives of patriarchal conventions like Phaeon, or the lewd voyeur Salami. At a diegetic level, the narrative validates the presence of the female body, which had been historically dismissed by a tyrannical male society that concentrated their efforts on keeping women's bodies under control. Hence, the text shows two women who, rather than "keep[ing] [their] mouth shut" or their "legs together" (Winterson 1998/1999: 39), represent an alternative that gives voice to a body that is fluid, multiple, open, and which desires.

The use of pictorial images, in particular those from real-life Picasso's paintings, contributes to the affirmation of the feminine body. A particularly significant scene displays the female Picasso, previously portrayed as releasing bull-red blood, suddenly transforming into a bull in the midst of a scene of passionate sex. Bullfighting is a recurring topic in Picasso's work, dealt with in many of his paintings and drawings. Particularly inspiring for this amalgamation between human and animal described in "The Poetics of Sex" may have been one titled *Bullfight* (*Corrida de toros*) (1934), in which a mass of body parts of an anthropomorphic bull and horse mingle with an almost geometrical fighter.

In the story, the focus on the bodily act and the intensity of the sexual encounter is enhanced by the image of the bull, which represents the appropriation of a conventionally masculine symbol and its relocation as an epitome of the passion and power of female sexuality:

> She rushes for me bull-subtle, butching at the gate as if she's come to stud. She bellows at the window, bloods the pavement with desire [...] I know enough to flick my hind-quarters and skip away [...] My bull-lover makes a matador out of me. She circles me and in her rough-made ring I am complete. I like the dressing up, the little jackets, the silk tights, I like her shiny hide, the deep tanned leather of her. It is she who gives me the power of the sword. I used it once but when I cut at her it was my close fit that frilled into a hem of blood. She lay beside me slender as a horn. Her little jacket and silk tights impeccable. I sweated muck and couldn't speak in my broken ring.
>
> (Winterson 1998/1999: 31–32)

As the intercourse between the two women progresses, a blurring between the fighter and the bull occurs so that it becomes impossible to tell one from the other. Indeed, at the end of the passage, their roles have been inverted, with Picasso turning into a matador and Sappho becoming the animal "sweat[ing] muck" (Winterson 1998/1999: 32). The interchangeability of roles as well as the blend of the two lovers reinforce the idea of the fluidity of the body and the impossibility of confining it to a neat compartment in a binary construction of gender.

Picasso's masterpiece, his 1937 *Guernica*, also finds its place in Winterson's story. In the section under the first of the two identical headings, "What Do Lesbians Do in Bed?", Sappho recalls the time when Picasso and her met at Art School and had their first sexual encounter. While the passage describes the passionately enticing encounter of the two lovers, which leads to a mutual discovery of their bodies and selves, it also contains some visual echoes of Picasso's *Guernica*. In the scene, Picasso is depicted as "look[ing] tubercular, so thin and mottled" (Winterson 1998/1999: 35). This image along with that of the "sulky" girl on the canvas in Picasso's studio (Winterson 1998/1999: 35) seem suggestive of the suffering female figures in the cubist painting. The presence of the horse, another major character in the pictorial composition, is also implicit in the text: "I took her by her pony tail the way a hero grabs a runaway horse" (Winterson 1998/1999: 34). On the other hand, the explicit focus throughout the passage on bodily parts echoes the amalgamation of bodies in the painting. Likewise, the light falling from above and disseminating dark patches all over the scene brings to mind the light bulb in Picasso's mural and its constant play of light and darkness. Finally, the newspaper "advertising rationing" is reminiscent of the war setting in *Guernica* and contributes to evoking the general sense of grimness and sordidness of the composition:

> Slowly now Picasso, where the falling light hits the floor. Lie with me in the bruised light that leaves dark patches on your chest. You look tubercular, so thin and mottled, quiescent now. I picked you up and carried you to the bed dusty with ill-use. I found a newspaper under the sheets advertising rationing.
> The girl on the canvas was sulky. She hadn't come to be painted.
> (Winterson 1998/1999: 35)

Other pictorial references serve subversive purposes and enhance the playful nature of Winterson's narrative, as is the case of "The Annunciation" as an artistic theme. A mock version of the famous scene appears at the beginning of the section entitled "Were You Born a Lesbian?", where the narrator offers a subversive interpretation of the Biblical episode in which Archangel Gabriel is presented as "a fairy in a pink tutu" visiting Picasso in order to give her a message. In contrast with the solemnly divine character of the announcement delivered by the Archangel in the New Testament, the news broken by Winterson's Gabriel sounds rather like a pastiche between a Christmas carol and an ironical, humorous speech:

> I bring you tidings of great joy. All by yourself with no one to help you you will give birth to a sex toy who has a way with words. You will call her Sappho and she will be a pain in the ass to all men.
> (Winterson 1998/1999: 37)

On top of that, the divine character of Virgin Mary is here subverted in the way noted by Kristeva in her discussion on the depiction of this feminine ideal as a mother figure. According to Krsiteva, in this maternal representation of Mary, "two fundamental aspects of western love: courtly love and child love" are fused (1985: 136), hence the paradoxical combination of masochism with gratification and ecstasy as "the mother bows her head before her son but not without the boundless pride in the knowledge that she is also his wife" (1985: 142). In the story, subversion through the female figure is taken even farther, as it is not only eroticised by simultaneously acting as a mother and lover of the newborn Sappho, but also involved in a homoerotic relationship with her daughter/wife.[5]

Picasso, who is enraged after Gabriel's message, finally decides to take Sappho home, after her alleged birth and "[f]lesh of her flesh she fucked her" (Winterson 1998/1999: 38). Nevertheless, despite the transgressive or even blasphemous tone of Winterson's recreation of the Biblical narrative, the conclusion of the section restates the necessity of attending to our own desires, notwithstanding the impositions based on gender categories and stereotypes. A clear example, the narrator suggests, is in the purity and authenticity of the love between the two female protagonists of the story: "[Sappho] had nothing to offer but herself, and Picasso, who thought she had seen it all before, smiled like a child and fell in love" (Winterson 1998/1999: 38).

Destabilising Myths: "Orion"

The discourse of the imagination as a vehicle for the demolition of certain rigid preconceptions of reality is clearly illustrated in another story from Winterson's *The World and Other Places*: "Orion", a rewriting of a classical myth. Up to this point I have used the word "myth" as referring to "a widely held but false belief or idea" ("Myth" 2017), but in the ensuing discussion of Winterson's "Orion", I will use term in the sense of "a traditional story, especially one concerning the early history of a people or explaining a natural or social phenomenon, and typically involving supernatural beings or events" ("Myth" 2017).

According to Joseph Campbell, one of the main purposes of a mythological order is to validate and maintain a certain social system – a shared set of rights and wrongs, proprieties or improprieties, on which a particular social formation depends for its existence (1959: 9–10). Robert Graves agrees that a major function of myths is to justify the existing social system and to account for rites and customs (1975: v). The use of authoritative myths has led feminists to look into them as "potent discourse[s] in the conceptualisation of women within the cultures of the West" (Zajko 2007: 396), and feminist rewritings of those myths have represented a means of subverting the order imposed upon women through these tales. As Vanda Zajko observes in her study of women in Greek myths:

> She [the mythical woman] has been effaced in favour of a figure defined by her sexual behavior, whose moderate compliance with the dominant social mores functions to reinforce the potency of the family. Even when she appears to choose her own destiny, the semblance of freedom is illusory: her only role in myth is to show a male-dominated society the apocalyptic consequences of allowing her a choice.
>
> (2008: 395–396)

For Diane Purkiss, a feminist rewriting of myth often involves

> the reinterpretation of individual stories [...] by changing the focus of the narrative from a male character to a female character, or by shifting the terms of the myth so that what was a 'negative' female role-model becomes a positive one.
>
> (1992: 401–402)

Along with these strategies of displacement and reversal, Kristeva also insists on the necessity for the writer to "reject, disrupt, supplement and alter the terms of one's relation to the cultural contract" as a strategy of dissidence (Sellers 2001: 26). For her, inscribing plural, unpredictable meanings into these rewritings as a means of relying on the unconscious for inspiration represents an act of insurrection against the predictability of prescribed systems of values (Kristeva 1986: 26). Winterson's revision of the myth of Orion and Artemis represents her own contribution to the critical reassessment of the historical configuration of the gender asymmetries consolidated by those myths.

"Orion" illustrates that shift of focus and the inscription of new meanings and dimensions into a myth as effective tactics to subvert the patriarchal conventions reproduced in it. Narrated mainly from the point of view of the goddess, the story deprives Orion of his aura of magnificence and reduces him to a rude, brutish and ultimately ruthless male whose cruelty – he rapes Artemis – is finally avenged with his death at the goddess' hands. In this sense, Artemis emerges not only with the resoluteness and determination of a hunting deity, but also with a complex psychological depth that will allow her to forgive Orion's cruelty and move forward. Her compassion will both enable the callous hunter to obtain the final mercy from the gods as well as his eternal absolution in his new existence as a constellation. As I will argue, in "Orion", Winterson portrays the female protagonist with the strength of character and inner power her male counterpart lacks.

The different versions of the mythological narrative of Orion reach no further than presenting the character as a hunting hero, venerated on the grounds of his hazardous adventures, and likely the son of two deities, the sea-god Poseidon and, in Apollodoros' version, of Earth – Ge – (Fontenrose 1983: 6). One of the Hellenistic versions of the myth has Zeus, Poseidon and Hermes urinate and ejaculate in a bull's hide and bury it in the earth, then tell Hyrieus of Tanagra to dig it up ten months later so that he could see his desire of having a son fulfilled (Euphorion of Chalcis 1971: 171, ll.7–20). As to Artemis, most of the narratives highlight the brave and independent character of the goddess. According to Callimachus, at the age of three, she asked Zeus, her father, to grant her six wishes, among which she included to remain always a virgin, to have a bow and arrow so that she could hunt, or to rule the mountains (Callimachus 1921: 62, "Hymn 3 to Artemis", 22 ff.).

Winterson's "Orion" introduces complex characters with fully-developed personalities. In the narrative, Artemis and Orion are a married couple, the latter being a rude, narrow-minded and even block-headed man who lacks any sense of decorum or politeness. Furthermore, aware of his fame as a mighty hunter and a hero, Orion constantly boasts about his actions in front of her, whom he considers a mere hunting trophy:

> He wandered into Artemis's camp, scattering her dogs and bellowing like a bad actor, his right eye patched and his left arm in a splint [...] When she returned she saw this huge rag of a man eating her goat, raw. When he finished, with a great belch and the fat still fresh around his mouth, he suggested they take a short stroll by the sea's edge. [...] The ragged shore, rock pitted and dark with weeds, reminded him of his adventures and he recounted them in detail while the tide came in to her waist. There was nowhere he hadn't been, nothing he hadn't seen. He was faster than a hare, stronger than a pair of bulls.
> 'You smell' said Artemis, but he didn't hear.
> (Winterson 1998/1999: 58–59)

Winterson's Orion expects his wife to be submissive and obedient, and to comply with patriarchal expectations. He encapsulates thus what Raywen Connell has defined as "hegemonic masculinity": he is one of those "white, heterosexual, competitive, individualist and aggressive men [...] who dominate the moral, cultural and financial landscape" (2005: 77). In a similar vein, Christopher Blazina establishes an analogous set of features that often functions as the benchmark by which masculinity is measured in Western cultures. Drawing on some anthropological studies, Blazina devises his so-called theory of the "Three P's" in order to explain how a sense of hegemonic masculinity is acquired. For him, this is contingent with man's "ability to achieve three major roles: protector, provider and progenitor", whereby "he is granted the honorary title of 'man'" (2008: 84). As Blazina notes, the "successful fulfilment of the Three Ps is directly related to having a fully functioning 'masculine body,' one able to perform the tasks of a man" (2008: 34). On the contrary, the inability to adequately perform these roles compromises men's emotional equilibrium as males, as they perceive that their sense of what it is to be masculine is at risk. Orion seems to be an apt representative of Blazina's – and Connell's – concept of hegemonic masculinity. As he himself feels: "No, he didn't want her to talk, he knew about her. He had been looking for her. She was a curiosity" (Winterson 1998/1999: 59). Artemis, however, could not be more different from the traditionally submissive wife he selfishly expects, as she is a strong, independent woman who attempts to have the same kind of adventurous life as him:

> She didn't want to get married and sit out some war, while her man, god or not, underwent the ritual metamorphosis from palace prince to craggy hero. She didn't want children. She wanted to hunt. [...] She had envied men their long-legged freedom to roam the world

and return full of glory to wives who only waited. She knew about the history-makers and the home-makers, the great division that made life possible. Without rejecting it, she had simply hoped to take on the freedoms that belonged to the other side. What if she travelled the world and the seven seas like a hero?

(Winterson 1998/1999: 57)

Yet, unlike him, she is not so much concerned with glory and admiration as with the satisfaction of finding her own self, and longs to be fully realised as a woman:

When no one was left, she would have to confront herself. [...] She realised that the only war worth fighting was the one that raged within [...] Home was not a place for the faint-hearted; only the brave; only the very brave could live with themselves.

(Winterson 1998/1999: 58)

Such fulfilment necessarily requires a readjustment of traditional gender roles, epitomised by Artemis' wish to leave the family home in search of adventure (Front 2009: 35). However, Artemis' freedom would compromise Orion's own sense of masculinity, so he decides to stop such a threat to his power and implicitly punish Artemis for leading a man's life by raping her (Du Toit 2007: 210). Through this act of sexual domination, Orion performs and reaffirms his hegemonic patriarchal position. Nevertheless, it is the degree of psychological complexity added to the characterisation of both protagonists that endows Winterson's rewriting of the myth with particular significance. In different traditional versions of the story, Orion's action is merely taken for granted, followed by the goddess' subsequent revenge by killing him with a scorpion. In Winterson's tale, however, both Orion's rape and her final retaliation have a deep impact on Artemis, who suffers the effects of these traumatic experiences: "She thought about that time for years" (Winterson 1998/1999: 59). Immediately after killing Orion, the goddess feels some type of horror at the discovery of her own soul – "She was not who she thought she was" (Winterson 1998/1999: 60) – and must now cope with the conflicting feelings of remorse and liberation:

In a night, 200,000 years can pass, time moving only in our minds. The steady marking of the seasons, the land well loved and always changing, continues outside, while inside, light years move us on to landscapes that revolve under different skies.

Artemis, lying beside the dead Orion, sees her past changed by a single act. The future is still intact, still unredeemed, but the past is irredeemable.

(Winterson 1998/1999: 60)

Nevertheless, in spite of Artemis' revenge, Winterson portrays her as loyal and definitely much more profound and honest than her male partner. As in "The Poetics of Sex", the discourse of imagination, on this occasion related to the reassessment of a classical myth from a feminist perspective, serves the author to demystify traditional conventions associated with gender stereotypes. While both Orion and Artemis have perpetrated atrocious crimes, what makes Artemis to some extent heroic is not her act of violence and revenge towards Orion, but rather her compassion and humanity, as well as her later repentance. Hence, after having killed her husband with a scorpion, she thoroughly arranges a mound of rocks and stones she collects with her own hands until they bleed, so that may serve as a shrine for Orion's body and keep it protected from the wind or the attack of animals:

> Artemis [...] fetched rocks and stones to cover Orion's body from the eagles. She made a high mound that broke the thudding wind as it scored the shore. [... B]y the time she had finished she was soaked with rain. Her hands were bleeding and her hair kept catching in her mouth.
>
> (Winterson 1998/1999: 62–63)

Once she accepts the consequences of the events and considers how these will affect her life from that moment onwards, Artemis feels a kind of redeeming peacefulness. She has forgiven not only her torturer, but herself. She seems to have assumed that the traumatic experiences are and will continue to be present in her life, but now she has learnt to live with them: "She was hungry but not angry now" (Winterson 1998/1999: 62–63).

Once Artemis' compassion has materialised, it reaches a universal dimension so that Orion also obtains absolution from the gods. After his atonement through a period in Hades, he is eventually taken to "the heavens for all to see" (Winterson 1998/1999: 63). Winterson's rewriting of the myth of Orion and Artemis unveils a narrative of female bravery and resistance, but also of human weakness and the teachings our own limitations provide us with, thus moving beyond traditional depictions of the goddess as essentially an adventurer and daring hunter. Winterson highlights here the capacity of Artemis to forgive her torturer and how, in so doing, she finds a path towards self-realisation.

Conclusion

As has been discussed throughout this chapter, Jeanette Winterson's use of the discourse of imagination in the stories under examination here entails an inspiring intertextual dialogue with different artistic expressions, which necessarily involves a process of feminist appropriation and reassessment. The latter consists in the debasement of certain social prejudices that coerce an egalitarian conception of coexistence among individuals, notwithstanding their gender or sexual identity. Hence, in "The Poetics of Sex", the women on Sappho's Lesbos mock the heteronormative Phaeon and his ridiculous sexual fantasies. Picasso's bulls and some other elements from his *Guernica* are also appropriated by Winterson to exemplify the authentic passion and intensity in a same-sex relationship, in which the artist's colour periods invade the text in the form of menstruation as a means to validate the female body. All this occurs as a version of Archangel Gabriel in a pink tutu delivers to Winterson's Picasso what, in the end, will become a message of free and unconditional love between the two women. On the other hand, Winterson's rewriting of the Orion myth becomes a powerful reflection on the most unfortunate consequences of hegemonic patriarchy for women's legitimate aspirations. Winterson deprives both characters of their mystic aura by emphasising their flawed nature. Yet, redemption will be eventually possible thanks to Artemis' mercy and compassion, which ends up restoring cosmic order. In these stories, Winterson advocates a release from pre-established conventions and gender categories through the power of art and imagination upon the reader: "The book does not reproduce me, it re-defines me, pushes at my boundaries, shatters the palings that guard my heart. Strong texts work along the borders of our minds and alter what already exists" (Winterson 1996: 26).

Notes

1 The issue of absence in postmodern literature has been discussed in works such as Slocombe (2006), Silverman (1990), and Battersby (1998, especially 81–102).
2 Note the sexual overtones implicit in the word "coming" and strengthened by the repetition of the verb. The image comes to reinforce the idea of language as subjected to patriarchal desire.
3 Note the doubly grotesque implications of his name, both on the grounds of his identification with pork and of the grossly phallic allusion of the word itself. I am indebted to Jorge Sacido-Romero for this suggestion.
4 The repetition of the same question at the beginning and at the end of the story suggests a circularity that reinforces the harvesting metaphor and connects with the cycle of the seasons.
5 Laura Lojo-Rodríguez (2012) has analysed extensively a similar echo of Kristeva's depiction of the duality in the maternal image of the Virgin Mary in Michèle Roberts's story "Charity".

References

Arnell, Carla (2005) "Earthly Men and Other Worldly Women: Gender Types and Religious Types in Jeanette Winterson's 'Atlantic Crossing' and Other Short Fiction", *Journal of the Short Story in English* 45: 163–177.

Battersby, Christine (1998) *The Phenomenal Woman: Feminist Metaphysics and the Patterns of Identity*, New York: Routledge.

Blazina, Christopher (2008) *The Secret Lives of Men: What Men Want You to Know about Love, Sex, and Relationships*, Deerfield Beach, FL: Health Communications Inc.

Butler, Judith (1990) *Gender Trouble: Feminism and the Subversion of Identity*, New York: Routledge.

Butler, Judith (1997) *The Psychic Life of Power: Theories in Subjection*, Stanford, CA: Stanford University Press.

Callimachus, Lycophron, Aratus (1921) *Hymns and Epigrams. Lycophron: Alexandra. Aratus: Phenomena*, translated by A.W. Mair and G.R. Mair, Loeb Classical Library 129, Cambridge, MA: Harvard University Press.

Campbell, Joseph (1959) *The Masks of God: Primitive Mythology*, New York: Penguin Compass.

Connell, Raywen (ed.) (2005) *Masculinities*, second edition, Cambridge: Polity Press.

Denby, Michelle (2007) "Religion and Spirituality", in *Jeanette Winterson: A Contemporary Critical Guide*, edited by Sonya Andermahr, London: Continuum, 100–113.

Du Toit, H. Louise (2007) "Feminism and the Ethics of Reconciliation", in *Law and the Politics of Reconciliation*, edited by Scott Veich, Glasgow: Routledge, 185–214.

Euphorion of Chalcis (1971) *Scholia Graeca in Homeri Iliadem (Scholia Vetera)*, Vol. 4, *Scholia ad Libros O – T Continens*, edited by Erbse Hartmut, Berlin: De Gruyter, 171.

Fontenrose, Joseph (1983) *Orion: The Myth of the Hunter and the Huntress*, University of California Publications in Classical Studies, Vol. 23, Berkeley, CA: University of California Press.

Freud, Sigmund (1926) *The Question of Lay Analysis*, in *The Standard Edition of the Works of Sigmund Freud*, Vol. XX, edited by James Strachey, London: Hogarth, 183–250.

Front, Sonia (2009) *Transgressing Boundaries in Jeanette Winterson's Fiction*, Frankfurt am Main: Peter Lang.

Graves, Robert (1975) "Introduction", in *The New Larousse Encyclopaedia of Mythology*, edited by Felix Guirand and Robert Graves, translated by Richard Aldington and Delano Ames, London: Hamlyn, v–viii.

Grosz, Elizabeth (1994) *Volatile Bodies*, Bloomington, IN: Indiana University Press.

Hallett, Judith (1979) "Sappho and Her Social Context: Sense and Sensuality", *Signs: Journal of Women in Culture and Society* 4(3): 447–464.

Irigaray, Luce (1985) *This Sex which is not One*, translated by Catherine Porter with Carolyn Burke, Ithaca, NY: Cornell University Press.

Kristeva, Julia (1982) *Powers of Horror: An Essay on Abjection*, translated by Leon S. Roudiez, New York: Columbia University Press.

Kristeva, Julia (1985) "Stabat Mater", translated by Arthur Goldhammer, *Poetics Today* 6(1/2): 133–152.

Kristeva, Julia (1986) "The System and the Speaking Subject", in *The Kristeva Reader*, edited by Toril Moi, Guildford, Surrey: Columbia University Press, 25–33.

Lojo-Rodríguez, Laura Mª (2012) "Recovering the Maternal Body as Paradise: Michèle Roberts's 'Charity'", *Atlantis: Journal of the Spanish Association of Anglo-American Studies*, 34(2): 33–47.

March-Russell, Paul (2009) *The Short Story: An Introduction*, Edinburgh: Edinburgh University Press.

"Myth", *Oxford Living Dictionaries: English*, Oxford: Oxford University Press, https://en.oxforddictionaries.com/ (accessed 27 July 2017).

Oates, Joyce Carol (1998) "Deep in the Forest of Aeros: Review of *The World and Other Places* by Jeanette Winterson", *The Times Literary Supplement*, 26.

Oliver, Kelly (1993) *Reading Kristeva: Unravelling the Double-Bind*, Bloomington, IN: Indiana University Press.

"Picasso" (2010) *Artium. Dokuart. Biblioteca y Centro de Documentación*, http://catalogo.artium.org/dossieres/1/pablo-picasso/biografia (accessed 7 December 2017).

Purkiss, Diane (1992) "Women's Rewriting of Myth", in *The Feminist Companion to Mythology*, edited by Carolyne Larrington, London: Pandora Press, 441–459.

Rajewsky, Irina O. (2005) "Intermediality, Intertextuality, and Remediation: A Literary Perspective on Intermediality", *Intermédialités* 6: 43–64.

Richardson, Brian (2006) *Unnatural Voices: Extreme Narration in Modern and Contemporary Fiction*, Columbus, OH: Ohio University Press.

Sappho (2004) "One Girl", in *Sappho: Poems. Classic Poetry Series*, The World's Poetry Archive, www.poemhunter.com/i/ebooks/pdf/sappho_2004_9.pdf (accessed 6 December 2017).

Sappho (2004) "Words", in *Sappho: Poems. Classic Poetry Series*, The World's Poetry Archive, www.poemhunter.com/i/ebooks/pdf/sappho_2004_9.pdf (accessed 6 December 2017).

Sellers, Susan (2001) *Myth and Fairy Tale in Contemporary Women's Fiction*, New York: Palgrave.

Silverman, Hugh J. (ed.) (1990) *Postmodernism: Philosophy and the Arts*, New York: Routledge.

Skinner, Marilyn B. (1996) "Woman and Language in Archaic Greece, or, Why Is Sappho a Woman?", in *Reading Sappho: Contemporary Approaches*, edited by Ellen Greene, Berkeley, CA: University of California Press, 175–193.

Slocombe, Will (2006) *Nihilism and the Sublime Postmodern: The (Hi)Story of a Difficult Relationship*, New York: Routledge.

Stowers, Cath (1996) "'No Legitimate Place, No Land, No Fatherland': Communities of Women in the Fiction of Roberts and Winterson", *Critical Survey* 8(1): 69–79.

Winterson, Jeanette (1996) *Art Objects: Essays on Ecstasy and Effrontery*, Toronto: Alfred A. Knopf.

Winterson, Jeanette (1998/1999) *The World and Other Places*, London: Vintage.

Winterson, Jeanette (2005) *Weight*, Toronto: Alfred A. Knopf.

Wittig, Monique (1979) "Paradigm", in *Homosexualities and French Literature: Cultural Contexts/Critical Texts*, translated and edited by George Stambolian and Elaine Marks, Ithaca, NY: Cornell University Press, 114–121.

Woolf, Virginia (1929/1989) *A Room of One's Own*, San Diego: Harcourt Brace Jovanovich.

Zajko, Vanda (2007) "Women and Greek Myth", in *The Cambridge Companion to Greek Mythology*, edited by Roger Woodard, New York: Cambridge University Press, 387–406.

Part IV
Voicing Differently

8   (Un)gendering Voice and Affect in A.L. Kennedy's Short Fiction

Sylvia Mieszkowski

Introduction

A.L. Kennedy is one of those rare creatures: a writer who not only works across a plethora of genres and media, has won prizes for novels *and* short story collections,[1] but also authors non-fiction, radio plays, TV treatments and film scripts. Apart from performing stand-up acts, teaching creative writing classes and leading writers' workshops,[2] Kennedy participates in the public debate on policy and politics through her blog in *The Guardian*. From this mix the odd crossover emerges, blending journalism, drama and TV, such as "Permanent Sunshine", one of the nine original *Brexit Shorts*.[3] As this writer is a generalist, it might not do her justice to single out one genre for discussion. Nevertheless, this article will focus on some of her short fiction, making the case that this is the form in which she excels. Having introduced her short story poetics and the role that feeling plays in its context, I will discuss the importance of gender for the construction of narrative voice and character creation. Against the backdrop of affect theory, the analysis of "A Perfect Possession" and "The Effects of Good Government on the City", two stories about abuse and torture from the perpetrators' points of view, explores how and to what effect gender is erased, withheld, and revealed as problematic or undermined. Looping back to the centrepiece of what I call Kennedy's "ballistic" poetics of the short story, the final section argues that both "The Practice of Mercy" and "These Small Pieces" take pains to cross out the clichéd gendering of emotions. This article's central claim is that the gendering, ungendering and regendering of narrative voices and characters' emotions is the most important technique through which the analysed short stories achieve the very effect that, according to Kennedy, defines the short form's success.

Going Ballistic – A.L. Kennedy's Short Story Poetics

For a decade now, Liverpool's Edge Hill University has been awarding an annual prize for the best short story collection, and over the years A.L. Kennedy has been involved as a shortlisted contestant and as a judge. Moreover, in May 2006 she addressed an audience largely consisting of Edge Hill's students of creative writing. In this talk – an edited transcript of which was published later, titled "Small in a Way that a Bullet Is Small" – she lays out what short stories do not have to be, what they are, what they should aim to accomplish, and how writers can go about achieving it. An unusual image which aims to capture the genre's essence introduces her core point:

> The thing about the short story is that yes, it is small, but it is small in a way that a bullet is small, and the whole thing about a short story is that you're trying to give it the punch that will hit your reader and blow their fucking head off because you don't have long.
> (Kennedy 2008: 3)

The simile's obvious message is that the short story is powerful *despite* being small. Although neither a bullet nor a few pages of text may look like much in terms of size, both can have dramatic effects within a very short time, if put to proper use: physical effects, where the former is concerned; emotional ones in the latter's case. Since the short story has no choice but to unfold its effect instantaneously, the simile also carries a second message: the short story has to be powerful at once *because* it is small. Kennedy keeps insisting that brevity compels short fiction writers to create the effect they want in a flash.

Since Kennedy's text primarily addresses practitioners, she makes an effort to explain how exactly the ballistic effect of short fiction is to be achieved: a "strong sense of voice" and a clear "character point of view" (Kennedy 2008: 3–4, 6) are important, as are four other literary devices that expose the alleged genre divide between narrative and lyrical mode as artificial and irrelevant:

> It's the most concentration that you will ever do as a writer; you're certainly in the kind of territory that poets have appropriated, where every word counts on the page. The demands are very similar; you have to have the musicality because it's short, you have to have the shape on the page working because it's short, you have to have these boiled down beautiful multi-layered descriptions of things because it's short. Every metaphor and simile has to work because it's short.
> (Kennedy 2008: 5–6)

As Kennedy adds musicality, shape on the page, multiple meanings and working metaphors and similes to the list of narrative tools that create intensity, the causality that links these devices with brevity recurs like a mantra. What makes the short story a "hugely powerful form" is its ability to capture those "key moments in life" that themselves "are often fantastically brief and very deeply penetrating, and intense" (Kennedy 2008: 3).

Heeding her own advice for the careful use of tropes, Kennedy describes her short story poetics' last element through the metaphor of yet another metallic object, the well-cast bell:

> What you want with a short story is that it chimes with the reader because you've made it perfect enough that it resonates before and after itself. The people arrive and it's as if they were alive forever beforehand and the people leave and it's as if they're going off to the rest of their lives. This chime, this note, is the key moment; it's all you need to know for them to travel with you for the rest of your life.
> (Kennedy 2008: 4)

Lending "chime" to characters refers to the writer's art of creating the illusion that they – in spite of being made of letters – have a psyche, emotions, a past and future beyond the page, to enable readers to connect with them and, as Virginia Woolf suggested, "learn through feeling" (Woolf 1926/1972: 9, qtd. in Reynier 2009: 25) because they find the fictional characters "emotionally and psychologically consistent, convincing and three-dimensional" (Kennedy 2008: 1). In order to fit out characters with the affective range that makes them plausible as people, writers have to draw on their own reservoir of feeling, which is why short stories are "intense experiences" (Kennedy 2008: 3) and why the genre is "the most emotionally demanding form" for writers (Kennedy 2008: 5). Kennedy warns her audience of aspiring authors that in a short story "[i]t's so visible if you're not going to emotionally commit to your character" (Kennedy 2008: 3), but also maintains that if "chime" and focalisation work, a writer, mediated by a narrator, can make readers look at a given situation through the eyes of a character, which they have accepted as a person. In Kennedy's words, which underscore the short form's moral and political potential, this is "a massively unsociopathic thing to do" (Kennedy 2008: 6). When it succeeds, this is not a purely intellectual affair but can only work if reader emotions are engaged. As a genre, the short story seems to achieve this more effectively than other narrative forms, since it does not burden readers with convoluted plot developments, relationships between several plots, or recurring themes, as might be the case in the novel. The need to establish this affective connection quickly, however, is also the reason why an effective short story is not only emotionally demanding for authors, but also for readers.

Kennedy is not alone in emphasising that a short story needs to trigger reader affect if it is to be successful: as Christine Reynier has shown, Virginia Woolf understands the short story as an "art of emotion rather than of thought, both in writing and in reading" (2009: 24), in which "the soul becomes the locus of affects" (2009: 22). It is this common emphasis on affect, feelings and emotions for character construction and reader response that provides Kennedy's poetics with a genealogy that reaches back to the root of the modern short story that Reynier unearthed. Traces of what, retrospectively, becomes readable as Kennedy's poetic antecedents can be found in Woolf's metanarrative short story "An Unwritten Novel" (1921) and in her essay "Mr Bennett and Mrs Brown" (1924). When Woolf summarises, in the latter, contemporary writers' task as having to "bring back character from the shapelessness into which it has lapsed, to sharpen its edges, deepen its compass, and so make possible those conflicts between human beings which alone rouse our strongest emotions" (Woolf 1924/1988: 387), she directly links character construction to affective reader response, a thought that also resonates throughout Kennedy's talk.

To put Kennedy's ballistic poetics into a nutshell: a fully realised short story needs a strong sense of voice, a clear character point of view, musicality and chime. If the writer pays appropriate attention to the shape of the words on the page and ensures that the tropes succeed in carrying multiple meanings, a short story can provide an intense/penetrating/powerful effect within a moment, by creating an emotional resonance with readers that may produce a lasting mark equivalent to that left by a key event in real life. Gender, either as an important part of character construction or as a social category, is not discussed in "Small in a Way that a Bullet Is Small". In order to learn what role it may play for a writer who stresses the importance of making her invented characters plausible as people, a two-pronged approach seems most promising. Kennedy's own account of what kind of attention she pays to gender and its politics will be complemented by a critical analysis of how she narratively genders and ungenders narrative voices and characters in some of her short fiction. This juxtaposition will unfold against the background of how affect, emotion and feeling have been theorised in the field of cultural studies.

Theorising Affect

Affect theory in the humanities took off in the 1990s, when scholars embraced some of the ideas the psychologist Silvan Tomkins had published some thirty years before, in 1963. His most succinct definitions of affect, feeling and emotions are disseminated broadly by the Tomkins Institute:

> [a]ffect is the innate, biological response to the increasing, decreasing or persistent intensity of neural firing. This results in a particular feeling, facial and body display, and skin changes. [...] Affect makes things urgent. Awareness of an affect is a feeling [... A] feeling plus memory of prior similar feelings is an emotion.
>
> (2014)

Two scholarly traditions, in clinical psychology and in cultural theory, branch off from Tomkins's distinction between affect as capacity and feeling/emotion as the result of its activation. For psychologist Ross Buck, affect is a set of "subjectively experienced feelings and desires" (1999: 1) which all humans share. Whereas Buck neglects social elements completely, these are foregrounded by philosopher Brian Massumi (1995: 91), who sees affect as a "processual concept" characterised by "transversality" (1995: ix, x) which bridges the problematic Cartesian divide (between body and mind) because it acts as its "point of emergence" (1995: 94). Literary scholar and queer theorist Eve Kosofsky Sedgwick is mostly interested in the fact that the affect system is "interwoven with cognitive processes" (2003: 18), and art historian Erika Doss joins in the inquiry into "cognition itself" as "embodied, sensate, interested and invested" (2009: 10). For the purpose of examining short fiction, this point emphasised by cultural theory is helpful because it is precisely the intersection of cognition and affect, the embodiment of cognition, that enables writers to do what Kennedy demands of them in her poetics: to activate real readers' emotions in the absence of those sensual signals and body signs that ordinarily act as triggers, since writers have nothing but letters and imagination at their disposal. In their introduction to the *Affect Theory Reader*, Gregory Seigworth and Melissa Gregg state that

> [a]ffect arises in the midst of *in-between-ness*: in the capacities to act and be acted upon. Affect is an impingement or extrusion of a momentary or sometimes more sustained state of relation *as well as* the passage (and the duration of the passage) of forces or intensities.
> (2010: 1)

Each of Kennedy's stories discussed in this article stages the "in-between-ness" of affect between characters and readers as well as between narrative voices and readers. While some focus on the "momentary", others focus on "the passage [...] of forces or intensities", but all reflect on the interwovenness of affect and cognition by evoking states of strong, mixed emotion to engage their readers.

Ungendered Narrative Voice/s: "We"

When asked whether she sees herself as a "feminist" writer, Kennedy rejects this label, mostly because she considers tags of any kind of little use outside marketing (Mieszkowski 2017).[4] Academic discussions of literature inspired by gender studies or queer theory – the other potential context of which one might think here – hardly seem to be of interest to her. Occupying any "political standpoint", she argues, would be "too doctrinaire to help me make individual characters", restricting range rather than lending focus (Mieszkowski 2017). Consequently, she prefers to think of herself as a "humanist" (Mieszkowski 2017). She does not mean this in the sense attached to the European philosophical tradition, notorious for denying subject status to non-white and non-male humans, while aiming to exclude them categorically from the intellectual sphere. Rather, Kennedy – who states "I believe in the potential of my species" – uses "humanism" to express her fundamental optimism about people in general, and about granting male and female characters equal access to the entire spectrum of affects, feelings and emotions. In what follows, this article explores how this "humanism" translates into "shades of gender" (Mieszkowski 2017) in the very act of narrative ungendering.

Some of Kennedy's stories experiment with the ungendering of narrative voice and problematise gender on a sliding scale between mere performance and critical reflection. Analysing "A Perfect Possession", the opening story from *Now That You're Back* (1994/1995), and "The Effect of Good Government on the City", in its versions published in *Freedom* (2009) and *All the Rage* (2014), respectively, will show how and to what effect gender is first purged from the narrative voice/s, sometimes continuously withheld, sometimes slowly revealed, only to have its/their regendering then undermined or at least questioned.

As if fulfilling Kennedy's poetic rule of "multiple meanings" (2008: 5) right away, the very title of "A Perfect Possession", a short-short story of seven pages, lends itself to two interpretations: it may refer to a six-year old boy presented as his parents' "possession" and, simultaneously, point to these parents' religious mania. Well-suited to have readers recoil in mounting horror, the story is a tale of child abuse. This is never explicitly stated but has to be worked out by the reader without any help from the autodiegetic narrative voice. In fact, one only arrives at this insight by reading the narrator's story against the grain because this narrative voice, as it turns out, belongs to the abuser/s. The resulting unreliability is not the result of an effort to mislead the reader, but an unconscious symptom of "possession". Once the reader has understood this and starts concentrating on the subtext of what is being said, a gap opens between the narrator's characterisation of events and the reader's own interpretation of these events (as well as the narrative act). That this gap is never closed results in the persisting simultaneity of two contradictory versions of what is going on, which in turn produces growing empathy with the victim and repulsion vis-à-vis the abusers: a sinful (*or* perfectly ordinary) boy is protected (*or* isolated and kept prisoner behind barred windows and a locked door) by his loving (*or* deluded and abusive) parents, who teach him to do better (*or* harshly punish transgression) and shield him from temptation (*or* deny him the most basic emotional warmth and tie him up in bed).

From the opening phrase, the narrative voice consistently and without exception uses the first-person plural: "It hurts when we love somebody, because loving is a painful thing [...] He is spending this evening in his room where we don't see him" (Kennedy 1994/1995: 3). Later, phrases like "our part in his conception" (Kennedy 1994/1995: 8) infer that this voice belongs to a parent. Like other indexical pronouns, the first-person plural – in the absence of external gender markers – makes it impossible to decide whether what is told is the result of the father's or the mother's focalisation and narration. Yet the text consistently avoids all possible markers or any other form of gendering. The narrator at all times speaks in the name of/for his or her partner; at least if one assumes that the story is told by *one* voice. But of course, erasing gender also prevents readers from being sure whether the story is, in fact, told by *one* narrator. It is perfectly possible that both parents alternate in speaking for each other. In this case, sharing the "we" form and the absence of any stylistic breaks would represent these parents as an inseparable, and therefore all the more stifling, community of two that seems totally devoid of empathy or emotional warmth. This, I argue, matches the core of the parents "perfect possession": having established a monolithic, repressive system, they are determined (in the name of education) to stamp out individuality as much as they are determined (in the name of purity) to deny any gender difference between them – that is, block every chance that a differently embodied cognition might lead to an alternative parenting style – as the last consequence of sexual repression.

Regardless of whether one assumes one narrator or two, self-ungendering in "A Perfect Possession" – as far as bodies, perspectives, experience or role models are concerned – is a consequence of an attempted self-unsexing in the name of an ideology that conceives of sexuality as inherently sinful. Mirroring a traditional "sex/gender system" (Rubin 1975: 159), this grows directly out of the belief which the narrative "we" confidently represents, by which it claims to be guided, and in whose name it justifies its parenting style: namely, fundamentalist Christianity. Both the *Old* and *New Testaments* promote the notion of original sin. According to Genesis, eating from "the forbidden tree of the knowledge of good and evil" (Genesis 2: 17) introduces human awareness of sexual difference, mortality as its punishment (Genesis 3: 3), and sexuality as the signifier of humanity's fallen status (Genesis 3: 16). Paul's "Letter to the Galatians" lists sins considered "work of the flesh" (Galatians 5: 19) and John Calvin teaches that this "corruption of our nature" is a "hereditary depravity" (Calvin 2002: 1.8)[5] passed on through imputation from one generation to the next. The narrative "we" thinks of (cultural) gender as necessarily and unproblematically deriving from (biological) sex.[6] Because gender, through its link to sex, is also tied to the sexual act, the attempt to control "sin" leads to a collateral elimination of gender which, I maintain, manifests on the level of form in the choice of an ungendered narrative voice. If the parents' sexual act is inherently sinful in their own understanding, so is its "fruit". Like all other offspring, the boy is corrupt by proxy, the "immediate flower of sin" who inevitably "has bad seed in him" (Kennedy 1994/1995: 8). The parents' duty (*or* unhealthy obsession) of "bringing [their son] up from the animal level to something higher, better, closer to God" (Kennedy 1994/1995: 5) and teach him to control satanic urges (*or* quash his perfectly healthy need for emotional and physical comfort) to "release him from himself" (Kennedy 1994/1995: 9) provides the short story with both its thematic backbone and its dominant formal feature.

As the unusual narrative voice attempts to expunge all traces of sexuality, it not only ungenders but also characterises itself (and its partner) – quite clearly contrary to all intention – as cruel, perverse and dangerous for the boy's emotional wellbeing and psychosocial development:

> A time came when he wanted something he could hug on to in the night and we knew what that meant. That was a warning. We had to take his pillow away because he would sleep alongside of it, in spite of what we told him, and that was dirty, that was more of the filth we constantly fight to save him from. It grieved us when he cried about it, cried in the night, and didn't understand the procedures to which he would have to conform. In the end he was persuaded to pray with us and became peaceful which was a little victory for us all.
>
> (Kennedy 1994/1995: 7)

A textbook case of what Michel Foucault has described as one of four dominant forms of discipline that characterise the western history of sexuality, "A Perfect Possession" showcases a "pedagogization of children's sex" (Foucault 1978: 104) that is out of step by a good century with the contemporary majority's attitudes in the West towards both sex and parenting. The corrective regime, its trajectory, its underlying attitude and resulting actions leave a clear trace in formulations like "we knew", "we had to take away", "in spite of what we told him", "we constantly fight", "it grieved us", "he would have to conform", "he was persuaded" and "it was a little victory for us all" (Kennedy 1994/1995: 7). Especially the last two phrases seem to suggest that the rightfully reprimanded (*or* emotionally deprived) son succumbs to their teaching (*or* abuse). That he is ready to give up his sinful wishes (*or* understandable human needs) and to develop into an "upright and mannerly" (Kennedy 1994/1995: 7), though "dreadfully clumsy" (Kennedy 1994/1995: 5) child (*or* a broken, emotionally warped and intellectually retarded one) becomes clear in the arc that spans from "wanted something he could hug" to "warning", "dirty" and "filth" and "cried" (Kennedy 1994/1995: 7).

If one assumes that both parents might alternate as narrators, their unusual position of complete unity, successfully purged of gender difference, only reinforces the point the story is making: that no distinction is allowed to exist between these parents; that they speak as one; that their opinion on their son differs as little as their voices do; that there is no daylight between their views on what is and is not acceptable; that there is no space for a second opinion or negotiation; and that all of this sucks the air out of the boy's life. Within the framework of fundamentalist Christianity, gender functions as a reminder and signifier of inherited sin. Ungendering the narrative voice/s in this story has the opposite effect of what one might expect: instead of questioning or exploding hetero-normative gender roles, it exposes the parents' "perfect possession" as resulting in gender in-difference, in a loss of individuality, humanity and affective capacity, and in a total, structurally fascist, lack of alternative.

It is, of course, also possible to attribute the ungendered narrative voice in "A Perfect Possession" to *one* narrator. Given that an extreme form of Christian fundamentalism is likely to embrace patriarchal power structures and that *The New Testament* does contain passages, which advocate the asymmetrical access to "voice" for the two genders (1 Corinthians 14: 34–35),[7] it is feasible to assume that a single narrator might be gendered masculine rather that feminine. Patriarchal church ideology not only makes the asking of questions in public a male pre-rogative, but also installs and protects the husband's privilege to speak for his wife. Consequently, a feminist reading needs to point out that the narrative "we" in Kennedy's story, while technically gender-neutral, could also mask the deletion of the female/maternal voice. If the male partner arrogates to himself the position of the narrative "we" – by pre-tending to speak for both parents without being contradicted – this con-stitutes a successful act of gender oppression, to the point of silencing the wife/mother completely. That this muting relates to the domestic sphere and a small child's education – both traditionally defined as spheres of female influence and privilege – indicates an extreme form of paternal tyranny incompatible with accepting any gender-different position as valid. Grammatical ungendering, in this reading, hides the bias (for the masculine position) inherent to the gender dualism that structurally un-derlies all phallocentric systems of representation (Klinger 2005: 354). The narrative "we" as a signifier of male/paternal appropriation of a monolithic voice which silences all others – first and foremost the woman and the child – thus functions as a vehicle of patriarchal ideology. What Kennedy theorises as "chime" implies that, ultimately, this narrator – a manifestation of "hegemonic masculinity" (Connell and Messerschmidt 2005: 832) – will not tolerate any contradicting male voice or emotional approach to parenting either, which leaves the growing son little op-tion beyond identification with and imitation of the father, or (self-) destruction.

Ungendered Narrative Voice/s: "You"

"A Perfect Possession" is not the only short story by A.L. Kennedy that features a self-ungendering narrator. In her most recent collection, *All the Rage* (2014), no less than three texts use this device.[8] One of these is "The Effects of Government on the City", of which there are two versions. The first, originally commissioned by Amnesty International for a collection of short fiction by authors around the world, was published in 2009 to celebrate the 50th anniversary of the *Universal Declaration of Human Rights*.[9] Five years later, Kennedy included a reworked, slightly longer version in *All the Rage*. Ultimately, the story is a study of trauma and guilt, which makes its title's allusion to an allegorical fresco bitterly ironic. While the medieval mural to which it refers depicts urban scenes of peace, order, calmly practiced faith, trade-based prosperity and public entertainment, all of these are shown to be tainted in the political and psychological climate evoked by Kennedy's story.[10]

Interestingly, the representation of gender is precisely where the 2009 and the 2014 versions of Kennedy's story differ most significantly, and I offer an analysis of the following three points in which this difference becomes traceable: as far as the revelation of the focaliser-narrator's gender (or rather the *suspension* of this revelation) is concerned; in terms of incongruity between gender identity and gender role; and with respect to how the protagonist's sense of belonging to either of the dominant genders is undermined. All three points are linked to the secret at the story's core, which readers can only piece together bit by bit. Depending on when it becomes clear that the narrator-protagonist's trauma derives from having participated in torturing prisoners of war during a military deployment abroad, the story unfolds its Woolfian "violent shock of personal emotion" (Woolf 1926/1972: 7, qtd. in Reynier 2009: 25), which, according to Kennedy's ballistics, hits readers and "blows[s] their fucking head off" (Kennedy 2008: 3). As a result, the story slowly builds towards the moment of reader comprehension in which the created "emotional intensity" characteristic of the short story (Reynier 2009: 25) explodes in a veritably Woolfian shock.

In both versions of the story a large part of the narration is delivered in the second-person singular. Given the absence of external gender markers, which are once again withheld, the indexical "you", just like the "we" in "A Perfect Possession", results in the focaliser-narrator's grammatical self-ungendering. In terms of plot, the story's two versions are almost identical. A nameless protagonist/focaliser/narrator spends a weekend with an equally nameless boyfriend in Blackpool. As far as external events go, nothing much happens, and this blatant lack of action serves as a contrast for the protagonist's psychological struggle against the emotional emptiness. It turns out the post-traumatic stress disorder has been caused by the assignment as a so-called "observer" (Kennedy 2009: 29; Kennedy 2014: 162), a euphemism for someone who witnesses and indirectly participates in torture by resuscitating victims, once they pass out, to enable further interrogation.

Narratologists categorise second-person narration as a rarely used device and theorise it as "transgressive and subversive" and "non-communicative" (Fludernik 1994: 445, 446), as a "departure from the narrative norm" (Kacandes 1993: 329), as being "capable of representing the non-standard universes created by post-modern authors" (Margolin 1986/1987: 184), and as providing "a perfect space of discursive protection to liminal protagonists" (Wiest-Kellner 1999: 35; my translation). Whereas a "you" used in dialogue tends to refer to a character directly addressed by the speaker or to a general stand-in, a representative of everybody, a narrative "you" potentially carries a different double address: it may refer to the narrator, who for some reason or other does not think of him/herself as "I", but it is also available for identification with the reader, who is the narrator's addressee on the extra-diegetic level. In both versions of Kennedy's story, it is clear from the start that the boyfriend, who is – technically speaking – the protagonist's dialogue partner, is not the one addressed by this "you", since it is used in passages of interior monologue. In effect, the "you's" double address, on the one hand, invites readers to disturbingly identify with a shattered mind; with a character that oscillates between trauma and justification. On the other hand, it also signifies the protagonist's effort to protect the innocent self (possibly the absent, blocked "I") by splitting off the perpetrator self. Regardless of whether the "you" points to a medical condition or to a struggling psyche's attempt to heal itself, the resulting self-ungendering symptomises a destabilised sense of identity.

From the beginning, the story focuses on the narrator's inner life. Fragments of dialogue with the boyfriend, and italicised instructions that sound as if they were quoted from a military training manual, keep interrupting the dominant interior monologue. Due to the interlacing of these three types of text, the manual quotations take on exactly the kind of "multiple meanings" identified in Kennedy's poetics as a criterion of the fully realised short story: "*Stay on known safe areas. Avoid verges*" (Kennedy 2009: 23; Kennedy 2014: 153) read like recommendations given to soldiers in the field, but can also be an inner comment on the relationship between protagonist and boyfriend, who, clearly a couple in crisis, want to avoid breaking up. Other quotations from the army manual that flash through the protagonist's mind – prompted by perceptions, recollections and associations as the couple strolls around Blackpool – are much darker. A happy childhood memory, triggered by the sight of a few beach stalls – "*When you were little here it was miraculous*" (Kennedy 2009: 26) and, respectively, "*When you were little here it was all sweet undercurrents*" (Kennedy 2014: 157) – is immediately followed by a few manual sentences that associate the idea of childhood with that of exploitable vulnerability: "Recalling your childhood unleashes your capacity for wonder, appreciation of kindness and belief. There is a concomitant increase in your potential depths of helplessness and fear" (Kennedy 2009: 26). The 2014 version, in which this passage is slightly changed, emphasises different emotions in its explanation of how torture instrumentalises the effects of trauma on the human psyche:

Recalling your childhood unleashes your capacity for wonder, appreciation of kindness and belief. Returning someone to their childhood self will cause an increase in their potential depth of help-lessness and fear. The shock of capture, prolonged, can assist in use-fully producing this effect.

(Kennedy 2014: 157)

In both versions of the story, a happy memory – through a chain of as-sociations of childhood with helplessness, fear, wonder, emotional open-ness, vulnerability – reminds the protagonist of instructions on how to torture prisoners most effectively. This, in turn, illustrates how the pro-tagonist's own, innocent, childhood self is retrospectively contaminated by the new perpetrator self.

When it comes to the focaliser-narrator's gendering, Kennedy's ver-sions of this story differ. Both start by mentioning the nameless boy-friend, but unless one automatically presupposes a heterosexual (or a homosexual) relationship, the narrator-focaliser, by using the gram-matically neutral second-person singular, remains at first ungendered. After eleven iterations of this "you", the 2014 version contains one sentence that seems to imply a third-person narrator and, thus, deliv-ers a hint as to the protagonist's gender: "There'd been nowhere for thinking while you were away. Close the doors and draw the blinds and block the chimney [...] Not that they'd had any chimneys out there. Not the way she was used to" (Kennedy 2014: 153). This sudden switch from "you" to "she" is odd, especially since the text never refers to this "she" again and it remains inexplicable until it emerges that the protagonist's trauma may manifest in a split consciousness that differ-entiates "you" from "she". Any first-time reader is likely to assume that the female character to which "she" points might still be introduced later in the story. Only at a repeated reading – once it is clear that there *is* no other female character and that the focaliser-narrator is, thus, the only one to whom "she" could possibly refer – does this odd third-person feminine personal pronoun register as a clue, after which the 2014 version keeps readers in suspense about the protagonist's gender for another four pages.

The 2009 version delays divulging any information on its focaliser-narrator's gender even longer: for a full six pages into the story with-out *any* hint at all. In this version, it is not a pronoun, but an item of clothing which first suggests the protagonist's femininity: "And having an Olde Time photo taken together – you wearing a dress that didn't fit well, because you're lean, you're in shape, you're not an average customer" (Kennedy 2009: 28). While one might very well miss the 2014 version's subtle use of "she", the dress in this passage is hard to miss as a marker of femininity. Yet at the very instant the pro-tagonist is gendered by association with this garment, her femininity is suggested to be non-standard since the dress does not "fit well" because her body does not conform to the "average" of her gender (both Kennedy 2009: 28). The 2014 version contains the same "Olde Time photo" scene, although it occurs a little later, and the gender incongruity is even more clearly one between a typical piece of feminine clothing and a non-typical female body. Moreover, an explanation is offered for this discrepancy: "They gave you a dress that fitted in silly places, because you're lean and also muscular and not an average customer. You have grown into the shape the job requires" (Kennedy 2014: 161). Here, gender incongruity produces an awkward, or at least uncomfortable, effect. That the dress "fitted in silly places" rather than in the "right" ones is a synecdoche, since the protagonist feels generally like a misfit, which makes this scene one of the tropes that "work" (2008: 6) demanded by Kennedy's ballistic poetics. The gender incongruity is not, however, due to a discrepancy between gender and sex, since the non-compliant body parts are not sexual organs or chromosomes or hormones. Rather, it is an incongruity between (average) gender and (non-average) gender, since muscles and fat are body parts that both sexes possess and that are easily sculpted by (cultural) activity. By changing the gender neutral "lean" into the slightly more masculine "muscular" *and* by then linking the muscles to a soldier's labour, Kennedy's 2014 version suggests more strongly than the one from 2009 that its protagonist's job, the diet, and the exercise involved have changed her body in a way that collides with a gender role which, although marked as "Olde", still shapes normative femininity. Looping back to the odd switch from "you" to "she" and back to "you", which only the 2014 version sports, the poor fit (at the level of discourse) between the protagonist and the feminine-gendered pronoun corresponds with poor fit between the protagonist and the feminine-gendered dress (at the level of plot).

Both versions of "The Effects of Good Government on the City" contain passages that highlight the social aspects of the protagonist's ungendering. In the story's 2009 version, two pages before it finally becomes clear that the focaliser-narrator is a woman, the text misleadingly suggests the focaliser-narrator might be a man, by evoking male-gendered practices and vocabulary: "This [Blackpool] isn't a kid's place any more. It's all lap dancers and cider and sick lights squirming down in the rain and losing control with your mates" (Kennedy 2009: 26). The slang term "mates" carries two suggestions of gender, since it tends to refer to a man's male friends. This passage, too, has been slightly changed for republication in 2014, where "mates" is replaced with "boys", thereby suggesting even more clearly that the protagonist moves in a predominantly male social environment. This small change introduces a whole paragraph that has no equivalent at all in the earlier version and exemplifies what Kennedy's poetics calls "clear character point of view" (2008: 6) in the protagonist's self-reflection on her exceptional gender status:

> This isn't for the kiddies and families any more. It's for lap dancers and being on the lash and sick lights squirming down flat in the rain and being with the boys, except you can't, you've got to watch that – they forget you're not a boy, or else they remember and both are No Bloody Chance in the end. You are not one thing and not the other. You are not most things. You have been somewhere in which most things are not most things and no one gives a toss so why should you and how would you know you ought to and this is how you've ended up. Bad enough, but then you talked to a milk-white lawyer. Afterwards, he hated you more than anyone, even though you did nothing. That was the point. You did nothing in every way. Nothing about the goings-on, the box of frogs clusterfuck of what was going on. You did nothing. And then you talked.
>
> (Kennedy 2014: 157)

That Blackpool has metamorphosed into a stag-night resort triggers a thought process that reveals the protagonist's sense of gender identity as destabilised. Soldiering is still a job overwhelmingly associated with masculinity, and the protagonist's use of army slang – "being on the lash", "box of frogs", "clusterfuck" – testifies that she has embraced the gendered discourse of her work environment. Yet, whereas the moment after the phrase "being with the boys" signals hope for a female soldier's successful integration into the army, it is immediately crossed out by "except you can't". What follows is an act of explicit verbal self-ungendering: she does not think of herself as "a woman" but as "not a boy" (Kennedy 2014: 157). The focaliser-narrator is not alone in seeing her ambiguous, doubly erased gender position – "not one thing and not the other" – as a problem. Regardless of whether her colleagues "forget you're not a boy, or else [...] remember", neither option leads to a stable sense of self as a full member of the soldierly community. It is not enough that she shares her colleagues' view of the lawyer as emasculated ("milk-white") or accepts the underlying sexism, which equates emasculation with feminisation, weakness and inferiority. While her job and work environment have alienated her from fitting into a feminine gender role, the capitalised "No Bloody Chance" indicates that none of the positions on the spectrum of masculinities, be it "hegemonic", "complicit", "subordinate" or "marginal" (Connell and Messerschmidt 2005: 832, 844), is available to her either.

As a whistle-blower who used to be a perpetrator but has now decided to talk to a lawyer about the army's condoning and even active practice of torture, she neither confronts her colleagues, nor does she simply participate in what they do and keep her mouth shut. This double exclusion is structurally analogous to her alienation from either of the two positions made available by the gender binary: the path she chooses instead – "You did nothing. And then you talked" (Kennedy 2014: 157) – has earned her contempt from both her fellow soldiers and the public, leaving her isolated. While she is not the only one who has been "somewhere in which most things are not most things" (Kennedy 2014: 157), referring to the location of torture, the position she occupies between the genders and between clear-cut moral stances is not a tenable one in either of the binary systems in which she is caught. This leaves her, who is "not most things" (157), falling through the grid. Kennedy's 2014 version shows how the perpetrator's trauma and guilt can lead to a loss of self-respect and the erosion of a stable sense of identity of which the protagonist's ungendered position becomes the most important expression.

Ungendering Emotion: Angry Women, Crying Men

This article has been arguing that affect, in conjunction with the un/re/gendering of characters and narrative voices, is essential for that part of Kennedy's ballistic poetics, which discusses how short stories should/can establish their connection to readers. They do so by successfully pretending that characters, like real people, have feelings and emotions which, in turn, activate (sometimes violent) corresponding or radically different feelings and emotions in readers that can shade from empathy at one end of the spectrum to repulsion at the other. When Kennedy's latest collection of short fiction, *All the Rage*, was first published, literary reviewers caught hold of a red thread.[11] Chris Power maintained that the stories were "linked by love" which "involves psychic and sometimes physical pain rather than violins and swooning" (2014). For Molly Young the collection "focuses on tales of love: people deceived by it, people injured by it, people who inflict its injuries on others" (2014). Megan Labrise found that the volume portrays the interrelatedness of emotions: "When love's what's first, resultant anger may be doubly potent" (2014). Katey Guest thought that "A.L. Kennedy's texts should come with the warning that '[t]hese stories may break your heart'", attributing their power to the ability to evoke a combination of different affects: "You could say that these stories are laugh-out-loud sad" (2014). Even critics who dislike *All the Rage* agree that its focus is on emotion. Tim Martin thinks the collection merely "affects to apply the precise language of police statements and official forms to the elusive grades of human emotion" and laments "the yawning abstractions that this involves [which] force the reader to slow down, pick through, decode" (2014). Lionel Shriver draws the opposite conclusion from a similar observation: "It is Kennedy's portrayal of the difficulty, if not seeming impossibility, of connecting with other people that makes these stories so moving" (2014). Where

Martin sees obstacles to communication between text and reader, and criticises *All the Rage* for demanding interpretative work, Shriver locates the obstacles to communication between characters, and sees their – perhaps inevitable – failure to overcome them as the collection's most effective tool to activate reader emotion. Michael Hingston, who describes his reading experience as "an offbeat joy", confesses to having felt "an instinctive affection" (2014) for Dorothy, the protagonist of "The Practice of Mercy", thereby testifying to Kennedy's success in providing her story with the "strong sense of voice", a clear "character point of view" and "chime" (Kennedy 2008: 3–4, 6), which her own poetics rate so highly.

All the Rage contains a dozen stories, the main characters of which are of different genders and sexual orientations: one features a heterosexual couple, three have female protagonists, five have male ones and two never reveal the gender of their narrator-focalisers, thus leaving it open whether love between women, love between men or between opposite sex couples is being described. Bearing in mind Kennedy's warning about falling into gender "cliché" or "stereotype" (Mieszkowski 2017), it seems more than a coincidence that four of these stories work against traditional gendering of affect and its expression. Instead, two portray angry women who are *not* rendered unattractive by a rage that is *neither* destabilising *nor* dangerous; and two depict crying men who are *not* rendered weak or emasculated by their tears but gain, by giving in to them, in emotional depth, maturity and complexity.

"The Practice of Mercy" is told by a third-person narrator and focalised by Dorothy who, after a serious fight with her male partner, has taken off to an unnamed European town. During her touristic roaming, she experiences a mix of disappointment, guilt and sorrow because of her apparently failing relationship, but also excitement about exploring and relief that she is still able to savour new impressions. The key moment, in which anger is portrayed not only as a productive force but an important component, occurs as Dorothy embarks on her excursion:

> A banana would do her fine until lunchtime. Tennis players and athletes in general ate them for potassium with positive effects at a cellular level. She recalled a school chemistry lesson in which her teacher [...] had dropped a sliver of potassium into water. The whole class had then watched as the metal wasped back and forth on the liquid's surface in a tiny blur of lilac flames, too angry to sink. It made Dorothy smile, then and today: the idea that every human body hid a pastel shade of outrage no one should view without safety glasses, or else protective screens. It was a necessary element. Inside. The fuel for frenzy, beauty, frenzy, for evaporating types of heat was medically essential.
>
> (Kennedy 2014: 63)

In this conceit, rage is volatile but indispensable and – provided it comes at the right dosage – literally vital, a source of creative power at the root of "beauty". The ideological framework of heteronormativity prefers to paint anger as a male prerogative, an accepted expression of male "public authority" (Barton 2005: 374), or even as a masculinising (if not unproblematic) force.[12] At the same time, this tradition presents female anger as "unfeminine", "unproductive" and "undesirable *in* and therefore undesirable *for* women" (Frevert 2011: 91). Kennedy's metaphor counters this cultural tradition by insisting that potassium is part of "every human body", and thus anger, which it represents, is part of every human affect system and can, if lifted into consciousness, develop into a feeling available to all genders. By featuring rage as not only accessible to a female character without punishing her for it (Dorothy's relationship recovers precisely because she was allowed her productive anger), but by presenting it as positive, "The Practice of Mercy" undermines those cliched representations of gendered emotion against which Kennedy warns (Mieszkowski 2017).

Another story in *All the Rage* makes a comparably move with regard to the gendering of unabashed expression of strong, mixed emotion through tears. "These Small Pieces" is mostly told in third-person narration and set shortly before Christmas. Its protagonist, who consciously chooses to refer to himself with the help of the pseudonym "Douglas", enters a Carol service with the explicit purpose of shaking loose some pent-up feelings. The key moment from which the story takes its title is also its end:

> It was customary; you wanted it in a Christmas service: an opportunity to weep. Douglas, or whoever, shivered and the snag and heave and braveness in his breath surprised him. Wipe at the eyes when he sat and no shame about it. [...] He is simply crying and unable, for Heaven's sake, to cry any less or prevent small howling bubbles of sound from escaping him and there is no justification for his behaviour, he is not especially mourning or damaged and this is exactly his problem, to be frank, because he deserves no particular sympathy. All that has happened is that time has passed and he isn't who he was and never will be and occurrences have hurt him *tump tump* and so he weeps and he would like a rest and so he weeps and this boy, this man beseeches an intervention, but has no faith in saviours and so he weeps and he knows he is commonplace and unrequited and so he weeps and he knows he is impossible and build around these small pieces, baffling pieces, ridiculous animal pieces, and so he weeps and he knows that he needs to be saved and he sings for it, tries to sing for it. Everyone, he thinks, does try to sing for it. His problem would be that he's making the wrong noise.
>
> (Kennedy 2014: 57–58)

This passage contrasts the character's self-perception with the narrator-guided reader's impression. "Douglas" thinks of himself – "for Heaven's sake" – as "impossible" and "ridiculous" and diagnoses that the absence of "mourning" or "damage", a justification that would allow a man to cry, is a "problem" (Kennedy 2014: 57). His definition of masculinity does no longer completely exclude tears, but as he cries, he still needs to tell himself that there is "no shame about it" (Kennedy 2014: 57). The way this final paragraph is narrated, with its multiple repetitions of "and so he weeps" (Kennedy 2014: 58) and with the character's flow of thoughts pushing syntax to its limits without breaking it, paints a different picture: that of a man who is properly human because his affect system has access to that part of the emotional spectrum, which is most heavily burdened by cultural clichés of emasculation. Although "Douglas" thinks "he's making the wrong noise", the narration suggests he is making exactly the right kind of move by seizing the opportunity to open the floodgates for his pent-up emotion.

Conclusion

A.L. Kennedy's short stories are a laboratory for experimenting with the gendering, ungendering and regendering of characters and narrative voices. "A Perfect Possession" is told in second-person plural narration, while both versions of "The Effects of Good Government on the City" use second-person singular narration. Yet all three texts grammatically erase or suspend gender, using the unaccommodating binary structure of heteronormativity to tell stories about damaged humans. At the same time, these three stories testify to the cultural gendering of belief systems (like Christianity), institutions (like the army), their ideologies, discourses and the power structures that pervade the characters'/focalisers'/narrators' social surroundings.

Against the phallocentric tradition that has equated "the male" with "the universal" for centuries (Klinger 2005: 337), "The Practice of Mercy" allows the female protagonist to stand in for "every human" (Kennedy 2014: 63) by making anger available to her. By crossing out that part of heteronormative ideology that tends to cast women as the preferred representatives of nature and, for that matter, as inherently emotional (and therefore irrational) creatures (Klinger 2005: 338), Kennedy's story allows a male character to represent everyone's "ridiculous animal pieces" (Kennedy 2014: 58). Thus, "These Small Pieces" makes vulnerability, unrestricted abandon to affect, the need to be saved, and the only seemingly unjustified tears, which express all of these, available to the gender that has been excluded from this type of catharsis for a long time. Going against "cliché" and "stereotype" (Mieszkowski 2017) by narratively cross-gendering (at least from the heteronormative point of view) emotions, both "The Practice of Mercy" and "These Small

Pieces" draw attention to the fact that the gendering of affect is one of the cultural constructs from the dismantling of which much may be gained. They thereby underscore that affect, as the "innate, biological response to the increasing, decreasing or persistent intensity of neural firing" (Tomkins Institute Website 2014), is a human feature that should be available in every shade of feeling to all genders. Kennedy's narrative experiments, this article has argued, progress from ungendering as a tool that articulates gender oppression (in "A Perfect Possession") to ungendering as an expression of trauma and a lost sense of identity ("The Effects of Good Government on the City"), and finally to the ungendering (via cross-gendering) of anger and tears as both liberating and subversive. All three steps ultimately contribute to Kennedy's project of ungendering affect, feeling and emotion with a view to putting what she likes to call "humanism" into the practice of her ballistic poetics.

Notes

1 A.L. Kennedy has six collections to her name: *Night Geometry and the Garscadden Trains* (1990), *Now that You're Back* (1994), *Original Bliss* (1997), *Indelible Acts* (2001), *What Becomes* (2009) and *All the Rage* (2014).

2 For example, "He, She & Me: Writing in and out of Gender", taught at London's Writing Factory in March 2016. https://shortstops.info/2016/03/13/word-factory-41-masterclass-19th-march-london/.

3 After the referendum on the United Kingdom's secession from the European Union in 2016, *The Guardian*, in collaboration with the theatre company Headlong, commissioned a series of monologues from British playwrights. The resulting texts form the basis for *Dramas from a Divided Nation*, nine short-short films on Brexit and the emotional fall-out for leavers and remainers in different regions of Britain. The clips were put online in the third week of June 2017, a year after the vote. Kennedy's monologue, set in Glasgow and spoken, like the other pieces, by its single character straight into the camera, can be viewed at: www.theguardian.com/stage/2017/jun/19/permanent-sunshine-a-new-play-by-al-kennedy-brexit-shorts (accessed 25 June 2017).

4 See the interview with A.L. Kennedy, conducted on 20 Oct 2016 via email, which has since been published in volume 22 of *The Bottle Imp*. Online at: www.thebottleimp.org.uk/2017/11/interview-l-kennedy/. Quotations refer to this online version and are thus without pagination.

5 "Original sin, therefore, seems to be a hereditary depravity and corruption of our nature, diffused into all parts of the soul, which first makes us liable to God's wrath, then also brings forth in us those works which Scripture calls 'works of the flesh'. This corruption is repeatedly designated by Paul by the term sin." Calvin, *Institutes of the Christian Religion*, II.1.8.

6 This is a conservative view refuted, most famously, by Judith Butler in *Gender Trouble* (1990).

7 "Let your women keep silence in the churches: for it is not permitted unto them to speak; but they are commanded to be under obedience, as also saith the law. And if they will learn anything, let them ask their husbands at home: for it is a shame for women to speak in the church." (1 Corinthians 14: 34–35).

8 Due to second person narration, the narrators' gender in "A Thing Unheard-of" and "This Man" remains unclear throughout.
9 Each of the first thirty short stories in this collection is headed by one of the *Declaration*'s articles. Kennedy's text is positioned as a comment on Article Two ("Universality of Rights").
10 Ambrogio Lorenzetti painted two murals around 1340, which were used to decorate one of the walls in Siena's Palazzo Pubblico. Kennedy, by refusing to name her story after the eponymous image's counterpart, titled "The Effects of Bad Government on the City", seems to have aimed deliberately for his ironic effect.
11 All following citations are taken from the respective reviews' online versions and are, therefore, without pagination.
12 See Barton (2005) for Christian discourses on *ira, furor* and *iracundia*.

References

1 Corinthians, *Bible: King James Version*, https://quod.lib.umich.edu/k/kjv/ (accessed 3 February 2018).

Barton, Richard E. (2005) "Gendering Anger: *Ira, Furor*, and Discourses of Power and Masculinity in the Eleventh and Twelfth Centuries", in *In the Garden of Evil*, edited by Richard Newhauser, Toronto: Pontifical Institute of Mediaeval Studies, 371–392.

Buck, Ross (1999) "The Biological Affects: A Typology", *Psychological Review* 106(2): 301–336.

Butler, Judith (1990) *Gender Trouble: Feminism and the Subversion of Identity*, London: Routledge.

Calvin, John (2002) *The Institutes of the Christian Religion*, translated by Henry Beveridge, Christian Classics Ethereal Library, www.ntslibrary.com/PDF%20Books/Calvin%20Institutes%20of%20Christian%20Religion.pdf (accessed 3 February 2018).

Connell, R.W. and James W. Messerschmidt (2005) "Hegemonic Masculinity: Rethinking the Concept", *Gender & Society* 19(6): 829–859.

Doss, Erika (2009) "Affect", *American Art* 23(1): 9–11.

Eagleton, Mary (1989) "Gender and Genre", in *Re-reading the Short Story*, edited by Clare Hanson, New York: St. Martin's Press, 55–68.

Fludernik, Monika (1994) "Second-Person Narrative as a Test-Case for Narratology: The Limits of Realism", *Style* 28(3): 445–479.

Foucault, Michel (1978) *The History of Sexuality*, Vol. 1, translated by Robert Hurley, London: Pantheon Books.

Frevert, Ute (2011) *Emotions in History: Lost and Found*, Budapest and New York: Central European University Press.

Galatians, *Bible: King James Version*, https://quod.lib.umich.edu/k/kjv/ (accessed 3 February 2018).

Genesis, *Bible: King James Version*, https://quod.lib.umich.edu/k/kjv/ (accessed 3 February 2018).

Guest, Katy (2014) "*All the Rage* by A.L. Kennedy", *Independent*, www.independent.co.uk/arts-entertainment/books/reviews/book-reviews-all-the-rage-by-a-l-kennedy-9160962.html (accessed 3 February 2018).

Hill Collins, Patricia (2015) "Intersectionality's Definitional Dilemmas", *Annual Review of Sociology* 41: 1–20.

Hingston, Michael (2014) "All the Rage: An Offbeat Joy to Read A.L. Kennedy's Propulsive Prose", *The Globe and Mail*, https://beta.theglobeandmail.com/arts/books-and-media/book-reviews/all-the-rage-an-offbeat-joy-to-read-al-kennedys-propulsive-prose/article16899439/?ref=http://www.theglobeand-mail.com& (accessed 3 February 2018).

Kacandes, Irene (1993) "Are You in the Text? The 'Literary Performative' in Postmodernist Fiction", *Text and Performance Quarterly* 13: 139–153.

Kennedy, A.L. (1994/1995) "A Perfect Possession", *Now That You're Back*, London: Vintage, 3–9.

Kennedy, A.L. (2008) "Small in a Way That a Bullet is Small", in *The Short Story*, edited by Ailsa Cox, Newcastle-upon-Tyne: Cambridge Scholars Publishing, 2008, 1–10.

Kennedy, A.L. (2014) *All the Rage*, London: Jonathan Cape.

Kennedy, A.L. (2017) "Permanent Sunshine" for "Brexit Shorts: Giving Voice to a Divided Britain through New Dramas", edited by Chris Wiegand, *The Guardian*, www.theguardian.com/membership/2017/jun/23/brexit-shorts-giving-voice-divided-britain-dramas (accessed 25 June 2017).

Kennedy, A.L. (ed.) (2009) "The Effects of Good Government on the City", *Freedom: Short Stories Celebrating the Universal Declaration of Human Rights*, London: Amnesty International UK/Mainstream Publishing, 23–33.

Kessler, Suzanne J. and Wendy McKenna (2006) "Toward a Theory of Gender", in *The Transgender Studies Reader*, edited by Susan Stryker and Stephen Whittle, London: Routledge, 165–182.

Klinger, Cornelia (2005) "Feministische Theorie zwischen Lektüre und Kritik des philosophischen Kanons", in *Genus: Geschlechterforschung/Gender Studies in den Kultur und Sozialwissenschaften: Ein Handbuch*, edited by Hadumod Bußmann und Renate Hof, Stuttgart: Kröner, 328–364.

Labrise, Megan (2014) "A.L. Kennedy", *Kirkus*, www.kirkusreviews.com/features/l-kennedy/ (accessed 3 February 2018).

Margolin, Uri (1986/1987) "Dispersing/Voiding the Subject: A Narratological Perspective", *Texte: Revue de critique et du théorie littéraire* 5(6): 181–210.

Martin, Tim (2014) "*All The Rage* by AL Kennedy, Review", *Telegraph*, www.telegraph.co.uk/culture/books/10719453/When-a-great-novelist-falls-under-her-own-spell.html (accessed 3 February 2018).

Massumi, Brian (1995) "The Autonomy of Affect", *Cultural Critique* 31: 83–109.

Mieszkowski, Sylvia (2017) "A. L. Kennedy: An Interview", *The Bottle Imp* 22, www.thebottleimp.org.uk/2017/11/interview-l-kennedy/ (accessed 3 February 2018).

Power, Chris (2014) "*All the Rage* by A.L Kennedy Review: Stories about Psychic and Physical Pain", *The Guardian*, www.theguardian.com/books/2014/apr/12/all-rage-al-kennedy-short-stories-review (accessed 3 February 2018).

Reynier, Christine (2009) "Virginia Woolf's Definition of the Short Story", *Virginia Woolf's Ethics of the Short Story*, London: Palgrave Macmillan, 18–35.

Rubin, Gayle (1975) "The Traffic in Women: Notes on the 'Political Economy' of Sex", in *Toward an Anthropology of Women*, edited by Rayna R. Reiter, New York: Monthly Review Press, 157–210.

Sedgwick, Eve Kosofsky and Adam Frank (2003) *Touching Feeling: Affect, Pedagogy, Performativity*, Durham, NC: Duke University Press.

Seigworth, Gregory J. and Gregg, Melissa (2010) "An Inventory of Shimmers", in *The Affect Theory Reader*, Durham, NC: Duke University Press, 1–25.

Shriver, Lionel (2014) "Book Review of *All the Rage* by A.L. Kennedy", *Financial Times*, www.ft.com/intl/cms/s/2/28d19c5c-adca-11e3-9ddc-00144feab7de. html (accessed 3 February 2018).

Tomkins Institute Website (2014) "Nine Affects, Present at Birth, Combine with Life Experience to Form Emotion and Personality", www.tomkins.org/ what-tomkins-said/introduction/ nine-affects-present-at-birth-combine-to-form-emotion-mood-and-personality (accessed 3 February 2018).

Tomkins, Silvan (1963) *Affect, Imagery, Consciousness*, Vol. 2. London: Springer.

Wiest-Kellner, Ursula (1999) *Messages from the Threshold: Die You-Erzählform als Ausdruck liminaler Wesen und Welten*, Bielefeld: Aisthesis.

Woolf, Virginia (1924/1988) "Mr Bennett and Mrs Brown", *The Essays of Virginia Woolf*, Vol. 3 (1919–1924), edited by Andrew McNeillie, London: The Hogarth Press, 384–389.

Woolf, Virginia (1926/1972) "How Should One Read a Book", *Collected Essays*, Vol. 2, edited by Leonard Woolf, London: The Hogarth Press, 1–11.

Young, Molly (2014) "Love is Strange: *All the Rage* by A.L. Kennedy", *New York Times*, www.nytimes.com/2014/07/27/books/review/all-the-rage-by-a-l-kennedy.html?_r=0 (accessed 3 February 2018).

9   What's in an Echo?

Voice, Gender and Genre in Ali Smith's Short Stories

María Casado Villanueva

Introduction

Ali Smith is not only a prolific short story writer, but she has also shared her views on the particularities of this genre, both in interviews and through her eminently metafictional literary practice. The opening narrative of her collection *The First Person and Other Stories* (2008), titled "true short story", is among other things a commentary on the nature of the short story and, specifically, on the intersection of genre and gender which is the general focus of the present volume. In this story, as well as in other narratives of the collection, the concepts of voice and response are central. For this reason, drawing on Bakhtin's notion of dialogism as "verbal-ideological decentering" (1981b: 370) and on its implications for feminist theory, I attempt to pinpoint some ways in which the treatment of voice and multivocality in Smith's stories – mainly those in *The First Person* – relates to both genre and gender.

Why Is the Short Story like a Nymph?

In the last decade or so, Smith's work has been relatively widely discussed, with a focus on her uses of perspectivism, metafiction, ecocriticism and authorial presence, as well as on the tensions between fragmentariness and connection (in both short stories and novels) and on the ethical issues which emerge from such formal concerns. *The First Person and Other Stories*, which is Smith's fourth story collection, received some nuanced positive reviews. For some critics, the book is lacking the freshness and originality of previous collections, since the author tends to resort again to the linguistic virtuosity and metafictional devices she had displayed in past works (see Ahmed 2008; Gee 2008; Lea 2016; Tyler 2008). *The First Person and Other Stories*, however, is also the collection where the intersection between genre and gender is more openly addressed, and its opening narrative, "true short story", illuminates some of the author's views on this issue.

"true short story" is an autobiographical account, highly unconventional in structure and radically metafictional, composed, as Smith herself defines in the book's front matter, as a "playful response" (Smith 2010) to an unfortunate metaphor used by Alex Linklater, deputy editor of *Prospect* magazine, in his discourse on the launching of a major new prize for short story writers.[1] Linklater spoke in the following terms:

> The novel is a capacious old whore: everyone has a go at her, but she rarely emits so much as a groan for their efforts [... T]he short story, on the other hand, is a nimble goddess: she selects her suitors fastidiously and sings like a dove when they succeed. The British literary bordello is heaving with flabby novels; it's time to give back some love to the story.
>
> (Pauli 2005)

In "true short story", the narrator (Ali) sits at a table in a coffee house and overhears two men talking about the above-mentioned genres in similar terms. The novel, a young man says to the lecherous delight of his elderly interlocutor, "is serviceable, roomy, warm and familiar [...] but really a bit used up, really a bit too slack and loose", "[a] flabby old whore. [...] Whereas the short story, by comparison, [is] a nimble goddess, a slim nymph. Because so few people [have] mastered the short story she [is] still in very good shape" (Smith 2010: 4). Intrigued by the misogynist allegory, Ali phones her friend and scholar Kasia Boddy to know her opinion about it. She and Boddy propose playful alternatives to the joke-like question "Why is the short story like a nymph?", and the narrator offers a retelling of Ovid's metamorphosis of Echo calling the episode "a short story that most people already think they know about a nymph" (Smith 2010: 11). The narrative starts in the usual way, but then takes somehow a different turn as the nymph transforms slightly but impudently the words she was deemed to repeat:

> That's you sorted, Juno said.
>   You sordid, Echo said.
>   Right. I'm off back to the hunt, Juno said.
>   The cunt, Echo said.
>   Actually, I'm making up that small rebellion. There is actually no rebelliousness for Echo in Ovid's original version of the story.
>
> (Smith 2010: 12)

The narrative of Echo in "true short story" is followed by the narrator's first memory of Boddy, who let her inquisitive voice be heard during a lecture which they both attended as students. Boddy's intervention is regarded as audacious in a context in which the narrator herself avows that as

a postgraduate student at Cambridge [...] I had lost my voice
[... T]wo years of a system of hierarchies so entrenched that girls
and women were still a bit of a novelty had somehow knocked what
voice I had out of me.

(Smith 2010: 13)

Towards the end of "true short story" the narrator quotes the views of famous writers on the short story genre, among others, Grace Paley's idea that
"short stories are, by nature, about life, and that life itself is always found in
dialogue and argument", and concludes that the distinctiveness of the short
story resides on the fact that "the echo of it answers back" (Smith 2010: 17).

Smith's naughty portrayal of the mythological nymph and the final
statement of "true short story" are suggestive and thought-provoking,
and they imply that in the short story resides a voice with subversive potential. The author seems to endorse the ideas which the Irish short story
writer Frank O'Connor articulated in his essay *The Lonely Voice* (1962),
where he argues that "the conception of a short story as miniature art
is inherently false"; rather, the short story is defined by its engagement
with the *voice* of "submerged populations" (1962/2011: 26). Smith's
choice of words, "answers back", evokes the postcolonial practice of
appropriation by "writing back" and hints at the notion of literature
as response, suggesting the reciprocity of conversation and thus putting
forward a consideration of the short story as especially suited to open up
a dialogue between texts and between readers and texts. In an interview
with Kasia Boddy, Smith elaborates on this idea:

There is always an answering back and that answering back is really
exciting [...] Dialogue is absolutely life. The whole of life happens
in dialogue [...] and response is the place at which we get to be our
most human and playful. [...] [W]hen you got two minds engaged,
they open up whole worlds, incredibly vast new worlds, and beyond
that, there's a multilogue as well which is that the worlds themselves
start to connect [...] The dialogic element, the life of form and the
form of life both become spotlit in the story form.

(Boddy 2010: 73)

Not coincidentally, most of Smith's shorter narratives are dialogues, or
textual collages which include fragments of stories, trivia, pieces of news
and of songs and texts, which interrupt (and sometimes constitute) the
main story; a choir of voices which conflate, conflict and harmonise.
Thus, Mikhail Bakhtin's theories about polyphony and dialogism, as
well as their reinterpretations by feminist critics, constitute an especially
apt theoretical frame for a discussion about the ways in which Smith's
short fictions channel alternative voices and articulate unconventional
understandings of gender and identity.

Bakhtin, Genre and Gender

The concept of dialogism as formulated by Bakhtin suggests that speech emerges as the conflation of a multiplicity of speakers with divergent intentions and meanings. Language itself is conceived of as stratified in a number of varieties and thus, by essence, heteroglossic (Bakhtin 1984: 40). Polyphonic and dialogic texts stage a variety of voices, yet dialogism, as Bakhtin conceives it, goes beyond the linguistic and literary domains to become a central element not only of his notion of the self, but also of his exploration of the personal, social and ideological fields. In this system of thought, voice becomes a central notion: "I hear voices in everything", Bakhtin writes, "and dialogic relations between them" (1968b: 169). This centrality of voice in literature is foregrounded by the fact that it is through the act of speaking that the character actualises itself (Bakhtin 1984: 7). Moreover, these voices are never fully consistent and homogeneous but always, at least, double, conveying various messages simultaneously (Bakhtin 1981c: 65).

For Smith, the voice is seen as a corrective to the seeming superficiality of the image. The narrator of "The Good Voice" (*Public Library* [2015]) states that she wishes to write a story "about voice, not image, because everything's image these days and I have a feeling we're getting further and further away from human voices" (Smith 2015: 25). Thus, in most of her stories, she focuses explicitly on the workings of multiple vocality and her narratives often take the shape of dynamic dialogues where speakers interact, change roles and become narrators of secondary stories.

Although, for Bakhtin, the concepts of dialogism and heteroglossia are epitomised by the novel, and though he glosses over any reference to gender in his work, his ideas can illuminate discussions on both the short story and the articulation of female voices. In fact, the most problematic aspect of Bakhtin's theories derives from his inflexibility to acknowledge the potentially dialogical character of all literary genres, although he predicted that the future of all literature is to become "novelized" (Bakhtin 1981a: 7). According to Bakhtin, there is a subversive power in the novel which is related to its "unofficial" or counter-canonical status as a genre in a literary context dominated by poetry and the epic (1981a: 3). Yet one could argue in favour of the even more marginal status of the short story in terms of genre, for centuries neglected as a worthy object of study (Patea 2012: 6).

Moreover, it has been argued that the absences which the genre's brevity imposes underscore the value of the voices and stories heard at the margins of the explicit. In his study about the English short story, Adrian Hunter underlines the polyphonic nature of Joyce's epiphanies, which far from reflecting a "unifying determinate moment of insight or closure" work as "spaces in which every utterance enters into what M.M. Bakhtin elsewhere characterizes as a 'tension-filled environment of alien words, value judgements and accents'" (Hunter 2007: 58). Similarly, Smith praises the "explosive *resonances*" of Katherine Mansfield's work, her "democratic sense of hearing", her ability to "renew language", to play with the effects of the contiguity of apparently unrelated pieces of story, to "float on the surface on one level while doing fifteen things below that surface, holding them all below the surface" (Fountain 2014; my emphasis). Mansfield's stories often disclose an ambiguity, progressively and indirectly, through symbolism and double meanings. When her characters express themselves, they often fall into inconsistencies, allowing glimpses of an unofficial discourse which undermine the apparent totality of the hegemonic one.[2] These same features which reveal the dialogic nature of language are characteristic of Smith's own narratives, but her postmodern aesthetics and metafictional practice allow her to overtly focus and comment on such devices.

Dialogical thought is subversive because it entails an overcoming of the binaries of Western mentality which articulate patriarchal ideology. Therefore, the theory of dialogism has been productively incorporated into feminist criticism, since Bakhtin's conception of meaning as generated in the liminal space between two conflating voices is in line with the premises of feminist critical theory. Thus, for instance, in her essay "The Laugh of the Medusa", Hélène Cixous states that

> writing is precisely working (in) the in-between, inspecting the process of the same and of the other without which nothing can live, undoing the work of death, infinitely dynamized by an incessant process of exchange from one subject to another.
>
> (1976: 883)

Cixous' "phallogocentric order" corresponds to Bakhtin's monoglossic discourse, which can only be transgressed through the subversion of its norms (Gasbarrone 1994: 4).

Feminist criticism also situates the notion of "voice" in a privileged position within texts, underlining its heteroglossic nature. Julia Kristeva introduced Bakhtin's thought in the Western world and intersected his ideas with semiotic theory. She placed them within a psychoanalytical framework, embracing the notions of dialogism and intersubjectivity to develop her own theories of intertextuality (1966/1980). Dialogism also resonates in Irigaray's idea of the "Speculum" and of a female voice characterised by the tensions between the perception of the feminine as subject and as object (1974). Elaine Showalter's theory of women's writing as "double-voiced", encompassing "the social, literary and cultural heritages of both the muted and the dominant" (1981: 201), recalls Bakhtin's notion of "double-voiced discourse" (1984: 199). Most interestingly, a dialogue between Bakhtinian and feminist theories serves to dismantle essentialist ideas of female writing as a type of discourse with specific features which emphasise female experience (such as possessing particular rhythms, expressing a nostalgia for the maternal or being directly related to the unconscious and the body). Rather, it serves to foreground ideas of inclusion, diversification and, ultimately, decentering, in a type of writing which Cixous defined at one point as an "ensemble of the same and the other" (1976: 883). Thus, it has been argued that there cannot be a univocal interpretation of the notion of female writing just because, in its struggle against the hegemonic language of logic, this discourse shows a tendency to become diverse, "polyphonic", "dialogic" (Jardine 1981: 230) and "pluralized" (Furman qtd. in Bauer and McKinstry 1991: 11). For Dale Bauer and Susan Jaret McKinstry (1991: 10–11), it is precisely the patriarchal zeal to silence dissonant voices what undermines its authority because it points at what is unsaid. It is this speaking of "none" (the woman deprived of identity) where the speaking of "not one", but of necessarily multiple voices emerges. It is not surprising that terms such as "the female dialogic" (Herrmann 1989: 21) and "feminist dialogics" (Bauer and McKinstry 1991: 1) have been productively used to characterise the different ways in which texts have inscribed alterity at the margins of conflicting voices, questioning the idea of a "feminist monologic voice" (Bauer and McKinstry 1991: 4). Furthermore, accepting the plural nature of voice implies recognising that "the singularity of the female voice is at best an illusion, at worst the silencing of the many experiences and contexts about which and within which women have spoken through the ages" (Hohne and Wussow 1994: ix).

Bearing in mind Smith's metaphor of the short story as an echo, I will explore in the next sections some of the ways in which her short stories become suitable means to enact the dialogical principle of staging conflicting voices which seek to defy pre-established ideas about culture, genre and identity. First, her short narratives focus on acts of revision and appropriation of previous cultural discourses, thematising the inescapable intertextual nature of language and literature and addressing the possibilities of subversion in language, an issue of concern both for Bakhtin and feminist theory. Second, Smith's writing, like the voice of Echo in her story, is characterised by humorous wordplay, a strategy which destabilises language and shakes the idea of a fixed identity; an effect which the fragmentariness of the short story intensifies. Finally, her technique favours an illusion of orality which is more successfully sustained in shorter narratives (Lepaludier 2006), integrating forms of imaginative storytelling which liberate her characters from cultural and linguistic constraints.

Appropriation and Agency in The First Person and Other Stories

Bakhtin explains his appraisal of the multi-layered nature of language in the following terms:

> Each utterance is filled with *echoes* and reverberations of other utterances to which it is related by the communality of the sphere of speech communication. Every utterance must be regarded primarily as a *response* to preceding utterances of the given sphere.
>
> (1968a: 91; my emphases)

This view foregrounds an element of predetermination in every speech act while pointing at its potential to reply to previous discourse. Katherina Clark and Michael Holquist summarise Bakhtin's view on the elasticity of language and meaning by stating that for him "language it is not a 'prison house' [...] it is an 'ecosystem'" (1984: 227).

At the heart of Bakhtin's philosophy lays a conception of language and of individual conscience which moves between two poles of forces in an unequal dialectical struggle: on the one hand, the "centripetal" unifying forces, which aim at coherence, and, on the other, the "centrifugal" forces, which lead to fragmentation and heterogeneity (1981b: 270). Therefore, language can never be totalising: even the most authoritarian discourse contains within itself the germ of rebellion. In contrast to psychoanalytical readings of the voice which attribute it disruptive powers out of the subject's control, Bakhtin endows the subject with a certain degree of agency to bend the discourse subversively.

Smith's rewriting of Ovid's metamorphosis of Echo implies a similar understanding of the constraining and liberating dimensions of language: it is an ecosystem, or rather an "echosystem" which, like the Ovidian nymph, both reproduces and resists surrounding discourses. Moreover, in "true short story", the figure of the nymph juxtaposed to the episode at Cambridge and its reference to silenced women informs Smith's reading of Echo with a feminist ethos. Adriana Cavarero points out that

> in the economy of the patriarchal symbolic order, Echo is but the younger sister of the mute woman [...] Women in general, it could be said, adapt themselves to a silence that conforms to a 'natural' feminine inadequacy when it comes to logos. For Echo, on the other hand, it is a matter of revocalizing logos through a voice that is totally drained of its semantic component.
>
> (2005: 167)

As Miller-Frank has noticed, the feminist attempts to restate the value of feminine voice "may be seen as a response to this representational tradition, as an effort to hear Echo's lost words" (1995: 1). Moreover, feminist theory, relying on a psychoanalytical appraisal of language, has often been concerned with the alienation of women in language. In this sense, Judith Butler states that speaking is always "the melancholic reiteration of a language that one never chose, that one does not find as an instrument to be used, but that one is, as it were, used by, expropriated in" (1993: 242). Nevertheless, as Irigaray points out, although mimicry is the only possibility for women within patriarchy, this has an ambiguous effect: "To play with mimesis is thus, for a woman, to try to recover the place of her exploitation by discourse, without allowing herself to be simply reduced to it" (1985: 76). Also, Cavarero hints at the subversive power of the echoic voice, stating that a focus on its reiterative nature constitutes itself a challenge to patriarchal logos. The reason is that repetition is the mechanism of performativity, and therefore emphatic repetition lays bare that mechanism (2005: 168). Dale Bauer argues that a feminist understanding of Bakhtin's dialogism would always emphasise this contradictory dimension of language:

> Language is not merely a prison house; it does not only cage human potential (although it does that, too), but also produces eruptions of force which do not always follow the norms or conventions that language commands. The very language which restricts human intercourse produces occasions for its own disruption and critique.
>
> (1988: xiii)

If we take these ideas into account, Smith's rewriting of the myth of Echo in "true short story" is in itself an act of reiterative insubordination: appropriating mythology is a strategy of the subaltern that mirrors Echo's appropriation of Juno's discourse in this narrative. For Barthes, "the fundamental character of the mythical concept is to be appropriated" (1993: 119), and Cixous's seminal "The Laugh of the Medusa" (1976) also rests on her reinterpretation of a mythical figure. In her novel *Girl Meets Boy* (2007), Smith had reinterpreted the myth of Iphis to inquire into notions of gender fluidity and unconventional sexuality and identity (see Doloughan 2011: 100–106; Mitchell 2013). At one point, the androgynous character Robin reflects:

> Do myths spring fully formed from the imagination and the needs of a society [...] as if they emerged from society's subconscious? Or are myths conscious creations by the various money-making forces. For instance, is advertising a new kind of myth-making?
>
> (Smith 2010: 89)

She further explains: "Nobody grows up mythless [...] It's what we do with the myths we grow up with that matters" (Smith 2010: 98).

Through her rewriting of the myth of Echo, Smith both exerts agency over the inherited story and endows her nymph with agency over Juno's discourse. Echo's voice in Smith's story is repetition with a twist, and the rewriting of a myth which is the same "but not quite" invites the reader to reassess the values inscribed in the source version and in the process of myth-making itself.

Emily Horton, who emphasises the ethical concerns that inform Smith's stories, has discussed how her characters resist the determining conditions imposed by impersonal and suffocating urban scenarios by showing an "intensity of response" which liberates them from such spatial constrains (2013: 15). In *The First Person*, "No Exit" and "I know something you don't know" are clear examples of this, according to Horton (2013: 15). In the same way, other characters of the collection, like Echo, also challenge the determinism of language and tradition. Three stories in particular focus on linguistic and cultural alienation and stage encounters with conflictive social discourses with varying results.

"the child", second story of the collection, addresses the issue of performative repetition from a humorous yet pessimistic perspective. It illustrates an encounter with the embodiment of monologic discourse, which bars the possibility of dialogue and hyperbolises the tensions between character and voice. It opens with the narrator finding the cutest of toddlers in the shopping trolley she had left out of sight for a moment. No one claims the baby, and everybody insists it must be hers, so she feels forced to take the child against her will (mockingly addressing the social pressure which makes of maternity an obligation for women). The beautiful creature's talking abilities prove to be uncannily precocious when, in its sweet RP, voices right-wing statements and a number of rude, racist and misogynistic jokes. Ironically, the pre-symbolic use of voice often associated with baby language, evocative in its rhythms and musicality of a prelapsarian state of contact with the mother, is here substituted by pure *logos*, by fully articulated political discourse. At first fascinated by its beauty and apparent helplessness, then amused by some of the jokes but progressively horrified by its disturbing remarks, the narrator ends up abandoning the baby at the next supermarket. The child's unsettling ventriloquising underlines the alienating nature of language, and the ways ideology operates through statements which reverberate in our daily conversations and in the media and which configure social realities by virtue of repetition. Since the narrator is too taken aback to retort or counter the discourse in any way, dialogue fails and the ending suggests the story will simply repeat itself.

"Fidelio and Bess", although melancholic in theme, offers a more positive take on the issue of dialogic appropriation and agency. It illustrates what Bakhtin described as a process of hybridisation, showing how cultural history is not a matter of continuity but a dynamic process generated when dissonant traditions meet (1981b: 303). The piece is one many

Smith's "you-I stories", composed as a dialogue between two lovers. The first-person narrative voice tries to retell a blending of the operas *Fidelio* by Beethoven and *Porgy and Bess* by George Gershwin as way to express her feelings of estrangement and hopelessness in a relationship described as "doomed" (Smith 2010: 79). This I-voice is the third party in a relationship, younger and less educated than the interlocutor (referred to as "you"). The latter interrupts the account of the re-imagined story and rejects this act of appropriation, betraying the role of repetition as a mechanism of power assertion:

> You can't, you say.
>   Can't what? I say.
>   Culture's fixed, you say. That's why it's culture. That's how it gets to be art. That's how it works. That's why it works.
>
> (Smith 2010: 76)

Nevertheless, the narrator manages to finish this new version of the story and, significantly, it is one in which a marginalised female character in Beethoven's opera is given a central role and a more prominent voice. The echoed pieces acquire new significance when set against each other in a different context, as the borrowed words give voice to the narrator's own experience.

"the history of history" presents the conflict between a young narrative voice and her rebellious mother with uncertain results.[3] The story addresses explicitly, and humorously, the possibilities of revising history, and of resisting compliance with cultural expectations. The teenage narrator is taking "language and history" at school, and language and history set limits to her* imagination and speech. She* tries to write an episode of British history as a newspaper report for homework and it is unclear whether she* cannot help using the sexist references and tone typical of the yellow press, or if she is mockingly criticising them. At the same time, her* mother begins a personal emancipatory campaign, seemingly at the expense of her family's needs, which the narrator finds outrageous. At one point the mother throws down the stairs a novel by Georgette Heyer (author of regency romances), shouting "Christ almighty I hate these fucking books [...] they are full of shit", and the young narrator is scandalised by the language, of which she* "very much disapproved" (Smith 2010: 98), using the snobbish phrasing of an adult. At the end of the story, when the angry narrator blames her* mother for being neglectful, the latter reproachfully answers: "You used to be so much more of an independent thinker", but adds: "You are tenacious, like me" (Smith 2010: 101). The parallelism between the characters is emphasised by the fact that the narrator had, at the beginning of the story, expressed her* own disgust for Gide's *La Symphonie Pastoral*, which she* considered "a load of sentimental rubbish" (Smith 2010: 94).

Most ironically, she* tells her* friend: "Worst fucking thing is, she's [her* mother's] started swearing now" (Smith 2010: 100). The tensions remain unresolved, but the issues of cultural and linguistic determinism and the possibility of rebelliousness emerge again as central topics.

What Is a Pun There For?: Meaning Decentred and A Decentred Identity

The stories discussed above do not only address the possibilities of re-writing cultural and literary tradition as a form of participating in culture and a vindication of silenced voices: they also show the limitations and contradictions inherent to this task. This practice is in line with what Anne Herrmann defines as female dialogics, which is a step beyond the rewriting of literary tradition as it does not only reveal silenced stories within the official ones but recognises the intrinsic dialogic character of language (1989: 21). From a formal point of view, an emphasis on this essential dialogism means to offer resistance against the attempts to enforce an unchallenged association between signifier and signified characteristic of monologic discourse, an effort which Smith openly undertakes.

Wordplay is an apparent feature of Smith's aesthetics, and one which seeks to undermine the stability of the relationship between word and meaning. This ludic practice, which Echo's retorts in "true short story" illustrate, is a further example of the possibilities of the individual to take an active part in the reversal of hierarchies, escaping the determinacy of language and allowing for carnivalesque relief. Puns become a central theme in Smith's novel *There but for the*, where the intellectually precocious nine-year-old Brooke asks "What exactly is a pun, therefore?" to another character whose echoing reply is: "What exactly is a pun there for?" (2011: 35). It is significant that, for Brooke, puns and the creative coinage of words become not only a source of enjoyment but also of liberation at a moment when she is being bullied by for her intelligence and loquacity. Narrative voices and characters take delight in playing with the multiple meanings of words also in the short stories. Double-meanings counteract the illusion that there is a logic in language while evoking meaningful associations.

The third narrative of *First Person*, titled "present", illustrates Smith's ability to exploit the diverse meanings of a word to expand the interpretations of her narratives. The action takes place in a solitary pub on a Christmas night where the narrator witnesses a dispirited conversation between a local man and a waitress, the only people at the bar. To avoid being drawn into the exchange, the narrator retreats to her car. Soon, though, she resents the solitude and starts imagining a dialogue with the other two, who ask her to tell a Christmas episode from her childhood. The narrator's musings lead her to avow her need for personal contact and she re-enters the pub (Horton 2013: 16–17). Different meanings of the title emerge as the story progresses. The idea of a gift is alluded to in the context of Christmas: the whisky the narrator is drinking was a present to herself (Smith 2010: 39). The man's socks were possibly someone's present to him, and he could tell to a group of friends that the food at the pub was "the best present anyone gave him" (Smith 2010: 47). In the course of the imagined conversation, however, the man mocks the narrator for using the historical present when asked to tell them a happy anecdote from her childhood: "Happy is not the word I'd have used at the time, I say. I'm about twelve", the narrator says, to which the man responds: "I don't mean this to sound rude but you look a bit older than twelve" (Smith 2010: 48). A reference to Dickens' *A Christmas Carol*, "Christmas past, Christmas present, Christmas near future" (Smith 2010: 49), further underlines this temporal meaning. Moreover, the narrator dwells in the solipsistic fantasy that she needs to be *present* in the pub for the other two to continue their talk. The title also refers back to two quotations in "true short story": Nadine Gordimer's "short stories are absolutely about the present moment" (Smith 2010: 15) and Cynthia Ozick's comparison of the short story with a "talismanic gift given to the protagonist of a fairy tale" (Smith 2010: 16). As a result of the title's resistance to convey a single meaning, the story becomes a commentary about our perceptions of time, how it works in narration and how this particular narrative exemplifies some features of the short story genre. The sense of history characteristic of the novel is here absent, and momentariness is emphasised. Both in "present" and in the embedded memory of the narrator, the isolated moment acquires significance when individualised.

In Smith's narratives, the instability of language is paralleled by an equally unstable conception of identity. In her short stories in particular, Smith's characters are eminently vague. They sketch themselves and develop mostly through speech, but because they lack a history and the genre limits the length of their interventions, they remain highly schematic. This open understanding of identity as an ongoing process realised through voice is also in line with Bakhtin's idea that the subject configures itself in speech and through interaction. Bakhtin's theories about literature and culture stem from a complex appraisal of the subject which not only puts forward the notion of agency, but also undermines the idea of coherent subjectivity. He elaborated on these views in his earlier work which foregrounds the subjects' contingency on the specific circumstances of the moment (Bakhtin 1993: 12–13), the necessity of their active role in this self-constituting process (Bakhtin 1993: 29), an essential interaction with the other (Bakhtin 1993: 15–17) and the "unfinizability" of this process (1993: 13).

In Smith's stories, the intentional decentring of words' meanings and the rendering of decentred identities are brought together through one of her most striking technical devices – namely, her treatment of personal pronouns and the way she exploits their possibilities as empty signifiers. In most of Smith's stories, the reading process is often mired and enriched by the author's/narrator's decision to conceal the gender of some of the characters through a preference for first-person narratives with an addressee. The prominent use of non-gendered "I" and "you" helps to destabilise the binary system upon which gender rests for, as Herrmann points out:

> The first-person pronoun is the least stable of all linguistic signifiers, since its referent changes with every utterance [...] By masking its gender it obscures the fact that any subject speaks from a position marked by sexual difference; by masquerading as genderless it embodies the possibility of disrupting difference by eliminating gender altogether.
>
> (1989: 22)

Smith's conception of self-construction in dialogue also constitutes an alternative to a binary and hierarchal pattern of identity as defined by opposition to an objectified "Other", very much in line with Herrmann's notion of "female dialogic" (1989: 28–29). In this way, Smith emphasises gender and identity as eminently fluid, an idea which is foregrounded in *The First Person*'s front matter through Mansfield's quotation: "True to oneself! Which self?" (Smith 2010). At the same time, Herrmann acknowledges the impossibility of a complete effacement of sexual difference in writing because authors "must necessarily inscribe themselves in that conflict as historical subjects" (1989: 10). Indeed, Smith engages with the relations between real life and story, and the authorial presence within her texts is something that Felicity Skelton (2009) and Michelle Ryan-Sautour (2013) have aptly explored. Ryan-Sautour has highlighted Smith's ability to exploit the incomplete character of the short story to frame an exchange between the fictional and the real. Smith's narratives, she holds, disclose the potential of the genre "to connect with life and constructions of the self" (Ryan-Sautour 2013). At one level, they explore the fictional possibilities of the non-fictional; at another level, the tensions between continuity and fragmentariness found in Smith's collections – particularly in *The First Person and Other Stories* – mirror the author's complex appraisal of identity as both fragmentary and continuous. Smith's texts, Ryan-Sautour points out, stage Judith Butler's concept of *étrangereté*, which again underlines the dialogic nature of identity:

> I may try to tell the story of myself, but another story is already at work in me, and there is no way to distinguish between the 'I' who has emerged from this infantile condition and the 'you'. The set of 'you's' who inhabits and dispossesses my desire from the outset.
>
> (Butler 2005: 74; qtd. in Ryan-Sautour 2013)

Thus, Smith's "you-I" stories invite an interpretation of their multiple voices as exteriorisation of this decentred self (selves). They also recall Irigaray's notion of specularity, a further step in the representation of the dialogic, since the speculum offers a mirror image which, as the reverberating voice of Echo, allows one to see (hear) oneself as Other. Enacting the principle of female dialogics would mean to give voice to subjects which perceive themselves both as object and subject. The intention of staging a dialogised self also explains the recurrence of ghostly presences in Smith's narratives. When asked to deliver some lectures in comparative literature in Cambridge University, Smith avoided the lecture-like tone characteristic of monologic discourse by devising a fictional self which addresses her* deceased partner, come back from the dead. Similar discussions on life and art also take the form of dialogues in "the ex-wife", a story included in *Public Library* (2015), where the narrator has recently broken up a relationship with her partner, a Katherine Mansfield scholar, partly because of the partner's obsession with her object of study. Some time later, the narrator has an encounter with the spectre of the writer, with whom she converses (interestingly, all of Mansfield's sudden interventions have been extracted from her diaries and letters, thus echoing a literary tradition which helps the narrator to understand her ex-partner's fascination).

The irruption of these spectres also creates a fissure in the characters' coherent sense of time and reality and often leads to a disintegration of discourse. Nevertheless, the breakage of the natural time flow provides a logic which is alternative to dominant causal and chronological conceptions and which "is rather the Other logic of the [female] dialogic" (Herrmann 1989: 16). These presences tend to trigger off an empathic response in the characters, resulting in a sort of emotional wholeness and an acceptance of the dialogical nature of identity. Thus, in "the hanging girl" in *Other Stories and other stories* (1999), mentally unstable Pauline gets emotionally bound to a girl who nobody else can see. Significantly, the ghostly girl irrupts into Pauline's reality after she has been confronted with the echo of her own voice, which – unsettling like the nymph's in "true short story" – shakes Pauline's grip on reality:

> Pauline sneezed, and heard the sneeze repeat itself in the church a fraction of a second after it had left her nose. Bless me, she said. Less me, the echo said. She lay as flat as she could [...] nothing there, she said. Air, the echo said. I give up. I'm going mad. I am, Pauline said. Vup.Ad.Am, the echo said.
>
> (Smith 1999: 24)[4]

In *The First Person*, this discontinuous aspect of identity is perfectly exemplified by the tenth story, "writ". The narrator of the story "present" had started her childhood account using the present form to refer to herself in the past: "I'm about twelve" (Smith 2010: 48). In "writ", the middle-aged narrator has received an unexpected kiss which brings back a memory of her teenage years and, this time, her fourteen-year-old self turns up in flesh in the middle of her living room. The story presents the process of growing up as one of linguistic change, foregrounding the relationship between voice and identity and the instability of both. In the encounter with the narrators' two selves, dialectal, diachronic and social linguistic varieties interact. The young self questions the narrator's uses of language:

> You go girl, I say.
>   She looks at me as if I'm insane. Where? she says.
>   Ha, I say. No, you go girl is a phrase, like a cliché. It's from music. It means good on you, too right, that kind of thing. It's American. It's borrowed from black culture. It's from later. I mean, you're too young for it.
>
> (Smith 2010: 154–155)

Hearing the teenager's voice (her own, yet not quite) talking back to her provokes a strong emotional response in the narrator: "Her accent is so where I'm from and so unadulterated that hearing her say more than four words in a row makes my chest hurt inside" (Smith 2010: 155). The disturbing undermining of the narrator's sense of reality brought about by the girl's presence is counterbalanced by the restoration of a regained sense of the self as dynamic and fluid.

Spinning the Yarn: Narrative Voice and Creative Storytelling

Finally, Smith's conception of the short story as an echo is illuminating, for it also suggests a preoccupation with the idea of voice as emanating from the text, even when countered by constant reminders of the artifice involved in writing. She stated at an interview:

> I think everything is voice. I don't think anything exists without voice. The first thing that anything written does is go to voice. And to think that prose doesn't have that voice, even if it is in the third-person voice, is just not using our ears, because everything has voice.
>
> (Beer 2013: 138)

The paradoxes of the voice in text were also addressed by Bakhtin, who discussed the effects of *skaz*, a literary device conceived to create an illusion of orality by endowing the narrative voice with conversational traits and a particular idiolect. This technique emphasises the dialogical relationship between addresser and addressee, writer and reader.[5] For Bakhtin, *skaz* is a technique which further evidences the dialogism inherent in language, for it is "above all orientation towards the speech of another, and only then, as consequence, towards oral speech" (1984: 199).[6] Moreover, this artifice seeks to veil the permanent nature of the written text bringing to the fore the transient nature and continuous actualisation of discourse (Lepaludier 2006: 2). Non-coincidentally, the examples of *skaz* that Bakhtin – contrary to his concentration in the novel – mentions are short stories, as their brevity and focus on significant moments make them especially suited for this delusion which would be difficult to sustain through a longer narrative.

Smith's short stories intentionally underline the oral/aural effects of the text, which become apparent in a writing style filled with colloquialisms and that reflects the hesitant quality of spoken speech. It is in transcriptions of conversations and in first-person narrative accounts that the oral dimension of narrative voice is accentuated (Lepaludier 2006: 4), and Smith's "you-I" stories clearly bring this impression to the fore. Moreover, these voices in dialogue often become the tellers of secondary stories, sharing memories or made-up tales, thus complicating their position as participants in a conversation and becoming intradiegetic narrators. This technique helps to thematise a concern with the different positions that the narrative voice can occupy regarding its subject narrative and the effects and ethical issues involved in this choice.

This preoccupation is addressed in *The First Person* through the triad formed by the stories titled "the third person", "the second person" and "the first person". "the third person", which precedes the other two in the collection, opens with the objective tone of a "camera-eye" technique, thus privileging the visual and distancing itself from the oral. It presents a total of eight apparently unrelated tableaux taking place in different geographical and temporal settings. Through a number of linking metaphors, which refer in reverse order to the previous sketches, the story reflects on the implications of the narrative uses of this perspective. The choral of images and, progressively, of voices and thoughts is fully orchestrated by the narrator, who begins and suspends the narratives at will, as a "presentiment of God" (Smith 2010: 68).

Precisely these last words are echoed in "the second person", where embedded narratives are presented within a dialogical frame and the participants in the conversation become alternatively narrators, narratees and subjects of the narrative. As Ryan-Sautour observes, the story "foregrounds fabulation in relation to the self and other" (2013). The characters mirror those in "Fidelio and Bess" for there is an imbalance of power between a seemingly more knowledgeable voice (in this case, the "I") and a younger one (the second person, the "you"). "You're something else, you. You really are. This is the kind of thing you'd do" (Smith 2010: 121), the I-voice states at the beginning of the narrative. Typical of the other's behaviour would be to fall in love with two enormous accordions and buy them, even if unable to play. The partner, like a character rebelling against its author, finds the account outrageous:

> after... all the years of *dialogue* between us, you think you've got to the right to just decide, *like you're God*, who I am and who I'm not and what I'm like and what I'm not and what I'd do and what I wouldn't.
>
> (Smith 2010: 123; my emphases)

When it is the you-voice's turn to imagine a narrative about the I-voice, the latter interrupts the tale and, offended, provides her* own interpretation of it, preventing all possibility of dialogue. At the end of the story, after the speakers have parted, the narrator receives in the post a big accordion, which signals the apparent compliance of the interlocutor in doing what was expected of her*. Significantly, the card accompanying the parcel contains the words with which the story opened ("You are something else, you" [Smith 2010: 134]), an unsettling echo which once again recalls the permanent intrusion of alien discourse within one's own, while opening up a number of possible endings. Is this submission, apology, or sneering mockery? Is it an invitation to look for the twin instrument or an allegory of solitude? This open-endedness contrasts with the tendency that the I-person had shown to interpret stories univocally.

As a counterpoint, in "the first person" – the story which closes the collection – the process of inventive storytelling in which the speakers engage becomes mutually enriching. Both the first person and the interlocutor reinvent themselves through their exchange, and the story brings to the fore development and fluidity, as well as the joys of wordplay. The speakers relish in the illusion of being "story-free" (although a narrative between parentheses provides a likely account of their real first encounter), and puns and fabulation become sources of energy and renewal. They fantasise about how they met each other, in a narrative in which bodily changes, related to the recurrent theme of metamorphosis in Smith's fiction, become a metaphor for ever-changing identity:

> Instead of an arm, you had, like, a, a violin, and where your hand should be was the scrolly piece of wood at the end of a violin-... it's that I'm going through some changes, you say. Change is necessary. Mutatis mutandis, I say. Mutability. Muton.
>
> (2010: 197)

This foregrounds again an appraisal of identity as unfinished and emerging through voice and in dialogue with the other.

"You are not the first person to spin me a yarn" (Smith 2010: 204), the I-voice states at one point. Most significantly, this idiomatic expression referred to the creative process involved in storytelling echoes another Ovidian tale, that of Philomela.[7] A mirror image of the figure of Echo, she is the silenced woman who tells her tale through the tapestry she weaves. In the entwining of Philomela's voice into the fabric, the "textile" emerges as a perfect metaphor for the ways voices are inscribed in writing, in the "textual". "the third person", "the second person" and "the first person" illustrate a progression from omniscient narration, characteristic of written accounts, to pure character dialogue and a rendition of oral speech. Thus, the three stories become a commentary on the tensions between textuality and orality. At the same time, the narratives stage the contrast between the solipsism involved in writing, which shows a tendency to fictionalise the reader without opening to dialogue, and the possibilities of creative storytelling and revitalising exchange.

Conclusions

In light of the above said, it seems that Smith's stories, specifically those in *The First Person and Other Stories,* illustrate Bakhtin's dialogical understanding of language and identity, principles successfully appropriated by feminist theory to put forward a conception of female voice as polyphonic and decentred. As "true short story" suggests, the genre is particularly apt to channel such voices, since its indeterminacy allows for multiple meanings to resonate in the text. These resonances also work more effectively in brief narratives, as single words and sentences acquire a significance which can be lost among the profusion of words in longer narrative forms. Like the subversive voice of the nymph Echo, Smith's stories underline the oral quality of texts, and lay bare both the alienating nature of language and its dialogic essence, bringing to the fore the liberating possibilities of intertextual dialogue and language play. Since these narratives are fragmentary and open-ended, they become especially suited to reflect an equally emancipating appraisal of the self as ever evolving and emerging through dialogical exchange and imaginative storytelling.

Notes

1 Quotations from Ali Smith's *First Person and Other Stories* are from the 2010 Anchor Books edition.
2 These features are also underlined in the chapter that Dominique Head devotes to the work of Mansfield (1992: 109–138). Carolina Nuñez-Puente sees similar strategies in the work of Charlotte Perkins Gillman. Her stories, she argues, can be read under the lens of Bakhtin's theories as dialogical and hybrid, in terms both of genre and representations of gender (2012: 139–154).
3 I will later discuss the difficulty of establishing the gender of some of Smith's characters. Whenever that is the case I may use feminine pronouns with an asterisk as default reference markers.

4 The spectre has been interpreted as a motif of the Doppelgänger (Sienkiewicz-Charlish 2011), and as an embodiment of an unconscious desire for invigorating human contact repressed in the character's cynical and meaningless every day existence (Sacido-Romero 2016).

5 Tory Young (2015) points at the "metaleptic" implications of Smith's use of the second person in the "you-I" stories, and Ben Davies (2015) investigates the "postal effects" produced by the complicated relations between addresser and addressee.

6 This view contrasts, to a certain extent, with Derrida's idea that orality intensifies the illusion of the presence of a unified subject in the text, and of the existence of a conscience that can be accessed through speech (1981).

7 Feminist criticism has also underlined the role of women as tellers. Karen Rowe argues that fairy tales are typical female narratives in an essay significantly entitled "To Spin a Yarn: The Female Voice in Folklore and Fairy Tale" (1986). Rowe refers to Philomela and Scheherazade to illustrate the liberating potential of the act of storytelling (see also Warner 1994).

References

Ahmed, Fatema (2008) '"Nimble Goddess' Sells Us Short", *Observer*, www.theguardian.com/books/2008/oct/19/fiction (accessed 8 December 2016).

Bakhtin, Mikhail Mikhaïlovich (1968a) "Problems of Speech Genres", in *Speech Genres and Other Late Essays*, edited by Caryl Emerson and Michael Holquist, translated by Vern W. McGee, Austin, TX: University of Texas Press, 60–102.

Bakhtin, Mikhail Mikhaïlovich (1968b) "Towards a Methodology for the Human Sciences", in *Speech Genres and Other Late Essays*, edited by Caryl Emerson and Michael Holquist, translated by Vern W. McGee, Austin, TX: University of Texas Press, 159–177.

Bakhtin, Mikhail Mikhaïlovich (1981a) "Epic and Novel", in *The Dialogic Imagination: Four Essays by M.M. Bahktin*, edited by Michael Holquist, translated by Caryl Emerson and Michael Holquist, Austin, TX: University of Texas Press, 3–41.

Bakhtin, Mikhail Mikhaïlovich (1981b) "Discourse in the Novel", in *The Dialogic Imagination: Four Essays by M.M. Bahktin*, edited by Michael Holquist, translated by Caryl Emerson and Michael Holquist, Austin, TX: University of Texas Press, 259–422.

Bakhtin, Mikhail Mikhaïlovich (1981c) "From the Prehistory of Novelistic Discourse", in *The Dialogic Imagination: Four Essays by M.M. Bahktin*, edited by Michael Holquist, translated by Caryl Emerson and Michael Holquist, Austin, TX: University of Texas Press, 41–83.

Bakhtin, Mikhail Mikhaïlovich (1984) *Problems of Dostoevsky's Poetics*, edited and translated by Caryl Emerson, Minneapolis, MN: University of Minnesota Press.

Bakhtin, Mikhail Mikhaïlovich (1993) *Toward a Philosophy of the Act*, edited by Vadim Liapunov and Michael Holquist, translated by Vadim Liapunov, Austin, TX: University of Texas Press.

Barthes, Roland (1993) *Mythologies*, translated by Anette Lavers, London: Vintage.

Bauer, Dale (1988) *Feminist Dialogics: A Theory of Failed Community*, Albany, NY: State University of New York Press.

Bauer, Dale and S. Jaret McKinstry (1991) "Introduction", in *Feminism, Bakhtin, and the Dialogic*, edited by Dale M. Bauer and S. Jaret McKinstry, New York: State University of New York Press, 1–6.

Beer, Gillian (2013) "Gillian Beer interviews Ali Smith", in *Ali Smith: Contemporary Critical Perspectives*, edited by Monica Germanà and Emily Horton, London: Bloomsbury Publishing.

Boddy, Kasia (2010) "Ali Smith: All There Is, An Interview about the Short Story", *Critical Quarterly* 52(2): 66–82.

Butler, Judith (1993) *Bodies that Matter: On the Discursive Limits of "Sex"*, London: Routledge.

Butler, Judith (2005) *Giving an Account of Oneself*, New York: Fordham University Press.

Cavarero, Adriana (2005) *For More than One Voice: Toward a Philosophy of Vocal Expression*, translated by Paul A. Kottman, Stanford, CA: Stanford University Press.

Cixous, Hélène (1976) "The Laugh of the Medusa", *Signs* 1(4): 875–893.

Clark, Katherina and Michael Holquist (1984) *Mikhail Bakhtin*, Cambridge MA: Harvard University Press.

Davies, Ben (2015) "Address, Temporality and Misdelivery: The Postal Effects of Ali Smith's Short Stories", in *British Women Short Story Writers: The New Woman to Now*, edited by Emma Young and James Bailey, Edinburgh: Edinburgh University Press, 163–178.

Derrida, Jacques (1981) "Plato's Pharmacy", in *Disseminations*, translated by Barbara Johnson, London: Athlone Press, 61–171.

Doloughan, Fiona J. (2011) *Contemporary Narrative: Textual Production, Multimodality and Multiliteracies*, London: Continuum.

Fountain, Trevor (2014) "An Interview with Scottish Author Ali Smith", *Cafebabel*, www.cafebabel.co.uk/culture/article/an-interview-with-scottish-author-ali-smith.html, (accessed 11 October 2016).

Gasbarrone, Lisa (1994) "'The Locus for the Other': Cixous, Bakhtin, and Women's Writing", in *Dialogue of Voices: Feminist Literary Theory and Bakhtin*, edited by Karen Hohne and Helen Wussow, Minneapolis, MN: University of Minnesota Press, 1–19.

Gee, Sophie (2008) "Mad for It", *Financial Times*, 11 October, 19.

Head, Dominic (1992) *The Modernist Short Story*, Cambridge: Cambridge University Press.

Herrmann, Anne (1989) *The Dialogic and Difference: "An/Other Woman" in Virginia Woolf and Christa Wolf*, New York: Columbia University Press.

Hohne, Karne and Helen Wussow (1994) *Dialogue of Voices: Feminist Literary Theory and Bakhtin*, Minneapolis, MN: University of Minnesota Press.

Horton, Emily (2013) "Contemporary Space and Affective Ethics in Ali Smith's Short Stories", in *Ali Smith: Contemporary Critical Perspectives*, edited by Monica Germanà and Emily Horton, London: Bloomsbury Publishing, 9–22.

Hunter, Adrian (2007) *Introduction to the Short Story in English*, Cambridge: Cambridge University Press.

Irigaray, Luce (1974) *Speculum of the Other Woman*, translated by Gillian C. Gill, Ithaca, NY: Cornell University Press.

Irigaray, Luce (1985) *This Sex which Is Not One*, translated by Catherine Porter and Carolyn Burke, Ithaca, NY: Cornell University Press.

Jardine, Alice (1981) "Pre-Texts for the Transatlantic Feminist", *Yale French Studies* 62: 220–236.

Kristeva, Julia (1966/1980) "Word, Dialogue & Novel", in *Desire in Language: A Semiotic Approach to Literature and Art*, edited by Leon S. Roudiez, translated by Alice Jardine, Thomas Gora and Leon S. Roudiez, New York: Columbia University Press, 64–91.

Lea, Daniel (2016) *Twenty-First-Century Fiction: Contemporary British Voices*, Manchester: Manchester University Press.

Lepaludier, Laurent (2006) "What Is This Voice I Read? Problematics of Orality in the Short Story", *Journal of the Short Story in English* 47, https://jsse.revues.org/799?lang=fr (accessed 1 October 2016).

Miller Frank, Felicia (1995) *Mechanical Song: Women, Voice, and the Artificial in Nineteenth-Century French Narrative*, Stanford, CA: Stanford University Press.

Mitchell, Kaye (2013) "Queer Metamorphoses: Girl Meets Boy and the Futures of Queer Fiction", in *Ali Smith: Contemporary Critical Perspectives*, edited by Monica Germanà and Emily Horton, London: Bloomsbury Publishing, 61–74.

Nuñez-Puente, Carolina (2012) "The Yellow Hybrids: Gender and Genre in Gilman's Wallpaper", in *Short Story Theories: A Twenty-First-Century Perspective*, edited by Viorica Patea, Amsterdam: Rodopi, 139–153.

O'Connor, Frank (1962/2011) *The Lonely Voice: A Study of the Short Story*, New York: Melville House.

Patea, Viorica (2012) "The Short Story: An Overview of the History and Evolution of the Genre", in *Short Story Theories: A Twenty-first-Century Perspective*, edited by Viorica Patea, Amsterdam: Rodopi, 1–24.

Pauli, Michelle (2005) "Short Story Scores with New Prize and Amazon Project", *The Guardian*, www.theguardian.com/books/2005/aug/23/news.michellepauli (accessed 2 February 2017).

Rowe, Karen E. (1986) "To Spin a Yarn: The Female Voice in Folklore and Fairy Tale", in *Fairy Tales and Society*, edited by Ruth B. Bottigheimer, Philadelphia, PA: University of Pennsylvania Press, 53–74.

Ryan-Sautour, Michelle (2013) "Transparence Auctoriale et Postures Pronominales dans The First Person and Other Stories de Ali Smith", *Études Britanniques Contemporaines* 44, https://ebc.revues.org/510 (accessed 6 February 2017).

Sacido-Romero, Jorge (2016) "Ghostly Visitations in Contemporary Short Fiction by Women: Fay Weldon, Janice Galloway and Ali Smith", *Atlantis* 38 (2): 83–102.

Showalter, Elaine (1981) "Feminist Criticism in the Wilderness", *Critical Inquiry* 8(2): 179–205.

Sienkiewicz-Charlish, Agnieszka (2011) "Double Identities: The Theme of the Double in Contemporary Scottish Gothic", in *The Supernatural, the Fantastic and the Oneiric*, edited by Piotr Spyra and Agata Wachowska, Łódź: Biblioteka, 79–86.

Skelton, Felicity (2009) "Echo Writes Back: The Figure of the Author in 'True short story' by Ali Smith", *Short Fiction in Theory and Practice* 2(1/2): 99–111.

Smith, Ali (1999) *Other Stories and other stories*, London: Penguin.

Smith, Ali (2010) *The First Person and Other Stories*, New York: Anchor Books.

Smith, Ali (2011) *There but for The*, London: Hamish Hamilton.

Smith, Ali (2015) *Public Library*, London: Penguin.

Tyler, Christopher (2008) "Are your Books Good in Bed?", *The Guardian*, www.theguardian.com/books/2008/oct/04/fiction.alismith (accessed 8 December 2016).

Warner, Marina (1994) *From the Beast to the Blonde: On Fairy Tales and Their Tellers*, London: Chatto and Windus.

Young, Tory (2015) "You-Universal Love: Desire, Intimacy and the Second Person in Ali Smith's Short Fiction", in *Twenty-First-Century British Fiction*, edited by Bianca Leggett and Tony Venezia, Canterbury: Gylphi Limited, 293–312.

10 In a Different Voice

Janice Galloway's Short Stories

Jorge Sacido-Romero

Introduction: Voicing Women

When asked what the word "story" meant to her, Scottish author Janice Galloway answered plainly: "A voice. [...] The real grist of a novel or a short story is not plot, it's voice and perception. That's story" ("Interview with Janice Galloway" 2010). This voiced perception that, for Galloway, constitutes the stuff of her fiction is first and foremost the articulation of "a female perspective" that strives to be recognised as legitimate, valuable and *normal* in a male-dominated world that considers it otherwise:

> I want to write as though having a female perspective is *normal* which is a damn sight harder than it sounds. I don't think people tend to regard 'women's priorities' as in any way normal: so-called *women's issues* are still regarded as deviant, add-on, extra. Not the Big Picture. [...] The structures and *normal* practices of both politics and the law make it *difficult for women to speak as women directly because there's little accommodation for a female way of seeing*. I think women's traditional attraction to fiction is just that – a go at reconstructing the structures.
>
> (March 1999: 85–86; last emphasis mine)

To accommodate, or, what is more, to prioritise silenced female otherness against received assumptions, sweeping categorisations and commodifying strategies is central to Galloway's attempt "to write as a woman, to be as honest about it as possible" and "to produce a cutting-edge, a *voice*" (March 1999: 86, 89).

Ten years before, in an interview on occasion of her highly acclaimed novelistic debut, *The Trick Is to Keep Breathing* (1989), Galloway likewise denounced the male-biased consideration of women's experiences and interests as unworthy literary stuff, yet affirmed that there was "a Scottish dimension" in her work and even went as far as to suggest that "Woman" and "Scotland" were analogous in the sense that both were colonised territories (Thomas 1989). However, as early commentators of her work did not fail to point out, gender and nation are two conflicting dimensions in Galloway's fiction. Thus, for Margery Metzstein, for instance, Galloway's work "analyses and questions the often negative effects of Scottish male culture on the female" (1993: 145), while Mary McGlynn connects Metzstein's view on Galloway's gender-focused rendition of present-day Scotland to the ways in which "the struggle to assert a nationalist identity obscures or doubly marginalizes the assertion of gender (the woman's voice)" (2001: 13).

Galloway's early fiction (*The Trick is to Keep Breathing* [1989] and the short story collection *Blood* [1991]) articulates women's voices mainly in relation to the conflicts that affect female experience *within* the patriarchal contemporary Scottish context, in which women are denied full subjective status.[1] As Cristie L. March argues, "[f]or Galloway, gender provides a means by which to break open the contemporary Scottish experience and reveal what previous decades of Scottish writing had elided" (2002: 109). The central task of articulating and preserving a woman's voice instead of "falling into the conventions of assuming guy stuff is 'real' stuff" (March 1999: 86) accounts for Galloway's priority concern with gender over national and class issues, which were the central focus of her male fellow writers, even of those of an earlier generation like Alasdair Gray and James Kelman. The latter were instrumental in the consolidation of a distinctive tradition of the Scottish novel in the 1980s and 1990s, of which Galloway's *Trick* is often cited as a prominent example (Craig 1999: 192–197; Craig 2006: 126–138; Craig 2012: 267–273; McIlvanney 2012: 228–230). Although Galloway recognised having been influenced by these writers' formal innovations,[2] she raised her voice loud and clear against the obstacles encountered by women writers who wanted to speak as women in Scotland, where the process of redefinition of a distinctive Scottish literary field linked to the political struggle for Devolution (led in both cases by men) dictated nationalist and working-class priorities over those gender concerns that was her task to explore (Galloway 1991: 14).

The firm and rapid progression of Scottish literature towards its official and international recognition in the 1990s meant no improvement in the situation Galloway denounced. For her, the Scottish literary scene remained, in Carole Jones's words, "overwhelmingly male" (2007: 210).[3] The great national and international impact of Welsh's *Trainspotting* (1993) and its filmic version of 1996 led Kristin Innes to argue that the

> much-fêted new visibility of Scottish culture, which coincides with the working-class male's literary enfranchisement, appears to be won at the expense of women, gay men and ethnic minorities, whose *voices are silenced* by the new literature's blatant misogyny, homophobia and racism.
>
> (2007: 302; my emphasis)

The literary developments of the 1990s that led to the establishment of the full-blown category "Scottish Lit." celebrated by the media increased Galloway's feeling of exclusion from a movement that, she felt, continued to marginalise women as it came to be identified with a certain type of male writing which the market promoted and demanded. Thus, to Cristie L. March's suggestion of a possible affinity with Irvine Welsh, Galloway stated in 1999 that the novel she was writing at the time (*Clara* [2002]) gave up Scottish elements altogether. "One reason I might be doing it", Galloway explained,

> is I got bogged down by the whole 'Scottish' sales-tag [...] We were all 'urban and gritty', even those of us who weren't. I felt the strong push of *This is what's expected – this is what you guys do* – and what was usually meant was certain *guys*. The women were to be add-ons again or compare-and-contrast elements. [...] Now that Scottish writing has a profile, it's a bloke's profile, and one I find I wish to distance myself from. The most visible of it seems to be about being blokey – adolescent blokey at that. It doesn't say a great deal to me about what I consider to be the wider priorities. [...] Scotland has always meant something to me. It was a place to stand from a quite literally different perspective. Then that very geographical difference was used to make us out as clones. Scary. I guess shifting off the *overtly*, the *apparently current* Scottish expectations is my stab at centring myself-again.
>
> (March 1999: 92)

As a result of this process of cultural and literary commodification, Galloway argues, Scottish society as a whole was restrictively associated with the concrete social situations depicted in working-class male fiction "with which women have great difficulty identifying" (Jones 2007: 210). Galloway took on the self-appointed task of reconstructing social structures through fiction by making women give up the role of silent supporters to which they were confined, so that their voices could be heard.

Novels Leave, Short Stories Remain

Critics of Galloway's work have not failed to note what *seems* an evident fact: namely, the "anti-'Scottish' trajectory" of her writing (Jones 2009: 210).[4] If *The Trick Is to Keep Breathing* (1989) was set in the Glasgow area, the action of her second novel, *Foreign Parts* (1994), moved to France as the travelling destination of two Scottish female friends, while her last novel to date, *Clara* (2002), went farther away both in time and space to narrate the life of nineteenth-century German composer and pianist Clara Schumann.[5]

A crucial point to be taken into account, however – one that even criticism attentive to issues of gender in Galloway's work largely obviates – is that this fictional removal from the Scottish context takes place gradually in Galloway's novelistic output but *not* in her short story production, which remains bound to the concrete social situation of contemporary Scotland, in her own words "a country that is struggling with difficulties about gender", where there are still "real gender problems" (Richards 2003). Contrary to the progression traceable in her novels, Galloway's three collections of stories to date – *Blood* (1991), *Where You Find It* (1996) and *Jellyfish* (2015) – constitute a sustained effort to tackle gender issues, reformulate priorities and reconstruct structures within the still phallocentric context of contemporary Scotland. By focusing mainly on her novels, the critical assessment of Galloway's fiction reproduces the generic prejudice of considering the short story as inferior or less relevant than her longer works, despite the fact that she has published as many short story collections as novels.[6] The persistent refusal to grant the short story the canonical status it deserves as a distinct literary form goes hand in hand with the publishing industry's deeply entrenched doubts about its saleability, a situation of literary and economic marginality that has proven more impervious to change in Britain as a whole than elsewhere in the Anglophone world (Malcolm 2012: 50–56).

The case of Galloway's short fiction is thus not extraordinary, but, rather, the norm. What makes it particularly remarkable within the context of her production is that it functions as an enduring channel for a woman to speak in a different voice against a contemporary social system that considers women, as Galloway vehemently states, "a frill, a fuck or a boring bit that does housework or raises your kids round the edge. That stuff is not round the edge! It's the fucking middle of everything" (March 1999: 86).

The Ethics and the Poetics of Smallness

The affinity between, on the one hand, the consideration of women's concerns as add-ons to men's engagement with real, serious issues and, on the other, the short story as a nearly negligible supplement to the truly significant work of novel-writing goes deep in Galloway's case. Though, as she told me in an interview, she considers this association "more a trope of those who analyse fiction" (Sacido-Romero 2018a), Galloway defends shorter narrative forms against the prejudices commonly and recurrently generated by its unremitting contrast in terms of value with the novel, a demeaning preconception stemming from the celebration of the big, the "gladiatorial" that finds its historical "shallow" roots in "a colonising time": "Big meant victorious, powerful, fuck-off shorty" (Sacido-Romero 2018a). This disregard of and contempt for smallness (the short story included) continues in the present world, in which capitalist accumulation is paramount and, as Galloway states, "[s]ize is an issue. Oh yes, size is an issue" (Sacido-Romero 2018a).

Though not really comfortable with clear-cut generic categories, Galloway does appreciate the specific potentialities of the short story as a form: "You can express anything you like – including what happens or the resonances of a very long period of time – just in a more condensed form" (Sacido-Romero 2018a). She points out that the concentration the short story demands makes it similar to other "short works of art" in that they "suggest subtlety by definition" (Sacido-Romero 2018a). Furthermore, Galloway's fondness for the short form stems from her earlier reading preferences: "My favourite thing as a child were Greek legends and mythology, then Scottish folk ballads and stories. I like the intensity and airy space they both offer for the head to roam" (Sacido-Romero 2018a).[7] If her intention is "to offer stuff as elliptical and ambiguous as the world outside" (March 1999: 86) and "to make the reader feel" (Brown 1996), then the short story can work as effectively as the novel, even more so on account of its distinct formal features of intensity, subtlety, condensation and readerly engagement. These features emerge as constitutive elements of Galloway's poetics of the short story.

Galloway's poetics of the short story is intimately linked to an ethical stand in defence of the small, the trivial, the ordinary: of all those elements of otherness that power and money consider unworthy, and that she wants to place her focus on.[8] To give voice to women, or, more precisely, to write as a woman entails an engagement with what is silenced, dispossessed, ignored, considered *not normal*: "Deliberately pointing up that otherness, where what passes for normal has no bearing on you or ignores you – that fascinates me" (March 1999: 86). Ellen-Raïssa Jackson reads Galloway's short stories precisely as fiction that places the focus on the otherness that undermines the assumed consistency of reality, on "the gaps in the logic of living", repeatedly "asking us to look carefully at the smallness of life" (2004: 7). For her part, Josiane Paccaud-Huguet interprets the stories in Galloway's *Blood* as modernist narratives because, in them, "[i]nstead of repressing the otherness of life and language, Galloway celebrates it in her playful experiment with form that reveals the tragedy of a universe left gaping over a core of darkness" (2004: 56).

Dealing with darkness and the logical gaps in the fabric of human experience entails finding alternative ways to those enforced by dominant structures and restricting discourses. In Galloway's case, this engagement with "the eventual absurdity of the world" (Sacido-Romero 2018a) is translated into "an acute interest in smallness, dispossession, being overlooked [..., which is] one reason I like to write about children and animals too. What's small needs to be on its guard" (Sacido-Romero 2018a). Smallness is an instance of that disregarded otherness that Galloway cares for, and that includes short stories, which for her remain an underrated literary form for the simple reason that "[t]hey're shorter – this and this alone!" (Sacido-Romero 2018a). She accounts for the undying ascendancy of the novel in the realm of fiction by relating the latter to the pervading admiration for "BIGNESS", which "springs more from a kind of transferred blood-lust – a kind of gladiatorial stature", while linking her appreciation of the short story to the "much rarer" tendency "[t]o value spareness, the beauty of small or infrequent things; the aesthetic of non-acquisition or controlled lusts, or rationality of kindness and the urge to give" (Sacido-Romero 2018a).

The Different Voice of Care

Inscribed in this opposition big/small is the contrast between two ethical views: on the one hand, a dominant one that promotes individual autonomy, competitiveness, self-interest and personal achievement; on the other hand, a marginalised one that struggles to be heard and which insists on relations, on responsiveness to otherness, and on kindness and care as central moral values. In the tradition of feminist ethical thought and articulation of modalities of selfhood alternative to those enforced by patriarchal ideology, the latter view comes normally under the rubric "care ethics", whose earliest and most substantial formulation is to be found in Carol Gilligan's work *In a Different Voice: Psychological Theory and Women's Development* (1982).[9] Drawing critically on Nancy Chodorow's psychoanalytical exploration and defence of female identity as relational *versus* dominant notions of masculinity based on separation and individuation (1974; 1978), Gilligan focuses on the central role played by intimacy, attachment, empathy, communication, connection and care for others in women's moral reasoning when it comes to solving conflicts and defining themselves. Gilligan provides incontrovertible evidence of how, in the fields of psychology and psychoanalysis, such stand is dismissed as morally underdeveloped and immature because of its failure to rely on abstract ethical standards (rights, rules, laws, norms) that sustain the male-biased notion of the fully developed human subject as an autonomous entity.

In listening to her male and female interviewees speak about moral problems and the relationship self/other, Gilligan could hear how "women's voices sounded distinct" (1982/1993: 1). An alternative view on morality and moral development could be drawn from their "stories" (Gilligan 1982/1993: 2), a type of ethical reasoning that implicitly singled out the isolated self, the rejection to take responsibility and the lack of communication as the origin of aggression and violence, the utmost expression of moral failure (Gilligan 1982/1993: 38, 45, 61; Held 2006: 139). Yet, this new ethical voice was, and continues to be, beset by external constraints and internal inhibitions that arise from the fear of hurting others or not being heard/understood/accepted. The main challenges for this voice were and still are to find itself, to resist being silenced, to prevent the disabling splitting of the self and of moral reasoning and agency (Gilligan 1982/1993: 16). To make their different voices heard, women must struggle against silencing interferences and against dominant patriarchal discourses, the terms of which they are forced to reproduce.

For Gilligan, a woman's alienation from herself and from her speech becomes particularly apparent in moments of "crisis of identity and moral belief – a crisis that centres on her struggle to disentangle her voice from the voices of others and to find a language that represents her experience of relationships and her sense of herself" (1982/1993: 51). Precisely because of its brevity and other formal features, like its "episodic structure", the short story is an apt vehicle for the expression of "fleeting moments of crisis and decision" (Achilles 2015: 41), particularly as it affects women's conflictive relation with and interrogation of dominant discourses that dictate normative models of womanhood (Drewery 2011: 1). In what follows, I will read some pieces from Galloway's short fiction production featuring female characters at moments of crisis, in which they try to speak in what is recognisably the different voice of care for that disregarded otherness, ordinariness and smallness which she, as a woman writer, wanted to prioritise. In the stories selected for discussion, Galloway ties each of her female protagonists' predicament to the specific socio-historical context of contemporary Scotland. Each of these women's idiosyncratic endorsement of a relational notion of selfhood, as well as of the need to communicate and be responsive to what is marginalised and under threat, confronts hegemonic male-biased prejudices that may muffle their voices and impede their agency. Of course, Galloway's women are *not* ideal fictional examples of a fully successful advocacy of care ethics. What we find in these stories is, rather, the articulation of a voiced perspective which renders the vicissitudes, conflicts and, often, failures that attend such moral stance in the hostile context of turn-of-the-twentieth century Scotland. They can be read as fictional instances of what Virginia Held, in *The Ethics of Care* (2006), calls "feminist experience": namely, "the lived experience of feeling as well as thinking, of performing actions as well as receiving impressions, and of being aware of our connections with other persons as well as our own sensations" (23). In sum, not the experience of woman as "an abstraction, but the experience of actual women in all their racial and cultural and other diversity" (Held 2006: 23).

The Life/Art Connection: "the bridge" (*Where You Find It*, 1996)

Life and art, lived experience and writing, go together for Galloway. Against "the kind of writing that inflates the intellect" and that privileges "abstract truth", she attempts "to write realistically about what it feels to be alive" (Brown 1996). In the story "the bridge" (*Where You*

Find It 1996), the view of life and art as essentially connected, along with the definition of life as the set of relations of care and belonging, are voiced by the woman character, Fiona. She meets a former fellow art student and now professional painter named Charlie in London, where he lives. Told in the third-person yet focalised through Fiona's mind, the central action of the story takes place on a bridge over the Thames River at night. It revolves around Fiona's failure, precisely, to *bridge* the gap between her and the man for whom she feels a strong attachment that is a mixture of artistic admiration and infatuation, or "lust", as it is called at one point (Galloway 2009: 289).[10]

Having slept with him the night before, Fiona spent the day watching Charlie paint. Out on the bridge after having dinner at some restaurant, she looks at him walking ahead of her and thinks "about Charlie painting, the sexiness of his total absorption" (Galloway 2009: 290). The distance between them grows larger as the story progresses because of the different views each holds concerning what is relevant in life. Charlie, a Glaswegian like Fiona, is fully devoted to his art, the only thing he feels attached to and may be said to belong to: Fiona affirms she feels at home in Glasgow and asks him if he does not feel the same way, to which he replies "No. I [Charlie] don't want to belong to any of that thanks. *Being Scottish*. [...] I don't think I want to belong to anything. Except art maybe, my work" (Galloway 2009: 294–295).[11] Charlie, a citizen of the world, says he does not belong anywhere in particular and considers ordinary life and personal relations boring, exhausting and meaningless: "People are always a waste of time in the end. They don't think, don't prioritise their fucking lives. People *wear you down*. [...] Art *makes sense*: people *don't*" (Galloway 2009: 297–298). Fiona retorts that, on the contrary, ordinary life is what is truly worthy and meaningful: "what's ordinary is what's universal, isn't it? That's where the biggest meanings are" (Galloway 2009: 297). She wants, we are told, to "make some kind of contact to stop him digging the trench any deeper" (Galloway 2009: 297) but feels the pressure of her convictions growing in her chest. When Charlie reiterates her view that people are worth nothing, her speech changes into a firmer, more vigorous denial of the Art/Life divide:

> This supposed Life and Art debate: this notion you're somehow above *ordinary* living order to be an Artist and Life is for the lower order or something – it's all crap. Maybe male crap, maybe elitist crap but definitely crap. [...] It's worse than crap, it's a con trick, Charlie. If there's no Life there is no bloody Art is there?
>
> (Galloway 2009: 298)

And when Charlie asks her point blank what "Life" is, Fiona responds in the unequivocal language of care: "Talking and interchanging, the raising of weans [children]. Getting by. Behaving decently towards other people. Love, I suppose. If you don't attend to that, you attend to nothing. Love, Charlie" (Galloway 2009: 298).

At this climactic point in the story, we come across a woman's sharp and clear articulation, in her own voice, of a moral conception of life as relation and care, and of art as part of it. This moral stand is criticised by Charlie – who in the story epitomises the opposite dominant ideal of individual autonomy – as imposing disabling choices that particularly affect women because of their being too emotional and, therefore, incapable of living by those superior moral principles that guarantee individual self-realisation, the highest goal in life. Thus, Charlie tells Fiona that her moral choices are simply wrong – "You're too bloody serious about the *wrong* things" (Galloway 2009: 300; my emphasis) – and criticises some Alison Sime for having given up the possibility of a successful career as a painter to become a mother.

Cristie L. March sees Fiona as one of those women in Galloway's fiction who try to liberate themselves from "behavioural expectations only to be forced back into submission by men who figure centrally in their lives" (2002: 112). It is true that, after her articulate vindication of relational ethics, she tones down her speech not to ruin her chances of spending another night with Charlie. As Carol Gilligan insisted in her "Letter to Readers, 1993", in women's voicing of an alternative view of morality and selfhood, the sonic, aural dimension is a crucial one: advocacy and vocalisation must reinforce each other for women to speak truly and truthfully for themselves (1982/1993: x–xi). This aspect of sound, of the physical articulation of the female voice, is recurrently thematised in Galloway's stories as part of woman's effort to speak for themselves. In "the bridge", Fiona's qualification of her strong ethical stand goes hand in hand with a modification in the modulation of her voice, from which she feels dissociated: "She had to slow down, *care less*. Try for lightness. [...] Her voice had gone that soft way, like a psychiatrist. A doctor in a film" (Galloway 2009: 299; my emphasis). Assailed by the fear to miss the opportunity of another sexual encounter with Charlie, Fiona eventually decides to remain silent: "saying anything else was just going to make it worse" (Galloway 2009: 300). But her strategic inhibition proves useless as Charlie's distancing increases, so much so that on the way back to his place, they "avoided looking at each other" and "sat with one empty seat between them on the tube back, not talking" (Galloway 2009: 301).

Leaving aside the fact that Galloway is not providing role models in her fiction,[12] the affirmation that Fiona's is a case of personal defeat and moral failure cannot be taken at face value. To begin with, she is driven by a force (sexual attraction) that overpowers her as it may overpower any *living* human being, men and women alike. Furthermore, she actually wants their sexual intimacy to grow into something larger and richer, to facilitate "some kind of possibility opening up between them" (Galloway 2009: 299). Her "wish to touch" Charlie (Galloway 2009: 288) is not just an aim in itself, but a way to express a desire for connection, communication and relationship: "She'd wanted him to say something else. A question, maybe, something that wondered what *she* cared about, her work or something. Only he'd never seen her pictures, never asked her to send any when she's offered" (Galloway 2009: 299). Moreover, the story exposes Charlie's attitude as one of masculine ego-centrism and carelessness about others. As Ellen-Raïssa Jackson points out,[13] Charlie boasts about his knowledge of women's mistaken priorities, but "never asks Fiona about her work" though she is a painter just like him (2004: 17). He is proud of his exceptional power of sight ("I *see* everything" [Galloway 2009: 298]), but he "seems not to notice much at all: from Fiona's presence as he paints, to the man [a beggar] by the bridge, he sees little" (Jackson 2004: 17).

Charlie's failure to see is rendered in the story as a foil to Fiona's responsiveness to the world around her and to her own self in relation to it. His failure to notice is exposed in the narrative as a failure to care, unlike Fiona, who not only cares for Charlie, but also for the beggar by the bridge and for a lonely boy that sat motionless at the restaurant while they were having dinner and remained so as they left (Galloway 2009: 287). The latter scene constitutes the story's elaborate opening and establishes a clear contrast between Charlie and Fiona in terms of moral sensibility from the very beginning: while Charlie was completely oblivious of the young man's melancholy presence, Fiona "glanced back while they paid at the till, watching to see if he was moving yet but he wasn't" and, as Charlie held the door for her, "[s]he flicked her eyes in the boy's direction again, knowing he wouldn't be any different, hoping anyway" (Galloway 2009: 287). The distance between their respective moral stances as sketched at the beginning grows into an unbridgeable gap at the end.

Against Violence: "Need for Restraint" (*Blood,* 1991)

Like "the bridge", "Need for Restraint" (*Blood*) also opens with the main woman character's caring reaction to a scene of human suffering, yet in this case not one of dejection or need, but of open male violence.[14] This character, whose name is Alice and who functions as the third-person narrative focaliser, engages more actively than Fiona in trying to solve this painful situation. The story focuses on the conflicts arising from Alice's attempt to maintain her ethical stand in an unresponsive and hostile context. More specifically, Alice's predicament is presented as series difficulties and obstacles encountered by a woman's different voice of care as it tries to make itself heard.

In a shopping mall where she is to meet her man, Charles, Alice's attention is "suddenly" caught by the "terrifying" sight of two men engaged in a violent fight, while "[r]unnels of people practising mass avoidance kept to the other side of the walkway" (Galloway 2009: 82). Her spontaneous pacifying attempt in the midst of general indifference ("Somebody will get hurt if you don't stop it", pronounced after much inner struggle and mental rehearsal) clashes against masculine expectations regarding women, which are first verbalised by one of the fighting men who responds vehemently: "Somebody's supposed to get hurt, that's the fuckin idea" (Galloway 2009: 83). Yet such expectations concerning women's silent passivity about, and compliance with, male brutality are forced on her not only externally (by the men who keep fighting, or by her cold and unsympathetic husband/partner, who reproaches her for trying to meddle in other people's affairs and for showing tenderness in public), but also and more importantly internally: they are part of a set of prescriptions she had interiorised as the defining features of her *normative* identity, which she feared to violate or not to be up to.[15] Thus, Alice's conflict is rendered in the story as the dialectic between two capitalised injunctions: on the one hand, the censoring mandate "THIS IS NOTHING TO DO WITH YOU" and, on the other, the expression of her desire to stop meaningless violence, "THERE IS NO REASON FOR THIS" (Galloway 2009: 82, 84, 88). This lasting struggle actually seems to take place inside her mind during the episode at the mall. It can be conceived as a battle of two utterances to win Alice's will for which the text nevertheless provides an origin. Right before the concluding paragraphs, marked off by quadruple space, there is an analeptic passage that goes back to the night before in which Alice saw men fighting in the street from a window at home and felt the "terrible need to do something" (Galloway 2009: 87).[16] She was stopped at the door by Charles who, first in a "voice calm" and later in a "voice changing, hard as the grip on her wrists", told her several times the affair was "NOTHING TO DO WITH YOU" (Galloway 2009: 88). Alice responded with a single, yet equally capitalised, "NO REASON FOR THIS", before giving up her plan of going down to the street to stop the fight (Galloway 2009: 88). She remained in a state of painful regret afterwards, and both "stayed apart for the rest of the night" (Galloway 2009: 88).

Cristie L. March cites "Need for Restraint" as one instance of the "dysfunctional communication between the sexes" that she sees as central in Galloway's work (2002: 118). As this chapter argues, such a failure to communicate is determined by a woman's endorsement of an ethics of care and of a relational notion of selfhood that is at odds with the models and ideals that dominant ideology imposes. For, indeed, this is the story of a woman's endeavour to change her subjective position by forcefully speaking up her mind against male violence, as well as to overcome guilt and shed an identity that entails being unresponsive to human pain. Furthermore, it is actually the story of her struggle to literally make her voice heard ("Her mouth felt hardly used [...] as though neither she nor her voice were there"), a voice that strives to come out ("Saying, saying anything, might loosen this lump in her chest"), yet seems to get stuck in her throat when trying to approach her man: "The words jammed. They stopped. [...] She had not even said what she wanted to say" (Galloway 2009: 83, 86, 87). The story's conclusion hints at the onset of her emancipation from the alienating bond to a man from whom she derived her identity and who functions as the mouthpiece of patriarchal discourse that resonates in her mind, blocking her speech. Thus, when, after the retrospective passage, the narrative returns to the shopping mall scene, we are told that Alice is bold enough to defy Charles's repressive male expectations by a simple caring gesture which publicly undermines his self-image of toughness. The scene is a public staging of the lack of communication that characterises their home life:

> To speak would only make things worse. Yet if she touched him now, he would go without her. That might be kind. It would be something. Deliberately, she reached, tipped the warm cloth of his coat. He broke free as she knew he would, moving to merge with the crowd.
> People were looking.
>
> People were looking.
>
> (Galloway 2009: 89)

"Need for Restraint", the story's title, condenses in its ambiguity the two poles in conflict in the narrative: against the official need to restrain care so as not to compromise the autonomy of the self and become too sentimental, there stands as an alternative the need to restrain violence and indifference as radical manifestations of moral failure to care and connect. In this and in many other stories, Galloway lays bare the illegitimate male violence pervading the patriarchal structures of contemporary Scottish society, which she aims at "reconstructing" by giving voice to woman's alternative perspective on ethics and selfhood. Yet this does not mean that all the male characters in Galloway's stories are egocentric or violent: some of them are not, like David in the eponymous story collected in *Blood* (clearly related to the character of Joy Stone's caring young lover in *The Trick Is to Keep Breathing*), the unnamed first-person narrator in "hope" (from *Where You Find It*, featuring a man who feels trapped in an unhappy marriage), or Riley (who, in "distance", the final story in Galloway's last collection, *Jellyfish*, acts responsibly by taking care of his son after his traumatised wife tells him she wanted a divorce). These male characters may be said to resemble the redeeming young masculine figures in her novels, through which, the author "attempt[s] to rehabilitate masculinity" (Jones 2009: 93). For Carole Jones, Galloway's work rehearses the articulation of new configurations of gender relations in the historical context of masculine disorientation brought about by the advance of feminism and the decline of male-dominated heavy industries in Scotland. Jones argues that Galloway strikes an optimistic note at the end of her novels through the introduction of sensitive young men, who epitomise the model of the "post-patriarchal youth, [who] prioritises partnership over domination" (2009: 93).

Jones, however, concentrates on Galloway's novelistic output, in which we witness a gradual departure from the contemporary Scottish context of gender relations. Unlike her novels, Galloway's short fiction never abandons that sociocultural context which she tries to restructure, and the idea that the intergenerational transmission of patriarchal power is disrupted, as Jones maintains (2009: 69), must be qualified. Though there may be a message of hope implicit in Galloway's work, massive textual evidence in her stories shows how the patriarchal system seems to go on promoting individualistic models of selfhood, imposing ideals of male toughness and aggressiveness which entail a rejection of the alternatives of care and interdependence that women characters struggle to voice. Furthermore, the complicity of male-dominated institutions such as the family and the school in the perpetuation of the former is exposed crudely in stories in which father figures teach children lessons on mistrust ("Scenes from the Life No. 23: Paternal Advice", *Blood*), or directly mistreat them, as in "someone had to" (*Where You Find It*), where a scopophobic stepfather inflicts upon his superhumanly resilient six-year-old stepdaughter increasingly cruel torments, as the girl defiantly stares back at him in silence.

On Mothering, Animals and Music: "fine day" and "distance" (*Jellyfish*, 2015)

The brutal stepfather in "someone had to" rationalises his sadistic actions through an explicit dismissal of care which chimes in with Charlie's critique of women's prioritisation of sentimentality in "the bridge": "People sentimentalise; children and animals it's what they do" (Galloway 2009: 272). Intertwined quite conspicuously with Galloway's exploration of gender relations in her last collection, *Jellyfish* (2015), there are two elements intrinsically related to care ethics that grow in prominence, precisely those this cruel stepfather had dismissed: children and animals as objects of women's concern. More clearly than in *Blood* and *Where You Find It*, Galloway places children and animals at the centre of the picture in *Jellyfish*. Mothers' relationships with (especially) their sons, as well as women's interactions with animals, figure largely in this collection. Certainly, many of the stories in *Jellyfish* are about single parenting, an issue Galloway attempted to capture "in a full-length novel [which] left her frustrated" (MacLeod 2015). As for Galloway's greater interest in animals in this collection, it conforms to her view that it is life's "very fleetingness and vulnerability [that] makes living things – all kinds of living things – so powerful subject for me" (Sacido-Romero 2018a).

Mothering has been a major topic of care ethics since its inception, and the extension of care to forms of life other than human gained relevance in later developments. While Virginia Held "locate[s] the beginnings of the ethics of care" in Sara Ruddick's reassessment of mothering as the site of moral reflection in "Maternal Thinking" (1980), Josephine Donovan and Carol J. Adams state that the "feminist ethic of care regards animals as individuals who have feelings, who can communicate those feelings, and to whom therefore humans have moral obligations" (2007: 2–3). Galloway admits that though

> [m]y concern for animal welfare and ecology has always been there, I guess it's finding its way into the work more now because things are getting uglier with regard to lack of human *compassion* and *care* for their fellow creatures [...] Without the *connections* – and *care of those connections*, nothing of any stripe survives.
>
> (Sacido-Romero 2018a; my emphases)

Interestingly, Galloway relates the idea of connecting responsiveness to vulnerable otherness to music because, for her, music "suggests a world of sense and rational thirst for communication" and "is one of those things that makes you sensitive to that which is 'not you'" (Sacido-Romero 2018a). In what follows, I will comment on two stories from *Jellyfish* in which the voiced perspective of care revolves around the issue of gender relations and the experience of motherhood, which are connected, respectively, to music ("fine day") and to both music and animals ("distance"). In the two pieces under scrutiny, the theme of vocalisation of women's views and desires is again brought to the fore.

"fine day" takes its title from the most famous aria in Giacomo Puccini's *Madam Butterfly* (1904), "One Fine Day We Shall See", in which Japanese Madam Butterfly recreates in her mind the future return to Nagasaki of her American husband, Pinkerton, with whom she is passionately in love. Pinkerton does eventually return, but does so in the company of his American wife, Kate, who had agreed to take care of Madam Butterfly's son by Pinkerton. Butterfly agrees to give up her child to the American couple on condition that Pinkerton comes to see her one last time. Pinkerton agrees and arrives to see Butterfly dying after cutting her throat (Illica and Giacosa 1906). In Galloway's story, a husband, Murray, abandons not only his wife, Katrin, but also their son, Danny, because, Murray argues, he "does not love [her] anymore" and has made the "*mature decision* to move on" (2015: 79–80). Murray, a self-controlled narcissistic teacher or college professor, is a later embodiment of male egotistic individualism. This male character recalls Charlie in "the bridge", who, as suggested in that story, had also left a wife and a son behind in New York in his pursuit of a career as an artist (Galloway 2009: 293). But Murray's is a worse case, as his immoral

self-interest and irresponsibility are hidden under the screen of politically correct, euphemistic and aseptic discourse. The story elaborately
debunks his rhetoric by reproducing his jargon (ironically emphasised
in italics), either directly in Katrin's sardonic rejoinders ("It's not even
called *separation* any more. It's called *moving on* or *redefining one's
priorities* or *conscious uncoupling* god help us and it's perfectly ok"
[Galloway 2015: 80]), or in a third-person voice which recurrently mod-
ulates into free indirect discourse as another way of articulating Katrin's
reaction to Murray's rationalising speech. In his "bloodless" and "impersonal, tight-arsed counselling mode", Murray's language had always
served to separate rather than communicate, as language should. He had
always been completely refractory to Katrin's attempts at having him
share his feelings and fears and, instead, went on adopting an attitude
of "long-suffering condescension", recalcitrant even to direct "sarcasm",
and aggressively self-serving (Galloway 2015: 80).

From his position "as an educator", Murray even dares to warn Katrin
against the danger of transforming their son into a weakling due to
excessive maternal affection. His is a more *civilised*, tempered version of
the less articulate criticism of sentimentality spat out by the sadistic stepfather in "someone had to": "She [Katrin] might benefit from a short,
sharp course on the importance of strong male roles models for boys and
how smothering mothers could be" (Galloway 2015: 81). As an authority figure within the educational system, Murray may be said to work
in favour of the transmission of patriarchal power, which promotes a
model of selfhood based on separation, autonomy and self-realisation,
while forestalling one based on relationships of interdependence and
care as inferior and/or wrong. Katrin hoped Danny would not identify
with the model his father represented, a man who "needed the freedom
to flit in and out of lives as though they [were] incidental train platforms
between his journey to himself" (Galloway 2015: 82).

After Murray leaves, Katrin wakes Danny up from his nap. Her voice
is described as "catching" at one point, almost breaking with emotion
in making a humorous remark; a voice to be contrasted with Murray's,
which was previously defined as "distant, as though he was talking from
a different planet through an intercom" (Galloway 2015: 84, 80). To
handle the critical situation provoked by Murray's defection, Kate plans
an evening with Danny watching *Madam Butterfly* on TV, eating snacks
and drinking apple juice. When the action of Puccini's opera reaches
the point in which Butterfly sings "One Fine Day", Danny falls asleep.
Katrin keeps watching and weeping "without relief" because of Butterfly's wishfulness (Galloway 2015: 85). Before Butterfly commits suicide,
however, she abruptly changes channels, at which point the story reaches
a final turning point, leading to its conclusion in the final paragraph.
After changing channels, Katrin witnesses "a miracle" unexpectedly
coming out the TV set: the news that "a middle-aged man" had acted

altruistically, "saving the life of a teenage boy" involved in a car accident (Galloway 2015: 86). As the man told the reporter: "You just did
what you had to" (Galloway 2015: 86). The contrast of this episode in
the news with her life with Murray and with the tragic denouement of
Puccini's operatic plot continues in Katrin's display of affection for her
sleeping boy and her decision to place him in "the centre of the picture
now" (Galloway 2015: 86). She sings Butterfly's aria to salute a future
in which she and her son "might even bloom" (Galloway 2015: 86),
yet her singing is performed as pure music, as "emotional or unspoken
connection by another means", to quote Galloway's description of the
communicative power of music (Sacido-Romero 2018a). In this way, the
words she sings from Puccini's "One Fine Day" are deprived of their articulated meaning in an expression of motherly affection for her son: "In
her by-numbers Italian accent, *understanding it only as sound*, she sang
to her son's closed eyelids, his oblivious, perfect face" (Galloway 2015:
86; my emphasis). The violence of Murray's perfectly articulated language is, in the end, counterweighted by the sound of music, the soothing, balanced medium of non-verbal expression and communication that
helps reinforce caring bonds.[17]

The piece that closes the collection, "distance", is the story of how
an exacerbation of care and responsibility may have adverse effects on
those involved, the caregiver included. "jellyfish", the title story of the
collection, had also dealt with the delicate question of how too much
maternal concern for a child could interfere with his development as a
person.[18] In that story, the mother did learn how to calibrate her influence as a parent on her son; in "distance", however, the mother's involvement reaches pathological proportions so that a more radical solution is
required. Though there may be some grounds to criticise Martha, the
central character, as irresponsible, whimsical, fickle, careless, or at least
morally ambiguous, I will rehearse a more sympathetic approach to her
predicament and consider hers as an acute case of what Rita C. Manning
calls "caring burnout". As Manning states, "caring persons are not obli-
gated to continue caring until they slip into caring burnout. This denies
their own status as persons who deserve care and is counterproductive"
(1992: 77). In my view, "distance" tells the story of how a burned-out
caring mother, Martha, attempts to regain her psychic balance by *distancing* herself from her primary objects of care – her son, Peter, in particular. She becomes aware that the problem lies with her, that her care
is counterproductive, that she is "a drain on him [Peter] just now. Both
of them [husband and son]" (Galloway 2015: 152). This process of sal-
utary distancing is initiated the moment Martha envisions the way out
of her trauma, an insight simultaneous with its verbalisation and with
the acquisition of a new voice which the text repeatedly thematises, and
which entails a radical change in her life as well as in that of her closest
family. In my interpretation of the story's conclusion, Martha regains
her position as caregiver in the inner recesses of the Scottish island of

Jura, after hitting a stag with her car at night and holding him in her caring embrace while the Queen of the Night arias from Mozart's *The Magic Flute* are heard on the car radio.

The story of Martha's trauma began when Peter, their son, was three years old and fell against a table, cutting his head. The small boy got medical attention and his injury was soon cured, but the episode was so traumatic for Martha that the fear that Peter could hurt himself again became the source of permanent torment. The situation became unsustainable as "she began waking Peter at night, checking more than once if he was breathing" (Galloway 2015: 148). Her husband warned her that she would "make Peter paranoid at this rate" and recalled how Martha's mother, Nancy, had "ruined" her life for being so neurotic and – as we are later to learn – for having committed suicide (Galloway 2015: 148). When Riley delicately told Martha that it was "time to get a grip", the words "[t]o move on" were heard (Galloway 2015: 148). The reader inevitably attributes the expression to Riley, as the paragraph closes with these words in direct speech without the use of inverted commas. That the phrase "to move on" – an echo of previous stories but without ironic connotations[19] – was not actually uttered by the male character, but by Martha, the traumatised wife and mother, comes as a surprise not only to the reader, but to Martha herself: "Move on. Martha only realised she had said the words when she heard them out loud, her own throat, working" (Galloway 2015: 148). The same ambiguity also affects the expression "Let it go", uttered immediately afterwards and which we infer to have been spoken by Riley after affectionately "kissing her fingers" (Galloway 2015: 148). Yet, due to the lack of typographical markers and *verba dicendi*, and in view of what comes next in the story, we may again safely attribute the expression to Martha herself. Thus, sometime afterwards, Martha bought a self-help or pop-psychology book titled *Toxic Bonds* she chanced to see in an Oxfam Shop. The book contained pieces of advice on how to be "a good mother" that Martha spent the night reading and rereading: "A good mother did not limit the growth of what she loved. A good mother did not cling, for clinging was a curb upon joy" (Galloway 2015: 149). In the small hours, while the rest of the family was asleep, "she took the book's advice *and spoke out loud*. Let it go. [...] Let it go. [...] Let it go." (Galloway 2015: 149; my emphasis). The book's advice is an echo of Martha's words in her conversation with Riley, as if it were metaphorically and literally *in tune with* her mind, hence her intense engagement with a work which developed what she had previously expressed in a nutshell.

After an unsuccessful visit to a counsellor, Riley, whose desire was "to work together" to find a solution, is surprised by Martha's intention to separate: "Divorce, Martha said. The words had come out no one else's mouth. [...] The words surprised her, but only slightly" (Galloway 2015: 150). Finding a way out of the impasse entails a radical redefinition of familial relations, which Martha performs by speaking up her mind against the expectations that up to then had defined her identity, hence the feeling of strangeness that her own words provoked on her when first heard. This recalls Alice in "Need for Restraint", who experienced a similar feeling of alienation from her own speech when trying to stop the fight at the mall and had to struggle against this disabling feeling: "And she thought she spoke. Somebody will get hurt. It was a thin testing voice she heard" (Galloway 2009: 83).[20] In a completely different context, both Alice and Martha speak the voice of care; yet, whereas Alice's speech had to struggle against silencing and inhibiting forces, Martha's is misunderstood as pathological introversion, like her mother's, who had committed suicide and left only a note saying "It's for the best" (Galloway 2015: 152). But, as Martha told her censorious elder sister on the phone, she was acting "for the best" and their mother's action "bore no comparison with her situation" (Galloway 2015: 152–153). In fact, Martha's caring burnout most likely had its origin in her having been forced, at a very early age, to take care of her mother when still alive and to deal with the legal affairs and funeral arrangements after her death. She had clearly been overburdened as a caregiver when still an adolescent, as her sister recognised in a light-hearted tone over the phone: "She [their mother] called you her rock. Martha's such a bloody rock" (Galloway 2015: 152).

Martha agrees with Riley's plan to take Peter with him to Canada to live with Riley's mother. On Peter's last visit before his departure, mother and son play a "what-if game" and imagine they "could live on an island" where they would "find animals, Peter said, make friends" (Galloway 2015: 156). This seemingly irrelevant episode is crucial in that it chimes in not only with the final development of the story, but also with the opening paragraphs, where, through prolepsis, we are told about Martha's arrival in a Scottish island and her sight of the deer that "came down to the road at night, slipping through the bracken just before dusk" (Galloway 2015: 145). Every night Martha drove back to the harbour road impelled by some basic, primitive instinct to see the animals, with whom she established a pacifying contact:

> Something primitive, she guessed, was drawing them. *Her too.* Deer did not judge, did not speculate about her motives: they simply were. And so, they decided, was she. Gentle things made bolder by the dying light, *they met her eye to eye, their pupils huge, absorbent in the dark.* This was their element, not hers. *But she had permission to stay.*
>
> (Galloway 2015: 145; my emphases)

As if fulfilling Peter's imaginary projection in the what-if game, Martha made friends with animals on an island which, as we are to learn later, was the island of Jura, one of Scotland's Inner Hebrides. She had decided to travel to this remote place after being diagnosed with "[e]ndo-metrial hyperplasia" and giving up her job as a supply teacher. Jura was "Orwell's island", an author she was forced to teach at school, but did not much like (Galloway 2015: 164). Part of Martha's dislike for Orwell had to do with the way he raised his small son Richard when he, already a widower, spent some time in Barnhill, Jura, completing his dystopian novel *1984*. In "distance" and in "almost 1948" (another story in *Jelly-fish*), Orwell is depicted as one of those strong male role models for boys that Murray in "fine day" had lectured Katrin about. He tried to instil male toughness in Richard by making him do hard and even dangerous things. Orwell reasoned that "[s]*omeone had to* toughen the boy up. It mattered he should not be sentimental [...] The fate of the weak was to fall" (Galloway 2015: 67; my emphasis).

On her last evening in Jura, Martha was driving her car into the in-terior, "pressed the radio button and found Mozart" (Galloway 2015: 166). A "gorgeous voice", the sound of "sheer, edgeless" singing, ac-companied her reckless driving till she hit something so that, eventually, the car "lurched to a stop" (Galloway 2015: 167). Leaving the car with Mozart's *The Magic Flute* still on in the radio, she found a wounded young male deer. She approached the animal she had injured carefully. "Gently, she placed her cheek against his flank" and tried to assuage his pain and fear by saying "I'm here", an echo of her comforting words to her son, Peter, after the latter hit his head against the table (Galloway 2015: 169, 147). This verbal and physical act of care seems to have en-abled Martha to regain her psychic balance and strength, and connect with something which was not her, another fleeting and vulnerable form of life: "This was all she had. She was Martha. A rock. She was forty-one years old. And despite herself, still here. Incapable of letting go" (Galloway 2015: 169).

To a large extent, Martha functions as the positive counterpart of two negative maternal figures mentioned in the narrative: on the one hand, Martha's mother, who was found dead inside a car with the ra-dio on after committing suicide; on the other hand, Mozart's Queen of the Night, the figure of an evil mother who unsuccessfully manipulated her daughter for her own ends and was eventually doomed to eternal darkness (Cantoni and Schwarm 2014). Unlike the Queen of the Night, Martha saves her son by letting him go with her husband, and regains her strength through an affective, caring connection with a being she had unintentionally hurt, in contrast with the Queen of Night whose plan to dominate the world ended in her eternal damnation.

In the animal world, whose course runs unimpeded in the island of Jura, knowledge articulated in human language is secondary, not to say irrelevant; thus, for instance, birds exist independently of "whether she [Martha] knew what they were or not", as we read at the beginning of the story (Galloway 2015: 146). As in "fine day", the story concludes with words, human speech coming close to music as a channel of affection independent of the meaning they carry. Blending with Mozart's music on the car radio, Martha's words to the injured stag mutate into echoing sounds that can also be heard by non-human beings: "Dislocated bars of Mozart were gusting like feather in the night air [...] I'm here, she said, her words bouncing off the surrounding rocks and rising, furious, into the solid dark" (Galloway 2015: 169). Both stories conclude with references to the/a mother's voice, a theme whose complexity and ambiguity is beyond the scope of this chapter to explore. Suffice to say that, in the end, the stress is put on the aural, sonic dimension of speech to which Carol Gilligan gave so much importance and which, in Galloway, becomes a vehicle for the connecting expression of care for that which transcends the individual self, for that, as she put it, "which is 'not you'" (Sacido-Romero 2018a).

Conclusion

In contrast with the anti-Scottish turn of her novelistic plots, Janice Galloway's exploration of female experience in her short stories remains systematically bound to the context of contemporary Scotland. The pieces collected in *Blood, Where You It* and *Jellyfish* articulate women's perspectives *on and in* a male-biased world, in which female views and concerns are dismissed as irrelevant. The stories discussed above focus on woman characters at critical points in their struggle to make their different voices heard, voices that, in different ways, endorse relational notions of selfhood and the values of care ethics alternative to those enforced by patriarchal ideology. Against individualism, aggressiveness and indifference, women's voices in Galloway's stories resonate, calling attention to their aurality and transmitting a message that should be heard.

Notes

1 This idea is sketched by Margery Metzstein (1993).
2 See also March (2002: 108).
3 Critics of a more feminist persuasion like Glenda Norquay and Kirsten Stirling expose the masculinist bias of otherwise valuable readings such as Cairns Craig's (1999: 1999; 2006: 137–138) for reproducing the *topos* of the feminisation of the nation recurrent in nationalist discourse. The latter transforms central women characters in novels into a "representative[s] of Scotland itself", into "potential incarnation[s] of Scotland" (Norquay 2000: 136; Stirling 2008: 123). See also McGlynn (2008: 223).
4 See also March (2002: 128) and Stirling (2008: 122).
5 Galloway is presently working on a new novel which is removed farther back in time than *Clara*, and like the latter is not set in Scottish soil: "'That novel' is set in eighteenth-century Italy, but she [Galloway] says with a groan that progress is slow and she's only half way through" ("Janice Galloway on Her New Short Story Collection" 2015).

6 By "mainly on her novels" I mean that Galloway's short fiction has been the object of some critical interest, most importantly, for the purposes of this essay, Cristie L. March (2002).

7 See also Galloway (2008: 189). Galloway goes as far as to say that what drives her to write short stories is her fondness for them as a reader: "I write short stories because I like reading them" (Sacido-Romero 2018a).

8 See also Galloway's criticism of the trinity "MONEY, POWER, and WORTH" in "Bad Times" (1996).

9 Gilligan's seminal work has given rise to a wide range of reformulations and critical responses that reaches up to today and which is beyond the scope of this paper to discuss. Two excellent surveys on, respectively, the ethics of care and feminist explorations of alternative models of selfhood are available online: Maureen Sander-Staudt, "Care Ethics", *International Encyclopaedia of Philosophy*, 2011, www.iep.utm.edu/care-eth/c, (accessed 2 October 2017) and Cynthia Willett, Ellie Anderson, and Diana Meyers, "Feminist Perspectives on the Self", *Stanford Encyclopaedia of Philosophy*, 1999, rev. ed. 2015, https://plato.stanford.edu/entries/feminism-self/, (accessed 2 October 2017). For a fairly recent, sympathetic and well-informed account of Gilligan's contribution to the delineation of "the feminine subject" see Hekman (2014: 56–76).

10 *Blood* (1991) and *Where You Find It* (1996) were published together as *Collected Stories* in 2009. References to stories in *Blood* and *Where You Find It* are to this 2009 edition.

11 Galloway never uses inverted commas for dialogue or passages in direct speech.

12 "I can't think", Galloway told March, "'woops—this woman's not much of a role model so I better change her.' Ha. It doesn't happen like that. That's and academic approach" (March 1999: 87).

13 Jackson (2004) reads Galloway's short fiction as an exploration of the experience of Scottishness that is beyond the white male nationalist version and includes age, class and gender differences.

14 Part of the argument concerning Galloway's unmasking of male violence in this chapter was sketched in my one-page contribution to the text of a roundtable (Sacido-Romero, Torres-Zúñiga, Lara Rallo and Andrés Cuevas 2016: 347–348).

15 This fear is the very definition of guilt. See, for instance, Sigmund Freud (1930/1961: 78–83).

16 Most likely, the action took place the previous night, but we cannot know for certain as the passage simply begins: "It had been a dark evening through long windows" (Galloway 2009: 87).

17 "Blood", perhaps Galloway's best-known story, comes to mind here. The unnamed girl protagonist, who had a tooth pulled, is literally assailed by aggressive discourses from all flanks and heads for school to find relief in music: "She suddenly wanted to be in the music rooms, soothing herself with music" (Galloway 2009: 5).

18 I have examined elsewhere the central character's liminal experience of motherhood in "jellyfish" (Sacido-Romero 2018b).

19 Apart from Murray in "fine day", the phrase "to move on" is also used in reference to the egotistical absent father in "jellyfish", there emphasised in italics and bold type in the original (Galloway 2015: 16).

20 In "the bridge", Fiona's articulate dismissal of the separation Life/Art and her affirmation of care against masculine expectations embodied by Charlie had a similar effect on her: "My god what was wrong with her? This monologue and that word ["love"] suddenly coming out" (Galloway 2009: 298).

References

Achilles, Jochen (2015) "Modes of Liminality in American Short Fiction: Condensations of Multiple Identities", in *Liminality and the Short Story: Boundary Crossings in American, Canadian, and British Writing*, edited by J. Achilles and I. Bergmann, New York: Routledge, 35–49.

Brown, Georgina (1996) "The Trick Is to Start Writing", *The Independent*, www.independent.co.uk/arts-entertainment/the-trick-is-to-start-writing-1349929.html (accessed 3 April 2017).

Cantoni, Linda and Betsy Schwarm (2014) "*The Magic Flute*: Opera by Mozart", in *Encyclopaedia Britannica*, https://www.britannica.com/topic/The-Magic-Flute (accessed 4 December 2017).

Chodorow, Nancy (1974) "Family Structure and Feminine Personality", in *Women, Culture and Society*, edited by M.Z. Rosaldo and L. Lamphere, Stanford, CA: Stanford University Press, 43–66.

Chodorow, Nancy (1978) *The Reproduction of Mothering*, Berkeley, CA: University of California Press.

Craig, Cairns (1999) *The Modern Scottish Novel: Narrative and the National Imagination*, Edinburgh: Edinburgh University Press.

Craig, Cairns (2006) "Devolving the Scottish Novel", in *A Concise Companion to Contemporary British Fiction*, edited by James F. English, Malden, MA: Blackwell, 121–140.

Craig, Cairns (2012) "Otherworlds: Devolution and the Scottish Novel", in *The Cambridge Companion to Scottish Literature*, edited by Gerard Carruthers and Liam MvIlvanney, Cambridge: Cambridge University Press, 261–274.

Donovan, Josephine and Carol J. Adams (2007) "Introduction", in *The Feminist Care Tradition in Animal Ethics: A Reader*, edited by J. Donvan and C.J. Adams, New York: Columbia University Press, 1–20.

Drewery, Claire (2011) *Modernist Short Fiction by Women: The Liminal in Katherine Mansfield, Dorothy Richardson, May Sinclair and Virginia Woolf*, Farnham, Surrey: Ashgate.

Freud, Sigmund (1930/1961) *Civilization and Its Discontents*, translated and edited by James Strachey, New York: Norton.

Galloway, Janice (1991) "Introduction", in *Meantime: Looking Forward to the Millennium*, edited by Janice Galloway, Edinburgh: Polygon, 1–8.

Galloway, Janice (1996) "Bad Times", *Review of Contemporary Fiction* 16(1): 39–43, https://www.thefreelibrary.com/Bad+Times.-a059410492 (accessed 31 July, 2017).

Galloway, Janice (2008) *This Is Not About Me*, London: Granta.

Galloway, Janice (2009) *Collected Stories*, London: Vintage.

Galloway, Janice (2015) *Jellyfish*, Glasgow: Freight Books.

Gilligan, Carol (1982/1993) *In a Different Voice: Psychological Theory and Women's Development*, Cambridge, MA: Harvard University Press.

Held, Virginia (2006) *The Ethics of Care: Personal, Political, and Global*, Oxford: Oxford University Press.

Hekman, Susan (2014) *The Feminine Subject*, Cambridge: Polity.

Illica, Luigi and Giuseppe Giacosa (1906) *Madama Butterfly: A Japanese Tragedy*, libretto translated by R.H. Elkin, http://opera.stanford.edu/Puccini/Butterfly/libretto_a.html (accessed 24 November 2017).

Innes, Kirstin (2007) "Mark Renton's Bairns: Identity and Language in the Post-*Trainspotting* Novel", in *The Edinburgh Companion to Contemporary Scottish Literature*, edited by Berthold Schoene, Edinburgh: Edinburgh University Press, 301–309.

"Interview with Janice Galloway" (2010) *The Short Review*, www.theshort review.com/authors/JaniceGalloway.htm (accessed 24 July 2017).

Jackson, Ellen-Raïssa (2004) "Love in a Changing Environment: Placing Janice Galloway's Short Stories", in *Exchanges: Reading Janice Galloway's Fiction*, edited by Linda Jackson, Edinburgh: Edinburgh Review, 7–20.

"Janice Galloway on Her New Short Story Collection" (2015) *The Scotsman*, https://www.scotsman.com/lifestyle/culture/books/janice-galloway-on-her-new-short-story-collection-1-3807920 (accessed 31 July 2017).

Jones, Carole (2007) "Burying the Man that Was: Janice Galloway and Gender Disorientation", in *The Edinburgh Companion to Contemporary Scottish Literature*, edited by Berthold Schoene, Edinburgh: Edinburgh University Press, 210–218.

Jones, Carole (2009) *Disappearing Men: Gender Disorientation in Scottish Fiction, 1979–1999*, Amsterdam: Rodopi.

Malcolm, David (2012) *The British and Irish Short Story Handbook*, Malden, MA: Wiley-Blackwell.

Manning, Rita C. (1992) *Speaking from the Heart: A Feminist Perspective on Ethics*, Lanham, MA: Rowan & Littlefiled.

March, Cristie Leigh (1999) "Interview with Janice Galloway", *Edinburgh Review* 101: 85–98.

March, Cristie Leigh (2002) *Rewriting Scotland: Welsh, McLean, Warner, Banks, Galloway, and Kennedy*, Manchester: Manchester University Press.

McGlynn, Mary (2001) "Janice Galloway", *Review of Contemporary Fiction* 21(2): 7–40.

McGlynn, Mary (2008) "'I Didn't Need to Eat': Janice Galloway's Anorexic Text and the National Body", *Critique: Studies in Contemporary Fiction* 49(2): 221–236.

McIlvanney, Liam (2012) "The Glasgow Novel", in *The Cambridge Companion to Scottish Literature*, edited by Gerard Carruthers and Liam McIlvanney, Cambridge: Cambridge University Press, 217–232.

MacLeod, Michael (2015) "Janice Galloway Calls for More Fiction about Parenting, Less about Sex", *The Guardian*, https://www.theguardian.com/books/2015/aug/21/janice-galloway-calls-for-more-fiction-about-parenting-less-about-sex (accessed 29 November 2017).

Metzstein, Margery (1993) "Of Myths and Men: Aspects of Gender in the Fiction of Janice Galloway", in *The Scottish Novel Since the Seventies*, edited by Gavin Wallace and Randall Stevenson, Edinburgh: Edinburgh University Press, 135–146.

Norquay, Glenda (2000) "Janice Galloway's Novels: Fraudulent Mooching", in *Contemporary Scottish Women Writers*, edited by Aileen Christianson and Alison Lumsden, Edinburgh: Edinburgh University Press, 131–143.

Paccaud-Huguet, Josiane (2004) "Breaking through Cracked Mirrors: The Short Stories of Janice Galloway", in *Exchanges: Reading Galloway's Fictions*, edited by Linda Jackson, Edinburgh: Edinburgh Review, 55–78.

Richards, Linda L. (2003) "January Interview: Janice Galloway", *January Magazine*, https://www.januarymagazine.com/profiles/jgalloway.html (accessed 28 July 2017).

Sacido-Romero, Jorge, Laura Torres-Zúñiga, Carmen Lara-Rallo and Isabel Andrés-Cuevas (2016) "Women's Tales of Dissent: Exploring Female Experience in the Short Fiction of Helen Simpson, Janice Galloway, A.S. Byatt, and Jeanette Winterson", in *On the Move: Glancing Backwards To Build a Future in English Studies*, edited by Aitor Ibarrola-Armendariz and Jon Ortiz de Urbina Arruabarrena, Bilbao: Universidad de Deusto, 345–350.

Sacido-Romero, Jorge (2018a) "An Interview with Janice Galloway", *The Bottle Imp* 23, https://www.thebottleimp.org.uk/2018/07/an-interview-with-janice-galloway/ (acessed 10 July 2018)

Sacido-Romero, Jorge (2018b) "Liminality in Janice Galloway's Short Fiction", *Zeitschrift für Anglistik und Amerikanistik: A Quarterly of Language, Literature and Culture* 66(4): (forthcoming).

Stirling, Kirsten (2008) *Bella Caledonia: Woman, Nation, Text*, Amsterdam: Rodopi.

Thomas, Ruth (1989) "Janice Galloway Interview", *Textualities*, 2(6), http://textualities.net/ruth-thomas/janice-galloway-interview (accessed 25 July, 2017).

11 Speaking from Border Country

Colour as Fluid Identity Factor in the Short Stories of Jackie Kay

Barbara Korte

Voicing the Margins?

Jackie Kay has often declared her attraction to the short story form. To Kay, a short story "is a small moment of belief. Hard, uncompromising, often bleak, the story does not make things easy for the reader. It is a tough form for tough times" (2017). The short story is special to her because of its intensity of effect and resonance:

> A story asks the reader to continue it after it has finished or to begin it before it began. There is space for the reader to come in and imagine and create. There is space for the reader to think for ages, to mull the impact of a story over, to try and recover from it! The short story is such a perfect form, you should really be able to lift it up and carry it into a huge cornfield, and it should still glow.
>
> (Kay 2017)

What the short story can illuminate in particular is, to Kay, the life of people "who are really on the edge" (Rustin 2012). She professes to like "seeing people at a moment of crisis or at a moment in time", and sees the short story as a form that "suits people who feel displaced or misplaced or who don't fit in, people who feel their very bones are lonely" (Rustin 2012). With this view, Kay seems to address a feature that is almost a staple of short story criticism. Ever since the publication of Frank O'Connor's *The Lonely Voice* (1962) and its famous reference to "submerged population groups" (4), short story theory has observed an affinity of the genre with life on the margins and experiences of marginality – with respect to gender, sexuality, ethnicity, class, region or situations of (post-)coloniality. As Clare Hanson observed in her 1989 survey of the modern short story, it is "a form of the margins, a form which is in some sense ex-centric, not part of official or 'high' cultural hegemony", and it has "offered itself to losers and loners, exiles, women, blacks – writers who for one reason or another have not been part of the ruling 'narrative' or epistemological/ experiential framework of their society" (2).

It is tempting to apply such statements to Jackie Kay and her work, where traces of her biography often show up. Kay was born in 1961 to a white Scottish mother and a Nigerian father, but was then adopted by white Scottish parents who raised her in Glasgow, far away from London and its emerging ethnic and cultural diversity. With her familial background, Kay is often described, by journalists and academics alike, as "Scottish" and "black", and because she is open about her sexual orientation, as "lesbian". These labels, individually and in combination, can also be attached to some – but not all – of her characters. However, as this chapter will point out with particular attention to some of Kay's black characters, Kay's short fiction, like her poetry and her longer works of prose – her novel *Trumpet* and her nonfiction (the memoir *Red Dust Road* and a book about Bessie Smith) – tends to destabilise simple identity ascriptions. Her work is less concerned with margins and exclusions than with experiences and states of liminality – moments of fluidity, shifts and transitions for which the short story, thanks to its brevity, slice-of-life-approach and open form, has a special propensity.[1] The crises, moments of decision or simply experiences of change with which people are confronted in Kay's stories can never be attributed simply to their skin colour, gender, sexual orientation or Scottishness, even if these dimensions may play a certain role.

Kay has always resisted attempts to pinpoint her own identity. An author portrait tied in with the publication of her third story collection, *Reality, Reality* (2012), quotes Kay complaining about how

> she was 'bogged down' in identity politics for a long time, and worries that the labels and categories it created – 'lesbian writer', 'black writer', 'Scottish writer' – can become a drag. 'You want to be open about being gay – why would you not be open about being gay? But you don't want to be defined by it,' is how she expresses the conundrum.
>
> (Rustin 2012)

In an interview originally conducted in 2008, Kay pronounced herself to have a "complex identity because I'm Scottish and I'm African and I'm adopted and I was brought up in Glasgow by white, working class socialists" (Rowell 2014: 270). She also speaks of a "mixture or a clash or a fusion of identities" that, to her, "has always been very enriching" (Rowell 2014: 270). What her personal background thus seems to have given Kay as a writer is a sensitivity to

> the borders and the borderlines that exist between one state and another and one country and another, one state of mind and other [sic]. I write from that border country. [... M]y identity is a complex,

shifting thing. At different times in my life it's been different things to me. I think identity is fluid.

(Rowell 2014: 270)

Kay's idea about writing from border country has some affinity with Victor Turner's broad definition of liminality in *The Ritual Process* (1969), here cited from the introduction to a collection of critical essays which views the short story as "the liminal genre *par excellence*" (Achilles and Bergmann 2015: 4): "In his [Turner's] words, '[l]iminal entities are neither here nor there; they are betwixt and between the positions assigned and arranged by law, custom, convention, and ceremonial'" (Achilles and Bergmann 2015: 3). Precisely because of their dislocatedness (neither here nor there) and in-betweenness, liminal structures and spaces have the potential to question and change preconceptions and so make readers inclined to "rethink their own concepts and beliefs" (Achilles and Bergmann 2015: 11), or, in Kay's words above, to mull their impact over.

Kay's anti-essentialist approach to identity can also be discussed within the theoretical framework of intersectionality as understood in cultural studies: that is, with attention to the fact that selves are always complex, that factors which shape personal identities are multiple, interrelating, influencing each other reciprocally and with variation from case to case.[2] Black feminist theory, from where the concept of intersectionality originally arose, has a special concern with black women's social oppression and marginalisation.[3] But this is not the dominant concern in Kay's stories. The women of colour these stories portray are not easily described as objects of racist and/or (hetero-)sexist ideology and behaviour. In a more fundamental sense, Kay's stories argue against all boundaries and binarisms that fix people in social categories. In "Sonata", from the collection *Wish I Was Here* (2006), the frame narrator notes that:

We break the world up into opposing groups the whole time, the rich and the poor, the young and the old, the black and the white, men and women, but actually as far as I can see the most neglected difference is between the beautiful and the ugly.

(Kay 2006: 164–165)

In this story, which is set in former Yugoslavia (a country broken up into, and broken by, ethnic binarisms) and concerned with the tragic end of a love relationship between women, oppositions of class, age, colour and gender are relativised by a much less well-defined opposition between the beautiful and the ugly, both in an aesthetic and ethical sense. Aesthetics and ethics intervene and undermine social categorisation. Such destabilisation of thinking "in groups" occurs in many of Kay's stories, and it also seems to determine the arrangement of her collections. The story with which Kay opens her first collection of short fiction, *Why Don't You Stop Talking* (2002/2003), seems chosen specifically to undermine expectations which readers might bring to a book by a black-Scottish-lesbian-adopted author not only well known for her earlier poetry but also the acclaimed transgender novel *Trumpet* (1998). "Shark! Shark!" begins with the word "he", referring to a (presumably white) "Scottish man in the middle of England" whose life is broken "into two pieces" (Kay 2002/2003: 4) after he has developed an irrational fear of sharks and, more generally, of death. This fear seems to be quite unconnected to the fact that he is Scottish and thinks with a Scottish accent.

Kay's conviction that identities are complex and its factors are fluid goes hand in hand with her versatile use of voice and perspective. This will be demonstrated in the third part of this chapter with a focus on stories whose female characters are identified as black *and* who are aware, or made aware, of their skin colour as an element of relevance in their current moment of being. It needs to be emphasised that this is only a portion of Kay's stories, and that there are other stories where a character's blackness does not seem to be related at all to the situation in which she finds herself,[4] or where the central characters are white (one even being the spitting image of Queen Elizabeth II), or where ethnicity is left completely unspecified. One wonders, therefore, why the publisher Picador, for their paperback edition of Kay's story collections on the market in 2017, decided on covers with photographs of black women. There seems to be an intention here to market Kay, as far as her fiction is concerned, not as a Scottish writer, but as a writer who speaks to women, and especially as a black British or multicultural writer in a line with successful authors like Andrea Levy and Zadie Smith.[5] Such niching may help to boost the sale figures of Kay's story collections, but it distracts from the variety of themes, people and voices they unfold between their covers, and it undermines the tendency in the stories themselves to de-emphasise skin colour and ethnicity as identitary factors. As a backdrop for the discussion of Kay's stories and their special ways of speaking "from border country", the next section sketches some other ways in which writers of short stories have addressed the situation of black women in Britain.

Excursus: Black Female Experiences and the Short Story in Britain

In Britain after World War II, the short story was soon adopted by new migrants from the West Indies. The stories in Sam Selvon's landmark collection *Ways of Sunlight* (1957) capture the experiences of what is now called the *Windrush* generation, after the iconic ship that brought Jamaican migrants to Britain in 1948. While Selvon's stories, with their distinctive Caribbean narrative voice, capture the experiences of the male migrant community, the most well-known (and most frequently anthologised) short story by a female writer about the female experience of early West Indian migration is Jean Rhys's "Let Them Call It Jazz" (1962/1968). Also employing first-person narration in (moderate) Caribbean vernacular, it conveys a woman's sense of displacement and her growing distress after she has lost work and lodgings. Having landed in prison, she feels alienated not only from the white Britain that rejects and excludes her, but also from herself. The lonely voice in Rhys's story speaks from a position of marginality, even abjectness. It was not until the 1990s that a new generation of black women writers turned to the short story and used it to voice their own experiences of a Britain that had become multi-ethnic and multicultural at least in its metropolitan parts (Korte 2003: 167–168). In the twenty-first century, stories about black women in Britain (especially London) reveal a wide range of experiences and identity positions between marginality and full participation.[6] The two following stories by prominent black British writers illustrate ways in which the short story addresses blackness in connection with contemporary migration.

Andrea Levy's story "Loose Change" (2005) initially presents a young woman who thinks of herself as an integrated member of her society. The first-person narrator is a teacher whose grandmother was a member of the Windrush generation, but who defines herself less as black than as a Londoner. Her self-identification seems to be post-ethnic and metropolitan, but it is disturbed during a chance encounter in the National Portrait Gallery, a setting dedicated to "the men and women who have and are shaping British history and culture from the Tudors to the present day".[7] The NPG's policy of representation in the present day is committed to inclusion and diversity; a photograph of Andrea Levy was purchased for its collection in 2004. The narrator of "Loose Change" seems to feel at home in the inclusive space of the gallery until she is confronted with a girl from a new generation of migrants from post-1989 Eastern Europe who at first arouses her sympathy because she has to beg and sleep on the street. But the narrator then refuses her the help which her own grandmother once received as a new arrival. The granddaughter of black migrants borders herself off from the white migrant of a later generation.

Zadie Smith's "The Embassy of Cambodia" (2013) is concerned with migration from Africa. The story is set shortly after the Olympic Games in 2012, which gave the British capital an opportunity to advertise its cultural variety and multicultural spirit. Smith's story is told from the collective viewpoint and in the collective voice of Willesden, one of London's most ethnically diverse communities. What the story's collective "we" witnesses are the experiences of a young woman who has arrived from the Ivory Coast via Ghana, Libya and Italy, and who manages to free herself from the quasi-enslavement she experiences as a domestic servant in a wealthy South Asian household. With its frequent references to walls and enclosed spaces, not only those of the Cambodian embassy, the story reads like an elegy to multicultural and multiethnic London. Different as they are in narrative concern and style, the two stories by Levy and Smith make being black in twenty-first-century Britain an explicit theme. So does Salena Godden, a spoken word artist and short story writer, in her contribution to *The Good Immigrant*, a collection of essays originally published in 2016 that responds to the resurfacing of racism during the months leading up to the Brexit vote. Godden's essay diagnoses a newly increased tendency to divide people by colour, and it uses a pertinent everyday metaphor:

> I now imagine a giant separating people like he is recycling glass at the bottle bank: brown skin glass here, yellow skin glass here, white skin glass over there. But most people aren't simply one or the other, either black or white. What about me? Where are you putting the two-tone people?
>
> I wish the giant would pick the glass people up and hold us all up to the light. Then he'd see that together and united as a people we are a beautiful picture, a multi-coloured mosaic, a glorious stained-glass window. But the giant just scratches his head and continues flinging people in separate buckets.
>
> (2016: 183)

As will be seen, Jackie Kay also uses the bottle-bank metaphor in one of her stories with a "two-tone" character, but without any idea of separating by colour. And where Godden refers to stained-glass window and mosaic, that is, fixed compositions, Kay's view of colour as an identity factor is better described with the metaphor of a kaleidoscope and the flexible arrangements of pieces it can create. Where Kay's stories are concerned with colour at all, they typically present it as multiply and fluidly enmeshed with gender, sexuality and other dimensions that can define a person's sense of self in twenty-first-century Britain. Depending on how the kaleidoscope is turned, very different patterns of identity emerge, and in Kay's stories they are conveyed in different constellations of perspective and voice.

Voicing It Differently

The characters in Kay's three story collections are a "mixed" community: black and white, male and female, straight and gay, young and old, poor and financially comfortable, Scottish and English, beautiful and ugly – all in different combinations. Befitting her interest in "seeing people at a moment of crisis or at a moment in time" (Rustin 2012),

Kay favours first-person narration or third-person narration with internal focalisation. This preference in narrative technique helps her to leave factors of a person's identity unspecified when the narrator or focaliser are unaware of them as normal circumstances in their lives.[8] Only when a change of circumstance occurs or when the perception of other characters denaturalises them, do the factors become conscious and may become the cause of feelings of misplacement or loneliness. The first-person stories in particular give Kay scope to demonstrate her talent for rendering voice and linguistic register, a talent that was arguably first honed on her poetry. Kay has herself commented on the affinity of the short story to poetry, noting that stories "share the brevity of poetry and the preciseness of language but they have a more open narrative lens and perspective" (Rowell 2014: 271).[9] Like some of her poems, some of her stories were originally broadcast on radio (BBC 3 and 4) or performed in theatrical versions, which underscored the distinctness of their voice and the special quality of their speech.[10]

As Kay revealed in an interview, she understands her whole work as essentially voice based; she thinks of language "as being voice" and of voice "as being related back to people"; voice is therefore seminal to her creation of character: "once I've got the voice for the person I can run with it" (Rowell 2014: 273). Personally, as Kay stated in an early author portrait in *The Guardian*, she used to feel frustrated when people paid more attention to her (black) face than to her (Scottish) voice: "I still have Scottish people asking me where I'm from. They won't actually hear my voice, because they're too busy seeing my face" (Brooks 2002). The unchangeable, purely external properties of a face do no reveal a person's being. It is through voice that a person expresses her identity and momentary state of mind. The importance Kay ascribes to voice is mirrored in the attention it is given by some of her characters. When a man's voice stops in the story "The Silence", this is the most devastating sign of the estranged relationship between spouses, especially because the man makes an effort to "blot [his wife's] voice out and truly not hear it" (Kay 2011: 79). In "The Oldest Woman in Scotland", the focalising character is celebrating her hundred-and-seventh birthday, and the readers are sharing her thoughts (rendered in free indirect discourse). In one passage, the old woman scrutinises her assembled family when a commemorative photo is made:

> There's her youngest, her favourite daughter, Elsie, who has still got braw skin like her mother used to, a natural bloom in her cheeks; there's her scruffy son-in-law, no even able to put on a proper shirt for the occasion, his hair falling in every direction; there's her overweight black granddaughter with her bonny face and her dark eyes, her long dangling earrings and her big bosom; there's the great-grandson, black as the Earl of Hell's waistcoat, with such

tight, tight curls on his head and his eenty teenty English voice; and there's the great-granddaughter with her long loose black curly hair and her cheeky wee smile. All lined up on the couch, putting on their faces.

(Kay 2002/2003: 120)

The occasion of the photograph emphasises face, but the blackness of the adopted grandchildren and their offspring is mentioned only in passing, alongside other features of appearance like body shape or style of dress. The old woman is much more affected by the fact that her great-grandson does not have a Scottish voice: "An awful shame", the old woman thinks, "when families move away to England and lose their good Scottish tongues. The young boy doesn't even ken who Rabbie Burns was" (Kay 2002/2003: 119–120). Similarly, in "Sonata", one of Kay's formally more complex stories, and one where the importance of (musical) sound is signalled in the very title, the frame narrator – also serving as a stand-in for the "real" reader – is captured by the voice of a woman who sits opposite her on a train and tells her the story of the love she destroyed with her jealousy: "Your voice was now inside my head. It seemed to go with the snow and the dark, your deep, husky, smoker's voice. You halted often, straining to use a language that was not natural for you" (Kay 2011: 159). If read as a metanarrative statement, the voice inside the diegetic listener's head – and by extension the head of the ac-tual reader – can be interpreted as the special resonance Kay associates with the short story form; an effect for which the use of voice in her own stories – including the oral/aural effects of rhythm and sound – is essential. The important thing is that a character's or narrator's voice, even when it speaks in a distinctive register – as in Kay's (few) stories rendered entirely in Scottish English[11] – never transports just a single aspect of a person's identity but a blend of the whole personality. The implications of Kay's various choices of voice and perspective will now be considered in conjunction with her attention to "blackness" and how it is intersected with other elements of a personality.

In "Out of Hand", from her first collection, Kay deals with a collec-tive "black" experience. She wrote the story in the context of the fiftieth *Windrush* anniversary in 1998. In this story, which is told in the third person, an elderly black woman investigates her once beautiful hands and remembers how she arrived on the *SS Empire Windrush* in 1948. In internally focalised passages, she wonders why she stayed in Britain despite the rejection to which she was exposed: "How come she thought England was her country? How did that happen? How was it that she thought when she got on that *Windrush* that she was coming home?" (Kay 2002/2003: 168). At the end of the story, the *Windrush* is only a "huge fiction of a ship" to her (Kay 2002/2003: 169); the phrase evokes the migrant's disappointed hopes and also questions the *Windrush*'s new status as a historical icon for a country that in the 1990s was beginning to discover its multiethnic history. "Out of Hand" is unique amongst Kay's short stories because it emphasises blackness and uses its character to voice a group experience of marginalisation and exclusion. Kay seems not too comfortable with this generalising kind of approach; she was also hesitant to make a contribution to the 200th anniversary of the abolition of slavery, claiming that she thought "enough had been written about slavery, and that [she] didn't want to be pigeonholed as a black writer" (qtd. in Zimmermann 2008: 124).

The issue of being pigeonholed as a black person is a sub-theme in another story from Kay's first collection, "Trout Friday". The main character (and single focaliser of the story), Melanie, bears "blackness" or "darkness" in her very name, which derives from the Ancient Greek *melaina* ('the black one'). But this blackness does not marginalise and only partly defines Melanie, who, like her white mother, enjoys variety. This is one reason why she takes pleasure in the market where she buys her vegetables, with its vibrant mix of goods as well as people whose different skin colours are noted, quite intersectionally, in one breath with qualities of wealth, character and emotional disposition:

> Brimming, bustling, boasting, bragging, black people, white people, poor people, cool people, scary people, soft people. The whole world is here, Melanie thought to herself, looking down the stalls as one carefully piled stack of fruit and veg competed with another for love or money. Melanie liked the market so much she thought of it as a person, bags of personality and generosity. Funnily enough, it reminded her of her mother. 'Variety, Melanie, the spice of life,' her mum would say. Her mother always liked to try things that were different.
>
> (Kay 2002/2003: 71–72)

Melanie is a young woman who works successfully as a travel agent and is materially comfortable enough to afford "elegant" food and wine. While her parents are migrants with distinct accents – her father, who left the family, from Trinidad, and her mother from County Mayo, never losing her Irish accent "despite living in England for thirty years" (Kay 2002/2003: 70) – Melanie speaks the language of a young professional Londoner and her voice shows no trace of her parents' respective origins. Rather, she takes pleasure in the distinctly London voices of the fruit men she hears on the market every morning: "The strange rhyming slang they used for money was music to Melanie" (2002/2003: 71). This suggests that Melanie is a voice- rather than a face-oriented person herself, but she cannot escape being perceived and referenced as a person of colour, just as she cannot help seeing her own face in the mirror: "when she looked in the mirror, the pair of them were behind her, mixing themselves up in her face. [...] It still struck her as interesting that colour could be blended like that, as if people were paint" (Kay 2002/2003: 68–69). As the word "interesting" suggests, the pigmentation of her skin is nothing that Melanie herself has a problem with; because she is sensitive to visual beauty, she approaches skin colour aesthetically. She is therefore disturbed by the way others treat her skin as a raced surface, how she is colour-coded not only by white people, and in linguistic categories she finds partly offensive, partly laughable:

> She'd read somewhere that people with her colour of skin were now being called *beige*. Somehow she didn't like *beige*; it made her think of fashion and clothes. It made her ask questions like: does beige go with khaki? *Beige Britain*. She said, 'No!' out loud when she read that in her magazine. 'Please!' But she didn't like it when one of the girls at work called her *half-caste* because it sounded insulting and she didn't like *mixed-race* because it made her feel muddled. Certainly not *mulatto*, it made her think of mules. Definitely not people who said to her, 'You're neither one thing nor the other.' [sic] because that made her feel left out, belonging to nobody. [...] Most upsetting of all, she didn't like it when other black people described her as being *red* or *high yellow* because that made her feel like a primary colour.
>
> (Kay 2002/2003: 69–70)

As this passage indicates, Melanie has a good ear for language and a talent for language play that gives her a certain autonomy over compartmentalising language use. Melanie has a "concern over labelling", as Abigail Ward writes in her analysis of the story (2016: 352), but she also has the linguistic versatility to deal with the racism implied in labels for her skin colour. Melanie's punning – like her appreciation of visual beauty and her culinary skills – can be seen as an aesthetic strategy to cope not only with discrimination but with life in a far more fundamental sense. Melanie's major problem is that she is (momentarily) lonely because she has already experienced many traumatic losses in her young life: her beloved mother and uncle are dead, and her boyfriend left her after she had a miscarriage. But Melanie is determined to master the situation, and her main strategy is to ensure herself against further loss by trying to be "in perfect control" (Kay 2002/2003: 78), for instance by creating her own rituals. This is already conveyed, as Ulrike Zimmermann notes, with a "bitterly humorous tone" (2008: 131) at the beginning of the story, which mentions Melanie's systematic teeth brushing: "She'd lost too much already and she was only twenty-three and she didn't want to lose her teeth into the bargain" (Kay 2002/2003: 67). Another strategy to keep her life in order is to eat healthy food, and in particular a different kind of fish, each weekday; she also makes the effort to cook and serve it nicely even if she has to eat it alone. On Fridays, Melanie eats trout, a fish her mother liked, so that she thinks about her mother on Fridays. But on the Friday on which the story is set, the self-imposed structure of Melanie's life is destabilised when she receives a "perplexing" (Kay 2002/2003: 70) letter from her father, whom she always believed to have returned to the Caribbean. The letter (which is not rendered verbatim, thus denying the father a voice of his own) reveals that he has always lived in Tottenham and would now like to meet his daughter. Melanie is given an unexpected chance to regain someone she lost, and to learn more about her paternal heritage, but she then decides not to and chooses to leave the current equilibrium in her life undisturbed, even if one void in her life might be filled, and even if it means that it will need more time until she can enjoy the variety of life as fully as her mother did. "Trout Friday" addresses ethnicity as a (possible) identitary factor but at the same time relativises its importance. The story's main concern is the lonely young woman's resilience, her determination to cope with loss and loneliness, and the relevance of her skin colour is de-emphasised in this wider context.

Such de-emphasising also occurs in the much bleaker monologue story that gives Kay's first collection its title, one of several in Kay's compilations that portray characters in the state of severe psychological disturbance.[12] "Why Don't You Stop Talking" shares some motifs with "Trout Friday" (a mixed-race central character suffers from loneliness and is preoccupied with language, eating, and the mouth in general), but it treats them very differently. Where "Trout Friday" uses a controlled third-person narration (befitting a character who tries to keep her life under control), "Why Don't You Stop Talking" is a first-person monologue in a vernacular voice that is only stopped by shock. As the speaker introduces herself: "My dad was from Jamaica and my mum were a real East Ender" (Kay 2002/2003: 44). The distinctly oral quality of the narration corresponds with the oral compulsion that is the story's main theme: an orality that cannot be contained either in relation to speech or food. In this respect, the story's speaker, Thelma, is named with irony since the Greek *thelema* means "volition" or "will". Thelma makes an effort, but has considerable difficulty to exert her will, both over her intake of unhealthy sweets and the irrepressible verbosity she appears to have inherited from her mentally unstable (white) mother: "I do have one of those tongues that gets me into a load of trouble. I can't help myself. I just come out with what's in my head and it has caused me terrible problems all my life" (Kay 2002/2003: 41). It is this disturbance, the inability to control her voice and what it utters, and not primarily her skin colour, that is at the core of Thelma's feeling of powerlessness: "It's not the talkers that have the power; it's the silent ones. They're the ones that rule the world" (Kay 2002/2003: 49). In Thelma's perception, the world also belongs to the beautiful and not the ugly like herself. Unlike

Melanie in "Trout Friday", Thelma is neither young nor elegant; she is fat and constantly believes herself exposed to shapist prejudice.[13] This is not to say that her blackness does not contribute at all to Thelma's distress, but it is not in the foreground and only occurs in intersection with other factors, some of which are of much graver consequence.

From the beginning of her monologue, Thelma is on the edge of despair, and that this despair is mouth-centred is epitomised in the haunting image with which the story ends after she has cut her tongue with a razor: "The blood is generous and very red and it pours down my face. I wish they could all see me now" (Kay 2002/2003: 50). Blatant self-destruction is the only way in which Thelma can act against her oral compulsions and at the same time accuse those who have diminished her self-esteem. This tough ending certainly makes the reader mull the impact of the story over. The image of the cut tongue is disturbing not only because of its violence, but also because there is a cognitive dissonance between the narrator's assertion of having destroyed a speech organ and the ongoing voice of the narration. This discrepancy might suggest that the self-harming act has happened only in the narrator's imagination as she has drifted more deeply into mental disturbance. Nevertheless, whether imagined or real, the cut tongue is the result of a day that has driven Thelma finally over the edge. She herself interprets her particular vulnerability on that day as premenstrual syndrome, trivialising it as a recognised female disorder that stops once menstruation (bleeding) sets in. But Thelma's psychological fragility cannot be relieved and stopped by bleeding because it is rooted in her unhappy childhood and the social isolation which results from that early period in her life. Thelma is perfectly aware that her problems are not primarily caused by other people's rejection but by the fact that she cannot restrain herself and, especially, her speech. For this character, being able to speak is a dilemma because what she voices (all her accumulated anger and frustration), and how she voices it, alienates the people around her. Tragically, Thelma is able to diagnose what is wrong with her, but she cannot cure herself, and she does not ask for help because an insensitive remark by her grandmother to the young Thelma has instilled her with a deep fear of the Red Looney Van Men who "will come for you and take you to the asylum, to the mental home where you'll learn to hold that tongue of yours" (Kay 2002/2003: 43).[14] The kind of talk that could actually help Thelma and release her despair, that addressed to a therapist, is stifled by her deeply ingrained fear of mental institutions.

The sense of tragedy that pervades Kay's story – up to its literal moment of catharsis in an outpouring of blood – is reflected in a three-act structure of events. On the single day narrated in the story, Thelma's distress and aggression first find vent in a supermarket, where she feels provoked by the stare of a slender, beautiful and "very well-spoken" woman (Kay 2002/2003: 39) at her well-filled shopping trolley. Thelma verbally attacks her, only to be asked in turn why she doesn't stop talking. Thelma can only prevent further escalation of the situation by having her next verbal outpouring discreetly and off-limits:

> The times I am silent when I need to talk is as hard as bursting for a piss. I can feel the talk coming and it's like a physical thing. I rushed outside and talked to myself behind the recycling bins where nobody could see me except an old alkie who was rummaging through some discarded bottles which hadn't made it inside either the brown or the green or the white bins.
>
> (Kay 2002/2003: 42)

The concisely described setting of discarded things that have not been orderly sorted – that are literally uncontained – underlines how Thelma's disorder turns her into a social outcast like the old alcoholic. However, her clandestine vomit of words does not help. After a second episode where she is undeservedly abused by a queue-jumping man at a cash machine (he refers to her "fat black mouth", the only openly racist remark in the story [Kay 2002/2003: 45]), Thelma witnesses how a skinny, stressed-out and presumably white woman is unkind to her child. This incident – and especially the quality of the woman's voice – triggers memories of her own unloved childhood with a mother who "could be vicious with her tongue" (Kay 2002/2003: 44). She says:

> It was her voice I heard first. It were so loud and shrill. I told myself to walk on but I couldn't help but notice that she was shaking her child, back and forth, on the street, really shaking him like he were a rag doll.
>
> (Kay 2002/2003: 45)

This arouses Thelma's ethical impulse to help the child. In polite and carefully restrained language, she tells the woman to treat her boy more kindly, but, like a counterpart to Thelma and presumably her mother, the woman is unable to control her aggression and attacks Thelma, even physically, which then triggers the final catastrophe: "I can't afford to take no more risks. Every time my tongue gets me into trouble, it will be punished. Then it will soon learn. I pick up the razor and I cut my tongue" (Kay 2002/2003: 50). In her reading of the story, Ulrike Zimmermann claims that Thelma with her cut tongue is "a modern-day Philomela who has internalised her victimisation" and that, as in Ovid's rendering of the myth, the cut-off tongue "simply refuses to stop calling for help" (2008: 128). Just as the silenced Philomela can still weave to reveal the story of her rape to her sister and sing as a nightingale after she has been transformed by the gods, Thelma's voice survives her self-destructive act and speaks of her despair and the reasons behind it; despite the tragedy that unfolds in the story, the surviving voice thus also has an element of resilience.

The emphasis on voice as a means to overcome subjection and grief is even more pronounced in the last story to be discussed here, "The First Lady of Song", from *Reality, Reality*. This story also alludes to the Philomela myth but with a particular interest in the metamorphosed Philomela, the nightingale – not only because its first-person narrator is a singer, but also because it is a piece of magic-realist writing. The story is thus inscribed in a tradition of women's fiction whose liminality between fabulation and realism has permitted authors from Virginia Woolf to Jeanette Winterson to rewrite hegemonic, masculine versions of history and myth. "The First Lady of Song" also has a feminist dimension, but above all its fantastic element allows Kay to treat skin colour, an apparently fixed aspect of face, as a shifting and changeable factor of identity. This is possible because apart from the Philomela myth, the story also connects with women's fantasies of eternal life, like Mary Shelley's "The Mortal Immortal" and Woolf's *Orlando*. In her life of three centuries, Kay's narrator-protagonist changes her skin colour as well as her sexual orientation, and along with these changes, the story can even develop a felicitous resolution to Kay's face-voice opposition.

Voice is a conspicuous element in this story from the very title, which references a famous black jazz singer, Ella Fitzgerald, acclaimed as "the first lady of song". Kay's first-person narrator, now living as Emilia Marty, looks back to a life in which she once became (and un-became) Ella. Before that phase in her life, she was many other singers after her father gave her, originally Elina Makropulos, a potion that stopped her aging process. The narrator describes herself as her "father's experiment" (2013: 41), as the victim of male scientific hubris that causes her great suffering until she finally finds the means to revert the spell and set herself free.

The story was commissioned by Glyndebourne for its 75th Festival of Opera and first published in an anthology of opera-inspired stories edited by Jeanette Winterson, *Midsummer Nights* (2009). The opera that inspired Kay's story is Leoš Janáček's *The Makropulos Affair*, in whose narrative a doctor also concocts a life-prolonging drink and tests it on his daughter. "Elina Makropulos" and "Emilia Marty" are names from Janáček's opera, but Kay adds the (first) names of other famous singers to her story and especially introduces the dimensions of blackness, same-sex love and ageing as decisive factors in her character's long way towards personal happiness and final self-identification. Despite its bleak beginning, Kay's story develops a celebratory note that befits a festival of opera. It is a tribute to the beauty of the female voice or rather, a series of female voices: "When I sang Elina's head off, Eugenia came. When I sang Eugenia's head off, Ekateriana came. When I sang Ekateriana's arias, Elisabeth came. After Elisabeth I was Ella" (Kay 2013: 42). To Kay's narrator, singing is a means by which she can live through the pain that her unwanted immortality causes her because she is bound to lose everyone she loves: "many husbands, countless children, grandchildren, great-grandchildren" (2013: 42). At one stage in her life she even gives up loving because otherwise she would no longer be able to bear the grief. Her inability to age also causes an insecure sense of identity because the narrator slips from period to period, from persona to persona and from name to name (only ever keeping its initial E) without being able to share the secret of who she really is (or was). She has therefore also found it difficult to *tell* her story and so create a meaningful self-narration: "Talking, I always trip myself up, make some nasty mistake" (Kay 2013: 41). Only when she begins to age again and her series of lives is stopped can she tell the story we read. Before that point, her singing voice was the only means by which she was able to create some continuity between her lives, remembering them "through music – what I was singing when" (Kay 2013: 42). And, as in Philomela's case, singing is also a way through which she survives the violence she has suffered herself and the history of subjection (of women and black people) to which she was a living witness.

In "Trout Friday", Melanie's aesthetic outlook is one of her strategies to cope with life, including instances of casual racism provoked by her skin colour. In "The First Lady of Song", a story about vocal art, skin colour is treated in a completely different way because blackness becomes a catalyst for the art itself. While the narrator's physical appearance does not change in shape or height, her skin at one point becomes darker, and this change of face goes hand in hand with a change in the colour of her voice. The time when she lives and sings as Ella is the "favourite period" in her life (Kay 2013: 42) because it enhances her artistic potential and because it gives her access to a musical tradition (spiritual, blues, jazz) that arose from (and defied) subjection and suffering.

The treatment of blackness in this magic-realist story exemplifies Kay's conviction that identities are fluent. The narrator's blackness is not genetic but emerges after she has already lived for more than two centuries; once it has entered her life, it intersects with other identitary elements, some of which are stable while others – like the narrator's lesbianism – are emergent themselves. Blackness as presented in this story is also much more than an element of "face" because it is conjoined with a darkening of voice and hence artistic potential. Emilia Marty perceives the darkening of her voice as an expansion of range: from classical singer she can turn into a jazz singer, Ella, with a vocal range famously "spanning three octaves" (Kay 2013: 45). As Ella, she also experiences her first intense feeling of liberation: "When I came to be Ella I was so much more independent. Those were plucky, scatting days. Even the moon bopped in the sky" (Kay 2013: 47). The widened range associated with blackness stays with the narrator when she becomes a classical singer again; as Emilia Marty, she turns an even darker shade of black than Ella, and this blackness is never treated as a raced surface. Like the narrator in "Trout Friday", Emilia Marty perceives her black skin in aesthetic terms; it is a beauty – the black beauty of the nightingale – she wears proudly: "I wear a great dark skin now, like a dark lake, like a lake at night with a full moon in the sky" (Kay 2013: 43). Thanks to its magical realism, "The First Lady of Song" presents blackness as a fluent property that does not constrain an identity but, in intersection with other factors, may help a person to expand her potential. Emilia Marty eventually gains happiness and self-identification not only because she is black, but also because she has discovered lesbian love and has begun to age. At the happy end of her story, she falls in love with another beautiful middle-aged woman who is a lover of music and good food, and who immediately recognises Emilia as who she is. This woman is said to have "curly hair" (Kay 2013: 55), but otherwise her ethnicity remains vague and arguably matters less than her other features. This fabulated story achieves a perfect moment of closure that expresses, almost paradoxically, Kay's conviction that "identity is a complex, shifting thing" (Rowell 2014: 270).

Conclusion: The Short Story as Kaleidoscope

Jackie Kay appears to be attracted to the short story because this liminal genre *par excellence* permits her not only to present characters who feel dis- or misplaced, but also to express her conviction that identity is kaleidoscopic, intersectional and fluid, that its single components can be arranged in different patterns and are of shifting relevance in an individual's life. In Kay's view, a person cannot and should not be pinpointed to their gender, sexuality, ethnic background or skin colour, should not be reduced to a merely outward face. It is through voice that personalities express themselves, and it is through characters who speak and think "from border country" that her stories illuminate moments of deep existential crisis, but also experiences of change that may lead to a positive end. The way Kay as short story writer tends to be marketed by her publisher and discussed in reference works, namely as black and female/lesbian, conceals the way in which she treats colour, sexuality or both in the stories themselves: in a de-emphasised manner that does not deny the significance they may have in a person's life but claims that this significance may not be always there, that a person may not be permanently aware of them, or even defined by them. Being black, or a (lesbian) woman, may sometimes contribute to a character's feelings of displacement and loneliness, but Kay never lets them take a person's life – or a story – over. With the exception of "Out of Hand", an untypical story in her oeuvre, Kay does not approach colour as a factor of marginalisation, but as one element among others that may affect a person's self during a phase in their lives. This approach distinguishes her work from other stories about black women in twenty-first-century Britain. That some of Kay's characters perceive their skin colour aesthetically may seem unpolitical, especially at a time when Brexit has brought racist and exclusionist thinking to the fore again. But one might also claim that this position, and generally the humanity of Kay's stories with their many voices and attention to the variety of lives and selves, is what can be held up to new racisms (or new sexisms).

Notes

1 Adrian Hunter's *Cambridge Introduction to the Short Story in English*, for instance, identifies the genre as "particularly suited to the representation of liminal or problematized identities", and as speaking "directly to and about those whose sense of self, region, state or nation is insecure" (2007: 138).
2 For an introduction to intersectionality theory and its major tenets, see Collins and Bilge (2016), and for a critical discussion, Cooper (2016).
3 As Cooper emphasises, "[i]ntersectionality constituted a specific paradigm or framework for understanding black women's subordinated social position and the situated effects of mutually constructing systems of power and oppressions within black women's lives. Never did [Kimberlé Williams Crenshaw's] work indicate that intersectionality was an effective tool of accounting for identities at any level beyond the structural" (2016: 390).
4 On Kay's technique of de-emphasising skin colour see also Arana (2009: 252). More often than not, Kay's stories mention their characters' blackness off-hand, just as a character's homosexuality is usually mentioned casually and matter-of-factly. See, for instance, "Big Milk", "Pruning", or "Making a Movie".
5 The recent *Cambridge History of the British Short Story* also mentions Kay in its chapters on multicultural and on queer stories, but not in the chapter on Scottish stories, although a number of them have a Scottish setting and/ or Scottish characters.
6 For a survey see also Korte (2016), especially 46–47.
7 As declared on the gallery's web page: www.npg.org.uk (accessed 23 July 2017).
8 In *Why Don't You Stop Talking*, half of the stories use a first-person narrator; in *Wish I Was Here*, seven out of twelve, and in *Reality, Reality*, only one story is not told in the first person.
9 On how Kay's poetry "is concerned with the voiceless other", see Aydin (2010: 116).
10 See Kay's acknowledgements to *Wish I Was Here* and *Reality, Reality*. As the acknowledgement page for the latter volume states, "Mind Away" was "commissioned by Sky Arts and shown in a dramatized version as part of the *Theatre Live* series" (Kay 2013).
11 "A Guid Scots Death" (*Why Don't You Stop Talking*) and "Mini Me" (*Reality, Reality*).
12 See "Shark! Shark!", "The Woman with Fork and Knife Disorder" and "Shell" (*Why Don't You Stop Talking*), "My Daughter the Fox" (*Wish I Was Here*), and "The White Cot" (*Reality, Reality*).
13 For more humorous treatments of weight problems, see "Mini Me" (*Reality, Reality*) and "Reality, Reality" from the same volume.
14 The colour red here already anticipates the story's bloody end.

References

Achilles, Jochen, and Ina Bergmann (eds.) (2015) *Liminality and the Short Story: Boundary Crossings in American, Canadian, and British Writing*, New York and London: Routledge.

Arana, R. Victoria (2009) "Clothing the Spirit: Jackie Kay's Fiction from *Trumpet* to *Wish I Was Here*", *Women: A Cultural Review* 20(3): 250–261.

Aydin, Özlem (2010) *Speaking from the Margins: The Voice of the 'Other' in the Poetry of Carol Ann Duffy and Jackie Kay*, Bethesda, MD: Academia Press.

Brooks, Libby (2002) "Don't Tell Me Who I Am", *The Guardian*, www.theguardian.com/books/2002/jan/12/fiction.features (accessed 6 October 2017).

Collins, Patricia Hill and Sirma Bilge (eds.) (2016) *Intersectionality*, Cambridge: Polity Press.

Cooper, Brittney (2016) "Intersectionality", in *The Oxford Handbook of Feminist Theory*, edited by Lisa Disch and Mary Hawkesworth, Oxford: Oxford University Press, 385–405.

Godden, Salena (2016) "Shade", in *The Good Immigrant*, edited by Nikesh Shukla, London: Unbound, 181–197.

Hanson, Clare (1989) *Short Stories and Short Fictions, 1880 to 1980*, Basingstoke: Macmillan.

Hunter, Adrian (2007) *The Cambridge Introduction to the Short Story in English*, Cambridge: Cambridge University Press.

Kay, Jackie (2002/2003) *Why Don't You Stop Talking*, London: Picador.

Kay, Jackie (2011) *Wish I Was Here*, London: Picador.

Kay, Jackie (2013) *Reality, Reality*, London: Picador.

Kay, Jackie (2017) "A Writer's View", in *Booktrust*, www.booktrust.org.uk/books/adults/short-stories/articles/a-writers-view-kay (accessed 2 June 2017).

Korte, Barbara (2003) *The Short Story in Britain*, Tübingen: Francke.

Korte, Barbara (2016) "The Short Story and the Anxieties of Empire", in *The Cambridge Companion to the English Short Story*, edited by Ann-Marie Einhaus, Cambridge: Cambridge University Press, 42–55.

Levy, Andrea (2005) "Loose Change", in *Underwords: The Hidden City*, edited by Maggie Hamand, London: Maia, 67–76.

O'Connor, Frank (1962) *The Lonely Voice: A Study of the Short Story*, London: Macmillan.

Rhys, Jean (1962/1968) "Let Them Call It Jazz", in *Tigers Are Better Looking*. London: Andre Deutsch, 47–67.

Rowell, Charles Henry (2014) "An Interview with Jackie Kay", *Callaloo* 37(2): 268–280.

Rustin, Susanna (2012) "A Life in Writing: Jackie Kay", *The Guardian*, www.theguardian.com/books/2012/apr/27/life-writing-jackie-kay (accessed 2 June 2017).

Shukla, Nikesh (ed.) (2017) *The Good Immigrant*, London: Unbound.

Ward, Abigail (2016) "New Voices: Multicultural Short Stories", in *The Cambridge History of the English Short Story*, edited by Dominic Head, Cambridge: Cambridge University Press, 341–357.

Winterson, Jeanette (ed.) (2009) *Midsummer Nights*, London: Quercus.

Zimmermann, Ulrike (2008) "Out of the Ordinary – and Back? Jackie Kay's Recent Short Fiction", in *Multi-Ethnic Britain 2000+: New Perspectives in Literature, Film and the Arts*, edited by Lars Eckstein, Barbara Korte, Eva Ulrike Pirker, and Christoph Reinfandt, Amsterdam: Rodopi, 123–137.

Part V
Narrating Life

12 Stories Told and Untold

Re-gendering World War I through Centenary Narratives

Isabel Carrera Suárez

Introduction: The Old Gendered Story

War narratives have traditionally been fundamental in the construction of collective identities. Imperial wars, civil wars, liberation wars, even wars fought for relatively unclear reasons, mould – and are moulded by – national discourses, and condition communal attitudes towards those designated as outsiders. In their most conservative versions, war narratives constitute exaltations of patriotic feeling and often foreground a barbaric enemy, even while unfolding the suffering of battle. As Carol Cohn has argued, there is "an old story about war", one in which warfare is "a quintessentially masculine realm", where men make decisions, fight, die, "protect their helpless women and children" and continue to exercise power when the war is over (2013: 1). In this "old story", women are absent or marginal, since they symbolically represent the alternative to battle, "a place of love, caring, and domesticity [...] all that is good about the nation which their heroic fighting protects" (Cohn 2013: 1). This "old" gendered pattern continues to underlie many narratives, despite the critiques and alternative knowledge rendered by the twentieth century in the areas of scholarship, public opinion and artistic expression which have transformed the general perception of past and present wars. The realities of war are complex, and their literary accounts are, in their turn, as varied as the historical conditions and stances of the authors and nations from which they stem. In Britain, as in other Western contexts, a growing body of writing has recorded and analysed a more nuanced narrative of the realities of war, one that distinguishes between types and contemplates historical settings, that travels beyond the battlefield to include the lives of those absent from it, those who return home wounded or traumatised (Achter 2010; Mayhew 2014), all those whose destinies are forever changed by a social disruption of dramatic consequences. The "old" gendered conception of war, its bond to normative masculinity, meant that war narratives by and about women were slower to surface or, when made public, were often neglected. Recent scholarly work, however, not only recovers narratives by and about women, but also employs a perspective which allows the foregrounding of women's wide-ranging experience of war (Higonnet 1995), both as active participants and as objects of a violence too often silenced (Cockburn 2013; Cohn 2013).

Perhaps because the twenty-first century began with episodes signalling the danger of war in home territory, the British commemorations of the centenary of World War I, opening in 2014, were especially charged with political meaning. The anniversary prompted discussion of a struggle won at a bitter cost, and in times anticipating the decline of the British Empire. It also inspired creative writing and collective projects which evidence the change of thought produced in the intervening century, not least in matters concerning Empire, world view and gendered relations. My object of analysis here is a collected volume, *1914 – Goodbye to All That: Writers on the Conflict between Life and Art*, edited by Lavinia Greenlaw and published in 2014, within the five-year *14–18-Now* arts programme.[1] Greenlaw commissioned ten texts by authors from countries which participated in World War I, asking them to write in response to *Goodbye to All That*, Robert Graves' famous "bitter leave-taking of England" (Graves 1929/1958: xv), his autobiographical essay on the suffering and incompetence of the War, and on post-conflict reinforcement of pacifism, social equality and atheism. The contributions written by women, most particularly those by Ali Smith, Xiaolu Guo and Jeanette Winterson, for whom Britain is birthplace or adoptive country, will constitute my main focus. These three authors occupy relatively peripheral positions in the geo-psychic map of British literature, while very centrally discussing aspects of British culture. My analysis will pair their relatively ex-centric and critical war narratives with the alleged liminality of the genre of the short story, reading their hybrid texts, which move between essay and story, between fiction and auto/biography, within the context of the twenty-first century perceptions of war, gender and art.

Women, Empire and World War I: A More Inclusive Story

World War I did in fact have its own female chroniclers in the genre of the short story. The quintessential modernist practitioner of the form, Katherine Mansfield, who felt that artists would be traitors if their expression went unaffected by the war, left emotive accounts of the absence and loss experienced by civilians, albeit in the oblique manner of a "covert war writer" (Edwards 2017: 50), through disruptions of form and language. A similarly powerful but oblique treatment of war is present, for instance, in Virginia Woolf's stories.[2] This indirect technique may be considered the war mode of modernist writers, a style later to be analysed as mirroring the symptoms of post-traumatic stress disorder (Higonnet 2002; Raitt and Tate 1997). However, and despite its *avant garde* artistic relevance, this was not the only approach to World War I in narrative written by women. Some authors challenged taboo subjects, as Radclyffe Hall did in "Miss Ogilvy Finds Herself", where a woman is finally able to adopt a role fitting to her transgender desires by becoming an efficient ambulance commander. Discarded after the war is over, the story turns to fantasy and she morphs into an ancient Briton, shifting from "she" to "he", in a trespassing of genre boundaries by Radclyffe which parallels the transgression of the story's character. "Miss Ogilvy Finds Herself" is one of the iconic stories inscribing the diverse manner of women's participation in war, a subject re-examined later in the century by authors like Sylvia Townsend Warner, and by scholarly works such as those by Angela K. Smith (2000a; 2000b), Margaret Higonnet (1987) and Jane Potter (2005).

This broader knowledge on women and war, built up throughout the twentieth century, is part of the inherited wisdom of contemporary writers, as proved by the recent volume *War Girls: A Collection of First World War Stories through the Eyes of Young Women*, also published in the anniversary year of 2014 (Geras, Doherty, Fine, Hooper and Burgess 2014). Written by nine established authors of young adult fiction, these stories look at women's war lives, mostly away from the battlefield but in a variety of roles that show courage, passion and love amid loss and grief. This is a lively, documented and enlightening collection of narratives, some of which are inspired by historical characters: Norah Neilson Grey, the Glasgow artist who volunteered as a nurse (Breslin's "Shadow and Light"); Helen Zenna Smith, writer and ambulance driver (Burgess's "Mother and Mrs Everington"); the more collective experience of women artists-entertainers (Doherty's "Sky Dancer"), nurses, waitresses, spies (Hooper's "Storm in a Teacup") and the two million "spare women" left behind by men who went to war (Nicholls's "Going Spare"; Geras's "The Green Behind the Glass"). The fact that these stories about women's agency in the "Great War" were still received by readers with surprise ("like no other WW1 fiction I have read before", [Erica 2014]; "makes us see the First World War in a totally different light", [Scribe 2014]) attests to the endurance of the "old story", even while their content shows the extent to which women's involvement in war affairs is now exposed and recognised.

A decade into the current century, Britain faced preparations for the 2014 centenary of a war that now had almost no survivors. The crucial role played by the UK in World War I, strongly conditioned by its imperial habits, left a deep trace in the country's history; this so-called "war to end all wars" left millions dead and the nation bankrupt, while those who made and traded in weapons amassed a huge fortune. The cost, even for the winners, was incalculable, in deaths, in wounded and traumatised survivors, in social disruption and lost human potential. Not surprisingly, the commemoration of the start of the war in 2014 generated a heated debate in the UK. In the face of a Prime Minister (David Cameron) intent on strengthening British nationalist feeling, who compared the occasion to the Royal Jubilee, pacifist platforms like *No Glory in War* (http://noglory.org/) collected news countering official triumphalism and presented information on less known or publicised aspects of the "Great War". This website published an open letter against bellicism, signed by British writers, film makers and public figures. The letter, which begins by describing World War I as "a military disaster and a human catastrophe", opposed Cameron's commemorations, which were aimed at stressing the "national spirit" and led in part by military authorities ("No Glory Open Letter" 2014). In contrast with this patriotic celebration, signatories of the letter foregrounded the lucrative impulse and territorial power struggle behind a war which left sixteen million dead and twenty million wounded; they suggested that the anniversary be used "to promote peace and international co-operation" ("No Glory Open Letter" 2014). While official acts returned to the "old story of war" underlining heroic feats and war tactics, part of British society read this official commemoration route as a strategy to justify current militaristic interventions. They responded critically by organising alternative movements which might help to grasp the lessons of this distant war for the present, and where the world of arts and literature played a prominent role. Carol Ann Duffy, Poet Laureate, contributed to the *No Glory* website by signing the letter and producing three poems on the Great War: "An Unseen", inspired by Wilfred Owen, "The Christmas Truce", on the moment when soldiers from both sides stopped the battle on Christmas day, and "Last Post", a homage to the only two remaining survivors of World War I. It was in this climate that poet Lavinia Greenlaw coordinated the publication of a collective volume, *1914 – Goodbye to All That. Writers on the Conflict between Life and Art* (2014), by inviting ten international writers to discuss the subject of artistic identities shaped by conflict (8).[3]

While the massive territorial and social change brought about by World War II has been extensively dealt with in recent fiction from and about the former colonies of the British Empire,[4] World War I had not produced such proliferation of the Empire writing back to the centre (Ashcroft, Griffiths and Tiffin 1989; Rushdie 1982) in contemporary terms. This gap may have suggested one of the key principles guiding Greenlaw's collection, that of including a spectrum of the nations involved in the war. Her appeal to writers from different origins aims to represent at least a fraction of the international actors in World War I, which despite its common denomination, is often taken to have occurred exclusively between European forces. As she explains in the introduction, the selection aimed to palliate general unawareness "of the true extent of global involvement that political repercussions, complex allegiances and colonial grip incurred" (Greenlaw 2014: 8). In today's Britain, while the Gallipoli massacre of young Australian and New Zealand soldiers is renowned and mythologised, other transnational human contributions are far less visible. The website *No Glory* reproduced an article published by *The Observer* on 23 August 2003 headlined "A More Inclusive Story from the Trenches: The Role of Non-European Troops in the First World War", which stresses how "a combination of deliberate exclusion and accidental myopia dramatically shrunk the First World War. Rather than the kaleidoscopic, multiracial, global conflict that it was, it became a monochrome European struggle" (Olusoga 2003). Some texts in Greenlaw's anthology stem from this same impulse to correct such amnesia.

The reach of the editor's invitation, to writers across nationalities and to six women (out of a total of ten contributors), is already a signal of the century of distance from 1914, which has resulted in a different sensibility towards imperial power, the interdependence of the world and women's public roles. The female contributors are Ali Smith (UK), Kamila Shamsie (Pakistan/UK), Elif Shafak (Turkey/France), NoViolet Bulawayo (Zimbabwe/USA), Xiaolu Guo (China/UK) and Jeannette Winterson (UK). Two are contingent residents in London (Guo, Shamsie), all live in the West, but only Smith and Winterson are British-born, in arguably peripheral parts of the UK, Scotland and Northern England respectively. Their texts, therefore, set out from a gendered, decentred standpoint not coincident with the official war narrative.[5] Some also clearly stand between genres, despite the fact that they are responding to Graves' *Good-Bye to All That*, a book-length essay which is also admittedly an idiosyncratic text. Although commissioned by the editor to meditate on art and war, on the gap between past and present, and on the tensions between life and art, the contributors chose forms that move freely between essay, auto/biography and fiction-writing. In particular, the two texts I will discuss in more detail, Xiaolu Guo's "Coolies" and Ali Smith's "Good Voice", are narrated in the form of stories, notwithstanding their incursions into history, life writing or journalistic prose, and their effective deployment of a first person authorial persona.

Susan Lohafer maintains that the relationship between fiction and non-fiction (the imaginary and the verifiable) finds its most interesting and frequent performance on the borders between the short story and "the art of the personal essay", as well as in their reception by readers (Lohafer 2015: 108). This firm conviction led her to carry out a formal analysis of what she terms "micro-markers of storyness", the subtitle of her essay (Lohafer 2015). Hybrid genres are of course hardly new in the practice of literature, but postmodern theory and writing, as well as twenty-first-century transmedial developments, have accustomed readers to a more intense practice of genre hybridity, in parallel with the enhanced physical and symbolic border-crossing which is one of the defining characteristics of the era. Creative writers produced abundant ficto-essays near the end of the twentieth century and in the first decade of the twenty-first.[6] In different degrees, the contributors to *1914 – Goodbye to All That* offer texts that shuttle between essay and story, with Ali Smith and Xiaolu Guo's leaning most clearly towards story structures.

Xiaolu Guo's "Coolies": Bitter Labour for the Western Front

One of the most striking contributions to the collection, Xiaolu Guo's "Coolies", follows a historical tract rarely discussed in talk of the "Great War". The world view of this multimedia artist, born in China in 1973,[7] is enriched by a personal history of dramatic life shifts, having moved successively from rural to urban China, from a suffocating Chinese artistic environment to a freer Western one that she embraces without relinquishing her critical outlook and cultural liminality. "Coolies" combines her interest in the effects of history on individuals, her ability to imagine and empathise with their fate, and her documentary talent and versatility, which allows her to gauge East and West with admirable fluency. The title of the story anticipates a deceptively familiar reference to a colonial Indian word and concept,[8] soon to be questioned by the tale. Guo's narrative rescues one of those groups omitted from the official accounts of the "Great War", the 100,000 Chinese peasants recruited by the British Army to dig European trenches:

> The coolies of China went everywhere. They built the railways that crossed the American Wild West and went from the Arctic to Siberia; they worked in Peruvian silver mines and Trinidadian sugar plantations. You can find evidence of coolies in the museums and histories of almost every country in the developed world. Yet there is one particular group of coolies who have been long ignored and almost entirely forgotten: the 100,000 contracted to the British Army during the First World War and sent from eastern China to the ashes and mud of the European trenches.
>
> (2014: 126–127)

Brought to France under deception, put to work in the trenches in a regime of slavery, many died from forced labour and racist abuse. Guo's text inscribes these naïve economic migrants, most of them thoroughly ignorant of this geographically distant war by using the symbolic force of the defining term *kuli*, a Chinese word which (unlike its English counterpart) lacks any negative connotations: "Historically, the majority of Chinese have been labourers. The Chinese believe that hard physical work can keep one alive, therefore 'coolie' is a neutral term. In the West, however, 'coolie' carries all the negative connotations of imperialism and exploitation", those derived from the near-slave circumstances of colonial workers (Guo 2014: 126). In China, we learn, *kuli* means "bitter labour" or "bitter strength", with bitterness viewed as a healing, necessary taste. Historical records, however, reveal that the thirty-two camps of the "British Chinese Labour Corps" established along the Western Front, far from keeping their workers alive, were sites of death and racist mistreatment, as is crudely described in the documents quoted:

> A diary published by a British lieutenant, Daryl Klein, entitled *With the Chinks,* records what he calls the "Sausage Machine" training centre where the Chinese were taught drill. He writes: "There is a rivalry among the officers in regard to the number of canes broken on the back, legs and shins, not to speak of the heads, of the defaulters." For crimes such as gambling and fighting, transgressors were punished by anything from docked pay to imprisonment of between three and fourteen days. If a coolie fell ill, his wages were immediately stopped.
>
> (Guo 2014: 129–130)

War documents record 2,000 deaths at the front, but suspected figures are closer to 20,000; causes of death are not documented. Guo's author-narrator describes, in the first person, a visit to Flanders, crossing the Channel to accompany a friend, Li Ling, to the cemetery of Noyelles-sur-Mer, the site of 842 tombstones bearing Chinese names along with the number assigned to each worker, a demeaning practice born from Western inability to distinguish one Chinese person from another. Against the odds, Li Ling locates her great grandfather's tomb, surprisingly dated 1919:

> So he died here not during the war but *after* the war! "How?" I ask Li Ling. She doesn't know. Did he die from a random explosion during mine clearances? Or from starvation? Or was he killed for desertion? There is no clue. Only some blackbirds flapping their wings in the distance. Then, beside Li Changchun's Corps number, I see this phrase: *Faithful unto death.*
>
> I look away. I can't bear the hypocrisy let alone the indifference with which this phrase has been foisted on this man. My eyes wander along the rows of Chinese names. The inescapable wind buffets the graves, otherwise there is silence. I look back. Li Ling is carefully placing her bunch of yellow chrysanthemums on her grandfather's tomb.
>
> (Guo 2014: 134–135)

The combined pathos and poetic tone of this narrative ending confirm the fictional structures of the text against the essayistic historical fragments quoted earlier. In other sections, a combined autobiographical and historical narrative underlines the situatedness of diverging readings of history: far from representing heroic mementoes, poppies in China are reminders of a shameful past, the Opium Wars during which the British Empire deliberately distributed and promoted opium among the Chinese to secure huge economic and strategic benefits: "My teacher was very clear: 'How to understand British history? Two things – they invented Capitalism and they forced opium on China.' Any Chinese who went to school in the '70s and '80s would have been taught these two facts" (Guo 2014: 131). Guo's East and West differ in their perception of wars and commemorations. For a Chinese person, the key date in the early twentieth century is 1917, the October Revolution and the advent of Communism. To the ordinary Chinese,

> war means above all massacre. The most infamous example is per-haps the An Lushan Rebellion, during the Tang Dynasty, which left 36 million dead. Some historians believe this to have been the largest atrocity in human history in that one-sixth of the world's entire pop-ulation at that time was lost.
>
> (Guo 2014: 131)

In more recent times, the devastating Rape of Nanking (December 1937) left behind "a city of corpses" (Guo 2014: 131). This stunning death toll and the generalised ignorance of such events in the West, where the author-narrator is expected to be conversant with European history, puts into perspective the ground still to be gained in reciprocating world knowledge.

Guo's story combines a search for the life of an individual, a friend's late grandfather, with the act of restoring into history the lives of the thousands of Chinese dead or enslaved in the fields of France, a deed of memory and reparation. Deploying narrative strategies of historical research, journalistic reportage and personal memoir, the text crucially pivots around a symbolic linguistic issue: the term *kuli*, which constitutes the title and the concept which encapsulates the meanings and cultural contradictions of the compelling multi-layered story. "Coolies" is a his-toriographic postcolonial narrative with a difference. China is not offi-cially a former colony, part of the usual migration routes from the British Empire, but the story clearly invokes a colonial European memory. It begins by subverting colonial knowledge itself, questioning our accepted version of the origins of the word *coolie*, to extend its application to a shameful (hence conveniently forgotten) case of exploited labour during World War I, tangentially reminding us of the equally shameful Opium Wars. In so doing, it takes readers beyond the usual territory of English language writing, yet paradoxically it does so from the capital of the UK, the multicultural, vibrant London, albeit one currently swept by the uncertainties of Brexit.

Ali Smith's "Good Voice": Telling (Gendered) Silences

This transnational, language-inflected angle on war is at the core of other contributions to the volume, which thus confirm the critical context of Guo's and Smith's stories. "Coolies" deals with three themes that recur in *1914 – Goodbye to All That*: war as lucrative and colonial (against official narratives of inevitability); the urgency of historical memory; and the links between peace, freedom and creativity. If Guo explains her exile as the consequence of stifling censorship in China, Kamila Shamsie, NoViolet Bulawayo and Elif Shafak describe their writing as inextricable from the turbulent history of their countries, which have moved from colonialism into complex internal and geostrategic struggles. Shamsie's "Goodbye to Some of That" traces how she came to "link Pakistan and its politics to memory and narrative" (2014: 33), her "personal Origin Story" inspiring all her early Karachi fiction. Equally tied to national politics is her first memory of experiencing empathy, an essential writerly skill, during a childhood visit to a relative under house arrest. Her later work on World War II with non-Pakistani protagonists breaks this homecoming writing habit but continues to explore conflict and memory. Zimbabwean writer NoViolet Bulawayo, in her heartfelt bio-historical manifesto, "Clarity", singles out the courageous act of fellow artist Owen Moseko, who publicly broke the official silence on the massacre of the Mdebele (1983–1987), as a turning point in her own writing, leading to her adoption of Bulawayo as a memorialising penname, and her decision "never to choose silence" (2014: 100). Her text stresses language's symbolic power and defines her own writing as a "love-letter" to her people (Bulawayo 2014: 106) from the diasporic distance of the USA, blissfully connected through the Internet. Equally focusing on memory and language, Elif Shafak's "In Search of Untold Stories" conveys the cultural loss suffered by Turks after their Ottoman language was banned by Ataturk, whose modernising frenzy deprived his people from reading the texts of their past. Shafak's writing strategy therefore includes the use of recovered Ottoman words together with the oral tales of women, the "bearers of memory" and "custodians of cultural continuity" (2014: 84). In relation to World War I, she quotes the striking image passed on by her grandmother describing soldiers "frozen to death, hundreds of them trench after trench, still standing, like trees of ice" (Shafak 2014: 80). The finding or recovering of voices, cracking those silences, is a running theme in the collection: "In the land where I come from silences are telling, weighty. There is more discontinuity than continuity, more amnesia than memory" (Shafak 2014: 77).

This paradoxical chorus of silences and lost voices has poignant expression in the structure of Ali Smith's markedly "storied" contribution to the volume, "Good Voice", a dialogue between a writer and her father, a Navy man in the 1940s (and the son of a First World War veteran) who, despite being dead, proves a flippantly belligerent interlocutor. The story condenses many of Smith's vintage narrative pleasures: a refusal of categories and linearity, the unpredicted juxtaposition of words, sources and perspectives that suggest an unresolved story, and multiple stories, to be completed by readers. Like other Smith texts (such as, relevantly, "true short story"), "Good Voice" includes a narrator-character ambiguously identifiable with the author. Within this dialogic frame, the narrator is seeking inspiration to write on World War I and the father acts as a memory bank, silent about his own combat experience, but providing the daughter with episodes from her own formative years: "doing" the Great War at school, joining the anti-nuclear movement, being chosen for school commemorations. The dialogue unravels her learning of the official and the alternative story of war, against the silence on her father's and grandfather's war traumas or her mother's life when she also joined the war, in the WAF.

In the opening of the story, the narrator shares with her father the surprising discovery that, in World War I, a voice bank of British and Irish accents was collected, ironically, by a German linguist who traversed the prisoner of war camps, recording and thus saving accents that otherwise would have been lost forever. The century-old voices of those prisoners, now available through the Internet (and more fully from the British Library), become part of the growing choir of voices contained by the story, those of war artists and troop entertainers like Gracie Fields, whose songs the father favours; those of the War Poets, rising from their texts in a school anthology, as they used to rise in her teenage nightmares in the form of a mudman from the trenches; those of the old school exchange girls from Germany, nonplussed at their classmates' taunts about Nazis; contemporary pacifist songs, Boy George and Culture Club singing "The War Song", Marianne Faithful singing "Broken English". These remembered, recorded and spectral voices inhabit the story, as the narrator-author explores perspectives on the "Great War". In a random Internet search, she finds a photo of

> Austrians executing Serbs 1917. JPG.
> Description: English: World War 1 execution squad.
> Original caption: "Austria's Atrocities. Blindfolded and in a kneeling position, patriotic Jugo-Slavs in Serbia near the Austrian lines were arranged in a semicircle and ruthlessly shot at a command".
> (Smith 2014: 13)

In another search, she discovers that the Scottish Highlands had the highest casualty rate per capita in Europe.

Throughout this extended enquiry, father and daughter engage in a singing duel: "My father starts singing when he hears the word song.

Oh play to me Gypsy. That sweet serenade" (Smith 2014: 11). He punctuates the story with his versions of Gracie Fields and other patriotic (and patriarchal) Second World War love songs. The daughter counters by singing Culture Club's "War is stupid, people are stupid", to her father's disdain. In a parodic version of the "flyting" tradition going back to Scottish *makars*, bards who contended in witty invectives, father and daughter compete in singing arguments that not only display their differing perspectives on war, but also on sexuality and gender. When the father, whose singing is meaningfully described as "wildly out of tune" (Smith 2014: 11), suggests that Boy George might have benefitted from war, the daughter reminds him of Wilfred Owen's homosexuality. Whether the spectral father's thinking can be affected retrospectively remains uncertain, but the daughter's glimpse into the horrors of war does finally translate into emotion, after she extracts all the phrases she has underlined over the years in her old war poetry anthology, to form an impromptu concrete poem, a collective "found poem" on the pathos of that "Great War":

> Consciousness: in that rich earth: for the last time: a jolting lump: feet that trod him down: the eyeless dead: posturing giants: an officer came blundering: gasping and bawling: you make us shells: very real: silent: salient: nervous: snow-dazed: sun-dozed: became a lump of stench, a clot of meat: blood-shod: gas shells dropping softly behind: ecstasy of fumbling: you too: children: the holy glimmers of goodbyes: waiting for dark: voices of boys rang saddening like a hymn: a god in kilts: God through mud: I have perceived much beauty: hell: hell: alleys cobbled with their brothers: the philosophy: I'm blind: pennies on my eyes: piteous recognition: the pity war distilled: I try not to remember these things now: people in whose voice real feeling rings: end of the world: less chanced than you for life: oaths Godhead might shrink at, but not the lice: many crowns of thorns: emptied of God-ancestralled essences: the great sunk silences: roots in the black blood: titan: power: in thirteen days I'll probably be dead: memories that make only a single memory: I hear you still: soldiers who sing these days.
>
> (Smith 2014: 24–25)

This exercise conjures her old nightmarish "man of mud and sadness" who rises "like a great wave, like a great cloud much bigger than the earth", speaking "with all the gone voices. He is a roaring silence" (Smith 2014: 25). The roaring silence of the execution photograph, where the men are "shooting people so close to them that they could have reached forward and touched them without even moving their feet" (Smith 2014: 25). The roaring silences of war. The daughter's sudden tears of understanding move the father to insist on uplifting songs in his Gracie

Fields *falsetto* (Smith 2014: 26; my emphasis). But the cross-purpose exchange between the two trails to an end, the father leaving with his out-of-tune Gracie Fields, the daughter retorting Marianne Faithful, whose "Say it in broken English" (Smith 2014: 26) closes the story, dubiously granting the daughter the last word.

Ali Smith's fondness for the concentration of the short story form is well known, and her pastiche technique grants this story a capacious inclusion of past and present voices, together with their verbal and non-verbal exchanges on war, love, non-binary gender and the breaking of masculinist codes, as well as on the victims (and perpetrators) of these. "Good Voice" was reproduced, a year after the publication of this volume, in Smith's collection of short fiction *Public Library and Other Stories* (2015), demonstrating, on the one hand, the contingency of genre categories, and, on the other, confirming the unclassifiable nature of Ali Smith's texts. Just as her Weidenfeld lectures, published in *Artful* (2012a), blended fiction (and a ghostly presence) with critical theory, this story complies with the essay function, unearthing data and reflecting on them in an authorial voice, without renouncing the efficacy of the short story's intensity to stimulate the imagination and elicit empathy.

Jeanette Winterson's "Writing on the Wall": War, Economy and Human Creativity

In contrast with Smith's metaliterary opening piece, Jeanette Winterson's contribution, which closes the collection, is clearly inclined towards the essay form. "Writing on the Wall", a meditation on the value of art and creativity, takes us back to the industrial revolution and, quoting statements that could have been made in the present, compares the current climate of growing social inequality and uncontrolled capitalist development to that ruthless past. She reminds readers that in Marx's view, "[s]ocialism was needed to provide for man's animal needs (food and water, shelter, safety, health, rest, a clean environment), so that man might have leisure to supply his human needs", and that those human needs are "[l]ove and friendship, family life, education, intellectual pursuit, sport, enquiry, curiosity, books, music, art in all its changing shapes and forms [... T]he common denominator is creativity" (Winterson 2014: 158–159). Arguing against utilitarian education, which breaks the creative continuum we inhabit from childhood, she exposes the claim that art is an elitist activity as a new myth, used to justify withdrawal of funding:

> it's a mass-culture myth, and it suits the true elite of the world who has no interest in democracy or in human potential. The elite of the world depends on cheap labour, mental lethargy, depression so deep that change seems impossible, and strict segregation of entitlement.
> (Winterson 2014: 160)

In contrast, she points out, "we can always afford a war" (Winterson 2014: 161). In a modified version of the famous First World War memorial slogan "Lest we forget", she argues, with Adrienne Rich, that "the danger lies in forgetting what we had" (Winterson 2014: 167), forgetting our acquired human rights. The essay conducts a historical tour through past moments of support for learning and the arts: the first public library in the UK, created in her home town, Manchester, in 1852; the growth of public libraries (294 by 1900); Andrew Carnegie writing in *The Gospel of Wealth* that "Man does not live by bread alone … there is no class so pitiably wretched as that which possesses money and nothing else" (Winterson 2014: 168); Maynard Keynes persuading the British government after World War II to accept paintings for the National Gallery in lieu of payment from France; Engels looking at factories in Manchester and writing in 1844, in *The Condition of the Working Class in England*, that their exploitative horror is "what happens when men regard each other only as useful objects" (Winterson 2014: 170). As counterforce, Winterson defends that "the creative continuum recognises human beings as much more than useful objects" (Winterson 2014: 170).

Winterson's analysis of war, economy and art is upheld by recent social research. Many studies of masculinities prove how governments that concentrate funds on war, deviating them from social issues, leisure and art, are closely associated with militaristic masculinities and male bonding practices.[9] As Cynthia Cockburn demonstrates, war and gender relations are mutually shaping. In pre-war periods or times of perceived danger, patriarchy and nationalism are exacerbated, decisions masculinised and a high percentage of the Gross National Product goes to reinforcing armies and training children for roles of protecting family and so-called national honour. Cockburn (2013) maintains that gender power relations (masculinities) fit especially well into the *root* causes of war as described by Brian Fogarty (2000): that is, those predisposing a society to belligerence.[10] Gender relations and masculinist values (including economic decision-making) need to be challenged in order to avoid war, as campaigns like *No Glory* are aware. The unquestioning of binary gender identities (Smith), the ignorance of the past (Guo) and the loss of the humanising creative continuum (Winterson) can lead to a passive acceptance of such a pre-war economy. War narratives that examine gender relations, whether academic or creative, contribute to valuable knowledge of how conflict is produced and managed.

Critical Centennial Narratives: Knowledge, Difference and the Challenge of Creativity

The war stories by Ali Smith and Xiaolu Guo discussed here differ in thematic focus and in narrative strategies, displaying authorial (and autobiographical) traces that identify them as the work of their unique creators. This of course is equally true of the remaining texts in Lavinia Greenlaw's volume and of those in the anthology *War Girls*. Yet it is also a century-old truism that writings, as modernist Virginia Woolf put it in *A Room of One's Own*, "are the outcome of many years of thinking in common, of the thinking by the body of people, so that the experience of the mass is behind the single voice" (Woolf 1929/1998: 85). In terms of later critical formulations, they are the product of intertextuality, but I would like to underline here two essential features of this collective aspect of writing: on the one hand, the importance of accumulated, shared knowledge, built through academic and non-academic research, and disseminated through a variety of conduits, which include literature; on the other, the singular efforts of the authors here discussed to foreground, through their fictional strategies and skills, that diverse "mass behind the single voice" which makes up their stories (Woolf 1929/1998: 85).

The contemporary narratives we have been examining benefit from the expanded knowledge accumulated in the past century on war, women, global relations, post/colonial analysis, gender and queer theory, a knowledge transmitted and accessed, as the stories show, through the enhanced connectivity and mobility of the information age. They show the shifts taking place in the twenty-first century, changes in paradigm from globalisation to planetarity,[11] from dual male/female patterns of sexuality and gender to non-binary subjectivities transcending categorisation. These new perspectives, characterised by open-endedness, multiplicities and potentialities, but also by a strong ethical component, could not have developed or continue to develop without memory and the restorative salvaging of the voices and stories omitted by the dominant, unifying discourses of power.

The pieces collected in *1914 – Goodbye to All That* strive to bring those "voices of the mass" into their texts, more fully aware of who this "mass" may have been, with an ear more attuned to differences – in class, ethnicity, sexuality, gender, exclusion, strangerhood – that were not articulated, or generally foregrounded, in the otherwise pathbreaking writing of the modernists or in British war literature of the early twentieth century. The approach taken in these centennial writings is explicitly intersectional and inclusive, more prone to bordercrossing in both national and literary terms. The proverbially liminal short story form, in its easy intersection with the essay, allows writers to pose direct questions in authorial voice while juxtaposing the fictional resources that recreate voice and subjectivity, that are able to bring characters alive (even spectrally from the past) in order to provoke empathy. Ali Smith has repeatedly declared her passion for the form of the short story, for its poetic concentration and the brevity that she claims forces us to face mortality (Smith 2012b). Both her story, "Good Voice", and Guo's "Coolies" foreground a (mass) mortality whose ghosts return in different guises to teach us about being human. Through the essayistic, transmedia investigation of data and evidence, and by engaging our emotions through the recreation of human voices, the stories are able to convey the depth and variety of the lives affected by World War I, and to expose the underlying gender structures.

These tales of World War I, investigations which unearth shameful episodes of wartime racism and the inhumanity of battle and which challenge the gendered, root causes of war, cannot but suggest alternative readings of contemporary conflicts. They do so by exploring history and the complexities of language, trusting creative writing to communicate beyond the merely rational. The stories confront indifference and cultural amnesia, looking back from these centennial moments which, as Winterson reminds us, require collective action to challenge the patterns of a pre-war economy, to salvage our human side in times when "the writing on the wall" does not predict a peaceful future of egalitarian access to knowledge, humanity and creativity.

Notes

1 The *14-18-NOW* project can be found at: www.1418now.org.uk. It presents itself as "Extraordinary arts experiences connecting people with the First World War" and is still going strong in 2018, the year of the centenary of the armistice. Among other activities, it coordinates a celebration of the centenary of women's vote, achieved on 6 February 1918, with the event *Processions* planned for June 10 in London, Edinburgh, Cardiff and Belfast. Former actions include the very successful installation *Blood Swept Lands and Seas of Red* by Paul Cumming and Tom Piper that "planted" 888,246 ceramic poppies at the Tower of London.

2 After World War II, Rosamond Lehman will also portray women's alternative lives in households without husbands and fathers, watching young men leave for the front, and Elizabeth Taylor (1985), in "The Devastating Boys", leaves a memorable account of the miscommunication between working-class mixed-race children and the affluent families who host them temporarily.

3 Some of the authors also participated, in July 2014, in a public debate and book presentation within the "Great War" cultural events organised by the British Library and in a further event in Edinburgh. Information about *1914 – Goodbye to All That* related activities appears at: www.1418now.org.uk/commissions/goodbye-to-all-that/.

4 The list of novels would be interminable. *Small Island* (2004), by Andrea Levy, and *White Teeth* (2000), by Zadie Smith, are among the already classic millennial novels written by women that return to World War II from the UK with a broader territorial reach, with the Caribbean and South Asia featuring in both. In former colonies, Simone Lazaroo's *The Australian Fiancé* (2000) moves between Singapore and Australia, as does Hsu Ming Theo's *Love and Vertigo* (2000), to mention only a brief sample.

5 This was made evident in the reaction of a member of the public in the presentation of the book at the British Library in July 2014, an elderly man and veteran, who stood up to accuse the writers participating in the discussion of having no idea what the war had been about.

6 Canadian literature, particularly prolific in this arena, offers excellent examples of ficto-criticism by Margaret Atwood, Michael Ondaatje or Aritha van Herk, and already in the new century, Lawrence Hill or Esi Edugyan, at times coining new genre terminology, such as van Herk's *geograficitone*.

7 Guo lives in London, also spending periods in Berlin. She is usually described by promotion material as "Chinese-British" and was listed in Granta's Best of Young British Novelists in 2013. Her films and novels range from documenting London's nocturnal dwellers to fictionalising Chinese and Western characters, cities or history. She has also published a collection of short stories, *Lovers in the Age of Indifference* (2010).

8 The etymology of the word is traditionally traced to Tamil or Hindustani, and the concept was most famously applied to Indian unskilled labourers in colonial times, the term subsequently becoming generalised to refer to any unskilled, exploited labourers.

9 For a summary of some of these, see Cockburn, who discusses studies such as Robert Dean's *Imperial Brotherhood* (2001) on the elite men surrounding John F. Kennedy at the time of the Vietnam War, "warrior intellectuals" educated and socialised in male-only institutions, or see Altinay's study of the militaristic birth of the Turkish state founded by Artatürk, where education turns every male child into a soldier (2004).

10 Fogarty (2000) distinguishes between immediate prompts to war (for instance, access to oil), antecedent causes (such as ethno-national interests) and *root* causes, which predispose societies to belligerence.

11 For the theoretical and ethical difference between these two related terms, see Spivak's *Death of a Discipline* (2003) and Elias and Moraru *The Planetary Turn* (2015).

References

Achter, Paul (2010) "Unruly Bodies: The Rhetorical Domestication of the Twenty-First-Century Veterans of War", *Quarterly Journal of Speech* 96(1): 46–68.

Altinay, Ayse Gul (2004) *The Myth of the Military Nation: Militarism, Gender, and Education in Turkey*, Basingstoke: Palgrave.

Ashcroft Bill, Gareth Griffiths, and Helen Tiffin (1989) *The Empire Writes Back: Theory and Practice in Post-Colonial Literatures*, London: Routledge.

Bulawayo, NoViolet (2014) "Clarity", in *1914 – Goodbye to All That: Writers on the Conflict between Life and Art*, edited by Lavinia Greenlaw, London: Pushkin, 91–107.

Cockburn, Cynthia (2013) "War and Security, Women and Gender: An Overview of the Issues", *Gender and Development* 21(3): 433–452.

Cohn, Carol (ed.) (2013) *Women and Wars: Contested Histories, Uncertain Futures*, Cambridge: Polity Press.

Dean, Robert D. (2001) *Imperial Brotherhood: Gender and the Making of the Cold War Foreign Policy*, Amherst, MA: University of Massachusetts Press.

Edwards, Stephen (2017) "Katherine Mansfield and the Trauma of War: Death, Memory and Forgetting in 'An Indiscreet Journey', 'The Garden Party', 'At the Bay', 'Six Years After' and 'The Fly'", *Journal of the Short Story in English* 69: 37–54.

Elias, Amy J. and Christian Moraru (eds.) (2015) *The Planetary Turn: Relationality and Geoaesthetics in the 21st Century*, Evanston, IL: Northwestern University Press.

Erica, Cara (2014) "Review of *War Girls* by Adele Geras et al.", *The Guardian*, www.theguardian.com/childrens-books-site/2014/jul/01/review-adele-geras-war-girls (accessed 15 December 2017).

Fogarty, Brian E. (2000) *War, Peace and Social Order*, Boulder, CO: Westview.

Geras, Adele, Berlie Doherty, Anne Fine, Mary Hooper and Melvin Burgess (2014) *War Girls: A Collection of First World War Stories Through the Eyes of Young Women*. London: Andersen Press.

Graves, Robert (1929/1958) *Goodbye to All That*, 2nd edition, London: Doubleday.

Greenlaw, Lavinia (ed.) (2014) *1914 – Goodbye to All That: Writers on the Conflict between Life and Art*, London: Pushkin.

Guo, Xiaolu (2014) "Coolies", in *1914 – Goodbye to All That: Writers on the Conflict between Life and Art*, edited by Lavinia Greenlaw, London: Pushkin, 123–136.

Higonnet, Margaret R. (1987) *Behind the Lines: Gender and the Two World Wars*, Ithaca, NY: Yale University Press.

Higonnet, Margaret R. (1995) "Another Record: A Different War", *Women's Studies Quarterly* 23 (3/4): 85–96.

Higonnet, Margaret R (2002) "Authenticity and Art in Trauma Narratives of World War I", *Modernism/Modernity* 9(1): 91–107.

Klein, Daryl (2009) *With the Chinks in the Chinese Labour Corps During the Great War*, London: Naval and Military Press.

Lohafer, Susan (2015) "Between Story and Essay: Micro-Markers of Storyness", in *Liminality and the Short Story: Boundary Crossings in American, Canadian, and British Writing*, edited by Jochen Achilles and Ina Bergmann, London: Routledge, 108–120.

Mayhew, Emily (2014) *Wounded: A New History of the Western Front in World War I*, Oxford: Oxford University Press.

"No Glory Open Letter", *No Glory in War 1914–1918*, http://noglory.org/index.php/open-letter/no-glory-in-war-open-letter (accessed 15 December 2017).

Olusoga, David (2003) "A More Inclusive Story from the Trenches: The Role of Non-European Troops in the First World War", *The Guardian*, www.theguardian.com/commentisfree/2014/aug/23/neglected-figures-of-past-deserve-memorial-too (accessed 15 December 2017).

Potter, Jane (2005) *Boys in Khaki, Girls in Print: Women's Literary Responses to the Great War, 1914–1918*, Oxford: Oxford University Press.

Raitt, Suzanne and Trudi Tate (eds.) (1997) *Women's Fiction and the Great War*, Oxford: Clarendon Press.

Rushdie, Salman (1982) "The Empire Writes Back with a Vengeance", *The Times* 3 July: 8.

Scribe, Sophie (2014) "Review of *War Girls* by Adele Geras et al.", *The Guardian*, www.theguardian.com/childrens-books-site/2014/aug/28/review-war-girls-adele-geras (accessed 15 December 2017).

Shafak, Elif (2014) "In Search of Untold Stories", in *1914 – Goodbye to All That: Writers on the Conflict between Life and Art*, edited by Lavinia Greenlaw, London: Pushkin, 75–89.

Shamsie, Kamila (2014) "Goodbye to Some of That", in *1914 – Goodbye to All That: Writers on the Conflict between Life and Art*, edited by Lavinia Greenlaw, London: Pushkin, 27–40.

Smith, Ali (2012a) *Artful*, London: Hamish Hamilton.

Smith, Ali (2012b) "Interview with Arifa Akbar: Conversations with the Undead", *Independent*, www.independent.co.uk/arts-entertainment/books/features/conversations-with-the-undead-ali-smith-gives-the-lecture-a-haunting-twist-8226873.html (accessed 17 December 2017).

Smith, Ali (2014) "Good Voice", in *1914 – Goodbye to All That: Writers on the Conflict between Life and Art*, edited by Lavinia Greenlaw, London: Pushkin, 9–26.

Smith, Ali (2015) *Public Library and Other Stories*, London: Hamish Hamilton.

Smith, Angela K. (2000a) *The Second Battlefield: Women, Modernism and the First World War*, Manchester: Manchester University Press.

Smith, Angela K. (ed.) (2000b) *Women's Writing of the First World War: An Anthology*, Manchester: Manchester University Press.

Spivak, Gayatri Chakravorty (2003) *Death of a Discipline*, New York: Columbia University Press.

Taylor, Elizabeth (1985) *The Devastating Boys*, London: Virago.

Woolf, Virginia (1929/1998) *A Room of One's Own and Three Guineas*, Oxford: Oxford University Press.

Winterson, Jeanette (2014) "Writing on the Wall", in *1914 – Goodbye to All That: Writers on the Conflict between Life and Art*, edited by Lavinia Greenlaw, London: Pushkin, 153–171.

13 Women's Transcultural Experience in A.S. Byatt's Short Stories

Carmen Lara-Rallo

Introduction

In her contribution to the millennial issue of the *New York Times* (1999), the short story writer, editor and critic A.S. Byatt was asked to write about "The Best Story". Her contribution, later retitled "The Greatest Story Ever Told" in her essay collection *On Histories and Stories* (2000), opened with the question about which the greatest story ever told could be. Significantly, Byatt's reply focused on the *Thousand and One Nights*, whose prevalence across countries and along the centuries is analysed in terms of the intersection of life and storytelling: "Storytelling in general, and the *Thousand and One Nights* in particular, consoles us for endings with endless new beginnings [...] Scheherazade's tales have lived on, like germ-cells, in many literatures" (2000/2001: 166, 167).

One of the afterlives of the *Thousand and One Nights* can be found in "The Djinn in the Nightingale's Eye", from the title piece of Byatt's 1994 collection of stories. This narrative, which adopts the structure of embedded tales characteristic of the *Thousand and One Nights*, signals Byatt's fascination for Eastern cultures, since apart from incorporating this work and the production of the Turkish poet Faruk Nafiz Çamlibel among its main intertextual referents, it enacts a transnational and transcultural encounter between East and West. Such an encounter is particularly significant because it recurs at different points of Byatt's short-fiction writing career, including stories from *Sugar & Other Stories* (1987), *The Djinn in the Nightingale's Eye* and *Elementals: Stories of Fire and Ice* (1998).

Indeed, several narratives from these collections depict a Western female protagonist who experiences ambivalent responses to her contact with Eastern culture, ranging from isolation and misunderstanding to communication and understanding. This signals, so my contention goes, how Byatt has placed short fiction as a site for the transnational and transcultural dialogue between Western and Eastern civilisations, exploring the implications of such an encounter in a globalised world. In light of this, the present chapter will analyse three stories from Byatt's collections of short fiction portraying this

East-West interaction, with the aim of revealing its implications for the development of the female protagonists' personal, (trans-)national and (trans-)cultural identity. The depiction of this interaction in the context of women's travelling is particularly relevant from the point of view of gender because "vocabularies of travel are gendered" (Rojek and Urry 1997: 16), to the point that "[t]ravel and tourism can be thought of as a search for difference" with women being "the embodiment of difference" (Rojek and Urry 1997: 17). Such questions will be taken into account in the present analysis, which will be carried out not in terms of the chronological order of Byatt's stories, but according to the degree of contact between the protagonist and the foreign culture, and the different responses to the transcultural encounter. From the theoretical perspective, this analysis will be preceded by a preliminary incursion into the current "transcultural turn" and its relationship with the short story genre.

The "Transcultural Turn" and the Short Story: Theoretical Considerations

In the context of the growing interest in artistic cross-fertilisation, contemporary writers in English are challenging the boundaries that have traditionally divided creative and discursive modes of expression. Since the last decades of the twentieth century, an increasing number of narrative works of fiction have consciously engaged in a transdisciplinary dialogue that subverts those generic and discursive barriers. Such works take other arts and fields of knowledge as structural, thematic and stylistic referents, as attested by recent studies like *Restoring the Mystery of the Rainbow: Literature's Refraction of Science* (Barfoot and Tinkler-Villani 2011) or *Relational Designs in Literature and the Arts: Page and Stage, Canvas and Screen* (Carvalho Homem 2012). This tendency to the blurring of boundaries, however, is not restricted to the literary and artistic contexts, as it can be felt as well in the wider sphere of contemporary sociological and cultural processes. Indeed, the intensification of demographic and cultural exchanges in the wake of globalisation has resulted in the perception of national borders as fluid margins open to fruitful interactions.

This has led to the fostering of new approaches to the study of cultural plurality and of "the global flow of free-floating cultural tokens" (Bauman 2002: 172), in what has been characterised as the current "transcultural turn" (Nünning 2014: 36). The transcultural turn implies a revision of the concept of culture that goes beyond narrow definitions focused on ethnographical aspects (Tomes 2013: 6) to include "the totality of discourses, texts, images, performances, and other products of media culture, [together with] political culture, institutions, rituals, mentalities, as well as norms and values" (Nünning 2014: 34).

This broad view acknowledges the existence of the three dimensions of culture identified by Ansgar Nünning (material, social and cognitive [2014: 33–34]),[1] which underlie Byatt's perception of culture in her short stories, as will be clarified below. Moreover, the revised concept of culture in the "transcultural turn" connects with the growing attention to transnational issues in contemporary studies of cultural policy, where transnationalism tends to be understood as "globalization's kinder, gentler cousin. It embraces difference [...] and recognizes the role and development of arts, culture, and heritage alongside economic concerns" (DeVereaux and Griffin 2013: 2). Therefore, if globalisation carries negative connotations of threat to national and cultural identities, transnationalism signals "a newer manifestation of cultural, political, and economic integration" (DeVereaux and Griffin 2013: 22). Significantly, the negative and positive undertones resonating in such concepts are given expression in the characters' experiences of transcultural encounters in Byatt's short fiction.

Indeed, her stories attest to the suitability of the short story for the exploration of transcultural and transnational practices, in particular as they influence women's lives and the (con)figuration of their identities. This raises questions of genre and gender that should be examined in the context of the current interest in transcultural experience displayed by literary practice and theory, as attested by recent studies such as Mads Rosendahl Thomsen's *Mapping World Literature: International Canonization and Transnational Literatures* (2008) or Irene Gilsenan Nordin, Julie Hansen and Carmen Zamorano Llena's *Transcultural Identities in Contemporary Literature* (2013). According to the editors of the latter volume, "[m]any literary works published over the past three decades reflect a preoccupation with transcultural encounters against the background of globalization and increased migration", while "[t]he incorporation of transculturality and related concepts into the analysis of literary works is relatively recent" (Gilsenan Nordin, Hansen and Zamorano Llena 2013: xi).

In light of this literary interest in transcultural experience, the short story emerges as a fertile ground for its textualisation, as can be argued in connection with some of the intrinsic characteristics of the genre, particularly its liminal quality. The liminality of the short story has been examined by Adrian Hunter when exploring the reasons for the prominent role of the genre in connection with postcolonialism, describing it as "particularly suited to the representation of liminal or problematic identities" (2007: 138). Likewise, Jochen Achilles and Ina Bergmann have established a correspondence between the centrality of the concept of liminality in the contemporary age "of global mobility, digital networking, interethnicity, transnationality" and the short story as "the liminal genre *par excellence*" (2015: 3, 4). Achilles and Bergmann argue that the genre's in-betweenness places it as "an ideal terrain for mapping out liminality, which abounds in contemporaneous discussions of multiple identities [...], third sex and third gender [...], cultural mobility [...], post- and transnationalism [...], and postethnicity" (2015: 23).

The liminality of the short story and the aptness of the genre for the treatment of blurred identities (like that of the transnational and transcultural subject) is highlighted as well by Ellen Burton Harrington, who approaches the short story "as the outlet for the alienated individual" (2008: 7), stating that "[t]he form of the short story, long marginalized in literary consideration, invites other outlaws to plumb alienation and repression in the symbolic subtext, enlightening and challenging the reader through epiphany and patterning" (2008: 8). Interestingly, the female protagonists of the three short stories by Byatt analysed below feel alienation in different degrees at some points in the narratives, which connects with Richard Todd's contention that "[f]ew contemporary writers have examined both patriarchal and social attitudes to marginalized women more imaginatively than A.S. Byatt" (1997: 55). In fact, although the writer has shown her opposition to some aspects of women's studies, feeling uneasy with the dogmatic dimension of feminism, her interest in female experience is evident throughout her production.[2]

Even if Byatt's works are not informed by a feminist message or ideology, her involvement with feminism becomes evident not only in her treatment of gender "as a constitutive cultural force" (Franken 2001: xiv), but above all in her explicitness in providing her female characters with their own voice (Todd 1997: 55–56), since "[h]er sense of female identity is expressed directly, through the bodies, minds, and voices of her characters" (Campbell 2004: 21). In this process, her short fiction occupies an outstanding position because it offers a privileged site for the exploration of the situation of middle-aged women (Hidalgo 2005: 256), with the possibility, as I have argued elsewhere, of discovering female experience and perception as the structural link of a collection like *Sugar & Other Stories* (Lara-Rallo 2005). Like "Loss of Face" from this collection, all the stories explored in the present chapter portray a middle-aged female protagonist who enacts a transcultural encounter between West and East, foregrounding how "the nature of East-West cultural interaction is changing, as artefacts, artworks, cultural products, ideas and people move rapidly across the world in the present era of globalisation" (Huang 2011: 2). The degree of contact in that interaction, and its consequences, change from story to story, ranging from cultural impenetrability in "Baglady" to immersion in "The Djinn in the Nightingale's Eye".

"Baglady"

This story from *Elementals* enacts a negative encounter between West and East that becomes already evident in the characterisation of its

setting, an indeterminate country in the Far East where the protagonist experiences feelings of unease and danger "between the sleepy soldiers with machine-guns and the uniformed police with their revolvers
and little sticks" (Byatt 1998: 188). This character, Daphne Gulver-
Robinson, is a middle-aged English woman travelling with her husband
on a business trip, where she perceives herself to be an outsider not
just in relation to the foreign culture, but also among the other English
wives: "Most of the wives are elegant, with silk suits and silky legs
and exquisitely cut hair. [...] Daphne Gulver-Robinson is older than
most of them, and dowdier [...] Her style is seated tweed, and stout
shoes, and bird's-nest hair" (Byatt 1998: 186). This powerful feeling
of non-belonging, which reawakens the protagonist's childhood fears
of boarding school, results in a predominant sense of alienation that
permeates the whole story, affecting the character in increasing degrees
from discomfort to stifling terror.[3]

In the opening passages of the story, the exotic strangeness of the place
triggers Daphne's nostalgic memories of her home in rural Norfolk.
The contrast between home and the foreign setting can be approached
in the light of the traditional "identification of women with the home
and men with the limitless expanse of external space" (Rojek and Urry
1997: 17), as Daphne shows her reluctance to accompany her husband
on the trip in the following terms: "I'd better stay and mind the donkeys
and the geese and the fantails *as usual*, and you can have a good time,
as usual, in those exotic places" (Byatt 1998: 186; my emphasis). At
the same time, the protagonist's homesickness conforms to Zygmunt
Bauman's view of the tourist as someone who "has a home; [...] there
must be somewhere a homely and cosy, indubitably 'owned' place to go
to when the present adventure is over" (1996: 30). Bauman's contention
that the tourist "is everywhere he goes *in*, but nowhere *of* the place he
is in" (1996: 29) matches Daphne's emotions of alienation and dislocation, while his remarks about the safety of touristic places, where
"the strange is tame, domesticated, and no longer frightens" (Bauman
1996: 29), apply to the way Daphne and the other ladies are kept from
having a direct experience of the East, "protected" as they are from
its dangers and threats in "*comfort* and *isolation*. They swoop *silently*
through *crowded streets*, *isolated* by *bullet-proof* glass from the *smells*
and *sounds* of the Orient" (Byatt 1998: 187; my emphasis).

In the story, safety is initially associated with the Good Fortune Shopping Mall, where Daphne is taken with the other ladies on a shopping
trip the very day of their departure. The Mall emerges as a *locus* of
globalisation, a product of the homogenising forces that are evoked as
well in Byatt's "Loss of Face", as will be discussed below. As consumerist
comfort zones, malls are defined by Bauman as "tracts to stroll while
you shop and to shop in while you stroll. [... S]hopping malls are the
worlds made by the bespoke designers to the measure of the stroller"

(1996: 27), which contrasts with the reality of the local poverty outside: "Further away, along the walls of the Mall, are little groups and gangs of human flotsam and jetsam, gathered with bags and bottles around little fires of cowdung or cardboard" (Byatt 1998: 188). The Good Fortune Shopping Mall, whose ostentatiously fictional name reinforces the artificiality of the characters' transcultural experience, produces at the same time a disturbing sense of unreality that contributes to the transformation of this place from "a real Aladdin's Cave of Treasures" (Byatt 1998: 185) into a "suffocating Gothic horror castle" (Wallhead 2007: 219):

> She walks rather quickly past rows of square shop-fronts, glittering with gilt and silver, shining with pearls and opals, shimmering with lacquer and silk. Puppets and shadow-puppets mop and mow, paper birds hop on threads, paper dragons and monstrous goldfish gape and dangle. [... A]nother floor, more or less the same, except for a few windows full of sober suiting, a run of American-style T-shirts, an area of bonsai trees. (Byatt 1998: 188–189)

Here, Daphne shops alone, feeling alienated from the local culture and marginalised by the other ladies, with no sense of female bonding or comradeship, "as none of them waits for her" (Byatt 1998: 188). In this process, she will find herself immersed in a nightmarish dislocation of time and space, in which the gradual loss of her personal properties will result in the ultimate loss of her own identity. Overwhelmed by the feelings of isolation and alienation, the protagonist witnesses in panic how the Mall becomes a labyrinth of blocked corridors and nowhere-going stairs, extending "maybe as far into the earth as into the sky, excavated identical caverns of shop-fronts, jade, gold, silver, silk, lacquer, watches, suiting, bonsai trees and masks and puppets. [... G]round level cannot be found" (Byatt 1998: 192).

Apart from missing the meeting time with the other ladies (and so the opportunity to go back to the hotel, and to the airport), Daphne loses her camera, her money and a number of objects with symbolic implications: a present from her husband, representing her memories; her watch, standing for her time; and eventually, her passport, symbolising her own identity. This loss of identity is disturbingly accompanied by a process of invisibility, as nobody seems to see her or to hear her cries of desperation: "No one appears to hear or see her, neither strolling shoppers, deafened by Walkmans or by propriety, or by fear of the strange, nor shopkeepers, watchful in their cells" (Byatt 1998: 192). From a respectable middle-aged English lady, Daphne has been transformed into a "baglady", being now an outsider from the cultural and social perspectives: "She sees herself with his eyes, a baglady, dirty, unkempt, with a bag full of somebody's shopping, a tattered battery-hen" (Byatt 1998: 193). Byatt's choice of the concept of "baglady" is particularly significant not only in the cultural dimension of its implications of Western home-lessness, but above all from the perspective of its connotations of gender and the contrast with the image of ungendered poverty of those "little groups and gangs of human flotsam and jetsam" (1998: 188).

Now Daphne's fear of becoming part of the local poverty outside the safety of the touristic Mall seems closer and closer – "She sees herself sit-ting with the flotsam and jetsam [...] outside" (Byatt 1998: 193) – and so she is placed in the same awkward position as other female protagonists of Byatt's short fiction, like Mrs Sudgen in "In the Air" and A-Oa in "The Dried Witch", as they "meet with magically unhappy endings which un-cannily echo their deepest fears" (Alfer and Edwards de Campos 2010: 116). Daphne's helplessness and the reader's unrest are enhanced by the immediacy of the present tense used throughout the story, and by the poignancy of its open ending, which paradoxically leaves the protago-nist in claustrophobic agony, imagining herself trapped in the Mall for-ever: "She cannot imagine anyone coming. She cannot imagine getting out of the Good Fortune Mall" (Byatt 1998: 194).

"Loss of Face"

The open ending recurs in another of Byatt's stories portraying the transnational encounter between East and West, "Loss of Face", from *Sugar & Other Stories*, which places a Western protagonist (a middle-aged English woman) in an Eastern setting, offering a lesson on "end-less human diversity" (Byatt 1987/1995: 114). This setting, like that of "Baglady", is indeterminate,[4] although again pervaded by a sense of danger and threat: "Shadowy tanks, nose to tail, filled the clefts below. Helicopters clicked and whirred out of the dark, stooping down over the crawling monsters between the dark towers. Such alerts were frequent in this country" (Byatt 1987/1995: 118).

Here, the protagonist, Celia Quest, is a lecturer in English literature attending an international conference, where she discusses landmarks of Western culture such as John Milton and George Eliot with an Eastern audience. In the course of the conference, contrary views on this canon-ical literature are offered: while one of Celia's Eastern colleagues asks about the point of devoting his academic life to such authors ("Sometimes I think, to be quite truthful [...] that I have wasted the whole of my life. It has all been very interesting, perhaps, all this Wordsworth and Milton and George Eliot, but I am not sure it has had any real value" [Byatt 1987/1995: 124]), Celia will assert her cultural origins precisely in relation to these writers: "Milton and George Eliot are my roots, I do not want them to vanish from the world" (Byatt 1987/1995: 126).

This confrontation is particularly relevant, because it exemplifies how the encounter between East and West in this story could be described in terms of clash and misunderstanding, although with much more positive implications than in "Baglady": far from resulting in a threat to identity, the cultural (dis)similarities that culminate in Celia's literal and metaphorical "loss of face" awaken a series of productive reflections on transnational and transcultural issues, opening the way for a negotiation and re-evaluation of beliefs and assumptions. In this way, even if all the conference participants share the "lingua franca [of] Eng. Lit., pedagogy" (Byatt 1987/1995: 123), the dominant symbol in "Loss of Face" is that of the Tower of Babel, whose overtones of diversity and (mis)understanding preside over the protagonist's reflections on transcultural uniformity and variety.

In a context of incorporation of Western traditions into an Eastern setting, with Celia's eating of "a New World version of a Continental breakfast" in a hotel tower with no thirteenth floor and a lecture tower with no fourth floor (Byatt 1987/1995: 112) – thus following at once Western and Oriental superstitions – transnational uniformity is perceived as a result of globalisation, which produces an effect of artificial homogeneity similar to the unreal safety of the Good Fortune Shopping Mall in "Baglady". The story offers therefore a negative view of globalisation as that "intimidating force" whose effects "provide an unfolding narrative in which homogenization is the cultural norm" and so "distinct cultural identities no longer exist" (DeVereaux and Griffin 2013: 21). Blurring differences and all those characteristics that make each setting unique and distinctive, globalisation transforms the venue of the conference into "anywhere, [with] Japanese microphones, American-style presidential lectern, neon strip-lighting, Bauhaus-derived armchairs" (Byatt 1987/1995: 117).

Similarly, another reflection on globalisation as the source for spatial uniformity (and so, indeterminacy) is triggered on the way to the Folk Village, an open-air collection of traditional buildings and craftwork pieces where Celia and other English lecturers are taken by their Eastern hosts. As they approach this museum-like preservation and exhibition of cultural uniqueness, the protagonist thinks about how the motorways there "could have been in Texas, or the valley of the Rhône, in Birmingham or Kalgoorlie, no doubt also in Saskatchewan and Outer Mongolia" (Byatt 1987/1995: 119). The Folk Village, which contrasts with the view of the modern city as "terrible and without any character" (Byatt 1987/1995: 118), tries to counteract the effects of linguistic and cultural oppression suffered in "the days of colonial rule" (1987/1995: 124), becoming a site for the remembrance of the lost traditional past and the contrast with the globalised uniformity of the present, symbolised in the clothes of the folk-dancers and their audience: "They wore beautiful white linen clothes, tossing streamers of brilliantly coloured ribbons, [...] The people watching them wore blue jeans and sloganned tee shirts over boat-like plastic shoes" (Byatt 1987/1995: 121). In this way, Byatt endows the Folk Village with positive connotations, emphasising from the local perspective how "it was in houses like these that most of our people grew up" (Byatt 1987/1995: 121), and so she challenges the prevailing view of heritage representations as "artificial", "inauthentic" or as an alienating product of "the commodification of culture" (MacDonald 1997: 156).

It is precisely after the visit to the Folk Village, in the course of the closing banquet of the conference, that Celia fails to recognise one of her hosts, a mistake that will lead her to reflect once again on uniformity and variety. Feeling "[t]he exhaustion of the strange [...], the sudden refusal of mind and senses to take in new faces, new words, new foods, new courtesies" (Byatt 1987/1995: 123), she forgets her awareness of the Westerners' difficulty to discriminate Oriental faces and names, mistaking Professor Sun for a younger colleague. This failure is particularly ironic because Celia had prided herself on her ability to "tell a Japanese face from a Chinese face and both from these faces" (Byatt 1987/1995: 114), and had inadvertently anticipated her final mistake in the proleptic quotation from Milton's *Comus* in her lecture: "Virtue can see to do what Virtue would / By her own radiant light, *though Sun and Moon / Were in the flat sea sunk*" (Byatt 1987/1995: 114; my emphasis). Ashamed of herself, Celia realises that she has, literally and metaphorically, "lost face", using the Chinese expression that gives title to the story:

> She had failed to distinguish between oriental faces. [...] She had lost face absolutely. [...] In the national museum of that county hall after hall of Buddhas and Boddhisattvas smile, unvarying and various. Their hands speak a language Celia could not read, mudras that call power from the earth, or evoke infinity. No two were the same, though they were all one. (Byatt 1987/1995: 126–127)

This failure enables the protagonist to reconsider her previous views on the implications of cultural uniformity and diversity, which had led her to be suspicious of the concept of Third World literature on the grounds that "[s]he did not like, as a woman, to be thus marginalized. She did not like all these separate differences to be lumped heterogeneously together in one anger" (Byatt 1987/1995: 125), while at the same time, she had come to the conclusion that "[i]t was required that one think in terms of the whole world, and it was not possible" (Byatt 1987/1995: 127). These reflections on cultural uniformity and diversity, whose oxymoronic quality is echoed in the "unvarying and various" smiles of the passage quoted above, acquire particular relevance from two perspectives. Celia rejects the artificial homogenising force behind the concept of "Third World literature" in terms of her opposition to being marginalised as a woman, which brings to the fore the question of margins and its centrality in the articulation of the gender-genre dyad. In relation to the latter, influential approaches to the short story such as Dominic Head's have highlighted "[t]he short story's capacity to render marginalized experience" and its pertinence "to the experience of groups marginalized by ethnicity, gender or sexual orientation", the capacity of "transform[ing] the marginal into something affirmative" (Head 2016: 10). While Celia's reflections have been read by critics like Jane Campbell as a signal of the story's pessimism "about both the survival of individual differences and the possibility of global communication" (1997: 114), in my view, the narrative ends with optimistic overtones, as it concludes with a hopeful allusion to the immensity of the galaxy that counterbalances the negative connotations of the recurrent image of the Tower of Babel. Thus, if the open ending meant a poignant anticipation of eternal entrapment in "Baglady", the conclusion of "Loss of Face", with the reference to "the indiscriminate bright flux of the Milky Way" (Byatt 1987/1995: 128), introduces a positive note.

This implies the idea of a universal order superseding the national and cultural differences that lead to confrontation or conflict, or from Celia's literary perspective, the fancy that "the world was perhaps after all ruled by Milton's God" (Byatt 1987/1995: 127), or George Eliot's belief that "human nature was governed by universal and discernible laws, in exactly the same way as the law of gravity governed the movement of the heavenly bodies" (Byatt 1987/1995: 116). Interestingly, this mood of understanding and reconciliation pervades the third of Byatt's narratives analysed in the present chapter, "The Djinn in the Nightingale's Eye", where the protagonist gives an enthusiastic response to her experiences, both realistic and supernatural, in a context of transcultural interaction.

"The Djinn in the Nightingale's Eye"

The context of "The Djinn in the Nightingale's Eye" is once again an academic event, although, in contrast with the indeterminate Eastern location of "Baglady" and "Loss of Face", the setting of the story is very precise: an international conference on "Stories of Women's Lives" in Turkey, a key place from the perspective of transcultural communication because it is, as the narrative puts it, "a meeting-place of many cultures" (Byatt 1994/1995: 177). Indeed, in the light of the changing identity of contemporary Turkey in its assimilation of Western parameters, "Istanbul has now become a global city, a melting pot in which the diverse cultures of Turkey are juxtaposed, and then mixed further with the diversity of world cultures" (Robins 1996: 76).

As she travels to the conference, the protagonist, a middle-aged English narratologist called Gillian Perholt, experiences some feelings of fear reminiscent of those in "Baglady" and "Loss of Face": "In those days men and women, including narratologists, were afraid to fly East, and their gatherings were diminished" (Byatt 1994/1995: 97). Those feelings are effectively counterbalanced by Gillian's memories of danger at home when she was a child, as she remembers not only the horrors of the boarding school like Daphne in "Baglady" (Byatt 1994/1995: 232), but also the terror of the air raids during the war, precisely as she was watching *The Prince of Baghdad* and "small distant explosions had accompanied the princess's wanderings in the garden" (Byatt 1994/1995: 136). Above all, Gillian's fears are neutralised by her attraction for the East, "the lure of seeing the Golden Horn, the Bosphorus and the shores of Europe and Asia face to face" (Byatt 1994/1995: 97), a frame of mind that matches the description of cosmopolitanism offered by Gilsenan Nordin, Hansen and Zamorano Llena as individuals' development of "multidimensional forms of identification which include the local and the global, in all their diversity and interconnectedness" (2013: xv).

As a cosmopolitan woman, Gillian emerges as a transcultural subject in different dimensions of her life, with frequent academic journeys "to China, Mexico and Japan, to Transylvania, Bogota and the South Seas" (Byatt 1994/1995: 96), entering into contact with "narratologists in Cairo and Auckland, Osaka and Port of Spain" (Byatt 1994/1995: 103) and having her grown-up children in Saskatchewan and in Sao Paulo (Byatt 1994/1995: 101). By doing so, it could be argued that Gillian adopts a "nomadic strategy" which results in the "espacement of the female subject" (Jokinen and Veijola 1997: 43). In this context, "The Djinn in the Nightingale's Eye" covers a transnational location, since it portrays an English woman at the confluence of Europe and Asia, with its final part set in America (as Gillian travels to academic events in Toronto and New York), and including, as well, a reflection on Africa when the protagonist remembers watching a documentary on the condition of Ethiopian women (Byatt 1994/1995: 245–248).

In the Turkish setting, Gillian undergoes a process of personal growth and self-discovery that enables Byatt to explore what Celia Wallhead has described as "women's problems of identity, gender, power, desire, and finally, creativity" (2007: 132). Such a process is articulated through a number of experiences both in the realistic dimension of the touristic enjoyment of Turkish culture and the academic event of the conference, on the one hand, and in the supernatural dimension of the protagonist's encounter with magical creatures, on the other. First, in the company of a Turkish colleague and friend who criticises the stereotypes about the Turks (Byatt 1994/1995: 142), Gillian visits cultural landmarks of Istanbul like Haghia Sophia and the Grand Bazaar, where she is given different perspectives on the West. As they go around Haghia Sophia, which awakens an unexpected reaction of alienation in Gillian not as "a meeting-place of cultures, of east and west", but as "an empty exhausted barn, exhausted by battle and pillage and religious rage" (Byatt 1994/1995: 172–173), they meet a Pakistani family that describe the West as "[e]vil, decadent, and sliding into darkness", briefly reactivating

Gillian's fear at the beginning of the story when they suggest that "[t]rue religion would bring the cleansing sword and destroy the filth and greed and corruption of the dying West" (Byatt 1994/1995: 175).

Later on, in the Bazaar, Gillian immerses herself in a delightful shopping experience completely different from that of Daphne in "Baglady" (Byatt 1994/1995: 178–181). Here, the carpet-seller – who has a PhD on *Tristram Shandy* and so brings to mind the commentaries of Celia's Eastern colleagues in "Loss of Face" – complains about the inconstancy of Western tastes, offering a subtle comment on the workings of the globalised economy. Interestingly, this comment focuses on women's labour with the traditional categorisation of weaving as a typically female activity, a transcultural stereotype that brings to mind iconic images of weaving women in Western culture such as Arachne, Penelope or the Lady of Shalott, but attached to the reality of women's work and poverty in a globalised economy:

> He showed Gillian pallid kilims in that year's timid Habitat colours [...] The West is fickle, said Bulent the carpet-seller, they say they want these insipid colours this year, and the women in India and Iran buy the wool and the silk, and the next year, when the carpets are made, they want something else, black and purple and orange, and the women are ruined, their profit is lost, heaps of carpets lie round and rot. (Byatt 1994/1995: 179–180)

In parallel with Gillian's first-hand experience of local culture, the international conference becomes a site for the fruitful exchange of Eastern and Western stories, from the *Thousand and One Nights* to *The Canterbury Tales*, significantly two of the story cycles analysed by Byatt in *On Histories and Stories* in terms of how "[c]ollections of tales talk to each other and borrow from each other, motifs glide from culture to culture, century to century" (2000/2001: 167). Gillian delivers her lecture on the story of Patient Griselda, from Chaucer's "The Clerk's Tale", to an audience in which "[m]ost of the [...] students were like students everywhere, in jeans and tee-shirts" (Byatt 1994/1995: 107), thus echoing the image of the audience in the Folk Village of "Loss of Face". This lecture offers a reading of Chaucer's tale from the perspective of gender, as Gillian describes it as a story of women's stopped energies, comparing it with Shakespeare's *The Winter's Tale*. According to Gillian, both works share a lull in the narrative before the climactic scene where the woman – Griselda and Queen Hermione, respectively – is reunited with her children after being estranged by her husband. The allusion to women's roles as wives and mothers has personal implications for Gillian, who has been left by her husband in middle age, though in contrast with Griselda and Hermione, Gillian's abandonment is felt as a liberation: "She felt, she poetically put it to herself, like a prisoner bursting chains and coming blinking out of a dungeon. [...] She felt herself expand in the space of her own life" (Byatt 1994/1995: 103–104).

At the conference, Gillian's Turkish colleagues focus on different aspects of Scheherazade's stories, and so they discover the convergence of Western and Eastern narratives in their concern not "with states of mind or development of character, but bluntly with Fate, with Destiny, with what is prepared for human beings" (Byatt 1994/1995: 125). The focus on the universal topic of fate, which at first sight could seem to evade the treatment of particular social or cultural aspects behind the stories, acquires special connotations in the dimension of gender, as fate is evoked in a documentary on the condition of Ethiopian women recollected by Gillian in the course of "The Djinn in the Nightingale's Eye" (Byatt 1994/1995: 245–248). In contrast with men's helplessness as they face lost crops and the ensuing famine, the woman in the documentary complains about her enforced passivity and stopped energies, blaming her fate as a woman: "It is because I am a woman, I cannot get out of here, I must sit here and wait for my fate, if only I were not a woman I could go out and do something" (Byatt 1994/1995: 248).

Moreover, fate is precisely what Gillian manages to come to terms with through her supernatural encounter with magical creatures. The first of these encounters takes place during her visit to the Ankara Museum of Anatolian Civilisations, where the explanations of an uncanny guide make Gillian reflect on the trans-temporal and transcultural survival of mythical gods and goddesses:

> the goddess Ishtar – she was the goddess of Love, and also of War – she is the same goddess you know, ma'am, as Cybele and Astarte – and when the Romans came with their Diana she was the same goddess – terrible and beautiful.
>
> (Byatt 1994/1995: 144)[5]

Such reflections are accompanied by different comments on the centrality of Turkish locations for key figures of Western culture, including Homer, St Paul, and the Virgin Mary (Byatt 1994/1995: 152, 155, 165), and on the implications of the displacement of religious symbols, with transcultural references to female iconography:

> At a nightclub in Istanbul once, Gillian had been shocked [...] to find one of those vacant, sweetly pink and blue church Virgins, life-size, standing as part of the decorations, [...] as you might find a many-handed Hindu deity or a plaster Venus in an equivalent occidental club.
>
> (Byatt 1994/1995: 165–166)

The process of confluence between East and West is given full expression in Gillian's relationship with the djinn or genie, a magical creature in the Arabian popular and literary tradition that Gillian releases from a glass bottle, being thus granted three wishes. At first, the encounter with the djinn may seem to imply a cultural clash considering how "[Gillian's] English empiricism is at odds with the fantastic world of Middle Eastern myth in which she finds herself" (Alfer and Edwards de Campos 2010: 109). However, the djinn's "Otherness" (Todd 1997: 62) soon dissolves when Gillian uses one of her wishes to make the magical creature love her, after having asked him to transform her body into that of a thirty-five-year-old woman. Apparently, Gillian's wishes reflect the patriarchal values of female beauty and love, although her choice of her thirty-five-year-old body instead of a younger version of it shows how, in the process of "reconceiving female experience" in Byatt's short stories, the author enacts "a radical subversion of the body beautiful, normatively constructed as sexually attractive, fecund and maternal" (Coelsch-Foisner 2016: 299). Bringing together East and West in their relationship, Gillian and the djinn tell each other stories, and it is through storytelling that the protagonist comes to terms with her own fate of mortality. In this way, Gillian's close contact with the Eastern literary and cultural traditions, including the supernatural, enables her to accept what she describes as her "redundancy" and "irrelevance" as a middle-aged woman (Byatt 1994/1995: 95, 98), reconciling herself with her own ageing identity.

Conclusion

Gillian's reconciliation with herself, in a process that brings together women's identity, transnationalism, and the exercise of storytelling, signals the fruitfulness of her transcultural experience. Her success can be examined in terms of Gillian's assimilation of the three dimensions of culture identified by Nünning (material, social, and cognitive) mentioned above: apart from profiting from the encounter with the material dimension of the Turkish museums and monuments and the Eastern storytelling tradition, the protagonist of "The Djinn in the Nightingale's Eye" manages to integrate the social and cognitive dimensions through the interaction with her Turkish colleague and friend, and through her relationship with the djinn.

In contrast, Celia in "Loss of Face" succeeds in integrating the material and social dimensions in terms of her interest in the local language and history, and in the context of her engagement with the conference on its academic level, but fails in her attempt at assimilating the cognitive dimension in the context of the affective component of the conference's closing banquet. In "Baglady", Daphne is unable to interact with any of the dimensions, as even on the basic level of sensory perception, she remains hermetically closed to "the smells and sounds of the Orient" (Byatt 1998: 187), while Gillian experiences first-hand the local tastes and food, enjoying "stuffed peppers and vineleaves, kebabs and smoky aubergines in little restaurants" (Byatt 1994/1995: 152). The connotation of Western supremacy implied in the choice of the term "Orient" should not be missed.

In this way, after her involvement with Turkish culture, Gillian is no longer afraid of ageing or death, because she has understood that "[t]here are things in the earth, things made with hands and beings not made with hands that live a life different from ours, that live longer than we do, and cross our lives in stories" (Byatt 1994/1995: 277). Indeed, as Byatt herself stated in her contribution to the millennial issue of the *New York Times* mentioned at the beginning of this chapter, "[s]tories are like genes, they keep part of us alive after the end of our story" (2001: 166). In its immortality, storytelling offers a fertile ground for crossing barriers across time and space, and therefore for the fictionalisation of encounters between East and West in which not only female characters like Daphne, Celia or Gillian, but also readers themselves, discover the implications of the transnational and transcultural experience for the configuration of their identities.

Notes

1 In Nünning's typology, the material dimension corresponds to physical objects like literary texts, visual media or historical sources, and to performative acts like drama, rituals and festivals. The social dimension is associated with political institutions and social systems and hierarchies, while the cognitive dimension involves "mentalities, systems of values and norms, taboos and concepts of identity" (Nünning 2014: 33).

2 In different interviews, Byatt has described herself as a "feminist", stating that "[a]lthough as an artist I don't want to be part of the women's movement, I am a back-to-the wall feminist on things like tax, divorce laws, equal pay, married women's property, even abortion, though I am more equivocal about that". (Dusinberre 1983: 189). Furthermore, she has suggested that "[a]ll my books are about the woman artist – in that sense, they're terribly feminist books" (Tredell 1994: 66). Counteracting some critical voices that have stereotyped her as a non-feminist writer, two monographs have been devoted to Byatt's fiction from the feminist perspective: Christien Franken's *A.S. Byatt. Art, Authorship, Creativity* (2001) and Jane Campbell's *A.S. Byatt and the Heliotropic Imagination* (2004).

3 Such emotions could be associated with the literary connotations of Daphne's compound surname, in the light of Byatt's interest in providing meaningful names to her characters. Thus, if the protagonist of "Loss of Face" (Celia Quest) is named after Adela Quested from E.M. Forster's *A Passage to India*, with similar implications of the difficulties in cultural access (Campbell 1997: 112, 114), and the surname of the protagonist of "The Djinn in the Nightingale's Eye" (Gillian Perholt) echoes that of Charles Perrault, it is possible to argue that "Gulver-Robinson" hints at "Gulliver" and "Robinson", and the overtones of loss and displacement of Swift's and Defoe's characters.

4 Although Campbell argues that the story is set in Korea (1997: 111), my contention is that Byatt is deliberately ambiguous with the unspecified location

to provide a more general comment on women's experience and transcultural interaction.

5 Similar reflections recur later when Gillian contemplates the statues of the goddess Artemis in Ephesus: "a much older goddess than the Greek Artemis or the Roman Diana, an Asian earth-goddess, Cybele, Astarte, Ishtar" (1994/1995: 157). These statues not only embody "the female fecundity Gillian no longer possesses" (Hidalgo 2005: 260), but above all illustrate the process of cultural transference whereby "[s]uccessive cultures have written over the familiar names of gods and goddesses with new names of their own, as in a palimpsest" (Maack 2001: 125).

References

Achilles, Jochen, and Ina Bergmann (2015) "'Betwixt and Between'. Boundary Crossings in American, Canadian, and British Short Fiction", in *Liminality and the Short Story: Boundary Crossings in American, Canadian, and British Writing*, edited by Jochen Achilles and Ina Bergmann, New York: Routledge, 3–33.

Alfer, Alexa and Amy J. Edwards de Campos (2010) *A.S. Byatt: Critical Storytelling*, Manchester: Manchester University Press.

Barfoot, Cedric and Valeria Tinkler-Villani (eds.) (2011) *Restoring the Mystery of the Rainbow: Literature's Refraction of Science*, Amsterdam: Rodopi.

Bauman, Zygmunt (1996) "From Pilgrim to Tourist – Or a Short History of Identity", in *Questions of Cultural Identity*, edited by Stuart Hall and Paul du Gay, London: Sage, 18–36.

Bauman, Zygmunt (2002) "Cultural Variety or Variety of Cultures", in *Making Sense of Collectivity: Ethnicity, Nationalism and Globalisation*, edited by Siniša Malešević and Mark Haugaard, London: Pluto Press, 167–180.

Byatt, A.S. (1987/1995) "Loss of Face", in *Sugar & Other Stories*, London: Vintage, 112–128.

Byatt, A.S. (1994/1995) "The Djinn in the Nightingale's Eye", in *The Djinn in the Nightingale's Eye: Five Fairy Stories*, London: Vintage, 93–277.

Byatt, A.S. (1998) "Baglady", in *Elementals: Stories of Fire and Ice*, London: Chatto & Windus, 183–194.

Byatt, A.S. (2000/2001) *On Histories and Stories: Selected Essays*, Cambridge, MA: Harvard University Press.

Campbell, Jane (1997) "Confecting *Sugar*: Narrative Theory and Practice in A.S. Byatt's Short Stories", *Critique: Studies in Contemporary Fiction* 38(2): 105–122.

Campbell, Jane (2004) *A.S. Byatt and the Heliotropic Imagination*, Waterloo: Wilfrid Laurier University Press.

Carvalho Homem, Rui (ed.) (2012) *Relational Designs in Literature and the Arts: Page and Stage, Canvas and Screen*, Amsterdam: Rodopi.

Coelsch-Foisner, Sabine (2016) "Gender and Genre: Short Fiction, Feminism and Female Experience", in *The Cambridge History of the English Short Story*, edited by Dominic Head, Cambridge: Cambridge University Press, 286–303.

DeVereaux, Constance and Martin Griffin (2013) *Narrative, Identity, and the Map of Cultural Policy: Once Upon a Time in a Globalized World*, Farnham: Ashgate.

Dusinberre, Juliet A. (1983) "Interview with A.S. Byatt", in *Women Writers Talking*, edited by Janet Todd, New York: Holmes & Meier Publishers, 180–195.

Franken, Christien (2001) *A.S. Byatt: Art, Authorship, Creativity*, New York: Palgrave.

Gilsenan Nordin, Irene, Julie Hansen and Carmen Zamorano Llena (2013) "Introduction. Conceptualizing Transculturality in Literature", in *Transcultural Identities in Contemporary Literature*, edited by I. Gilsenan Nordin, J. Hansen and C. Zamorano Llena, Amsterdam: Rodopi, ix–xxvii.

Harrington, Ellen Burton (2008) "Introduction: Women Writers and the Outlaw Form of the Short Story", in *Scribbling Women and the Short Story Form: Approaches by American and British Women Writers*, edited by Ellen Burton Harrington, New York: Peter Lang, 1–14.

Head, Dominic (2016) "Introduction", in *The Cambridge History of the English Short Story*, edited by Dominic Head, Cambridge: Cambridge University Press, 1–15.

Hidalgo, Pilar (2005) "Death, Rebirth and the Ageing Woman in A.S. Byatt's 'The Djinn in the Nightingale's Eye'", in *Proceedings of the 28th AEDEAN International Conference*, edited by Juan José Calvo García de Leonardo, Jesús Tronch Pérez, Milagros del Saz Rubio, Carme Manuel Cuenca, Barry Pennock Speck and María José Coperías Aguilar, Valencia: Universidad de Valencia, 256–263.

Huang, Michelle Ying Ling (2011) "Introduction", in *Beyond Boundaries: East and West Cross-Cultural Encounters*, edited by Michelle Ying Ling Huang, Newcastle Upon Tyne: Cambridge Scholars Publishing, 1–14.

Hunter, Adrian (2007) *The Cambridge Introduction to the Short Story in English*, Cambridge: Cambridge University Press.

Jokinen, Eeva and Soile Veijola (1997) "The Disoriented Tourist: The Figuration of the Tourist in Contemporary Cultural Critique", in *Touring Cultures: Transformations of Travel and Theory*, edited by Chris Rojek and John Urry, New York: Routledge, 23–51.

Lara-Rallo, Carmen (2005) "Female Ageing as a Thematic Link: Fictionalising Women's Phases of Life in A.S. Byatt's *Sugar & Other Stories*", in *Women Ageing Through Literature and Experience*, edited by Brian J. Worsfold, Lleida: Servicio de Publicaciones de la Universidad de Lleida, 51–61.

Maack, Annegret (2001) "Wonder-Tales Hiding a Truth: Retelling Tales in 'The Djinn in the Nightingale's Eye'", in *Essays on the Fiction of A.S. Byatt: Imagining the Real*, edited by Alexa Alfer and Michael J. Noble, Westport, CT: Greenwood Press, 123–134.

MacDonald, Sharon (1997) "A People's Story: Heritage, Identity and Authenticity", in *Touring Cultures: Transformations of Travel and Theory*, edited by Chris Rojek and John Urry, New York: Routledge, 155–175.

Nünning, Ansgar (2014) "Towards Transnational Approaches to the Study of Culture: From Cultural Studies and *Kulturwissenschaften* to a Transnational Study of Culture", in *The Trans/National Study of Culture: A Translational Perspective*, edited by Doris Bachmann-Medick, Berlin: De Gruyter, 23–49.

Robins, Kevin (1996) "Interrupting Identities: Turkey/Europe", in *Questions of Cultural Identity*, edited by Stuart Hall and Paul du Gay, London: Sage, 61–86.

Rojek, Chris and John Urry (1997) "Transformations of Travel and Theory", in *Touring Cultures. Transformations of Travel and Theory*, edited by Chris Rojek and John Urry, New York: Routledge, 1–19.

Thomsen, Mads Rosendahl (2008) *Mapping World Literature: International Canonization and Transnational Literatures*, London: Continuum.

Todd, Richard (1997) *A. S. Byatt*, Plymouth: Northcote House Publishers.

Tomes, Yuma Iannotti (2013) *Cross-Cultural Interaction and Understanding: Theory, Practice & Reality*, New York: Nova Science Publishers.

Tredell, Nicholas (1994) "A.S. Byatt", in *Conversations with Critics*, Manchester: Carcanet, 58–74.

Wallhead, Celia (2007) *A.S. Byatt: Essays on the Short Fiction*, Bern: Peter Lang.

14 "Why Don't You Have a Go at a Novel?"

Gender through Genre in Helen Simpson's Stories

Laura Torres-Zúñiga

Introduction

"Why don't you have a go at a novel? It's the question I most frequently get asked", Helen Simpson stoically affirms (Simpson 2012b). It is not surprising, considering that in 1993, the literary magazine *Granta* included her on its list of the Best Young British Novelists on account of her first collection of short stories, and today, twenty-five years later, her novelistic debut is still to come. Although she has indeed written a longer piece, the novella *Flesh and Grass* (1990), Simpson's work to this date has centred exclusively on the short form; with Katherine Mansfield as her precursor, currently only Canadian Alice Munro and Irishman William Trevor join her in that exclusivity (Lawless 2007). Simpson is the only short story writer to have won the *Sunday Times* Young Writer of the Year Award (in 1991, for her first collection, *Four Bare Legs in a Bed*), while other awards such as the Hawthornden Prize (2001), or the E. M. Forster Award from the American Academy of Arts and Letters (2002), have also recognised the merits of her short stories.

Linguistic adroitness, honesty and humour are Simpson's most appreciated qualities, together with a deep understanding of "the dilemma of women struggling to carve out meaningful lives in a world structured to benefit men" (White 2015). A substantial amount of her short story production is devoted to the tragicomic depiction of the experiences and tribulations of contemporary women and, in fact, her collections can be said to follow the diverse rhythms of a woman's life: they share its cyclical nature – with one compilation appearing punctually every five years – and they simultaneously trace a linear progression through the different (st)ages and problems of women's lives. Simpson's protagonists have grown up from the girls and young childless women of *Four Bare Legs in a Bed* (1990) into the mothers or mothers-to-be of volumes such as *Dear George* (1995) and *Hey Yeah Right Get a Life* (2000), which reveal an array of perspectives on the difficulties and rewards of motherhood whose effects some have labelled as "contraceptive" (McInerney 2001). Finally, Simpson's women have entered the new millennium giving voice to preoccupations that belong to a more mature age, but still tackle taboo topics such as illness and menopause, as shown by collections such as *Constitutional* (2005), *In-Flight Entertainment* (2010) and *Cockfosters* (2015).

Simpson's "artistic creed" throughout all these stories has been to "[t]ell the truth. Be brave. Tell the truth as far as you know it" (Ward 2007: 70), and more concretely telling it on the subject of women's lives. "Up until now, everything I've wanted to say, I've been able to say in stories", Simpson asserted in 2006 (Allardice), and her satisfaction with the expressive possibilities of the genre has not declined. Yet her resistance to the pressure of writing a novel may have its downside, too: "If Simpson were a novelist, people would be much more ready to find in her work the whiff of portentous truth" (Day 2015), because (some) people still have a prejudiced vision of the short story genre as a form for minor themes.[1] Examining why and how Simpson employs the short story to (re)present women's lives may then facilitate the discovery and understanding of that "portentous truth" they tell. And, although "'story' is more than plot, [and] 'short' is more than temporality", as Mary Rohrberger affirms (2004: 5), both dimensions will prove to have a direct bearing on Simpson's predilection for this form.

Defying the "Big Bully": The Short Story versus the Novel

Simpson's concern about time, both diegetic and real, is one of the reasons for her preference for the short story. She frequently recognises, not without a seeming tinge of regret, that "novels always seem best to me when they're dealing with time. In a short story you can't really show character changing in time" (Orr 2011: 116). The novel, with diachronicity as its temporal base, "marks sequential actions and emphasizes externalities" (Rohrberger 2004: 8), allowing for more detailed descriptions of the evolution of characters and/or settings along linear time and propelling readers on and on in their "desire [for] novels to continue" (Rohrberger 2004: 7). Short stories, in contrast, make "readers move in time in such a way that it catapults them from beginning to end and back again, so strong is their desire to reread what is already there" (Rohrberger 2004: 7). Such is the feature from Alice Munro's short fiction that Simpson most admires: "She does this thing with the decades; she jump cuts. How she does it and still remains emotionally convincing I don't know" (Orr 2011: 116). Subverting linearity and building up to moments of epiphany, short stories are more closely based on synchronous time, the coexistence of multiple levels that create tensions, ironies, ambiguities and flux (Rohrberger 2004: 7). Simpson compares them with "a geologic core sample" (Gharraie 2012), which delves deep into reality and unifies in one column of layers the whole multiplicity of the past and the present, once stripped of the dispensable background minutiae, the subplots and "all the gossip" of the novel (Ward 2007: 69). Thus, the "accumulation of matter-of-fact details within temporal frames" through which novels represent reality (Rohrberger 2004: 7) does not seem convincing for Simpson, who instead complains that "sometimes, you get novels that are so full of padding you feel like saying 'Come on, come on, move it' [...] I wish it was shorter" (Lawless 2007). The advantage of short stories, Simpson affirms, is that "if you don't use too many details, it seems to me you waste less time about getting down to what matters" (Ward 2007: 69). The economy of the short story within the diegetic world has its positive implications in the real world of the author as artist and producer, too: "I like stories again partly because you can do them in a limited time. They're a nervous form. Sort of adrenalized; and I like that [...] I'm saving all that time", Simpson affirms (Ward 2007: 69).

Despite that tinge of regret about the difficulty that short stories have for showing character development, Simpson does not let herself be seduced by that "main temptation offered by the longer form" (Simpson 2012a: xxviii). In fact, she has repeatedly manifested her disinterest in charting the evolutions of individual characters and has instead declared she is trying to capture "the things we have in common" and focus on "what's typical in any particular experience" (Ward 2007: 69). One strategy for this would be keeping her characters nameless, like the protagonists in songs, for "when you think of a love song, it's not the individual moments so much – the character in a love song or the individual – but it's actually the universal experience" that matters (Ward 2007: 69). Simpson, who composed the libretto for Mike Westbrook's 1995 jazz opera *Good Friday, 1663* (based on her homonymous story), correlates short-story-writing and songwriting for their shared universalising aspirations and concentrated wisdom: "Songs get more to the heart of things, and stories as well" (Lawless 2007). She finds inspiration in different music genres for narrative content and style: "Mazurka lurches from elation and triumph into absolute despair within the space of an instant. It goes from melancholy to bliss! That's what you can do in a story" (Gharraie 2012); "Folk songs I adore. They tell stories so purely and powerfully, and apparently without artifice. I tried to do that with 'Charm for a Friend with a Lump' – capture a song-like quality" (Orr 2011: 116), which shows in the story's strophic paragraphs and conversational tone. In this perception of the musical reverberations of fiction, Simpson follows Angela Carter, who "thought of novels as symphonies, and stories as chamber music" (Gharraie 2012).

In another metaphorical conflation of stories and songs (and geology), Simpson compares both with "knives [...] something truthful and intense [...] that cuts through all the surface stuff", unlike novels, which get more embroiled and "bogged down in class detail, or clothes detail" (Lawless 2007). And when selecting an adequate blade to dissect reality, "it's lightness of touch you're after, as well as power" (Simpson 2012b). Simpson firmly believes in the power of short stories to offer such sharper representations of reality so that it strikes her "how asinine is the assumption that the short story is best kept for little subjects" (2012b). Quite the opposite, she deems it to be the right genre "for uncomfortable things, for uncomfortable subjects". Short stories, Simpson sustains, are not meant to be amiable: "Novels are more relaxing. You just give up to the novel, you go into its bath, you submit to it. You don't with a story" (Gharraie 2012). Simpson's descriptions of this provoking character of the short story hint at its power as a potential political tool for controversial social issues:

> I can feel when a subject's going to be good [...] It tends to be when it's touchy. You notice it in conversations: whether you're suggesting that motherhood isn't all bliss, or it's a good idea to cut back on air travel for the sake of the future. The room bristles. I'm interested in exploring the discomfort in the area, the touchiness. That's when the fun starts.
>
> (Crown 2010)

In addition, it seems that the same nervousness and adrenaline Simpson feels as a writer is transmitted to the readers, who are required to approach the story with a different attitude than they would adopt for embarking on a relaxing novel: "You're more alert as a reader, and more critical" (Gharraie 2012). This increased awareness and more active engagement in the interpretation of the text is facilitated by the economy of detail, one of Simpson's major concerns when producing short stories: "Reader, I save you time! I cut to the chase!", she insists (Simpson 2012a: xx). One cannot help but think here of many of her female characters, both stay-at-home and working mothers, for whom time for reading is an unaffordable luxury, a "forbidden fruit", "physically, mentally, impossible [...] to sit still and read a book" (Simpson 2000: 32, 82). But what about one short story...?[2]

Keeping in mind those two facets of the short story – its potential for handling socially critical topics and its demand for a more engaged interpretive commitment from the reader – Simpson proves to be more congenial to feminist fiction than she has herself admitted. Because, although some critics have described her as "profoundly feminist" (Young 2015: 133) or as a representative of a "regenerating feminism" (Munford 2016: 139), her own remarks in that regard are usually elusive or even apologetic, like those in the auto-interview that opens her retrospective collection *A Bunch of Fives* (2012a): "So are you a man-hating feminist?" she asks herself, and answers: "Blimey, you aren't half sensitive. [...] I'm neither a misandrist or a misogynist. What I am interested in – among other things – is how men and women (and children) live together.

Or don't" (Simpson 2012a: xxiv). In another interview she explains: "I'm talking as though I'm fascinated by issues of gender but I haven't read enough theory to hold forth on the subject. I'm aware I've just sensed my way forward instead" (Orr 2011: 115). Yet in this sensing forward, she has directed her steps towards paths that are of fundamental relevance for the feminist agenda, especially when considering the time – the 1990s and early 2000s – when her first collections appeared.

Simpson's Short Stories as a Feminist Vehicle of Expression

In Anne Besnault-Levita's view, "the subtle question of the links between gender and the short story" cannot be properly dealt with "unless it is historicized and contextualized" (2007: 484). If considered in both its historical and literary contexts, Simpson's short fiction becomes endowed with greater relevance and shows its value for questioning the ideological tenets of its era, mainly the naturalisation of primary mother care (Wolf 2016: 627–628). The publication of her first collections co-incided with the "mother-lit", "mommy lit" or "mumlit" trend that be-gan in the 1990s and was established "in the early years of the 2000s, [… when] the topic [of the material and ideological conditions of mother-hood that] had drifted to the margins of feminist studies" found its way into more popular arenas: "In memoirs, blogs, anthologies, and zines, women wrote about their experiences, their joys, and their disappoint-ments as mothers" (Kawash 2011: 970, 985). These productions were characterised by their exploration of "the 'real' experience of mother-hood honestly, without sentimentality or idealisation or judgement from the point of view of the mother", and dealt with "issues of work, identity and motherhood" (Hewett qtd. in O'Reilly 2010: 203). The reasons for the blooming of this mothering literature, Andrea O'Reilly maintains, were demographic, financial and ideological. Firstly, some third-wave feminists who had grown up in the 1970s with the theoretical and polit-ical (re)considerations of mothering and motherhood by Adrienne Rich, Nancy Chodorow and other representatives of the second-wave women's movement turned their attention to more personal accounts of maternity as they started to become mothers in the 1990s. Also, the increasing financial power of women allowed them to purchase more books. Most importantly, it was the prevalent discourse of intensive mothering or *new momism* that "made possible a public voice on motherhood, [yet] it simultaneously limited what that voice could say about motherhood" (O'Reilly 2010: 205).

The problem of these motherhood writings and memoirs that stemmed from the ideological breeding ground of new momism is that, despite their purpose of "telling it like it is" and unmasking the conflicts be-tween the expectations and the realities of motherhood, they criticise the consequences of the assumptions of new momism but *not the assumptions themselves* (O'Reilly 2010: 209). These narratives still emphasise "gender dualism and gender difference in parenting; the significance of the bodily experience of motherhood; [presence] of the 'natural mother' myth, which assumes women's superiority and ability as natural caregivers" (Ivana Brown, "Mommy Memoirs: Feminism, Gender, and Motherhood in Popular Culture" qtd. in O'Reilly 2010: 210). In this way, women would remain trapped within a discourse that "naturalizes and normalizes" the very conditions against which they protest (O'Reilly 2010: 205). The mothers in these writings may be stressed, overwhelmed or anxious for all their responsibilities and tasks in and outside the home, yet "the heroines of mum's lit show little sign of self-reflection or moral growth" (Garrett 2013: 25), and they still believe that full-time, intensive mothering – not *fathering* or childcare – is the necessary, more natural or wise option for rearing their children. Thus, the genre "remains one of complaint and not change", and does not fulfil its potential role in doing away with the naturalisation of gender inequities (O'Reilly 2010: 212).

Given its subject matter, Simpson's work has usually been included within this category of "mumlit", preceding authors such as Kate Figes and Rachel Cusk as "part of a wave of truth-telling by a new generation of writers who have arrived at motherhood, balked at its appalling but unspoken indignities, and made it their mission to bring them out into the open" (Briscoe 2003). In the pre-Internet years of the early 1990s, before the arrival of the plethora of maternity-related websites, blogs and social networks of today, Simpson remembers how female readers approached her after readings and thanked her for showing them that their frustrations, resentments or satisfactions about motherhood were not solitary but shared emotions: "It's like samizdat (clandestine manuscripts)", they told her, so secret and unspeakable seemed her books' contents (Lawless 2007). Those women for and about whom Simpson's stories were written were members of her generation "who, for the first time, found they could move around, do something different from their parents and, in the case of women, do something based on their brain" (Crown 2010).

As Emma Young has convincingly argued, Simpson's work is also a child of its time and reflects the tensions between the feminist discourses present at the turn of the millennium, between second- and third-wave feminism (Young and Bailey 2015: 12). Thus, for example, her short story collection *Hey Yeah Right Get a Life* (2000), according to Young, "purports the importance of recognising a woman's right to choose for herself and eschews a feminist politic in keeping with that of the third wave" that rose in the 1990s (2015: 135). Although theory may not have informed Simpson's work directly, the ideas of two fundamental feminist treatises – Arlie Hochschild's *The Second Shift: Working Parents and the Revolution at Home* (1989) and Sharon Hays's *The*

Cultural Contradictions of Motherhood (1996) – seem to underlie her work (Young 2015: 143), in particular as regards two "wincingly tender areas" within Simpson's fictional world: "how women combine (or do not combine) paid work with motherhood", which echoes Hochschild's analysis of the burdens of employed mothers, and how "parenthood [...] gender-politicises relationships" (Simpson 2006), which follows Hay's study of the ideology of intensive mothering. The latter view assumes this activity to be natural to women and essential to their being, and the mother to be the central caregiver of her biological children, who require full-time mothering even at the expense of her own needs or wishes.

Dealing with those topics has earned Simpson both positive and negative criticism, the latter mainly arguing that her inclination towards the "D word" – domesticity – is boring, or "letting the side down" (Simpson 2012a: xxiii). Very aware of how "our aesthetic judgements are ideologically bound" (Eagleton 1989: 57), Simpson cleverly traces the source of such criticism in political, not literary, terms: "If someone happens to set a story in a kitchen but writes well about it", depreciating it insinuates "you're objecting to the lives described, not the writing" (Crown 2010). She also detects a certain cultural bias in that criticism, which originates mainly in the UK, whereas in the United States, "you're allowed to write about domestic stuff and it's not seen as some loss of status":

> Alice Munro, Carol Shields [...] weren't criticized or called 'chick lit'[3] because they dealt with the indoors. It seems to me so idiotic to assume that if it's a domestic subject matter, it doesn't matter. It can be extremely political.
>
> (Ward 2007: 68)

With that affirmation, reminiscent of the motto *the personal is the political* of second-wave feminism,[4] Simpson suggests an intention not to restrict her work to "complaint and not change", as other mumlit works, and several features of the short story work to her advantage. For example, its characteristic resistance to closure allows for the use of open endings that hint at a possibility for change after narratives whose overall tone may be otherwise considered quite bleak, such as the well-known stories "Hey Yeah Right Get a Life" and "Hurrah from the Hols". Their protagonist, Dorrie, is one of those paradigmatic Simpsonian mothers, "frozen into their individual states of captivity" and "submerged in the oceanic life of the family" (Clark 2000). Still, both stories end in epiphanic moments of self-awareness which open up to more positive prospects for Dorrie, who transcends – if only for a moment – that state of frozenness and suffocation and experiences something like "the feeling in a limb that has gone numb, when blood starts to flow again [...] reviving [...] tingling into life" (Simpson 2000: 58). Part of this revivification comes from her realisation of the ideological pressure placed on mothers, "this puzzle [that] was to do with the loss of self that went with the process, or rather the awareness of her individuality as a troublesome excrescence, an obsoletism" (Simpson 2000: 178), as presented by the ideology of intensive mothering. In the concluding moments of solitude in "Hurrah for the Hols", Dorrie, "filled with excitement", feels "how it was thrilling, being alive and not dead" and even envisions the possibility of recovering that lost individuality: "Was it possible to reclaim the scattered-to-the-winds self?" (Simpson 2000: 178). Such final unresolvedness that makes the reader wonder "Is the story ending with curtailment or fulfilment?" (Mullan 2006) is also present in other stories yet with the opposite effect: the finishing lines of the lighter, more cheerful depictions of young girls and boys in "Lentils and Lilies" or "Up at a Villa" cast an ominous shadow on the careless existence of their protagonists. Their intention not to follow on the steps of the adults they contemplate with disdain may not find fulfilment if, as the narrative voice insinuates, those pathetic adults act not only "like the ghosts of summers past", but also, "indeed, of summers yet to come" (Simpson 2010b: 5). This defiance of conventional patterns of closure can be, as argued in Rachel DuPlessis's *Writing Beyond the Ending: Narrative Strategies of Twentieth-Century Women Writers*, a useful strategy to reject master narratives and subvert the masculinist, patriarchal models of the "happily ever after" endings of fairy tales and Victorian novels (DuPlessis qtd. in Bloom 1998: 66).

This open-endedness of the short story goes hand in hand with another of its characteristics that serves the purpose of "show[ing] the true complexity of life without pandering to the simpleton's urge to prove this way right and that way wrong" (Simpson 2006). Unlike the novel, which "by comparison, is too often a big bully" (2006), the short story and its typical presentation, the collection, allows for a freer, multifaceted presentation of reality enriched by the interrelations between the different stories. Although each individual piece is self-sufficient, their combination within a single volume creates "an open book" that invites the reader to find underlying patterns of form and theme, and "to construct a network of associations that binds stories together and lends them cumulative impact" (Luscher 1989: 149). Those associations are not necessarily a consequence of authorial intent – "I don't think you can coldheartedly decide to do a collection on a particular theme", Simpson sustains (Gharraie 2012) – but are rather the product of the reader's "more alert", "more critical" attitude towards the short story that Simpson celebrated. However, in Simpson's collections there are some authorial decisions that contribute to their internal *cumulative impact*, such as the recurrence of characters in *Hey Yeah Right Get a Life,* where the plotlines intersect as the opening and closing stories deal with Dorrie's family, whose babysitter is both the protagonist of "Lentils and Lilies" and the daughter of the central couple in "Burns and the Bankers". Also, thematically, *In-Flight Entertainment* introduces constant references to environmental concerns, be them the central topic of the stories ("In-Flight Entertainment", "Ahead of the Pack"), a motif for characterisation ("Squirrel", "The Tipping Point", "Geography Boy") or the cause of an apocalyptic setting ("Diary of an Interesting Year"), whereas the stories in *Cockfosters* trace a geographical route through their titles but also share a marked temporal character, punctuating their narration with the counting of minutes, hours, or days. These commonalities between their constituents bring Simpson's collections closer to being considered short story cycles, an intermediate position along the "continuum extending between the 'mere' collection of loose stories and the integrated form of the novel" (D'Hoker and Van Den Bossche 2014: 10). Unlike the novel, these short story collections retain "huge imaginative advantages" for the author, who, as Simpson celebrates, is "not forced to take a line and then stick to it; your explorations can be genuine. You are not coerced into making judgments" that may assign a univocal and definitive meaning to the texts (Simpson 2006).

Thus, the format of the short story cycle facilitates both the representation of life's interrelated and polyphonic quality and the more active critical engagement on the reader's part that Simpson so much values. Moreover, it is a form that provides "the ideal space for representing the kind of subjectivity that is commonly associated with the female subject: a selfhood that develops from 'relationship and dispersal' rather than 'the maintenance of boundaries and distance' or 'the subjugation of the other'" (Waugh qtd. in Lister 2007: 3). In the end, this form and this format constitute the perfect vehicle for her intention to break the "conspiracy of silence about what happens to women when they become mothers" and see their selfhood put at stake (Simpson 2006).

Simpson's stories represent this female, and especially maternal, subjectivity by means of different narrative strategies. She most directly engages with the effects of such conspiracy of silence on the relational selfhood of mothers in "Café Society", a story that revolves around two female friends who are *supposedly* conversing in a café about their disappointments with maternity and the impossibility to make it compatible with a job. By means of the use of italics, Simpson creates two parallel discourses which contrast what these women are saying with what they would *really* like to say in a kind of theatricalised script (Lepaludier 2008: 2). As could be expected, the amount of italicised internal monologue noticeably surpasses the actual dialogue spoken out loud, which is in addition reduced to fragmented, inarticulate sentences. All the agents in the story are aware of this repression, but also of the fact that "it's important to put up a decent apologia for your life [...] And if you can't, or won't, you will be shunned. You will appear to be a whiner, or a malcontent. Frances knows this, and so does Sally" (Simpson 2000: 19). And so does the narrative voice, who insists several times throughout the story that "[u]nfortunately, not one word of this makes it into the light of day" (Simpson 2000: 16), as if reminding the reader of its own privileged omniscient position and of the fact that, diegetically, communication is not working: "Sally's mind continues to follow her train of thought, silently addressing Frances even if all that Frances can see of her is a bumbling, clucking blur" (Simpson 2000: 16). Simpson seems to suggest that mothers themselves sometimes comply with this social conspiracy: "Put up and shut up is the rule, except with fellow mothers. Even then it can be taken as letting the side down" (Simpson 2000: 13). Frustrated communication is thus in correlation with frustrated personal aspirations: "*Why do they educate us, Sally, only to make it so hard for us to work afterwards? [...] Of course none of this will get said. There is simply no airspace*" (Simpson 2000: 18). This is Frances's suffocated cry, resounding only in her mind.

The reference to "work" is not randomly chosen, since this story as well as others such as "Hey Yeah Right Get a Life" seem to associate these women's forced silence with their disempowered financial position at home. Whereas Frances and Sally work part time or in euphemistically *freelance,* home-based jobs, Dorrie is a full-time mother who is more than aware of the cause of both her silence and her disadvantaged situation: "She felt uneasy complaining. Once she'd stopped bringing in money she knew she'd lost the right to object" (Simpson 2000: 49). Other stories in the collection, however, problematise such a straightforward connection between feminine subjection and joblessness, and show that "the experience of the stay-at-home mother is not that dissimilar to that of the working mother as both women experience feelings of guilt and are subjected to the same demands on their time and emotions" that are established as the norm by the ideology of intensive mothering (Young 2015: 144). The way in which Simpson presents these working mothers' voice is dissimilar, though. It may seem that the mothers in the stories "Burns and the Bankers" and "Wurstigkeit", who are highflying professionals working outside the home, have earned their right to speak. In "Wurstigkeit", for example, communication between both protagonists, Laura and Isobel, flows too easily and they start to share intimacies even before really becoming close friends. In the company dinner attended by Nicola Beaumont, the banker protagonist of "Burns and the Bankers", there is an exchange of power positions as women are the speakers and men the object of discussion, and a young female executive delivers a speech that, in quite the opposite move to the inarticulateness in "Café Society" and with Chaucerian resonances,[5] voices in front of everyone the desires and needs of her fellow women: "Men ask, what is it women want? [...] Women want love and they want work, just the same as men" (Simpson 2000: 102).

Nevertheless, this last remark points at certain controversial details in the narration that imply that these women have not really attained a place or a voice of their own as professionals *and* mothers. A closer look at some of their comments reveals how the underlying ideology still considers that such professional women have just occupied a place that was men's, and thus are acting "just the same as" them. Unlike the full-time mothers in Simpson's collection, Nicola and Isobel are two of those "girls [who] never did cross the ego line. Like men, they stayed the stars of their own lives" (Simpson 2000: 37). Consequently, both in their acts and in their voice, these professional women prove to have assimilated the masculine as the norm and repeat its discourse: Nicola "loved her children more than life itself [...] and so did [her husband] Charlie in his way; but, like him, she preferred to subcontract out much of the work of parenthood" (2000: 91). In this sense, Nicola assures her children that her love does not depend on the number of hours spent with them, "which was probably just what these three men, Iain and Donald and Brian, said to their wives" (Simpson 2000: 105). Of the two options that Sally in "Café Society" contrasts, the "mother-in-the-house voice" and the "woman-in-the-workplace voice" (Simpson 2000: 15), the latter proves to be a mere repetition of the man's: there is no space yet for the *mother-in-the-workplace* voice. The most conspicuous sign of this masculine position surfaces in Nicola's simple answer to that question in the Burns speech: "What every woman needs is a wife" (Simpson 2000: 103), a kind of subjugation of another woman that Isobel has actually achieved: "Nannies tend to jump ship at new babies, but I didn't rock the boat and now she's like my wife" (Simpson 2000: 150). Therefore, on the surface, the stories about working mothers may seem to offer role models of independent women who combine home and job successfully. However, they are not really that opposed to their home-staying equivalents since they are also subject to similar social pressures and prejudices: "there's no question of [Nicola's husband] adapting his hours to the family", but even if he does, she suffers "the assumption that because she was successful at work she must have sacrificed her children" (Simpson 2000: 98, 103). In addition, the work setting that they join forces them to adopt a typically masculine role. Simpson's stories at the turn of the millennium show thus that the post-feminist "notion of women 'having it all' is revealed to be a rhetorical spin" (Young 2015 143). Simply working outside the home is not the key for liberating women while

> paid labour means adapting to a regime built for traditional masculine work [...] It is a new patriarchy in which women must be two things: producers and reproducers at the same time, a spiral that ends up consuming all their life.
>
> (Federici 2014; my translation)

Furthermore, these stories can also help us reflect on how a certain ideological bias makes us *interpret* as masculine the behaviour of outspoken or self-oriented women. More than a decade later, Simpson would take this questioning of gender roles a step further, showing that her interest in probing the boundaries of gender stereotyping had not weakened. In the story "Erewhon" (collected in *Cockfosters* in 2015), which has been described as "bizarre, almost like science-fiction" (White 2015) and as "discomfiting" (Mukherjee 2015), Simpson reproduces the rambling thoughts of an anonymous man who tosses and turns sleepless in bed, while his wife, Ella, obliviously snores next to him. We do not get to know the narrator's name, and his wife is simply named with the generic feminine pronoun *she* (in Spanish, *ella*) – a significant detail, given the universalising aim of this narrative decision for Simpson. It does not take long for the reader, however, to realise that there is something strange in the "universal experience" this story portrays, in that the internal and domestic strife the nameless male narrator confides to the reader seems transposed from the opposite sex: it is a woman's experience that he seems to be undergoing, feeling overwhelmed by family and work yet guilty for not being able to balance both, responsible for the emotional work – and the meals – at home, angry though powerless in the face of the inequality of *his* situation. After a few lines it becomes clear that the whole society in "Erewhon" is upside down so that other men also behave in ways typically associated with women, whereas women adopt the typically masculine dominant position. For example, a father in the parents' evening at the school where the narrator teaches confesses to him that he is abused by his wife, "a policewoman ... [who] knew not to hit him anywhere it would show" (Simpson 2015: 17). The narrator's son, Colin, is characterised as a reserved and silent boy who has always suffered from "shaky self-esteem" and now at thirteen might be "flirting with anorexia" and other self-harming conducts, unlike his sister Daisy, who is impulsive and dominating, competitive, and knows exactly what she wants, like playing brainless computer games (Simpson 2015: 19).

Unlike other fictional alternative worlds that reconsider gender roles and envision more or less utopian societies, such as those imagined by Charlotte Perkins Gilman in *Herland* (1915) or Marge Piercy in *Woman on the Edge of Time* (1976), the female-dominated society of "Erewhon" proves to be a "parallel universe of matriarchal oppression" (Day 2015) sustained by "a blatantly unequal set-up", as the narrator complains (Simpson 2015: 24). Far from being utopian, "Erewhon" shows that "'matriarchy' would be no better than 'patriarchy'– that a binary reversal is not what we should be seeking, but rather an explosion of the night/day, male/female system altogether" (Wilson 2011). In their description of this oppressive matriarchy, the "Night Thoughts" of the male protagonist echo with uncanny familiarity all the classic situations that have been subject to feminist criticism:[6] the unsustainability of the double shift, the pressure of beauty standards on body image, the stereotyping of (supposedly) gender-linked character traits ("Is it just that women aren't as nice as men?" he wonders [Simpson 2015: 22]), or the delusion of free choice:

'You can have two out of three but not three. You can have the woman and the job, or the woman and the children. But you can't have the woman and the job and the children.' 'Why not? ... Women don't have to choose! Why can they have it all and not us?' 'That's life'.

(Simpson 2015: 23)

This latter and other remarks by the narrator ("that's life", "it was generally agreed", "This was the natural order") reinforce the story's denaturalisation of the dominant conventions of gender and provoke a certain estrangement on the part of the reader, who would certainly question whether it is really an unavoidable, fundamentally "unfair act of nature" the fact that "older *women* got better with age while *men* lost their sexual allure" (Simpson 2015: 18; my emphases) – the apparently *natural order* adduced by sexist discourses in our real world being the opposite. By means of this mismatch and interaction between the reader's own cognitive schemata and the gender relations and societal norms that govern in this gender-swapped world, Simpson's story follows the useful feminist strategy of "invok[ing] expectations of meaning in the reader's pragmatic experience, especially in her gendered experience", leading her – or him – to critically "question not only how she interprets her own experience but also what that experience is", and to identify the fault lines of the current situation and envision new possibilities (Joanne S. Frye qtd. in Rose 1993: 365).

With "Erewhon", Simpson joins a number of other creators that in subsequent years have used a similar strategy to make a strong statement about gender inequality and the microsexism that still pervades our Western society. Their creations, some of them audiovisual products such as short films and TV comic skits, all share their briefness to achieve a greater impact of their shocking effect. In 2013 conceptualist poet Vanessa Place presented her project *Boycott* (the title already a pun), in which she reformulated a series of canonical feminist texts replacing all female-gendered terms with male-gendered ones (Edmond 2012). She did not only swap pronouns or adjectives such as *female/male*, but also created substitutes for other female references: Hélène Cixous's "The Laugh of the Medusa" became "The Laugh of the Minotaur", and de Beauvoir did not explain the trauma of menstruation but of *ejaculation* (Perloff 2014: 6–7).[7] Place achieves a defamiliarisation of these discourses that "demonstrates the power of a simple substitutive gesture to illuminate cultural hierarchies", and advocates a certain authorial neutrality that "leaves the reader in the position of needing to come to her own independent conclusions" (Wagner 2014: 238).

Some similar parodies or satires that make an explicit point in unveiling all that is not natural or fair about male and female constructed identities also achieve their effect by picturing men being treated as women and suffering sexism. Such is the case of Eleonore Pourriat's short film *Majorité Opprimée* (*The Oppressed Majority*, which was produced in 2010 but became viral in 2014), Tracey Ullman's comedy skit for the BBC "What Were You Wearing" (2017, in her *Tracey Ullman's Show*, Season 2 Episode 6), and Aldara Figueira's short film *Cosas de Chicos* (*Boys' Stuff*, 2017). They share with "Erewhon" the unification of different aspects of sexism in just one intense narrative, which together with their brevity, may be the most effective format to get their message across, since "subjects with little or no emotional investment in the issue of sex discrimination, [... perceived] less discrimination when they encountered the relevant information in little chunks than when they saw the total picture at a single shot" (Crosby, Clayton, Alksnis and Hemker 1986: 637). All these narratives produce the same effect the critic Neel Mukherjee highlights in "Erewhon": "A slap to the face [...], deeply discomfiting, certainly to any male reader" (2015), but also for women. In fact, they stimulate in their audience, both men and women, the two "processes that would be useful to highlight when attempting to reduce endorsement of sexist beliefs": in the case of women, "heightening their sensitivity to different aspects of sexism in their personal lives", and for men a combination of that "awareness of the prevalence of discrimination and *perspective taking*" (Becker and Swim 2011: 239; my emphasis), which in these cases is achieved through a use of male protagonists that facilitates identification and allows for an increase of empathy.

Although they have become Simpson's signature pieces, these portrayals of motherhood are not her only criticism of the ideological tenets that sustain our contemporary gender relations. In other stories Simpson's female protagonists are younger girls who, nevertheless, are also subject to a conflict of expectations and social discourses about femininity. It is in these cases where Simpson typically makes use of intertextuality, a usual narrative strategy that relates directly with her own background as an Oxford English major with a thesis on Restoration farce. Interspersed all throughout her work we can find literary quotations and references to authors from the Renaissance, Restoration and Romantic periods, such as John Donne in the story "Good Friday, 1663", Shakespeare in "Dear George", Chidiock Tichborne in "Last Orders", Wordsworth and Coleridge in "Lentils and Lilies", Thomas Hardy in "Heavy Weather", Robert Burns in "Burns and the Bankers" and Milton in "The Tipping Point". In most cases, the stories where these quotations appears are focused on girls or young women before motherhood; as can be expected, the citations from those authors, all male, canonical and from centuries ago, provide a stark contrast between the societies and mores which those writers come from and represent in their works, and the reality of Simpson's contemporary characters.

In "Dear George" and "Lentils and Lilies" the two adolescent protagonists interlace comments about their English literature homework with ruminations about their pet loves and their future. The nameless girl in "Dear George" is both bored and attracted by the representations of Shakespearean love, and cannot help imagining her sweetheart and herself as tragic lovers: "There was George, big George, looming like a tower in the half-dark, and herself in a white nightdress [...,] his hot hands round her neck" (Simpson 1995: 7), she daydreams while tentatively pressing her throat with her own hands. Jade, the protagonist of "Lentils and Lilies", dismisses the melancholy worldview of Wordsworth and Coleridge in their respective works *Ode on the Intimations of Immortality* and *Dejection: An Ode*, for she is not precisely suffering from the loss of youth and innocence or an artistic paralysis, as these poems lament. On the contrary, in this story the protagonist is about to graduate from high school and feels exhilarated about the "choice landscapes and triumphs and adventures" that await her in the future (Simpson 2000: 4). She is "a young woman suffused with promise", but the story does not quite insinuate that "she is innocent", as some critics affirm (Kellaway 2000). Jade proves to be suffused with other cultural discourses that, unlike Romantic poetry, do offer her models for identification during "the long jewelled narrative which was her future [...] she was the focus of every film she saw, every novel she read" (Simpson 2000: 4, 2).

The problem of these cultural narratives from which young girls like these extract ideas and models to identify with is that they have a limited range of action, and provide *promises* for women only until they are "about thirty-three or thirty-four, leaving [them] at some point of self-apotheosis, high and nobly invulnerable [...] This was about as far as any of the novels and films took her too", closing the popular tales of romantic love and inaugurating that *conspiracy of silence* just when the realities of marriage, motherhood and adult life make their appearance (Simpson 2000: 4). As one of the mothers, Frances in "Heavy Weather", puts it: "What a cheesy business Eng. Lit. is, all those old men peddling us lies about life and love. They never get as far as this bit, do they" (Simpson 1995: 90). The intertextual references point thus at the influential role of those traditional – and typically man-made – "jewelled narratives" in shaping the modes of loving, relating to others and experiencing the world that women have contact with from an early age, and suggest the need for alternative discourses that can really offer a *choice* of landscapes and open up new perspectives. Simpson herself experienced the discovery of new literary horizons as a young girl, when after reading Shakespeare from her grandmother's library, she embarked on a search for literary models that made her discover the French writer Colette, a revolutionary woman whose writings helped her realise that "there were other ways of doing it" and recover "a sense of entitlement to pleasure which a procession of Victorian heroines had gone a fair way to extinguish" (Simpson 2010a).

Not only the contents of these discourses are relevant, but also their use of language is significant in delineating the gendered paradigms we are subject to. Simpson is particularly conscious of the stereotypes that circle the concepts of *masculine* and *feminine* writing – she depicts a heated debate about them in the story "Creative Writing" in *Dear George* – and demonstrates her intention to overcome them by means of two strategies. The one she is most celebrated for is her use of humour, which acts not just as a respite for the reader and a lifesaver against the domestic treadmill for her protagonists, but as a conscious decision against the old-time contention that "women wrote in a different way, less pointedly, more twisty twiny. [...] It did seem to mean that women wrote with their bodies and men wrote with their brains", a classical reductionist dualism: "I love witty writing, I like intelligence and I don't see why that should be a male quality", Simpson complains (2017). And indeed, throughout her work Simpson adopts the usual feminist strategy of "challeng[ing] male discourse through humor, parody, or irony" (Rose 1993: 363–364), as when she reworks Andrew Marvell's "To his Coy Mistress" into her story "To her unready boyfriend" (1995).

In order to be able to transcend established discursive practices, Simpson also engages in the re-metaphorisation of certain domains that have been stigmatised by patriarchal discourses, as is the case of menopause: "The language around it is so mythic and fearful; it's a way of dismissing women over a certain age, just getting rid of them" (Crown 2010). In "Arizona", Simpson searches instead for a different metaphor that can represent a novel, more positive perspective on that inevitable fact of every woman's life, and actually proposes two: as a time "somewhere around August" in a year-long life, bright and warm and "starting to go to seed" (2015: 105), and as a place, an unknown but appealing state like Arizona, "brilliantly lit and level and filled with dependable sunshine" (2015: 116). With this re-metaphorisation that may seem "shocking, in its way, to those of us conditioned to the notion of female old age as dark and witchy", Simpson demonstrates the need for women (and women writers) to reformulate language – the masculine symbolic – in order to voice their own uncensored views and "reclaim the territory by naming it for themselves" (Crown 2010), a naming act that symbolises the exercise of a power formerly denied to women (González-Barrientos 2017: 15).

Conclusion

If "what characterizes much if not most third-wave writing about motherhood [is] the claiming and exploring of the personal experience of motherhood in ways that contest cultural ideologies that whitewash and distort uncomfortable realities" (Hewett 2006: 46), Helen Simpson's short stories prove to be a leading exponent. Unlike other mumlit works that eventually are complicit with or even celebratory of the current conception of motherhood, Simpson's portraits do not offer such a conformist final judgement based on authorial authority (Garrett 2013: 2). Instead, they profit from the openness and indeterminacy of the short story genre and demand the reader's active participation in the construction of a meaning – or series of meanings – enriched through the juxtaposition of stories within and across collections. These narratives thereby promote a critical awareness necessary for the unveiling of the ingrained discourses that influence our constructions of gender. As such, they can aspire to yield a direct political effect like other "literary and cultural productions [that] provide access to the many realities of mothers' lives [and] that can help to inform public rhetoric" (Hewett 2006: 48) – for instance, by endowing it with new, not gender-biased tropes and metaphors. Do not "hand yourself over and suspend your critical faculties [... to be] lulled and dulled", Simpson seems to exhort us (2012: 25), either by a novel or by the other ideological fictions that surround and mould us: be vigilant and read short stories instead.

Notes

1 Epithets like "miniaturist", often applied to Simpson, do not quite help (see, for instance: Allardice 2006, Tayler 2010, or Day 2015).
2 For example, due to its terseness, Hermione Lee considers the short story a convenient form for women plagued by the interruptions of domestic duties (qtd. in Malcolm 2012: 37).
3 Genz and Brabon situate mumlit within "chick lit varieties over the past decade – recent permutations includ[ing], for example, 'mumlit'" (2009: 88).
4 For in-depth discussions of the feminist debates on the public/private distinction, see Pateman (1984: 118–140) and Higgins (2000). In fact, this motto makes its appearance in Simpson's story "Lentils and Lilies", where the young Jade realises the long way to go for the achievement of gender equality: "You'd think it was the fifties, men roaming the world while the women stayed indoors. The personal was the political, hadn't she heard?" (Simpson 2000: 8).
5 Finding the answer to the question "What thing it is that women most desire" is the Queen's challenge for the Knight in "The Wife of Bath" tale in Chaucer's *The Canterbury Tales*.
6 This was the title of the story when it was originally published in a 2011 issue of the *Granta* magazine dedicated to the "F word".
7 I am indebted to Dr Estíbaliz Encarnación Pinedo for pointing out Vanessa Place's work to me.

References

Allardice, Lisa (2006) "The Miniaturist", *The Guardian*, www.theguardian.com/books/2006/jan/07/featuresreviews.guardianreview9 (accessed 31 July 2017).

Becker, Julia C. and Janet K. Swim (2011) "Seeing the Unseen: Attention to Daily Encounters with Sexism as Way to Reduce Sexist Beliefs", *Psychology of Women Quarterly* 35(2): 227–242.

Besnault-Levita, Anne (2007) "Gender", in *Companion to the British Short Story*, edited by Andrew Maunder, New York: Facts on File Inc, 483–485.

Bloom, Leslie Rebecca (1998) *Under the Sign of Hope: Feminist Methodology and Narrative Interpretation*, New York: SUNY Press.

Briscoe, Joanna (2003) "Mums the Word: The Mother of All Taboos", *The Independent*, www.independent.co.uk/arts-entertainment/theatre-dance/features/mums-the-word-the-mother-of-all-taboos-112178.html (accessed 31 July 2017).

Clark, Alex (2000) "Battery mums", *The Guardian*, www.theguardian.com/books/2000/oct/07/fiction.reviews1 (accessed 31 July 2017).

Crosby, Faye, Susan Clayton, Olaf Alksnis and Kathryn Hemker (1986) "Cognitive Biases in the Perception of Discrimination: The Importance of Format", *Sex Roles* 14(11/12): 637–646.

Crown, Sarah (2010) "Helen Simpson: 'I Stuffed It with Sex and Violence'", *The Guardian*, www.theguardian.com/lifeandstyle/2010/may/28/helen-simpson-sex-violence (accessed 31 July 2017).

Day, Jon (2015) "*Cockfosters* by Helen Simpson, Review: 'A Grand Project'", *The Telegraph*, www.telegraph.co.uk/books/what-to-read/cockfosters-by-helen-simpson-review/ (accessed 31 July 2017).

D'hoker, Elke and Van Den Bossche, Bart (2014) "Cycles, Recueils, Macrotexts. The Short Story Collection in a Comparative Perspective", *Interférences littéraires/Literaire interferenties* 12: 7–17.

Eagleton, Mary (1989) "Gender and Genre", in *Re-reading the Short Story*, edited by Clare Hanson, London: Palgrave Macmillan, 55–68.

Edmond, Jacob (2012) "Emancipation via Elimination: Vanessa Place's 'Boycott Project'", *Jacket2*, http://jacket2.org/commentary/emancipation-elimination (accessed 31 July 2017).

Federici, Silvia (2014) "Es un engaño que el trabajo asalariado sea la clave para liberar a las mujeres", *El Diario.es*, www.eldiario.es/economia/engano-trabajo-asalariado-liberar-mujeres_0_262823964.html (accessed 31 July 2017).

Figueira, Aldara (2017) *Cosas de Chicos*, www.youtube.com/watch?v=g7RXnV_DKBo (accessed 31 July 2017).

Frye, Joanne S. (2010) "Narrating Maternal Subjectivity: Memoirs from Motherhood", in *Textual Mothers/Maternal Texts: Motherhood in Contemporary Women's Literatures*, edited by Elizabeth Podnieks and Andrea O'Reilly, Waterloo: Wilfrid Laurier University Press, 187–202.

Garrett, Roberta (2013) "Novels and Children: 'Mum's' Lit and the Public Mother/Author", *Studies in the Maternal* 5(2), www.mamsie.bbk.ac.uk/articles/abstract/10.16995/sim.25/ (accessed 31 July 2017).

Genz, Stephanie and Benjamin A. Brabon (2009) *Postfeminism: Cultural Texts and Theories,* Edinburgh: Edinburgh University Press.

Gharraie, Jonathan (2012) "Helen Simpson on *In-Flight Entertainment*", *The Paris Review*, www.theparisreview.org/blog/2012/02/28/helen-simpson-on-'in-flight-entertainment'/ (accessed 31 July 2017).

González-Barrientos, Marcela (2017) "Escritura femenina: Un recorrido por la crítica literaria feminista", *Tonos digital: Revista electrónica de estudios filológicos* 33, www.tonosdigital.es/ojs/index.php/tonos/article/view/1753 (accessed 31 July 2017).

Hays, Sharon (1996) *The Cultural Contradictions of Motherhood*, New Haven, CT: Yale University Press.

Hewett, Heather (2006) "Talkin' Bout a Revolution: Building a Mothers' Movement in the Third Wave", *Journal of the Association for Research on Mothering* 8(1/2): 34–54.

Higgins, Tracy E. (2000) "Reviving the Public/Private Distinction in Feminist Theorizing", *Chicago-Kent Law Review* 75(3), scholarship.kentlaw.iit.edu/cgi/viewcontent.cgi?article=3216&context=cklawreview (accessed 31 July 2017).

Hochschild, Arlie (1989) *The Second Shift: Working Parents and the Revolution at Home*, New York: Viking.

Kawash, Samira (2011) "New Directions in Motherhood Studies", *Signs: Journal of Women in Culture and Society* 36(4): 969–1003.

Kellaway, Kate (2000) "Life Is What You Had before Kids", *The Guardian*, www.theguardian.com/books/2000/oct/08/fiction.reviews (accessed 31 July 2017).

Lawless, Jill (2007) "A Woman of Few Words", *Oregon Life*, news.google.com/newspapers?id=pmBWAAAAIBAJ&sjid=svADAAAAIBAJ&pg=5820%2C1291494 (accessed 31 July 2017).

Lepaludier, Laurent (2008) "Theatricality in the Short Story Staging the World?", *Journal of the Short Story in English* 51, https://jsse.revues.org/891 (accessed 31 July 2017).

Lister, Rachel (2007) "Female Expansion and Masculine Immobilization in the Short Story Cycle", *Journal of the Short Story in English* 48, https://jsse.revues.org/682 (accessed 31 July 2017).

Luscher, Robert M (1989) "The Short Story Sequence: An Open Book", in *Short Story Theory at a Crossroads*, edited by Susan Lohafer and Jo Ellen Clarey, Baton Rouge, LA: Louisiana State University Press, 148–170.

Malcolm, David (2012). *The British and Irish Short Story Handbook*, Chichester: Wiley-Blackwell.

McInerney, Jay (2001) "Honey, I Loathe the Kids", *The New York Times on the Web*, www.nytimes.com/2001/06/17/books/honey-i-loathe-the-kids.html (accessed 31 July 2017).

Mukherjee, Neel (2015) "Time is of the Essence in Helen Simpson's *Cockfosters*", *The Spectator*, www.spectator.co.uk/2015/11/time-is-of-the-essence-in-helen-simpsons-cockfosters/ (accessed 31 July 2017).

Mullan, John (2006) "Limited Lives", *The Guardian*, www.theguardian.com/books/2006/apr/08/featuresreviews.guardianreview4 (accessed 31 July 2017).

Munford, Rebecca (2016) "Writing the F-Word: Girl Power, the Third Wave, and Postfeminism", in *History of British Women's Writing, 1970-Present*, edited by Mary Eagleton and Emma Parker, London: Palgrave, 130–144.

O'Reilly, Andrea (2010) "The Motherhood Memoir and the 'New Momism': Biting the Hand That Feeds You", in *Textual Mothers/Maternal Texts: Motherhood in Contemporary Women's Literatures*, edited by Elizabeth Podnieks and Andrea O'Reilly, Waterloo: Wilfrid Laurier University Press, 203–214.

Orr, Katherine (2011) "Overturning the Narrative: An Interview with Helen Simpson", *Short Fiction in Theory and Practice* 1(1): 109–118.

Pateman, Carole (1984) *The Disorder of Women: Democracy, Feminism and Political Theory*, Stanford, CA: Stanford University Press.

Perloff, Marjorie (2014) "Conceptual Poetry and the Question of Emotion", *Literatures of Modernity Distinguished Speakers Series*, 13 February 2014, Modern Literature and Culture Research Centre, Ryerson University. Guest lecture. www.stuttgarter-schule.de/Perloff_Conceptual_Poetry.pdf (accessed 31 July 2017).

Place, Vanessa (2013) *Boycott*, Brooklyn: Ugly Duckling Press.

Pourriat, Eleonore (2012) *Majorité Opprimée*, www.youtube.com/watch?v= kpfaza-Mw4I (accessed 31 July 2017).

Rohrberger, Mary (2004) "Origins, Development, Substance, and Design of the Short Story: How I Got Hooked on the Short Story and Where It Led Me", in *The Art of Brevity: Excursions in Short Fiction Theory and Analysis*, edited by Per Winther, Jakob Lothe and Hans H. Skei, Columbia, SC: University of South Carolina Press, 1–13.

Rose, Ellen Cronan (1993) "American Feminist Criticism of Contemporary Women's Fiction", *Signs* 18(2): 346–375.

Simpson, Helen (1990) *Four Bare Legs*, London: Heinemann.

Simpson, Helen (1995) *Dear George,* London: Vintage.

Simpson, Helen (2000) *Hey Yeah Right Get a Life*, London: Vintage.

Simpson, Helen (2006) "With Child", *The Guardian*, www.theguardian.com/ books/2006/apr/22/featuresreviews.guardianreview3 (accessed 31 July 2017).

Simpson, Helen (2010a) "Helen Simpson: My Hero Colette", *The Guardian*, www.theguardian.com/books/2010/may/15/colette-my-hero-helen-simpson (accessed 31 July 2017).

Simpson, Helen (2010b) *In-Flight Entertainment*, London: Vintage.

Simpson, Helen (2012a) *A Bunch of Fives: Selected Stories*, London: Vintage.

Simpson, Helen (2012b) "Open Book: David Hewson, Commonwealth Writers, Helen Simpson", *Books and Authors*, www.bbc.co.uk/programmes/p02sh2q2 (accessed 31 July 2017).

Simpson, Helen (2015) *Cockfosters*, London: Jonathan Cape.

Simpson, Helen (2017) "Being a Woman Writer", *BBC World Service*, www. bbc.co.uk/worldservice/arts/features/womenwriters/simpson_being.shtml (accessed 31 July 2017).

Tayler, Christopher (2010) "*In-Flight Entertainment* by Helen Simpson", *The Guardian*, www.theguardian.com/books/2010/may/01/in-flight-entertainment-helen-simpson (accessed 31 July 2017).

Ullman, Tracey (2017) "What Were You Wearing", *Tracey Ullman's Show*, www.youtube.com/watch?v=51-hepLP8J4 (accessed 31 July 2017).

Wagner, Catherine (2014) "US Experimental Poetry: A Social Turn?", *Primerjalna književnost* 1(37): 235–246.

Ward, Amanda Eyre (2007) "Helen Simpson (Writer): 'Even the Blindest of Bats Must See Eventually that It's Parenthood that Gender-Politicizes Relationships", *The Believer* 5(7): 67–72.

White, Melanie (2015) "*Cockfosters*, by Helen Simpson – Book Review: Gender Issues with an Icy Heft", *The Independent*, www.independent.co.uk/arts-entertainment/books/reviews/cockfosters-by-helen-simpson-book-review-gender-issues-with-an-icy-heft-a6688176.html (accessed 31 July 2017).

Wilson, Natalie (2011) "Do We Really Want a Matriarchy?", *MS Magazine Blog*, msmagazine.com/blog/2011/05/23/do-we-really-want-a-matriarchy/ (accessed 31 July 2017).

Wolf, Joan B. (2016) "Framing Mothers: Childcare Research and the Normalization of Maternal Care", *Signs: Journal of Women in Culture and Society* 41(3): 627–651.

Young, Emma (2015) "Feminist F(r)iction: Short Stories and Postfeminist Politics at the Millennial Moment", in *British Women Short Story Writers: The New Woman to Now*, edited by Emma Young and James Bailey, Edinburgh: Edinburgh University Press, 133–147.

Young, Emma and James Bailey (2015) "Introduction", in *British Women Short Story Writers: The New Woman to Now*, edited by Emma Young and James Bailey, Edinburgh: Edinburgh University Press, 1–14.

Part VI

Latest News

15 New Voices in British Short Stories by Women

Ailsa Cox

Introduction

Women short story writers are thriving in Britain today, producing work of tremendous range and diversity. As the founder and organiser of the Edge Hill Prize for the short story, I am sent copies of almost every new collection from the UK and Ireland. Twice in its eleven-year history, the shortlist has been all-female: an anthology *Head Land* (Glass 2016), with stories by previous winners and finalists, demonstrates the contribution made by major women authors, including Sarah Hall, Ali Smith and A.L. Kennedy – well-established figures who have several collections under their belts, and usually novels as well. In this chapter, I shall focus on a selection of less familiar titles, all published since 2012, three of them shortlisted for the Edge Hill Prize. They are *Diving Belles* by Lucy Wood (2012), Carys Bray's *Sweet Home* (2012), Carys Davies's *The Redemption of Galen Pike* (2014) and K.J. Orr's *Light Box* (2016a). After briefly introducing the writers and their collections, I shall discuss the publishing context and the culture of the short story in the UK, as it affects the careers of women writers. I shall then analyse the stories themselves, comparing the narrative strategies used by each author, and the cultural resonances of their work in Britain today.

Mainstream publishers tend to leave debut collections to the small independent presses, an exception being Bloomsbury,[1] who nominated 2012 as "the year of the short story" (Williams 2012). Lucy Wood's *Diving Belles* appeared alongside collections by Jon McGregor, D.W. Wilson, Roshi Fernando and Rajesh Parameswaran, an astonishing achievement for a writer without prior publication. Inspired by Cornish folklore, *Diving Belles* was based on Wood's MA Creative Writing dissertation at the University of Exeter. Since then, she has produced a novel, *Weathering* (2015) and a second collection, *The Sing of the Shore* (2018). Carys Bray's collection, *Sweet Home* (2012), was also based on her MA dissertation; one of the stories, "Just in Case", won the MA category of the Edge Hill Prize, which is awarded to a student. *Sweet Home* was followed by a prize-winning novel, *A Song for Issy Bradley* (2014); a second novel, *The Museum of You*, appeared in 2016, along-side a reissue of *Sweet Home* from Windmill Books, a subsidiary of

Penguin Random House. K.J. Orr's *Light Box* (2016a) originated in her PhD dissertation at the University of Chichester, and is published by Daunt Books, a small imprint founded by an independent bookshop. Carys Davies's background is in journalism. *The Redemption of Galen Pike* (2014) is her second collection, both of them published by Salt, one of the most prolific independent presses in the UK. (Bray's *Sweet Home* was also published originally by Salt). At the time of writing, Davies is under contract with Granta for two novels.

Davies, then, is the only one of the four writers without a Creative Writing degree, and it is worth briefly examining the role played by such degrees in short-story-writing, reading and publishing since 2000, a period which has seen a rapid expansion in provision. According to the National Association of Writers in Education (NAWE) there are currently about a hundred UK universities with MA programmes in Creative Writing, most of them also offering PhD supervision. While there is still some residual scepticism expressed towards the whole notion that Creative Writing can be "taught", and the motives of those who take such degrees, such hostility has become, as Rachel Cusk puts it, "obsolete" (2013). In fact, university affiliation of one kind or another has become the norm for short story writers. Women writers who have held professorial positions include, in addition to Cusk herself, Kirsty Gunn, Louise Welsh, Alison MacLeod, Jane Rogers, Marina Warner and Tessa Hadley. Indeed, Hadley has completed the full trajectory, having begun her writing career as an MA student at Bath Spa University. Cusk's article foregrounds novel-writing but, as I have discussed elsewhere (Cox 2016) the short story is especially suited to the workshop method which is so integral to the teaching of Creative Writing; a self-contained work of prose fiction can be produced and critiqued in the workshop, and then redrafted for final assessment. For the student writer, the short story serves as a space for experimenting with different styles and taking risks with subject matter and technique. But there is another related factor, especially for those students working on collections, which is a heightened awareness of form that is very attractive both to those teaching the short story and those students producing postgraduate dissertations. Writing short stories for a dissertation encourages the writer to develop, and reflect on, a personal aesthetic; in a newspaper interview, Lucy Wood says she could not have written *Diving Belles* without the MA programme at Exeter University (Popescu 2015). She has also credited the publication of the book to the MA, following a recommendation to an agent through one of her tutors, which resulted in her deal with Bloomsbury.

Cusk's article perceives a misogynist element amongst those objecting to Creative Writing; as a communal exercise, the writers' workshop threatens the image of the solitary male genius: "It was the writer's own insecurity that required him to distinguish himself from old ladies and housewives, to be the 'real' writer" (Cusk 2013). The headline given to an interview with Carys Bray, "Mother of four fits study and writing around her family to fulfil childhood dream to become published author" (Writers and Artists 2017) unwittingly revives that well-known figure, the "Angel in the House". The interview is in fact a paean to the flexible study patterns offered by the Open University, where Bray first studied Creative Writing within her undergraduate degree. Bray's modesty is clear to see: "I did a creative writing module and I did start to think about being a writer but I didn't think I'd have two books published before forty" (Writers and Artists 2017). Taking an academic course legitimates artistic self-expression that might otherwise seem an indulgence, granting permission to "think about being a writer" (Writers and Artists 2017).

Other short story writers who have completed MAs or MLitts include Kirsty Logan, Zoe Lambert, Anneliese Mackintosh, A.J. Ashworth and Daisy Johnson. Some, like Zoe Lambert, move on to a PhD before taking up a university position. But, for many of these writers, postgraduate qualifications are not necessarily a first step towards a permanent teaching post. While they might give occasional readings or guest lectures, or teach on residential courses such as those run by the Arvon foundation, many steer clear of the additional administrative and other responsibilities attached to a full-time position. Creative Writing teaching spills beyond institutional confines, and there is ongoing contact and co-operation between the universities and the wider community of short story writers and readers through live readings, literature festivals, magazines and other aspects of literary promotion.

Most writers these days are required to participate in book tours, festivals and so forth, promoting their publications through live readings, competitions, literary magazines and other means. For short story authors, this often entails advocacy for the form itself. The rhetoric of the embattled short story champion is at least as old as V.S. Pritchett's 1966 lament for "one of the inextinguishable lost causes" (1966: 6). An Arts Council-backed "Save Our Short Story" campaign, launched in 2002, spearheaded what is regarded by some as a short story renaissance in the UK.[2] Debates around the specificity of the short story and its supposed neglected form provide a lively and accessible theme for public discussion. The Small Wonder Festival, based in Sussex, is, like the Cork International Short Story Festival in Ireland, dedicated to the form; there have been similar initiatives in London and Leeds. Carys Davies curates a short story strand within the Lancaster Literature Festival.

The interconnectedness between the academy and the wider world of short-story-writing, reading and publishing can be seen in the Thresholds International Short Story Forum, run by Chichester University, and originally intended for postgraduates, but now a general resource for short story writers. The site includes advice on writing, feature articles and opportunities for publication. Carys Bray has written an author profile of Robert Shearman; K.J. Orr has contributed several articles, as well as being interviewed in 2016. Of equal significance is The Word Factory, founded by Cathy Galvin, which, amongst other things, hosts public readings and offers mentorships to emerging writers, most of them women.

Obviously, none of these initiatives could exist without the Internet, which has played such a crucial role in the resurgence of short-story-writing. Small press authors, in particular, rely on blogs, websites and social media to build their careers. Many independent presses look quite openly for evidence of a busy online profile when considering submissions; the expectation from most publishers, but especially the smaller ones, is that once a collection has been accepted for publication it is the writer's job to advertise themselves and their writing largely through their presence on social media.

In an article for *The Dublin Review,* the Irish writer Kevin Barry has highlighted the drawbacks of this frenzied self-promotion for the writer, confessing that his own compositional process is disrupted by a compulsion to check his emails. He even compares what he sees as an addiction to the Internet to the over-consumption of cannabis. He suggests that an inability to concentrate frustrates the attempt to produce sustained, continuous prose, and makes the classic novel inaccessible to contemporary readers, including himself (Barry 2017). Since the short story is a fragmented form, and since short story collections are published most often by small presses, relying on authors to promote their own books, we might speculate further on the relationship between distraction, social media and short story form. That topic is beyond the scope of this chapter, but it is interesting to compare the social media tactics of the four authors. Of these four, only Lucy Wood, with the publicity department at Bloomsbury at her disposal, has not created a website. If she has a Facebook page or a Twitter account I have yet to trace them. Carys Bray, on the other hand, is extremely active on Facebook and Twitter, and up until July 2016, also maintained a blog. K.J. Orr and Carys Davies have also managed to keep a distance from social media. In this they are unusual amongst the short story writers who have emerged in recent years. Nonetheless, their names are highly visible online through events, readings and, above all, success in competitions.

Competitions have come to dominate short-story-writing and publication in the twenty-first century. Literary awards in general have become increasingly significant in building a public appetite for serious fiction; Richard Todd's monograph, *Consuming Fictions: The Booker Prize and Fiction in Britain Today* (1996) has been superseded by later developments, but still provides valuable insights into prize culture, which has spread from novel to short story. In 2015, Davies's *The Redemption of Galen Pike* was the recipient of the annual Jerwood Fiction Uncovered prize and was shortlisted for Wales Book of the Year, as well as receiving the Frank O'Connor award (curiously, all three prizes were either abolished or suspended in 2016). Lucy Wood was granted a Somerset Maugham Award for Young Writers in 2013. These are all book awards; there has also been a steady accretion in the number of prizes for stand-alone stories since the inauguration, in 2005, of what is now the BBC National Short Story Award, launched as part of the Save Our Short Story Campaign's strategy to raise the status of the genre. The BBC prize has been joined by the *Sunday Times* EFG Short Story Award, the Costa Short Story Award, the Bristol Short Story Prize, the Bath Short Story Award, the Manchester Fiction Prize and numerous others. Literary magazines and even small publishers often use competitions as a fund-raising device; Galley Beggar Press also offers individual feedback for competition entries in return for extra payment.

Individual stories by Carys Davies have been shortlisted for a total of sixteen awards since 2002, including the highly respected V.S. Pritchett Memorial Prize (which she won) and the *Sunday Times*/EFG short story prize. Both she and K.J. Orr have been shortlisted for the Bridport Prize and the Asham Award, which is for women only. K.J. Orr was a winner and Lucy Wood a runner-up in the BBC National Short Story Prize. The BBC award has the widest reach of any of the short story prizes, through BBC broadcasts and attendant coverage, and is open to published writers only. Agents and publishers encourage submission for this reason; the success of both Orr and Wood came from stories available in their collections.

Competitions are good news for those on the shortlist, and even better for the winner. While the most prestigious competitions are for published writers, others have a remit to find new voices. Salt Publishing's Scott Prize for an unpublished collection (now discontinued) was one of these; Carys Bray's *Sweet Home* was published as a result of this initiative. But those who do not win are, by definition, losers, without the consolation of feedback or encouragement for work that might not be entirely without merit. There is also the possibility that competitions favour a certain type of story. Philip Hensher, editor of *The Penguin Book of the British Short Story*, is scathing about an over-dependence on competitions for discovering new talent, claiming that "they reward what they think ought to be good, and not what contains any real energy" (2015: xxv). While I would not completely agree with his judgement that prize-winning stories tend to be solipsistic, affectless and short on humour, he has identified the closed circle of competition culture, which subsidises a tiny number of short story writers through the fees of the rejected.

I shall now take a closer look at each of my four case studies in turn, examining characteristics of their work, their distinctive approach to the genre, and their cultural significance as women writers near the start of their careers.

Carys Bray, *Sweet Home* (2012)

The venerable American critic Charles E. May reviews *Sweet Home* favourably in a blog posting with the heading: "Carys Bray and Carol Shields: Whimsy and Artifice" (May 2013). May develops Bray's comments on the influence of Carol Shields to compare how both writers handle domestic material through what he calls the *"jeu d'esprit"*, the extra surreal twist added to a reality that already borders on the absurd (2013). In Bray's "The Baby Aisle", for instance, it becomes possible to pick up an extra child in the supermarket. The temptation to have another baby is made analogous to the seductive fragrance of newly baked bread; there are even special offers and a bargain bin, for those infants reaching their best-before date: "They made angry eye contact and cried real tears" (Bray 2012: 70).

May finds Bray's work "light and breezy" (2013), quoting her own account of the writing process as a playful experience. Yet, as that image of the cut-price babies shows, the *"jeu d'esprit"* often takes a sinister turn. Amongst the cut-price babies is "a half-price George with fanning ears and a Maya with red hair" (Bray 2012: 71). A salesman homes in on the protagonist as she stops to browse, and she is torn between her maternal instinct and her common sense when the Maya starts to cry, seeming to reach out for her: "'I'm sorry,' she said, itching to pick the baby up and console her, but determined not to do it in front of him. 'I already have four children. I really don't need any more'" (Bray 2012: 71).

Neither does she need the chocolates and pastries, and the other items that were not on her list. One reason that she has as many as four children is that she has twins, the result of a "buy one get one free" deal. In this story, Bray is satirising both the blandishments of consumerism and the broodiness of the young mother. In fact, the two drives – the one culturally manufactured, the other supposedly biological – are conflated: "She entered the supermarket without the protection of a list, and the next thing she knew she was pushing a double-seated trolley" (Bray 2012: 67). The word "protection" evokes the language of contraception. Bray's double-voiced discourse generates a parodic dialogue between sex and shopping that is rather more subversive than May's comments allow. The story ends with the disturbing image of the impulse purchase, smuggled home amongst the items on the list:

> And afterwards, when Peter arrived home from work and they sat around the dining table as good families should, she stocked the conversation with improved attentiveness, and longer-lasting laughter, in order to conceal the hoarse, feeble cries emanating from a toy box in the lounge.
>
> (Bray 2012: 72)

In their broad survey, *The British Short Story,* Emma Liggins, Andrew Maunder and Ruth Robbins note that "for women writers domesticity has often been a favourite theme, whether to record, to protest against or even to celebrate women's day-to-day experiences as wives, mothers and household managers" (2011: 231), discussing how women's writing since the 1960s has subverted expectations of those roles. Bray belongs within that tradition, citing the influence of many writers – Carol Shields, Alice Munro, Tessa Hadley and Helen Simpson – in her 2015 doctoral thesis, *A Song for Issy Bradley: A Novel and Poetics.*

The critic Emma Young (2015) has given a reading of Helen Simpson's work through the prism of the so-called "Mummy Wars", the conflict between stay-at-home mothers and women who choose to focus on their careers. Rather than simply encoding motherhood and family life as a hellish zone of oppression, Bray follows Simpson by adopting a more ambivalent stance. Placing maternity at centre stage in their fiction means that these women are affirming their identity and agency as mothers, while also challenging social attitudes that marginalise the maternal role. The title of Bray's now discontinued blog, *Postnatal Confession,* suggests that she is on the side of those women who choose to identify as mothers rather than escaping the domestic role entirely; she was also a member of the Mumsnet bloggers network. At first glance, "The Baby Aisle" depicts a woman at the mercy of external forces. Yet the story frequently affirms her agency and her control over the family. Although the first child, a boy, was her husband's choice, he seems to have played little part in subsequent purchases. It is easy for her to get her way through manipulation and concealment.

The narrative's closing sentence deploys, once again, the discourse of consumerism; "improved", "longer-lasting", terms straight out of TV advertisements. Bray's use of the word "stock" evokes both shopping ("in stock", "stock taking") and linguistic cliché ("stock phrase") (Bray 2012: 72). The protagonist is playing the game of happy families, acting a part, to serve her own ends. Bray frequently returns to this theme of play-acting, for instance in "Everything a Parent Needs to Know", where the mother "has rehearsed *Mary Poppins,* only to find herself acting in *Night, Mother*" (Bray 2012: 1). An account of the daily battle between mother and daughter, which happens in this instance to centre on what she wears for her swimming lesson, is intercut with excerpts from fictional child-rearing manuals:

> When all else fails, think a happy thought. Like Peter Pan and Wendy, you won't soar unless you are happy. Remember a happy moment and grasp it as tightly as you would grasp your sword if you were to come face to face with an unfriendly dragon (no offence to any friendly dragons out there!).

(Give a little whistle: Disney solutions to parenting challenges by
JO WHITE).

(Bray 2012: 4)

On the release of her novel *A Song for Issy Bradley* (2014), two years
after *Sweet Home*, Bray began to speak publicly about her Mormon
upbringing. The Mormon religion emphasises patriarchal family values
and the traditional role of women in the home to such a degree that
its social norms appear quaint and anachronistic to the secular mainstream. In an interview with *the Guardian*, Bray spoke about the gap
between ideology and the reality of parenting:

> Because motherhood is your role in this life and the next, to say,
> "Actually, I'm really not enjoying this that much and I think I might
> like to do something else at some point" is quite difficult. You're
> supposed to be a wonderful mother and absolutely love it.
>
> (Franklin 2014)

Play-acting becomes second nature when there is so much pressure
to conform to the ideal. The unfailingly cheerful demeanour that the
church demands of all its followers, male or female, has left its traces
in Bray's parodic "Disney" guide to parenting. Bray's humour is deeply
subversive, belonging to that category of unofficial laughter that Bakhtin
regarded as so threatening to the monologic medieval church (Bakhtin
1985).

A review of the reissued *Sweet Home* by Jane Housham identifies
an unsettling quality in Bray's ability to switch suddenly from levity
to darkness: "They trick you into thinking they are just funny, until
something disturbing pulls you up short" (Housham 2016). Pregnancy,
miscarriage, childbirth, the death of children and the loss of children –
because children grow up and they change and they leave us – all of this
stands for mutability. It stands for the provisional nature of reality and
the instability of language. The child is the vessel for adult hopes and
desires; and the figure of the dead or absent children, who recurs so
often in these stories, stands for all that is irrecoverable or inexpressible
(see "Just in Case", "The Ice Baby", "Scaling Never" and "Bed Rest").

All of these stories strip away social conformity, exposing the meanings camouflaged by euphemism and small talk. In "Just in Case", a
newspaper story includes an item about a man who finds a suitcase in
his dead mother's attic: "Inside the suitcase was a baby skeleton. A *baby
skeleton*. [...] As if it might grow up into an adolescent skeleton and then
an adult skeleton" (Bray 2012: 15). Elsewhere the narrator observes:
"When you are pregnant people often ask if you want a boy or a girl.
You must say that you don't mind. This is an unwritten rule" (Bray 2012:
12). She repeats that point towards the end: "I want a girl, but I will be

careful not to say that to anyone. You mustn't actually say it. It's one of those things you mustn't say. Like dead" (2012: 19). "Scaling Never", in which a young boy tries to resurrect a bird following the death of his sister, became the nucleus for Bray's novel, *A Song for Issy Bradley*. Focalised this time through a child, it begins with the phrase "There are so many kinds of never", contemplating its different meanings before concluding: "Never is a word that doesn't always mean not-on-your-nelly and absolutely no way. Sometimes never means not yet" (2012: 50).

Typically, Bray combines present tense narration with first person or free indirect narration, compressing colloquial speech and, as we have seen, introducing an element of word play alongside what May calls "*jeu d'esprit*" (2013). A particular poignancy is generated when language is distilled and intensified in this way, as well as a deceptive lightness and accessibility of style. Bray's interrogation of language enables her to un-pick social codes and expectations, and her use of the short story genre also creates a tension between a tightly controlled narrative structure and the raw emotions that it contains. Several of her contemporaries share this approach, for instance Kate Clanchy, whose "The Not-Dead and the Saved" is the story of a mother and her dying son; or Lucy Caldwell, whose "Multitudes" also describes a dangerously ill child. Such gruelling intensity would scarcely be sustained across a longer work of prose. Linguistic playfulness, formal invention and the "*jeu d'esprit*" make such topics bearable despite their emotional impact on the reader.

Lucy Wood, *Diving Belles* (2012)

The influence of Angela Carter is very clear in some of the stories in *Sweet Home*, especially the title story, which is a contemporary fable with a Hansel and Grettel gingerbread house as its central motif. A significant number of women writers follow in the footsteps of Carter's *The Bloody Chamber* (1979) by re-inventing folklore and the fairy tale, including Claire Dean, Zoe Gilbert, Kirsty Logan and Daisy Johnson. This can be a risky strategy; too many wolves, fairies and mermaids, and the stories can seem merely fanciful, or the ready-made symbolism too neat in its reversals and appropriations. Wood avoids such pitfalls, as do many others, by giving a hard edge to her stories, and anchoring them in contemporary reality.

My pun is intentional; Wood's title is itself, of course, a pun, and we can see the realms of fantasy and reality colliding within that extra vowel attached to "bell" which turns the practical object, the small underwater vessel used by deep-sea divers, into something suggestive of those very mermaids that I warned against. In the title story, "Diving Belles" is the name of a small company, housed in a scruffy Portakabin, that sends wives underwater in search of lost husbands. Wood's world is not always fabulous. It is described with detachment, using mundane details rather than seductively sensuous description. The protagonist, Iris, has woken up to find "a tiny fish in its death throes on the pillow next to her. There was only a lukewarm indent in the mattress where her husband should have been" (Wood 2012: 5–6). Wood's description of the sea's encroachment on the house blurs the boundary between the fantastic and the everyday:

> Despite the bleach, the smell lingered in cupboards and corners. Every so often, an anemone would appear overnight; she would find a translucent shrimp darting around inside an empty milk bottle. Sometimes, all the water in the house turned into brine and she lugged huge bottles of water home from the supermarket.
>
> (Wood 2012: 6)

In those moments when Iris finds her husband, Wood indulges the reader with a lush, romantic evocation of the underwater realms, and a glimpse of the mermaids themselves; however, this dreamlike description is undercut by harsh reality. Iris's husband is still a young man, but, having aged since their separation, she gropes for her glasses to see him, and when she drops them is unable to bend down and retrieve them.

Wood is a regional writer. Cornwall is part of the so-called Celtic fringe, which includes Scotland and Wales, but is much less represented in literary fiction, despite its importance to modernist incomers such as Woolf, Mansfield and Lawrence. Tourist constructions of Cornwall dominate its representation to an even greater degree than Scotland or Wales, concealing the decline of its traditional industries and the poverty of many locals. As Wood herself points out, "Cornwall's folklore is often seen as rather twee and clichéd, something for tourists and gift shops" (Dog Ear 2012), and what we can see in the stories is an attempt to reclaim regional identity, both in terms of its traditional culture and present-day experience at the furthest edges of contemporary Britain.

The story that ends the collection, "Some Drolls Are Like This and Some Drolls Are Like That", articulates Wood's personal poetics through the traditional figure of the droll teller or wandering storyteller. This droll is "hundreds of years old" (Wood 2012: 205) and has an intimate knowledge of local inhabitants, but the days of marathon storytelling sessions are long gone, and perhaps the droll himself is near the end, reduced to doing cut-price "story tours" for tourists. Wood describes the gradual fading of the culture and the dispersal of the locals as the coastal economy is disrupted, becoming ever more dependent on the tourist season:

> Faces became other faces. And they had all gone the same way: forgetting, becoming ill, weak, boring, giving up the struggle, while the droll teller had stayed more or less the same, watching it all, getting

left behind. Except maybe now it was different, maybe now it was his turn to go through all that.

(Wood 2012: 207)

The droll's memory is fading, and after he has recounted a lurid local legend to a pair of customers he realises that what he has remembered is just the plot of a soap opera that he saw in the pub. Nevertheless, the power of storytelling reasserts itself by the end of the story through the working of the imagination and the sense of place and the bond between the teller and the listener:

> It sounded to the droll teller as if something was climbing up out of the mine. His senses sharpened, knitted together. It could be a deep tapping, or it could be that bell, tolling. Was the bell in the mine or in the sea? He remembered a bell sunk in a shipwreck that still tolled underwater. A man had a premonition. Tap, tap. And then there was shuffling, movement. He could hear the story creeping out of the mine towards him. It was backing out slowly, hauling itself out bit by bit. It was taking its time. There were waves. There was a train carriage. There was a lamp swinging in the dark. The bell tolled louder and now here he was beginning again; somehow, despite everything, he was beginning again.
>
> (Wood 2012: 223)

This passage, with its echoes of the title story and its affirmation of renewal and circularity, evokes a local, perhaps even a universal, imperative towards storytelling that transcends social decline and the encroachment of contemporary mass culture.

This does not mean a rejection of mass culture or the trappings of contemporary life. The droll teller has a taste for Chinese takeaway as well as the local cider and "older tastes that he could barely remember – saffron maybe, or another, richer, spice that you couldn't get hold of any more" (Wood 2012: 215). In collapsing the boundary between fantasy and reality, Wood is also challenging the opposition between modernity and folkloric tradition. Like Annie Proulx, whom she has cited as an influence (Popescu 2015), Wood loves technical intricacies, such as the mechanics of the diving bell in the title story. The coastal villages of Cornwall are not tourist backdrops; they are working landscapes.

Wood also uses the interior, domestic spaces in her stories to infuse the present moment with the past. "Notes from the House Spirits", the story that was shortlisted for the National Short Story Prize, is narrated in present tense, using the first-person plural, "we". In this way, the passing moment is combined with the eternal. Like the droll teller, the house spirits observe the cyclical movements of people as residents come and go, age and disappear: "They have come back. We think they are the same people but we are not sure. We are not good with faces. They seem much older" (Wood 2012: 145). Ultimately the human presence is a part of the natural world, like the movements of geese that open the droll teller's story, and the open-endedness of the short story form affirms a persistence of hope and renewal, despite economic decline and cultural decay. As Paul March-Russell puts it, Wood's reworking of folklore

> constructs an unruly landscape that not only is at odds with the hegemonic discourse of national heritage but is also more abcanny than uncanny,[3] positing a vicarious future rather than a dead-handed past.
>
> (March-Russell 2017: 63–64)

Carys Davies, *The Redemption of Galen Pike* (2014)

As Charles Holdefer has pointed out in an article surveying flash fiction's formal characteristics and its relationship to new technology, "very short forms are nothing new, but they are currently enjoying greater currency under a variety of labels" (2014: 158). Amongst the seventeen stories in *The Redemption of Galen Pike*, seven are less than five pages. Read in sequence, the stories constitute a series of tableaux, placing one or two figures against the dramatic backcloth of historical settings, some of them more clearly identified than others. The opening story, "The Quiet", evokes some kind of colonial setting, its protagonist seeming isolated in a new land. A careful reader might guess at an Australian setting through references to convicts and smaller details, such as a sheepskin waistcoat, but this is never made fully explicit. Rather than establishing time and place, the opening lines present a stark visual image:

> She didn't hear him arrive.

> The wind was up and rain was thundering down on the tin roof like a shower of stones and in the midst of all the noise she didn't hear the rattle of his old buggy approaching. She didn't hear the scrape of his iron-rimmed wheels on the track, the soft thump of his feet in the wet dust. She didn't know he was there until she looked up from her bucket of soapy water and saw his face at her window, his pale green eyes with their tiny black pin-prick pupils blinking at her through the glass.
>
> (Davies 2014: 1)

The title story uses similar tactics, describing the events leading up to a hanging in another colonial setting that seems familiar from TV westerns, but is difficult to pinpoint in a specific time and space. A real "Piper City" exists on the map, but it is in Illinois, whereas this fictional small town is located somewhere in "the foothills of the Colorado Mountains" (Davies 2014: 90).

Historical settings are relatively unusual in short fiction. As Nadine Gordimer has said: "Short story writers see by the light of the flash; theirs is the art of the only thing one can be sure of – the present moment" (1994: 264). Historical fiction would seem to find a natural home in lengthy novels, with the space to establish authenticity and to chronicle a gradual progression through time, rather than in the short story, where time is experienced with greater urgency and immediacy. As demonstrated by the opening of "The Quiet", Davies turns the short story's engagement with the present moment to her advantage, avoiding the need for the elaborate reconstruction of a specific historical era. Her stories focus on vivid encounters or climactic moments, imagined events at the margins of historical record. In "Jubilee", a figure easily recognisable as Queen Victoria is unveiling a statue of herself in some northern town. The elderly alderman who is hosting the occasion compares her inconsolable grief for Albert with the loss of his wife; however, it is revealed that, far from dead, she has in fact eloped with her lesbian lover. In this instance, Davies is debunking official versions of history, suggesting that beneath the dreary public ceremonies performed, and endured, by the ruling classes, there is a far more interesting counter-narrative.

"Bonnet" originated as a contribution to an anthology of stories inspired by the Brontës (Ashworth 2013). The story imagines meetings between Charlotte Brontë and her young publisher, George Smith; the fashionable bonnet of the title represents Charlotte's misconceived desire to make herself attractive to him. Neither Charlotte nor George is named in the text, though a clue is provided in a reference to Haworth in the final paragraph. A note accompanying the story quotes a letter from Brontë to Smith to substantiate Davies's biographical speculations; without this contextual information, "Bonnet" shares the indeterminacy of the other stories – even "Jubilee" provides the minimal amount of historical detail necessary for the reader to decipher what is ultimately a joke about Queen Victoria's alleged ignorance towards lesbianism.

Dissatisfied with the term "historical fiction", the critic Michael Orlofsky deploys his own coinage, "historiografiction", to describe postmodern fictionalisation of historical events. According to Orlofsky, "historiografiction is primarily concerned with character, perhaps secondarily with theme; historical fiction, on the other hand, is activated by plot, setting, details, or lifestyle" (2003: 47). I am not completely convinced that historical fiction is as indifferent to character as Orlofsky assumes; however, his analysis does help situate Carys Davies's postmodern fables. A comparison of Davies's "Miracle at Hawk's Bay" with Lucy Wood's "Diving Belles" – both stories centred on the figure of the husband lost at sea – illustrates the pronounced indeterminacy I have already referred to. Wood introduces precise details, combining contemporary life with timeless elements; her characters listen to the hum of the freezer or take up herbal cigarettes in an effort to stop smoking. In Davies's story, the fictional Hawk's Bay is tethered to no specific time or place. It is simply a configuration of sea, sand, marsh and shingle.

Davies's "historiografiction" is concerned with emotional impact, rather than the social or political observations implied in Wood's story. The opening of "Miracle at Hawk's Bay" is characteristically dramatic: "Matthew High. We knew it would be him. Even before Hannah turned him over, we just knew it" (Davies 2014: 68). It is easy to see why so many of Davies's stories have gripped the attention of competition judges. This opening also demonstrates the oral qualities in her work, through the striking use of rhythm, repetition and, in this case, a collective voice and viewpoint. The story is told by a first-person homodiegetic narrator, but the use of the plural "we" recurs throughout the narrative, and ends the story with a final twist. The story describes the efforts of the women to take the corpse back home, sparing us none of the gruesome details. Davies manipulates the reader's response as the women decide who should break the news to his widow:

> I knew I couldn't be the one to tell her. I knew the words would lodge in my throat like a splint of wood and I would stand there looking at Bella High's lovely face with its sparkling grey eyes and its sweet mouth and all those glossy chestnut curls falling over her shoulders like a shower of bells and I knew I didn't have the strength for it.
>
> (Davies 2014: 71–72)

The physical task of retrieving the body and transporting it adds to the temptation to just leave him for the tide to take back, a thought shared by the women but never articulated.

They do, finally, bring the dead man home to be buried. Duty outweighs instinct. But, in the story's concluding pages, the reader's expectations are reversed as it is revealed that the object of pity is not in fact Bella, but the women themselves. Their ambivalence is not driven by compassion, but resentment because Bella is the lucky one:

> It was Annie who broke down, just as we were getting ready to leave the house; poor scrawny boss-eyed Annie who went up to Bella High and started screaming in her face that it wasn't fair, the way she was always the one to get everything in this life – how it had always been her that was blessed with the best of everything and now it was the same all over again and Annie held out her long empty hands before Bella High and shook them and wheeled round in front of us and shouted to us all as if we didn't know it, that the earth was a place of gifts for Bella High, always had been. Everything she wanted it

gave up to her in the end. She had always had the earth's gifts and
now she had the sea's too.

(Davies 2014: 74)

At least Bella has a body to mourn. The other women have all lost husbands at sea, but none have been returned.

The twist ending, used by Guy de Maupassant, O. Henry, Roald Dahl
and many others, has fallen out of literary favour but retains its popularity with many readers. In order for the twist to work, crucial information needs to be withheld for as long as possible – often, as in this
case, insights into the character's interior world and her private moti-
vations. In this story, the device is highly successful because it subverts
the conventional figure of the grieving widow. In others, less so – in
"The Travellers", for instance, the narrator has left the UK to become
an innkeeper in Siberia; one night she watches a woman freeze to death
on a sledge outside because she is sulking after a row with her husband.
The story then abruptly switches to a memory of the narrator's life with
her own partner, back in Birmingham; the very reason she has caught
a train to Siberia is that they had a similar argument on a car journey
when she was navigating. She decides she will go back home and learn
to drive, and if that fails "I would talk to him about public transport"
(Davies 2014: 35).

The earlier parts of the story are full of extraordinary imagery. Although it does depend on conventional depictions of Russian life –
bearded Cossacks, samovars, etc. – the horror of the situation and the
helplessness of the witnesses are fully developed. All of this is undercut
by the lead-up to the "punchline", because the character's emotions seem
less authentic and the visceral power of the imagery has been abandoned
for the sake of the twist. Nevertheless, Davies's achievement in this collection is considerable. Orlofsky regards historiografiction as an "attempt to escape from the self" (2003: 50), defying the Creative Writing
cliché, "write what you know". The escape from the self is liberating
for many women writers, Davies amongst them, and *The Redemption
of Galen Pike* demonstrates a strongly innovative approach to the short
story form.

K.J. Orr, *Light Box* (2016)

K.J. Orr's PhD thesis consisted of stories written during her period of
study, most of them included in her collection *Light Box*, plus a discussion of liminality and metaphoric experience in the short story; an
essay from this critical work, applying her thinking to a short story by
Alice Munro, is included in the volume, *Liminality and the Short Story:
Boundary Crossings in American, Canadian and British Writing*, edited

by Jochen Achilles and Ina Bergmann in 2015. In the essay, Orr says that "at the core of the short story lies flux [... T]he short story situates both characters and reader on the brink, foregrounding the uncomfortable intensity of threshold experience" (Orr 2015: 251). Meaning in the short story is always under negotiation, and the "metaphoric agility" of the form (Orr 2015: 260) disrupts the possibility of unitary meaning.

The insights provided by these comments suggest ways of responding to indeterminacy and to the mingling of the mundane with the fantastic in the work of the other three writers under discussion, as well as Orr's own work. Most importantly, they highlight the process according to which metaphors are actualised and made literal, shaping not only the story's imagery but also plot and narrative structure. For instance, as we have seen, Bray's "The Baby Aisle" acts out the attempts to suppress the yearning for another baby – "broodiness" – through the fantastic notion of babies for sale. The imaginary, yet somehow familiar, landscapes in Davies's stories are metaphorical spaces, her "historiografictions" poised between historical fiction and fable.

Like Davies, Orr sets her stories in a wide range of settings "from Argentina to Siberia, Papua New Guinea to London and New York", declares the book cover (2016a). Both Orr's publisher and Davies's affirm this geographical diversity as a key element in the stories' appeal to the reader. While neither writer completely eschews the domestic, we may sense a drive among women authors to prove they are not limited by gender through that "escape from the self" evoked by Orlofsky. None of Orr's stories can be categorised as historiografictions, but they often share the temporal indeterminacy of Davies's work. Like Davies, Orr includes a story with a Siberian setting, making the most of its extreme weather conditions. "The Inland Sea" is much longer and more complex than Davies's Siberian story; in fact, it was originally issued as a stand-alone pamphlet by Orr's publisher, Daunt Books. The account of a perilous journey made by two brothers across a frozen lake is interspersed with the memories of one of the brother's, Pyotr. This analeptic structure is very reminiscent of Alice Munro; in an article for *Thresholds*, she cites Munro's metaphor of the short story as a house with interconnecting rooms, discussing the "scope for doublings, for troubling juxtapositions, for time-bending narrative switchbacks and circularities – those analeptic and proleptic leaps that can be giddy-making, revelatory, devastating in the short space of reading time the story claims" (Orr 2016b).

Although there are indications of a modern-day setting, with references to cars and buses, and a geological expedition conducting experiments on the lake, many details remain undetermined in "The Inland Sea". The two brothers, from a fishing family, are figures in a landscape which evokes the primal and the elemental, and the temporal markers refer to the cycle of the seasons rather than linear time. This is how "The Inland Sea" begins:

> On the far side the lake is divided from the hills by a slash of soft pink that arrived with the dawn.
>
> They set out, stepping over a yawning crack where the sea has buckled. All along the shoreline the lake has twisted, churning the ice into contortions which it has thrown up and aside, forming banks of frozen rubble softened only by fresh snowfall.
>
> (Orr 2016a: 79)

Orr's interest in liminality is very apparent both in her engagement with landscape and her exploration of fluctuating inner states of consciousness. The characters are simultaneously integrated with this unstable landscape and threatened by its unpredictability. As the story develops, the weather worsens and they become stranded, the protagonist's consciousness, conveyed through free indirect discourse, also becomes clouded. In many of the other stories, characters experience altered states of consciousness or illnesses such as the congenital blindness in "Blackout". In "The Human Circadian Pacemaker", physical and psychological disturbances become almost indistinguishable from one another.

Like Wood's "Diving Belles" and Davies's "Miracle at Hawk's Bay", "The Human Circadian Pacemaker" features attempts to retrieve a lost husband, following a voyage into the unknown. In this story, the loss is symbolic rather than literal, as the husband is an astronaut, newly returned to Earth. He struggles to readjust his bodily rhythms with the aid of a light box. His wife meanwhile seems equally disoriented: "she had the odd sensation that he didn't recognise her at all" (Orr 2016a: 51).

Once again, the story is structured analeptically, and narrated through free indirect discourse. The style is cool and detached, recalling the couple's transatlantic love affair, preparations for the mission and her yearning for him when he is out of reach. When direct speech is introduced, it is as elliptical and minimal as the narration, which is often delivered as a series of statements, punctuated by fragmented sense-impressions:

> "There is something I have to tell you," he had said, one day over coffee. This time they had met in Manhattan. They had been involved for two years. Two years of transatlantic crossings. New York was like meeting halfway, but it was clear now that something had to give.
>
> He was nervous, which was unusual, and made her wonder what he was about to say. And then he had told her that he was very probably going to space, which was not what she had expected at all.

"So I'll move to the States," she had said, resolutely. "And then you'll move to space."

They had spent the rest of the day at their hotel. She remembers the cool of the window-pane on her neck as they leant together up above the city.

(Orr 2016a: 62)

Orr's story is ultimately concerned with the inaccessibility of another person's subjectivity, even when that other is a partner. "'I'll move to the States [...] And then you'll move to space'" – the astronaut is an extreme example of the husband who works away; and the compromises and adjustments made by the couple act out this fresh example of the metaphor actualised and, as Orr says in her critical exegesis, uncompleted. There could not be a better illustration of Frank O'Connor's view that the short story engages primarily with an existential loneliness.

This essential isolation, and the unknowability of the other, is reflected in the closing sentences, describing the protagonist lying awake before the dawn: "She wondered if her husband was awake too. She imagined him listening to the creaking of their timber-frame home. She tried to imagine what he saw as his eyes adjusted, the shapes that presented themselves" (Orr 2016a: 67).

The husband is never named; the wife, we discover, is called Eleanor, but those rare occasions when the name is used are unexpected in a text where so much is undetermined. As in "The Inland Sea", character is absorbed by landscape – in this instance, by the empty spaces and open skies of the desert and of course the changing light. The setting would appear to be New Mexico, but, like Carys Davies's Wild West in "The Redemption of Galen Pike", the specific location is withheld. In Orr's stories there is a pronounced engagement with time as flux through those "analeptic and proleptic leaps" that Orr mentions in her *Thresholds* article (Orr 2016b). This temporal fluidity is combined with the merging of boundaries between the body and landscape, self and world.

Conclusion

In their own distinct ways, all four writers exploit the elliptical properties of the short story form. Even Carys Davies, whose stories revive the "twist" ending traditionally associated with plot-driven fiction, employs a non-linear structure. All exploit narrative indeterminacy and all of them circumvent what Adrian Hunter has called "the novelistic will-to-knowledge" (2007: 176). Carys Bray, Lucy Wood and Carys Davies raise questions of gender, class and regional identity through their use of myth, fable and postmodern playfulness. It will be interesting to see how far these writers' commitment to the form remains tenable in the face of commercial pressures to concentrate on novels. Certainly, these examples prove there is a thriving industry of short-story-writing, sustained by independent publishers, Creative Writing courses and literary awards. That industry is in a precarious position, during a period of economic stagnation and public spending cuts in the UK. Let us hope that there are more stories to come from each of these four authors, each of them representing a distinctive and original strand within short-fiction-writing a whole.

Notes

1 Bloomsbury is one of the few large companies to retain its independence, most having been absorbed by large conglomerates such as Random House. Nonetheless, it should be considered a mainstream publisher by virtue of its size and its commercial status.
2 For a more sceptical view, see Paul March-Russell, "Writing and Publishing the Short Story" in *The Cambridge Companion to the English Short Story*, edited by Ann-Marie Einhaus, Cambridge: Cambridge University Press, 2016, 15–27.
3 March-Russell credits the writer China Miéville with the coinage of the term "abcanny" to describe that which is weird, unsettling and alien to the self, unlike the uncanny, which is disturbing because of its familiarity.

References

Ashworth, A.J. (2013) "Introduction", in *Red Room*, edited by A.J. Ashworth, Norwich: Unthank Books, 3–5.

Bakhtin, Mikhail Mikhaïlovich (1985) *Rabelais and His World*, translated by Hélène Iswolsky, Bloomington, IN: Indiana University Press.

Barry, Kevin (2017) "In the Skin of Anxiety", *The Dublin Review*, www.thedublinreview.com/the-skin-of-anxiety (accessed 7 October 2017).

Bray, Carys (2012) *Sweet Home*, Cromer: Salt Publishing.

Bray, Carys (2014) *A Song for Issy Bradley: A Novel and Poetics*, www.repository.edgehill.ac.uk/6502 (accessed 7 October 2017).

Bray, Carys (2014) *Postnatal Confession*, www.postnatalconfession.blogspot.co.uk (accessed 7 October 2017).

Bray, Carys (2016) *Sweet Home*, London: Windmill Books.

Bray, Carys (2017) "Horror and Humanity", *Thresholds*, www.thresholds.chi.ac.uk/horror-and-humanity (accessed 7 October 2017).

Caldwell, Lucy (2016) *Multitudes*, London: Faber & Faber.

Carter, Angela (1979) *The Bloody Chamber*, London: Victor Gollancz.

Clanchy, Kate (2016) *The Not-Dead and the Saved*, London: Picador.

Cox, Ailsa (2016) "The Institution of Creative Writing", in *The Cambridge History of the English Short Story*, edited by Dominic Head, Cambridge: Cambridge University Press, 581–597.

Cusk, Rachel (2013) "In Praise of the Creative Writing Course", *The Guardian*, www.theguardian.com/books/2013/jan/18/in-praise-creative-writing-course (accessed 7 October 2017).

Davies, Carys (2014) *The Redemption of Galen Pike*, Cromer: Salt Publishing.

Dean, Claire (2016) *The Museum of Shadows and Reflections*, Philadelphia, PA: Papaveria Press.

Dog Ear (2012) "An Interview with Lucy Wood", *Dog Ear Discs*, www.dogeardiscs.wordpress.com/2012/02/29/an-interview-with-lucy-wood/ (accessed 7 October 2017).

Fernando, Rajesh (2012) *Homesick*, London: Bloomsbury.

Franklin, Sarah (2014) "Why I Rejected Life as a Mormon Mother", *The Guardian*, www.theguardian.com/lifeandstyle/2014/jun/14/why-i-rejected-life-as-mormon-mother-religious-scepticism (accessed 7 October 2017).

Gilbert, Zoe (2018) *Folk*, London: Bloomsbury [forthcoming].

Glass, Rodge (ed.) (2016) *Head Land*, Glasgow and Liverpool: Freight Books and Edge Hill University Press.

Gordimer, Nadine (1994) "The Flash of Fireflies", in *The New Short Story Theories*, edited by Charles E. May, Ohio, OH: Ohio University Press, 263–267.

Hensher, Philip (2015) "General Introduction", in *The Penguin Book of the British Short Story*, edited by P. Hensher, Harmondsworth: Penguin xi–xxxvi.

Holdefer, Charles (2014) "How Short is Short?" *Journal of the Short Story in English* 62: 49–158.

Housham, Jane (2016) "*Sweet Home* by Carys Bray Review – Shades of Angela Carter", *The Guardian*, www.theguardian.com/books/2016/feb/26/sweet-home-carys-bray-review-paperback (accessed 7 October 2017).

Hunter, Adrian (2007) *The Cambridge Introduction to the Short Story in English*, Cambridge: Cambridge University Press.

Johnson, Daisy (2017) *Fen*, London: Vintage

Liggins, Emma, Andrew Maunder and Ruth Robbins (eds.) (2011) *The British Short Story*, London: Palgrave Macmillan.

Logan, Kirsty (2014) *The Rental Heart and Other Stories*, Cromer: Salt Publishing.

March-Russell, Paul (2016) "Writing and Publishing the Short Story", in *The Cambridge Companion to the English Short Story*, edited by Ann-Marie Einhaus, Cambridge: Cambridge University Press, 15–27.

March-Russell, Paul (2017) "The Abcanny Politics of Landscape in Lucy Wood's *Diving Belles*", *Short Fiction in Theory and Practice* 7(1): 53–65.

May, Charles E. (2013) "Carys Bray and Carol Shields: Whimsy and Artifice", *Reading the Short Story*, www.may-on-the-short-story.blogspot.co.uk/2013/02/carys-bray-and-carol-shields-whimsy-and.html (accessed 7 October 2017).

McGregor, Jon (2012) *This Isn't the Sort of Thing That Happens to Some One Like You*, London: Bloomsbury.

National Association of Writers in Education, www.nawe.co.uk (accessed 7 October 2017).

Orlofsky, Michael (2003) "Historiografiction: The Fictionalization of History in the Short Story", in *The Postmodern Short Story: Forms and Issues,* edited by Farhat Iftekharrudin, Joseph Boyden, Mary Rohrberger and Jaie Claudet, Westport, CT: Praeger, 47–62.

Orr, K J (2012) *The Inland Sea*, London: Daunt Books.

Orr, Katherine (2015) "Liminality, Metaphoric Experience, and the Short-Story Form: Alice Munro's 'Wenlock Edge'", in *Liminality and the Short*

Story: Boundary Crossings in American, Canadian and British Writing, edited by Jochen Achilles and Ina Bergmann, London: Routledge, 251–262.

Orr, K.J. (2016a) *Light Box*, London: Daunt Books.

Orr, Katherine (2016b) "Crossing Boundaries: Poetry and the Short Story", *Thresholds*, www://thresholds.chi.ac.uk/crossing-boundaries-poetry-and-the-short-story/ (accessed 7 October 2017).

Parmeswaran, Rajesh (2012) *I Am an Executioner*, London: Bloomsbury.

Popescu, Lucy (2015) "Lucy Wood Interview", *The Independent*, www.independent.co.uk/arts-entertainment/books/features/lucy-wood-interview-author-of-weathering-on-how-the-rural-landscape-fuels-her-creativity-9983342.html (accessed 7 October 2017).

Pritchett, V.S. (1966) "The Short Story", *London Magazine* 6(6): 6–9.

Todd, Richard (1996) *Consuming Fictions: The Booker Prize and Fiction in Britain Today*, London: Bloomsbury.

Williams, Charlotte (2012) "Bloomsbury Dubs 2012 'Year of the Short Story'", *The Bookseller,* www.thebookseller.com/news/bloomsbury-dubs-2012-year-short-story (accessed 7 October 2017).

Wilson, D.W. (2012) *Once You Break a Knuckle*, London: Bloomsbury.

Wood, Lucy (2012) *Diving Belles*, London: Bloomsbury.

Wood, Lucy (2015) *Weathering*, London: Bloomsbury.

Wood, Lucy (2018) *The Sing of the Shore*, London: Fourth Estate.

The Word Factory, www.thewordfactory.tv/site (accessed 7 October 2017).

Writers and Artists (2017) "Life-Changing Learning: Interviews with Carys Bray and Lisa Whenham-Bossy", *Writers and Artists: The Insider Guide the Media.* www.writersandartists.co.uk/writers/advice/816/a-writers-toolkit/interviews-with-authors (accessed 7 October 2017).

Young, Emma (2015) "Feminist F(r)iction: Short Stories and Postfeminist Politics at the Millennial Moment", in *British Women Short Story Writers: The New Woman to Now*, edited by Emma Young and James Bailey, Edinburgh: Edinburgh University Press, 133–147.

Index